The Making of the Modern Manager

Paul Turner

The Making of the Modern Manager

Mapping Management Competencies from the First to the Fourth Industrial Revolution

palgrave
macmillan

Paul Turner
Leeds Business School
Leeds Beckett University
Leeds, UK

ISBN 978-3-030-81061-0 ISBN 978-3-030-81062-7 (eBook)
https://doi.org/10.1007/978-3-030-81062-7

This Palgrave Macmillan imprint is published by the registered company Springer Nature Switzerland AG.
The registered company address is: Gewerbestrasse 11, 6330 Cham, Switzerland

In memory of my father, Ivor Turner (1929–2020)

Acknowledgements

My thanks go to:
Liz Barlow, Palgrave Macmillan
Professor Martin Reynolds, Leeds Business School
Wojciech Zytkowiak
Fostine Odhiambo
Jean Pousson
Mary Amala Divya, Springer Nature
And to the support and happiness given by:
Gail, Jane-Marie, Annette, Harrison, Ellis, Sebastian, Gary, Will and Jacob
Heart like Roses

Contents

About the Author

Paul Turner has held professorial appointments at universities in Leeds, Birmingham, Nottingham and Cambridge. His business career included executive and director positions in FTSE and Fortune companies, and he was Vice President of the Chartered Institute of Personnel and Development (CIPD). He was Chair of Human Asset, People Innovation and the European Talent for Tomorrow Conferences as well as being a judge on the Middle East HR, European HR Excellence and the CIPD People Management Awards. Paul is the author or co-author of *Employee Engagement* (2020), *Leadership in Healthcare* (2018), *Talent Management in Healthcare* (2017), *Make Your People Before You Make Your Products* (2014), *Workforce Planning* (2010), *The Admirable Company* (2008), *Talent Strategy, Management and Measurement* (2007), *Organisational Communication* (2003) and *HR Forecasting and Planning* (2002). He has written articles for academic and business journals and the International Press. Paul has a first degree from the University of East Anglia, a PhD from the University of Sheffield and is a Companion of the CIPD.

List of Figures

List of Tables

Introduction

We are on the cusp of a Fourth Industrial Revolution.

As new technologies combine in ways rarely seen in past technological revolutions, and as organisations become more fluid, seeing the end of hierarchies and bureaucracies, the place and contribution of the human workforce is the subject of significant discussion. What role do people have in automated production processes; what jobs will they undertake and what skills will they need in this new, interconnected world? Of course the Fourth Industrial Revolution will likely unfold for decades to come. Tantalisingly, whether the Fourth Industrial Revolution is on a continuum with the three previous industrial revolutions remains an open question. Perhaps the next 50 years may prove an end point in history in terms of our current understanding of management and its practice?

We are also on the cusp of a managerial revolution.

And so, a further, critical aspect of the transformation that is taking place, and a question that is of particular importance to this book is that concerning the role of the manager in organisations of extended, intertwined networks? Whereas in the past, managers and management were concerned with planning and organising, or leading teams of people to achieve clear objectives, today, with artificial intelligence (AI), the Internet of Things and robotics providing many of the production functions that were once undertaken by human beings, the scope and direction of management is less clear. What is there to manage if production and progress are done more efficiently by non-human interventions?

The key challenges may be summarised in three related areas.

First, the challenge of Technology. Shoshana Zuboff's (1988) seminal work demonstrated the value of understanding the fundamental differences between the nature of technologies in different periods of history. Ever since the invention of computers in the 1940s there has been much speculation about the possibilities of machine intelligence that are emerging in the Fourth Industrial Revolution. Specifically, the possibilities that artificial intelligence (AI) may have a direct and transformational impact on our understanding of what we see as the limits of human intelligence. This offers alternative views of futures where management competences may be transformed through the integration of augmented intelligence-based competences.

Second, the challenge of Organisation. It is reasonable to expect this will continue to be the case during the Fourth Industrial Revolution but with perhaps one notable feature as being the impact that new digital technologies will have in shaping a context where the dynamic between physical and virtual worlds will become increasingly integrated. How work and life is experienced has started to change dramatically along this continuum over the first two decades of the twenty-first century. As the Fourth Industrial Revolution evolves it may well open up fundamental questions about how we understand what and how organisations might do in a context where, for example, conventional notions of 'time', 'place' and even the meaning of 'skills' may be distorted by virtual world dynamics and the presence of augmented human intelligence (in whatever form).

Third, the challenge of People Management. People or workforce management has been a consistent area of challenge for the management role over the four industrial revolutions. Arguably it is the radically different nature of digital and information technology in the Fourth Industrial Revolution that presents a significantly different people management challenge from previous ones. Two illustrative points are worth emphasising. First, it is likely the balance of work and leisure time will be significantly different from previous norms. This may well challenge our understanding of key notions such as 'right people; right place, right time and right skills with right attitudes and behaviours'. Second, and more controversial, is the point that follows from the arguments put forward by writers such as Nick Bostrum (2014); if machine intelligence were to surpass (in some form) human intelligence in the Fourth Industrial Revolution, then managers would be challenged by not just people management issues but also those relating to how to manage and integrate 'smart machines' into organisation workplaces.

A recent white paper by the World Economic Forum provides insight and some response to these questions with the observation that 'the digital revolution is a human revolution. While new technologies are what's driving the Fourth Industrial Revolution, ultimately, it is people who will bring it to life in businesses.' To prosper in the face of radical and global change, managers will need to be effective in new business models able to respond with agility to change and transformation and to ensure that their organisations do as well. In many respects these challenges facing managers in the Fourth Industrial Revolution have a similar ring to them in terms of our lessons from history for the previous three industrial revolutions. However, the possibility of seeing a blurring between human intelligence and machine intelligence presents a possible scenario that is perhaps not part of our historical continuum; are human intelligent management practitioners capable and prepared for working with intelligent machines? Managers will of course need skills in integration as they are asked to bring in innovative new technologies in a way that is efficient and effective. It could be argued of course that the potential of intelligent smart machines has been overpredicted for decades; but it does not mean it will not happen. Innovation will continue to push the boundaries where machine intelligence can genuinely complement the capabilities of human intelligent management practitioners. So what might this mean for how human intelligent management practitioners will need to manage optimally, both a human workforce and automation? This of course may well depend on our interpretation of the possibility of the new realities created by digital and information technologies. If it were to happen—the creation of genuinely artificial intelligence comparable to that we know of human intelligent management practitioners—then this will create many challenges that will require knowledge and skills beyond the prevailing management competence frameworks we currently understand. Drawing on our lessons in history from previous industrial revolutions it is reasonable to assume a degree of continuity in the development of managerial skills in the early phases of the Fourth Industrial Revolution. Managers will need skills that include not only knowledge of technology, but of technology integration; not only of change management, but of agility in organisational transformation; not only people management but also the ability to engage a workforce in the delivery of challenging objectives.

Martin Reynolds
Leeds Business School, Leeds Beckett University
Leeds, UK
April 2021

References

Bostrom, N. (2014). *Superintelligence: Paths, Dangers, Strategies*. Oxford University Press.

Zuboff, S. (1988). *In the Age of the Smart Machine*. Heinemann.

1

What Is Management; What Do Managers Do?

On the Nature of Philosophy and Speculation

Management is a constellation of concepts and ideas.

Its many definitions span the boundaries of leadership and strategy on the one hand and business administration on the other; from people management to P&L accounts. Managers deal with operational processes and with human emotions; with intangibles—such as brands or goodwill, and tangibles—such as machinery on a production line or IT systems in a bank. Managers are concerned with both change and stability; sometimes simultaneously. They operate within Weberian hierarchies—'functional frames of reference', or in network or swarm structures, because in 'our digitally mediated world' the classic bureaucracy is less prevalent (Hilbert, 1987; Muellerleile & Robertson, 2018). There are few concepts that have attracted as much business interest as the management of organisations. Inevitably, diverse points of view about best practice have proliferated since Adam Smith first articulated the productivity benefits of the *division of labour*. But, in the evolution of the concept over time, there are some indications of consistent patterns or forms of knowledge and skill; of competences that may help the contemporary manager

P. Turner, *The Making of the Modern Manager*,
https://doi.org/10.1007/978-3-030-81062-7_1

to go about their job more effectively. The challenge in identifying these is interpretation that avoids the 'illusion of retrospective determinism', or oversimplifying to a 'one dimensional, uni-cultural' approach' or minimising the importance of race and gender in the richness of the management concept. There are issues when using past data to inform future intent. Nevertheless, there are potential benefits from seeking out and understanding the nature of the management identity—and from this understanding to speculate on implications for its future direction, using historical data to study longer processes and to put present developments into context (Brunninge, 2009; Cummings et al., 2017; Batiz-Lazo, 2019; Logevall, 2020). Technological influences are ever present in these developments.

New technologies have informed the narrative of management during each of Four Industrial Revolutions from around 1750 to the present day. 'Philosophers or men of speculation' (Adam Smith, 1776) have been observant of management in large-scale manufacturing units during the First Industrial Revolution in the eighteenth century, facilitating new means of transport and power during the Second Industrial Revolution from the nineteenth century, operating in globally integrated organisations during the Third Industrial Revolution of the twentieth century and navigating the rise of the technology behemoths of the Fourth in the twenty-first century. The phenomenon can be regarded in general as the planning, directing and coordinating of resources to achieve the efficient functioning of organisations and businesses (CIPD, 2014). The question that arises today is will the levels of discontinuity and a radically changed working environment, anticipated as the Fourth Industrial Revolution gathers momentum, affect the functions of how managers go about their jobs? Whereas the mechanical innovations of the First and Second Industrial Revolutions acted as a substitute for human strength, 'the machines of that time could not reason, compare, compute, read, smell, sense, hear, or make snap decisions. However, if artificial intelligence and robotics continue on their present trend, future machines will be able to carry out these human capabilities, at least in certain contexts and to a certain extent' (Mokyr, et al., 2015; 42). Managers face daunting challenges some of which—new technology, recruitment and training of a workforce for a radically different environment—are comparable over time; others—the digital, connected, virtual nature of technology—are not.

The questions raised in this book are concerned with lessons to be learned from previous experience that may inform future perspectives on management. And using the results of this learning to identify competences that may be relevant to the contemporary environment. Competences are those things that are causally related to effective performance and consist of *knowledge*—the retention and utilisation of information, *skills*—the ability to demonstrate a sequence of behaviour towards a goal—and *attitudes* and *behaviours*—the social manifestations of how a manager undertakes a role (Boyatzis, 1982). They can be specific, such as technology knowledge or that related to the business domain, or generic relating to interpersonal competences. A typology includes cognitive competence or work-related knowledge and the ability to apply it; functional competence the ability to perform work-based tasks; social competence or relational and communication skills; and meta-competence or personal and professional values. They are the *know-how, know why, know what* and *know how to behave* of management (Augier & Teece, 2009; Nobre et al., 2014; Kang et al., 2015; Van Lent & Durepos, 2019; Škrinjarić & Domadenik, 2020). These competences will contribute to organisational success not only by *singularity*—discreet interventions—but also by *complementarity*—interventions that are connected to a broader purpose. Complementarity means organisational constructs and actions that are collaborative, multi-layered, multi-faceted and most of all add to the competitiveness of the whole organisation.

Three areas of study will be influential in developing conclusions about how modern management has evolved. The first is on the nature of industrial revolutions how they influenced organisational strategy and decision-making; the second is on management practice in this context and how managers responded to revolutionary challenges; and third how various theories of management were developed either in advance of practice or as a result of practice.

On the Nature of Industrial Revolutions

The development of the modern capitalist world is most often set within the framework of Four Industrial Revolutions, with each being proclaimed for its uniqueness. Charles Babbage, writing on the First Industrial Revolution, for example, put forward the view:

> There exists, perhaps, no single circumstance which distinguishes our country more remarkably from all others than the vast extent and perfection to which we have carried the contrivance of tools and machines for which we have formed those conveniences of which so large a quantity is consumed … the advantages which are derived from machinery and manufactures seem to arise principally from three sources: the addition which they make to human power – the economy they product of human time – the conversion of substances apparently common and worthless into valuable products. (Babbage, 1832)

The First Industrial Revolution can be characterised by the emergence of European Pioneers and the genesis of modern management from around 1750 bringing significant growth in GDP, the application of advanced industrial technologies and higher levels of international trade. In Britain, innovations included textile equipment and tool-making as well as inventions in steam powered engines, railways and railway systems. Rapid growth in key manufacturing sectors gave Britain a comparative advantage in certain sectors, and a decisive break in the history of technology and the economy (Landes, 1972; Temin, 1997; Allen, 2011). In the eyes of one early twentieth-century economic historian, the First Industrial Revolution in Britain was inspired by 'deep rooted ideas and habits of thought' based on a laissez-faire outlook and 'sturdy individualism' (Meakin, 1928). As a result, the adoption of technology and new systems and processes led to significant increases in cotton production and growth in the number of power looms; technological developments in pottery, glass, chemicals and brewing; significant growth in production levels of iron, steel and coal; and large capital investments in metallurgy. By 1850, Britain's population was three times as large as 1700 with over 45% of that population living in towns. 'People purchased many more of the goods and services they consumed from strangers and worked increasingly in large establishments that were separate from their homes and which demanded discipline and punctuality' (Mokyr, 2009; 3). The country was a profoundly different place towards the end of the First Industrial Revolution than it was at the beginning (Mathias, 1969). The economies of Germany, France and other Western European countries followed their own paths to industrialisation and modernisation; and grew during the period both in response to endogenous pressures towards change in a similar way to Britain and as a reaction to new methods which were being developed in Britain. Even though there was a contrast between continental and British industrial development, the French Revolution swept away the institutional remains of the ancient regime and thereby laid the foundation for economic growth (Landes, 1972; Mokyr, 2009). A feature of all was that the industrial revolution was not some absolute phenomenon but an ongoing process; a sequence of challenge and response with complex, interconnected changes and continuities in which the whole tenor direction and possibilities of economic life were transformed; impacting on economic efficiency, productivity growth and entrepreneurial inquisitiveness. Furthermore, whilst the 'nation' is used as the dominant identifier, there was fluidity of ideas between nations. So, whether we regard the First Industrial Revolution 'as the triumph of virtue and ingenuity over poverty or as the victory of perfidious capitalist exploitation', or whether we view it as Britain at the helm with others in its wake, we cannot alter the fact that an event changed history fundamentally and irreversibly (Mokyr, 2009; Philbeck & Davis, 2019). And the way in which organisations went about their production or commercial processes was also fundamentally changed. The seeds of the concept of modern management were sown. For the purposes of this study, the parameters of the First Industrial Revolution will be set between 1750-1870 and the main geographic focus will be on Britain and Europe.

At the dawn of the Second Industrial Revolution there was the belief that it would usher in

> a new economic order in which the 'palaeotechnic' economics 'of crowded and monotonous industrial towns' was replaced with 'neotechnic'

economics 'bringing the potentialities of wealth and leisure beyond past utopian dreams. (Geddes, 1915)

The Second Industrial Revolution was notable for the emergence of the United States as the world's leading economy and *scientific management* at the forefront of business processes. Hence, even though Britain remained the bellwether of economic growth, the United States overtook the country in several key industries. Underpinning this progress was technological change and organisational development which were fundamental to US industrialisation during the late nineteenth and early twentieth centuries. From the ending of the barbarity of slavery after the mid-century Civil War—'the twentieth century arrived, and America's Industrial Revolution boomed'. Engineering innovation, the revolution in industrial and commercial use of electricity and mass production and mass consumption created economic opportunity unprecedented in scale and scope. The United States was well positioned to take advantage of this transformation. American companies founded during this period were Coca Cola, Westinghouse Electric, General Electric, Pepsico, Ford Motor, Gillette, IBM and Walt Disney. By 1913 energy consumption in the United States was equal to that of Britain, Germany, France, Russia and Austria Hungary combined (Kennedy 1988; 314). The use of electric motors expanded from around 5% of mechanical horsepower in US manufacturing in 1899 to over 82% by 1929. Labour productivity in the United States was about twice that of Britain (Broadberry 1994). The application of scientific ideas to the tasks of mechanical production; combined with the concept of cost accounting rather than historical reporting of accounts, had a far-reaching effect on the way in which American companies operated. The result was mass production, devised in America, and consisting of continuous production, specialisation, the re-planning of manufacturing plants and increasingly sophisticated methods of personnel management. This revolution saw not only a swathe of technologically inspired products but also technological infrastructure such as electricity grids and new forms of public transportation based on the internal combustion engine (Landes, 1972; Taniguchi, 2004; Nicholas, 2010; Philbeck & Davis, 2019). The transformation of American industry also brought with it the transformation of American management which went on to form the basis of the transformation of global management. For the purposes of this study, the parameters of the Second Industrial Revolution will be set between 1870 and 1950 and the main geographic focus will be on the United States of America.

Peter Drucker, writing at the outset of the Third Industrial Revolution saw an imminent era of challenge; that management faced the *first* great test of its *competence*—automation:

> A lot of 'science fiction' is being written today about automation. It is no accident that so much of this speculation comes from the advocates of controlled economy and central planning. Yet every one of these assertions, conclusions and fears is the direct opposite of what the new technology really means. Automation is not 'technical' in character. Like every technology it is primarily a system of concepts, and its technical aspects are results rather than causes. (Drucker, 1954)

The Third Industrial Revolution saw the emergence of Japan, Asian Dragons, Asian Tigers, China and India as leading world economies. New products, processes and the development of international markets in the period following 1950, shaped a post-war world. Six technology developments—the microprocessor, computer-aided design and manufacturing (CAD/CAM), fibre optics, biogenetics, lasers and holography were most influential (Finkelstein & Newman, 1984; Philbeck & Davis, 2019). Coinciding with a revolution in technology, was the revolution in the global economy in which, from the 1960s, companies in Asian countries were prominent in whole industries and sectors. There was an orientation within the Asian region to compete globally and this had significance in their growing stature in world markets. Beginning with the rise of Japanese corporations in electronics—driven by intense rivalry and domestic market saturation—they found exporting a necessity—through to the rapid and significant growth in the economies of the Asian Dragons and Asian Tigers, such as Singapore, Hong Kong, South Korea and Taiwan—growth rates of GDP in the period 1960-1995 of around 6% per annum—followed by Indonesia, Malaysia and Thailand (Porter, 1990; Davis & Gonzales, 2003; Chen, 2004), through to the incredible growth of the Chinese economy as the second largest in the world and of

India, which at $2.94 trillion GDP has become the fifth-largest economy by 2019. It was not only technology and globalisation that contributed to the success of Asian organisations during this period but new approaches to management practice. Once again, regional applications of the new management concepts quickly became global standards. For the purposes of this study, the parameters of the Third Industrial Revolution will be set between 1950 and the present day and the main geographic focus will be on Asia.

And most recently Klaus Schwab (2016) has written of the Fourth Industrial Revolution:

> We stand on the brink of a technological revolution that will fundamentally alter the way we live, work, and relate to one another. In its scale, scope, and complexity, the transformation will be unlike anything humankind has experienced before.

Transformational technologies will have a significant impact on the way people live and work as the merging of physical, digital and biological worlds create a new chapter in human development. Socio-cultural change—referred to as Society 4.0—will occur through the application of digital energy; digital health with better preventive care or diagnosis, digital communication and digital transportation systems as technology accelerates change across social structures and interfaces. It is also anticipated that the growing diversity of management teams will have a positive influence on the motivations and achievements of organisations. The question to be answered is about the nature of management in the face of these dramatic, powerful forces for change; a compelling narrative on equality and diversity in race and gender; and the impact on life and work of COVID 19. Dealing with such unprecedented social dynamics will require 'human ingenuity of the highest order'. This assumption also holds true for developments in the commercial world known as Industry 4.0. with a confluence of technologies which will transform how organisations operate; how they design and create their products and services and how they distribute them to market. Advances in machine learning, cloud computing, nanotechnology, 3-D printing, the Internet of Things, artificial intelligence (AI) and robotics will reach to the very essence of work (Rabeh et al., 2017; De Castro et al., 2018; Mazali, 2018; Iraj et al., 2017; Gratton & Scott, 2016; Morgan, 2019; McWilliams, 2020; Scott & Gratton, 2020; WEF, 2017, 2020).

Underpinning each of the above observations about industrial revolution was the belief that society was entering a new age in which existing technologies and their associated skills sets or systems would become largely obsolete; and would 'trigger a value migration of physical, financial and human capital, from the prior established order to the new way of doing things', the argument being predicated on the assumption that industrial revolutions introduce new standards of managerial, professional and technical skills built on what went before (Moingeon & Edmondson, 1996; Morgan, 2019; Philbeck & Davis, 2019; Roulac, 2019). To this end, sense-making about the theory and practice of management will provide a framework with comparable points of reference or loci. These are the historiographic landmarks; those elaborate, ideal constructions that give structure and coherence to our historical narratives (de Vries, 1994). And so, in the same way as eminent historians have done by taking a view of management as a broadly based process (Wilson & Thomson, 2009; 9), it is possible to take a similar eclectic view about the incidence of the industrial revolutions and their geographic focus.

On the Evolution of Management Practice

Sidney Pollard's seminal work (Pollard, 1965) analysing the genesis of management during the First Industrial Revolution noted the lack of universal agreement that management was a new concept occurring in the new manufacturing operations springing up in Britain from around 1750. He asked 'did not the ancient Egyptians build their huge pyramids, or the Chinese their Wall, or more recently, did not Louis XIV inaugurate a magnificent system of main road building in France?' If the control of large numbers of people was the question, generals had controlled many more over the ages, than managers in industrial companies. The point being made was that if management was concerned with planning and organising people to achieve a particular task or project, then there was a case for saying that management, as a concept, had existed across the globe for millennia rather than relatively recently coming into existence in a small valley in Derbyshire, England. But further analysis shows significant differences in both the managers' environment and their behaviour. In the first place, whilst the control of large numbers of people was a common characteristic of the military commander and the factory manager, there were few powers of compulsion for the latter—and it was this lack of legal enforcement of 'unfree' work that proved to be one of the most significant characteristics of the new capitalism—a seminal idea (Pollard, 1965; Joullié, 2018). Managing a workforce which had a choice was different to managing one without. Secondly, the factory manager had not only to make a product as a result of their actions, but to relate this to costs and then be able to sell the product competitively. The third area of difference is one that would separate the factory manager from the merchant. Whilst both the factory manager and the merchant had access to and used capital, there was an onus in the manufacturing environment to combine capital with labour and transform it into saleable commodities. Furthermore, increasing output per head meant directly more capital equipment per man of the labour force in industry and agriculture as well as greater capital investment in the necessary services to sustain these sectors (Pollard, 1965; Mathias, 1969). Management from the period of the First Industrial Revolution had sufficient difference from what had taken place previously to regard it, not only as innovative, adapting to new environments, but inventive, introducing new methods and techniques. In this respect, the locus of modern management can be situated during the First Industrial Revolution. It was inspired by mainly manufacturing industries and characterised by control over larger productive enterprises. It includes evolving industries such as textiles, mining and metal smelting, and newer industries such as distilling or sugar refining. The assumption here is that a useful analysis of management and the role of the manager would set the benchmark date, not at 2500 BC, the creation of the Great Pyramid of Giza, but during the middle of the eighteenth century—there were sufficient differentiators—the context of industrial capitalism—to warrant a perspective of management from the time of the First Industrial Revolution. And from this point management evolved often in line with the nature of ownership and control—from personal to personal, proprietal to managerial and latterly managerial financial (Wilson & Thomson, 2009; 104).

However, 'universal solutions to management problems do not exist' (Hofstede, 2007), and so managing in the American Automobile Plant in the 1920s, for example, required a distinct approach that was set in a unique historical context; one that was in contrast to the environment for managing in the Japanese corporation in the 1970s or the British Bank in the 1990s. The differences in knowledge, skills, attitudes and behaviours of the managers in each were determined by the context within which management practice took place. And this conclusion can be applied to every form of management practice in every era. If management competence is 'the specific ability required to achieve high work performance in a given job' then there are elements that will be specific to a time or place (*contextual*) and others that are consistent across time and place (*core*). Some of these elements will be cognitive, such as systems thinking and pattern recognition; others will be emotional, including self-awareness and others related to related to self-management (Takeuchi, 1999; Boyatzis, 2011). *Contextual management competence* is therefore important when considering the role of the manager. The context can be political or economic; it can be legal with the rules and regulations towards labour which prevail in that place and at that time; it can be technological; and it can be societal—such as attitudes towards race or gender. Each of these, or a combination of wider forces, will impact on how organisations function and how managers within them manage. However, there are also competences that might prevail in whichever time or place. The need to plan and organise, for example, and to motivate individuals or teams of people towards the achievement of objectives are fundamental requirements in the role of the manager. And throughout 'management is the process of making things happen' for a broad range of stakeholders (Armstrong, 2005). These might be referred to as *core management competences*. A typology of competence as part of an integrative model of competence will depend on the interaction between organisational and individual level competence in its creation. But it is the integration of the knowledge, skills and technological know-how that will distinguish the organisation from its competitors (Yang, 2015; Flores et al., 2020) and it is one of the roles of the manager to make sure that both strategic and operational processes use the core competences to deliver innovation and effective production of products and services. Such competences will range from those required to transition to new, systems, structures and processes, to selecting and applying new technologies; from setting up new types of organisational structure to attracting, recruiting and training a diverse workforce. Some of these competences will be technical or technology based. Some will be related to adaptability and change, but all will be based on the acquisition and dissemination of knowledge.

On the Evolution of Management Theory

The narrative on Management Theory and Praxis is rich and diverse. Its direction influenced by economists, engineers, behavioural scientists, organisational specialists, consultants and practitioners. Its sources emanating not only from learned societies and business schools, but from the shop floor and operational units with additions to the concept focusing on philosophical and ethical foundations, conservation, sustainability and cultural specificity in organisational forms (Cummings & Bridgman, 2011, 2016; Cummings et al., 2017). Rarely has a subject found itself under such a rigorous examination.

During the First Industrial Revolution management evolved mostly from practice rather than theory via a sequence of challenge and response. An increase in the demand for manufactured goods and the supply of technological advances to meet it; and the creation of workshops and factories to bring together both sides of the equation brought with them sharp management challenges. In the first place there was the necessity to acquire knowledge about new technology. Secondly there was the necessity to apply that knowledge to new systems and processes. Thirdly to attract, select recruit and retain a workforce. Fourth there was the need to maintain a fluid approach to adapting to change; there were few best practices and many 'best fits'. And finally, to be innovative in exploiting land and capital. Many British Industrialists rose to the challenge with vim, vigour and a hunger for knowledge; and mobilised talent or trained people in the new technological skills to take advantage of economic opportunities. This was a step function above the management skills needed in dispersed and disparate cottage industries. Technology skills coupled with effective supervision were essential. The foundations of management were laid but serendipity or challenge and response could only take management so far. And from the middle of the nineteenth century there was an awareness that more was needed other than the rule of thumb and so evolved the origins of a more scientific approach to management.

During the nineteenth century the seeds of *scientific management* were sown and cultivated. However, an awareness that time clocks, stop watches and slide rules could only go so far in informing how people should be managed, led to the growth of a more human emphasis on management and from the early twentieth century the emergence of *behavioural management* theories. At around the time of the Third Industrial Revolution new approaches arose. Hence *management science* underpinned new management theories, followed by the importance of the organisational environment. In this latter, *management as practice* is of particular importance and within this area, the innovations in practice introduced by successful global corporations that came out of the economies of Asia. There are many excellent analyses which cover the various stages of management theory. Drucker (1954) mapped its evolution backed up by specific examples such as the Ford Story and the Sears Story; Landes' (1972) splendid overview of technological change contextualised Taylor's experience at the Midvale Steel Works in Pennsylvania and the links between *scientific management* and machine tool operation, handling of materials, division of labour and organisation of work. Child (1969) concluded that 'management may be regarded from at least three different perspectives; first as an economic resource performing a series of technical functions which comprise the organising and administering of other resources; secondly as a system of authority through which policy is translated into the execution of tasks; and thirdly as an elite social grouping which acts as an economic resource and maintains the associated systems of authority'. Wilson and Thomson (2009) and Muldoon et al. (2020) provide comprehensive analyses and are essential reading on the subject. The key elements that come out of each of the various 'movements' are discussed in the following sections.

Taylor, Ford, Fayol and the Rise of Scientific Management

Whilst Henry Towne's early paper in 1885 has been put forward as the first 'well-presented statement of the separate identity and place of management' (Wilson & Thomson, 2009; 8), followed by J. Slater Lewis' 1896 book on factory organisation (Landes, 1972; 322), it is perhaps the work of Frederick Winslow Taylor and the application of scientific method by Henry Ford (though each gave little credit to the other), that bring the concept of management and specifically scientific management to the fore. 'The label of scientific management is the one with which we are most familiar today, but in 1915, and earlier, management programs were most likely to be identified with the names of the management engineers themselves, e.g., Taylor system, Gantt system, Emerson system, and so forth' (Nadworny, 1957). Taylor was a Harvard student before becoming an apprentice machinist, chief engineer at the Midvale Steel Company and establishing his own company. The processes underlying the theory of scientific management were laid out in Taylor's four-hour speech to the Packard company in Detroit in 1909 and two years later in his seminal work, *The Principles of Scientific Management*. Taylor's worldwide reputation was founded on these principles (although he made his wealth from patents in steel-process improvements and his health from being a competent athlete who played tennis nationally). Taylor's approach heralded the way for work study in factories, not only in the city of Detroit but across the world. The three years after Taylor's death in 1915 'saw the curve of his technique take a dizzying rush upwards … he would have seen the knowledge roll over Europe and even Moscow listened while Lenin declared we must introduce the study and teaching of the new Taylor system' (Bulletin of the Taylor Society, June 1925). In Germany, manufacturers adopted Taylor's ideas with gusto. 'Management was no longer a term used by Mrs Beaton to describe a way of looking after the household, nor was it simply a chain of command. Management had become a system of mass control in production by process method, and textbook, something that had enduring appeal' (Donkin, 2001; 153). Scientific management consisted of standardisation, systematic work study and high levels of productivity. Its popularity in the early years of the twentieth century rested upon impressive increases of workplace productivity engendered by it and by its logical offshoot Fordist mass production (Sheldrake, 2003; Parker & Ritson, 2005). The assembly of the model T Ford automobiles using the principles of scientific management at the Piquette Avenue, then the Highland Park Plants in Detroit, USA, have become the images around which Second Industrial Revolution management coalesce. Refinements in division of labour, the installation of moving chassis and parts epitomised breaking down tasks and timing each element to ensure the most effective production methods was 'pursued to extremes by Ford engineers' (Donkin, 2001; 148). Taylor's seminal work opens with the words 'the principal object of management should be to secure the maximum prosperity for the employer, coupled with maximum prosperity of each employee' (Taylor, 1911; 8). In France, Henri Fayol found that scientific management as articulated by Taylor, complemented his own administrative theory of management and Fayol became 'the prophet of gallicized Taylorism' (Landes, 1972; 528). Fayol's experience as managing director of a mining and steel-making company helped to inform his *General and Industrial Management* (Fayol, 1916), which defined managerial activities as one of six groups undertaken by industrial organisations (the others being technical, commercial, financial, security and accounting). Managerial activities were planning, organisation, command, coordination and control. Fayol argued that managerial ability should be acquired in the same way as technical ability—through theory and practice. It was to the former that he addressed his words because 'there exists no generally accepted theory of management leading to 'the most contradictory practices under the aegis of the same principle' (Fayol, 1916; 15). Whilst noting that there is no limit to the number of principles of management, he then laid out 14 of the most observed from the division of work through discipline through order and ending with esprit de corps. Whilst there were similarities between Taylor and Fayol, namely the *scientific approach*, Taylor's concept of management was built upwards from work study at the operating level; Fayol's began at the Managing Director and worked down through the hierarchical organisation. It was perhaps Fayol's observation that organising was the necessity to build up the dual structure of people and material, that brought the people aspect of organisation (rather than the process) to greater prominence and paved the way to a more behavioural theory of management. In the words of British industrialist Seebohm Rowntree that 'the factory is not just a soulless organisation for turning out cocoa and chocolate. It is a place in which thousands of people are spending a very large proportion of their waking hours. Everyone can, if he or she wills, help to foster a spirit of friendliness and good fellowship, so that the hours spent in the factory are happy hours. Let us have efficiency and good organisation by all means. In your everyday work, remember always the kindly spirit' (Morris, 2017). These words proved to be prophetic in their assessment of the role of organisations and hence the role of the manager in those organisations.

Follett, Barnard and the Rise of Behavioural Management

There were limitations in taking a purely scientific approach to methods of production. In fact, 380% labour turnover in the first year of production in Ford's the new plant raised concerns; (Donkin, 2001) in fiction, the perspective in Aldous Huxley's 1932 novel *Brave New World* was of workers being hatched as standardised workers. As the Second Industrial Revolution gained momentum, and as the new practices spread—mass production, scientific measurement of production processes—so did the demand for alternative management methods. And it was the growing emphasis on people in the organisation that led to the second important 'movement' in management theory, the behavioural or humanistic perspective, which over a 30-year period produced some of the benchmark texts of modern management theory. Max Weber's (1920) studies laid the sociological foundations of modern economic organisations, with particular reference to the role of the manager in bureaucratic structures. Amongst other significant works were those by Elton Mayo (*The Human Problems of an Industrial Civilization*, Mayo, 1933), Abraham Maslow (*A Theory of Human Motivation*, Maslow, 1943), Douglas McGregor (*The Human Side of Enterprise*, McGregor, 1960) and the works of Mary

Parker Follett and Chester Barnard. The latter's *The Functions of the Executive* (1938) was written in response to the perceived lack of reference to the function of the organisation of work and the role of executives and managers in it—which Barnard likened to 'leaving a vital organ out of anatomy or its functions out of physiology'. Barnard's business experience (he was President of one of the Bell Companies in the United States) was coupled with sharp observations about the nature of work in organisations. He concluded that social factors were critical to effective performance in organisations, and these social factors (human interaction) in cooperative systems leant an urgency to the need to create processes to maintain a cooperative environment—'for if cooperation cannot adjust to attack new limitations (such as organisational change) in the environment it must fail. These adjustment processes become management processes and the specialised organs are executives and executive organisations.' This was a thesis based on people and their interactions within organisations, of which management and the executive function had an integral role to play that went beyond measurement and process management; but included 'the capacity of organisations to satisfy personal ideals' (Barnard, 1938; 146). The role of human dynamics in organisations was recognised and the role of the executive or manager as a part of this dynamic was articulated creating a significant contribution to behavioural or humanistic perspectives of management theory.

The idea that business challenges could not be solved without the skills and cooperation of people form the basis of humanistic or behavioural theories of management and in this respect Mary Parker Follett's speeches and writings in the 1920s and 1930s exhibited markedly different views from those that had gone before –particularly of scientific management—and, for some, her theories meant that she 'stood apart from her time and anticipated much that was to come in the management literature' (Parker, 1984). Educated at Cambridge, Follett's experience covered vocational guidance and evening programs in public schools, and a period as a social worker in Boston, USA, from 1900 to 1908, during which time she developed her views of society in group dynamics which laid the foundations for her theories of management. She was one of the first women ever invited to address the London School of Economics where she delivered innovative viewpoints on management issues. Her concept of integrating opposing points of view, power-sharing control at the group and individual level, and recognition of the importance of the organisational environment led her to conclude that 'we need a technique of human relations based on the preservation of the integrity of the individual' and to unite 'fruitfully' the contributions of individuals to larger organisational objectives. In this context, management takes place in a system where 'organism reacts to environment plus organism' (Follett, 1930) and becomes a process of integrating the interests of individuals. To Follett, management was the art of getting things done through people. In the early years of the twentieth century management theory and practice evolved from being based largely on the science of systems and processes to the science of human interaction. But there was also the realisation that management wasn't a binary choice between one or the other. It was Peter Drucker who took the concept on to the next level.

Drucker and Management Science

The emergence of Management Science at the peak of the humanistic or behavioural era of management theory during the 1950s was based on recognition that the operating environment, the prevailing technologies in that environment and the relative position of the organisation in that environment should inform both the structure of an organisation and the way the organisation went about delivering benefits to its stakeholders—whether these be shareholders, customers or employees. In management science 'professional managers were assigned responsibility for planning, setting goals defining problems and making decisions. The methodological cornerstone was a contingency approach with unobtrusive control devices such as job specification, internal career ladders and operating routines monitoring performance' (Wilson & Thomson, 2009; 30). It was during this period that theoretical (and practical) approaches to management proliferated from the work of Peter Drucker (*The Practice of Management* Drucker, 1954) through to W. Edwards Deming (*Out of the Crisis* Deming, 1982) and Total Quality Management through to Thomas Peters and Robert Waterman (*In Search of Excellence* Peters & Waterman, 1982) and the Learning Organisation to the spawning of 'a range of derivatives, some of which were not much more than short term fads' (Wilson and Thomson (2009; 30). Of the many variants it is perhaps the work of Peter Drucker that was most influential in shaping the concept of management as a science. To Drucker, the quality and performance of managers determined the success of a business. Indeed, he regarded management as the only effective advantage of an enterprise in competitive markets. To him, management was grounded in the modern business enterprise through the systematic organisation of economic resources. 'Management, its competence, its integrity and its performance' would be decisive. It was the concept of systematic analysis that evolved into that of management as a science, rather than a vague rule of thumb activity with many interpretations. Drucker saw management as a 'specific organ of the business enterprise' (Drucker, 1954; 7). Its first priority was economic performance with business objectives to be achieved through management by objectives and self-control. In a series of ground-breaking publications, consultancy and his famed teaching assignments at, inter alia, the Graduate School of Business administration at New York University and Harvard Business School (as well as at Sarah Lawrence and Bennington) Drucker articulated the roles and responsibilities of the manager and the competences to carry these out. In *Management, Tasks, Responsibilities, Practices* (Drucker, 1974) he proposed that management was both codified experience and an organised body of knowledge; management consisted of tasks; it was a discipline but also consisted of people. Managers performed, but management determined what was needed. The dimensions of management were not only competences around skill and performance but also those of personality, example and integrity. In this respect, Drucker's management science outlined management as knowledge and skills on the one hand, but attitudes and behaviour on the other. Recognition of the scope and dimensions of management, the systematic analysis of its constituent parts and the articulation of them in a form that could be learned and taught thus forms the basis of management as a science. The planned and systematic nature management as it had evolved to this point proved an invaluable process. It codified a concept that had once been based on intuition alone. But, for some, it had over-elaborated and delineated a process that was more nuanced and failed to answer the question of how to account for the messiness or unpredictability that accompanied much of organisational life.

Management as Practice

The rigour that was being applied to management as a scientific subject from the mid-1950s onwards ('Peter Drucker put management on the map') proved to be a precursor to a focus on how to manage in new organisational forms arising from internationalisation then globalisation and about the differences between Leadership and Management. It was the work of Henry Mintzberg that approached the subject from the reality of management action; 'how do we make sense of the vast array of activities that constitute managing?' (Mintzberg, 2011; 1). His perspective on the subject was articulated in early publications *The Nature of Managerial Work* (Mintzberg, 1973) and 'The Manager's Job, Folklore and Fact', *Harvard Business Review* (Mintzberg, 1975) and refined over the next 40 years. First, he was of the opinion that leaders could not simply delegate management. Instead, managers were themselves leaders and leadership was management practiced well. Second, management was not uniquely a science nor uniquely a profession, instead, it was a practice that could be learned through experience and context. 'Put together a good deal of craft with the right touch of art alongside some use of science and you end up with a job that is above all a practice' (Mintzberg, 2011; 10). And thirdly, the role of the manager was one of action, of perpetual awareness of the environment, of constant needs to adapt and respond. He argued that the pressures of the managerial environment left little time for reflective planning. Instead, the job bred 'adaptive information manipulators' who preferred the live situation. What Mintzberg imparts in his analysis was not the 'dream of sequential and deliberate managerial control', but the 'real and important aspects of management … how management is performed in everyday work practices' (Tengblad, 2012). The emphasis on action; on the ability to respond to uncertain or unpredictable situations and the lack of lengthy reflective time in achieving objectives bring with them additional competences. Whilst science might be deemed important, it sits alongside craft and art in the panoply of requirements for managers in Mintzberg's world. But the essence of management of practice was not confined to Western centric approaches. Indeed, as the Third Industrial Revolution gathered pace a rich canvass of new management styles—originating in Japan—became sources of innovation for managing in a period of globalisation. The lack of a dominant Asian management theory means that there is a broad spectrum of opinion about what constitutes management practice in the region; perhaps supporting the observation that there 'is no one single management culture' (Sanger et al., 2017). Nevertheless there has been a sizeable impact and influence of Asian management practices and leading practitioners on the overall genre. It might be argued that the impact of Taiichi Ohno of Toyota, who is credited with developing the JIT (just-in-time) system in the 1950s and 1960s was as powerful an influence as F.W. Taylor; or that of Soichiro Honda, Zhang Ruimin, Lakshmi Mittal and Jack Ma as influential as Henry Ford. The rise of Japanese corporations introduced a whole new set of systems, processes and language of management. Amongst these were total quality management and continuous improvement that gained global traction. Decision-making by consensus, identifying problems at the root cause and dealing with them accordingly, just-in-time systems, *jidoka* or 'automation with a human touch', *kanban*, a production tool helping just-in-time production, and *poka yoke* or mistake proofing are all management concepts that can be added to the canon of management theory.

The nature of management challenges over the Four Industrial Revolutions beginning in 1750 range from start up to catch up; from hierarchy to network to swarm; from innovation to adaptation; from advantage to consolidation. Furthermore, the range of experiences included management challenges that were contextual such as the installation of water-power to run new types of cotton-making machinery; or the adaptation of systems and processes from the armaments and meat manufacturing industries to a new automobile factory; or the application of robotics and in commercial and industrial organisations in South Korea and Singapore in the twenty-first century. Ouchi's *Theory Z* (Ouchi, 1981) drew on sources from both Eastern and Western practice with an emphasis on consensus and individual responsibility. The emphasis on responsiveness, improvisation, flexibility and speed and the idea of adaptive translation were features of the approach to management in Asian companies that were as important to their success as Taylor's scientific management to that of US companies in earlier periods. The above paints a narrative of richness in management theory and practice which his more than a purely Western-centric point of view.

A Managerial Paradigm Shift

There is depth to management theory and practice that stretches over 250 years with many 'philosophers and speculators' providing evidence of some of the contextual competences required—whether these were the advanced management practices at Boulton and Watt's Soho Foundry—an 'astonishingly fertile pioneer of scientific management', during the 1790s (Pollard, 1965; 98); or the experiments in motivation in the relay assembly and bank wiring departments at Western Electric's Hawthorne Works during the 1920s (Sofer, 1972; Donkin, 2001; 168); or the management of Toyota's production systems during the 1980s with just-in-time, quality management and quality circles (Jackson & Tomioka, 2004). There are perceived shortfalls—the 'think manager think male' observation, or those in relation to race or ethnicity—which need additional research for a more complete picture. Hence, more recently particular Nobel Prize winners for Economics have also informed the subject of management, most notably Kahneman (2002) and Thaler (2017) and their contributions to psychology and economics and behavioural economics; and the work of inter alia Prieto and Phipps (2019) adding value with their narrative of African American management history. The urgency to increase the diversity of talent has rarely been greater. It should be no surprise that, in today's vortex of organisational change, the future of management is once again the subject of debate (Skilton & Hovsepian, 2018). A new, emerging narrative about management is that 'it's not business as usual now'.

In this regard, the new technologies of Industry 4.0. will transform business models, strategies and operational processes and have the potential to change how people in the workforce connect, interact and communicate. A particular aspect of these developments is a social media revolution which touches almost every aspect of working life. Social media platforms are those connectivity-enabled applications 'that facilitate interaction and the co-creation, exchange, and publication of information' by collaborative projects, blogs and microblogs, content communities and social networking sites—with each medium offering specific capabilities as well as constraints. They are technologies and channels which enable a large community of participants to collaborate productively. One of the reasons why social media has been so readily embraced is that it helps connect people with each other in ways that are valuable, meaningful and convenient (Blanchard, 2011; Thomas & Akdere, 2013; Poba-Nzaou et al., 2016). In commercial organisations, social media applications are beneficial when seeking to create and disseminate knowledge. They have the potential to enhance communication during times of change, increase the level of trust and participation in decision-making, decrease the level of resistance to change; and enhance the level of support for change acceptance in the workplace. Social media interchanges with co-workers can positively affect intrinsic work motivation and proactive behaviour. Of course, organisations must learn to utilise these tools for the purpose of achieving organisational goals. A process which continues to evolve (Bizzi, 2020; Naeem, 2020).

On the one hand, a positive outlook can foresee managers operating in a world where applications of new technology, backed up by the knowledge creation and communication power of social media, will create a revolution in the way they go about their daily tasks; where intelligent technology meets human ingenuity, not only to shape a future workforce, but to create new organisational forms and structures, new types of job within these structures and radical new content in the jobs themselves. At a corporate level, the massive disruption of the business environment, the rise of the knowledge-based organisation, the increasing relevance of competence in strategy setting, and the transformation from self-contained organisational hierarchies to flat and networked 'co-creation clusters', demand agility and adaptation. These changes will revolutionise not only the context within which management takes place, but also the nature of management and the role of managers—'now that AI is removing many of the administrative tasks typically handled by managers, their roles are evolving to focus more on soft over hard skills … robots are better than their managers at providing unbiased information, maintaining work schedules, problem-solving and budget management, while managers are better at empathy, coaching and creating a work culture' (Deiser, 2009; Chakhoyan, 2017; Schawbel, 2019).

Of course, there is another, less benign perspective of the future of management that emerged during 2020. None of the philosophers and speculators who presented their views on the anticipated outcomes of the

Fourth Industrial Revolution had built into their models the events that unfolded from the beginning of the year. The worldwide catastrophe of Covid19 has taken lives, devastated families and ruined economies. Some will never recover from the horror. It is likely that this devastating phenomenon will impact on every aspect of the economy and as a result, on organisational structures and operations. It has introduced a new language and heightened awareness of otherwise established concepts such as work life balance. With a world turned upside down the extent of this impact and how the management of those organisations will have to adapt remains uncertain. Nevertheless, where epidemics and pandemics have struck before, organisations have invariably adjusted. Many had no choice. The incidence of cholera in the nineteenth and strains of influenza in the twentieth century changed not only how people lived in their societies but how organisations operated in those societies. Seeking learning from these experiences may help to inform how organisations can adjust to the new normal that faces every country of the world after the passing of this latest horrific outbreak.

Already, new models of management and leadership are being proposed. A 'social super' leader or manager will combine social initiatives into the core of business operations; those who are data-driven and take methodical, data-focused approaches to decision-making; 'disruption drivers' are prepared to implement disruptive technologies; whilst 'talent champions' will focus their investment in helping employees to adapt to the future ways of working (WEF, 2019). Interpersonal communication will still be required for business, hence reinforcing the need for a managerial role, regardless of the level of technology; 'even in the Fourth Industrial Revolution, it is pointed out that interpersonal communication, including subordinate management, remains important as work that has to be performed by humans' and 'AI won't be replacing a manager's job; it will be supplementing it. The future of work is one where robots and humans will be working side by side, helping each other get work done faster and more efficient than ever before' (Toda et al., 2017; Schawbel, 2019). Management isn't a homogenous concept and there is no single definition that can capture the 'messy stuff' as well as the more planned and systematic activity. But perhaps one assumption holds true over time and Warren Buffet, the Sage of Omaha was very clear—'when you have able managers of high character running business about which they are passionate, you can have a dozen or more reporting to you and still have time for an afternoon nap' (Buffet, 2002). A greater understanding of management theory and practice over time may help to inform a future framework.

The Structure of the Book

Management competence is neither an abstract conceptual term nor a wish list of actionable attributes. Indeed 'it is a foolish and dangerous error to maintain barriers between thinkers and doers in any kind of human activity' (Watson, 1994). Instead management competence reflects the complex and often 'flexibly' defined role of the managers themselves. On the one hand the role of the manager is concerned with knowledge, its filtering, acquisition and dissemination, on the other it is concerned with delivering results through action. On the one hand it is concerned with planning and forecasting, on the other it is concerned with solving immediate problems. On the one hand it is concerned with strategic workforce management on the other with displaying emotional intelligence in the here and now. Management competence is not just the know why, it is the know-how and the know how to behave. These assumptions are taken into account in the structure of the book.

The framework outlined above envisages management as a concept, and managers in practice, being analysed in each of four historical periods. Evidence for any consistent approaches or outlooks will be sought and where relevant identified. There will of course be an element of subjectivity in this retelling of management competence but it is hoped that the outcome will provide at least a contribution to understanding the management competences that were predominant during each of the Revolutions and to speculate whether any have traversed time and may be relevant in future.

Chapter 2 will begin the analysis by looking at *management during the First Industrial Revolution* with a particular emphasis on Europe.

Chapter 3 will continue the theme by providing evidence of theory and practice of *management during the Second Industrial Revolution* with a focus on the United States, identified as being of the most significance to the subject during this period. The points of view of Frederick Winslow Taylor and the creation of the concept of scientific management from his findings will be covered as well as the contributions of Mary Parker Follett, Chester Barnard, Mayo, Maslow and McGregor. Chapter 4 will cover *management during the Third Industrial Revolution* and will shift the focus to those economies which from the 1960s achieved rapid growth from their bases in Asia. In the first place will be an analysis of Japanese organisations and how management practice was implemented in their context; secondly the analysis will extend to the economies of South Korea, Taiwan, Singapore and Hong Kong known as the 'Asian Tigers'. In addition, the rise of China as an economic superpower will also be considered and the management style and competence required in its successful commercial organisations. A further geographic perspective on the subject of management will be concerned with the management of those organisations whose operations expanded in the context of globalisation and global growth. Chapter 5 will complete the analysis of management during the specific time periods outlined by looking in depth at *management during the Fourth Industrial Revolution*. Chapter 6 will pull together the conclusions of the analyses in the form of *core management competences*. It is intended that Chaps. 7–11 will discuss in more detail some of the prevalent competences that appear to be important across time and geography. These are as follows: *demonstrates agile governance and adaptability to make change work effectively—'know-how', collaborates to create and share knowledge and information—'know why', engages and develops the workforce—'know how to behave', integrates multiple systems and processes and seeks continuous improvement—'know how' and takes effective action to deliver results—'know what'*. Chapter 12 will form the conclusion and address key learning points.

Important antecedents of contemporary management practice are contained within the experiences of those who managed throughout each of the Four Industrial Revolutions.

References

Allen, R. C. (2011). Why the Industrial Revolution was British: Commerce, Induced Invention, and the Scientific Revolution. *The Economic History Review, 64*(2), 357–384.

Armstrong, M. (2005). *Armstrong's Handbook of Management and Leadership.* Kogan Page.

Augier, M., & Teece, D. J. (2009). Dynamic Capabilities and the Role of Managers in Business Strategy and Economic Performance. *Organization Science, 20*(2), 410.

Babbage, C. (1832). *On the Economy of Machinery and Manufacture.* John Murray.

Barnard, C. I. (1938). *The Functions of the Executive, 1968 Edition.* Harvard University press.

Batiz-Lazo, B. (2019). What Is New in "a new history of management"? *Journal of Management History, 25*(*1*), 1.

Bizzi, L. (2020). Should HR Managers Allow Employees to Use Social Media at Work? Behavioral and Motivational Outcomes of Employee Blogging. *The International Journal of Human Resource Management, 31*(10), 1285–1312.

Blanchard, O. (2011). *Social Media: ROI.* Pearson.

Boyatzis, R. E. (1982). *The Competent Manager.* John Wiley and Sons.

Boyatzis, R. E. (2011). Managerial and Leadership Competencies: A Behavioural Approach to Emotional, Social and Cognitive Intelligence. *Vision (09722629), 15*(2), 91–100.

Brunninge, O. (2009). Using History in Organizations; How Managers Make Purposeful Reference to History in Strategy Processes. *Journal of Organizational Change Management, 22*(1), 8–26.

Buffet, W. (2002). *The Essays of Warren Buffet edited by Cunningham.* L.A. Wiley.

Bulletin of the Taylor Society. (1925). *Review of the Momentum of Taylorism.* Library of Congress.

Chakhoyan, A. (2017). Is the Era of Management Over? World Economic Forum, https://www.weforum.org/agenda/2017/12/is-management-era-over/.

Chen, M. (2004). *Asian Management Systems.* Thomson Learning.

Child, J. (1969). *British Management Thought – A Critical Analysis.* George Allen and Unwin.

CIPD. (2014). Are UK Organisations Getting Better at Managing Their People? https://www.cipd.co.uk/Images/megatrends_2014-uk-organisations-managing-people_tcm18-11407.pdf

Cummings, S., & Bridgman, T. (2011). The Relevant Past: Why the History of Management Should Be Critical for Our Future. *Academy of Management Learning and Education, 10*(1), 77–93.

Cummings, S., & Bridgman, T. (2016). The Limits and Possibilities of History: How a Wider, Deeper, and More Engaged Understanding of Business History Can Foster Innovative Thinking. *Academy of Management Learning and Education, 15*(2), 250–267.

Cummings, C., Bridgman, T., Hassard, J., & Rowlinson, M. (2017). *A New History of Management*. Cambridge University Press.

Davis, J. C., & Gonzales, J. G. (2003). Scholarly Journal Articles about the Asian Tiger Economies: Authors, Journals and Research Fields, 1986–2001. *Asian-Pacific Economic Literature, 17*(2), 51–61.

De Castro, J., Justo, R., & Delgado-Marquez, L. (2018). Female Leadership: The Impact on Organizations, *ie Insights*, https://www.ie.edu/insights/articles/female-leadership-the-impact-on-organizations/

de Vries, J. (1994). The Industrial Revolution and the Industrious Revolution. *The Journal of Economic History, 54*(2) Papers Presented at the Fifty-Third Annual Meeting of the Economic History Association, 249–270.

Deiser, R. (2009). *Designing the Smart Organisation*. Jossey Bass.

Deming, W. E. (1982). *Out of the Crisis, 2018 Edition*. MIT Press.

Donkin, R. (2001). *Blood, Sweat and Tears*. Texere.

Drucker, P. (1954). *The Practice of Management*, Butterworth-Heinemann Edition (2007).

Drucker, P. (1974). *Management, Tasks, Responsibilities, Practices, 2011 Edition*. Routledge.

Fayol, H. (1916). *General and Industrial Management*. 2013 reprint, Martino Fine Books

Finkelstein, J., & Newman, D. (1984). The Third Industrial Revolution: A Special Challenge to Managers. *Organizational Dynamics, 13*(1), 53–65.

Flores, E., Xu, X., & Yuqian, L. (2020). Human Capital 4.0: A Workforce Competence Typology for Industry 4.0. *Journal of Manufacturing Technology Management, 31*(4), 687–703.

Follett, M. P. (1930). *Creative Experience*. Longmans, Green and Co.

Geddes, P. (1915). *Cities in Evolution*. Williams and Norgate.

Gratton, L., & Scott, A. (2016). *The 100-Year Life*. Bloomsbury.

Hilbert, R. A. (1987). Bureaucracy as Belief, Rationalisation as Repair; Max Weber in a Post Functionalist Age. *Sociological Theory, 5*(1), 70–86.

Hofstede, G. (2007). Asian Management in the 21st Century. *Asia Pacific Journal of Management, 24*, 411–420.
Iraj, S., Kamat, S., Prakash, S., & Weldon, M. (2017). Will Productivity Growth Return in the New Digital Era? An Analysis of the Potential Impact on Productivity of the Fourth Industrial Revolution. *Bell Labs Technical Journal, 22*, 2–18.
Jackson, K., & Tomioka, M. (2004). *The Changing Face of Japanese Management*. Routledge.
Joullié, J. (2018). Management without Theory for the Twenty-first Century. *Journal of Management History, 24*(4), 377–395.
Kang, H.-J., Chung, K.-w., & Nam, K.-Y. (2015). A Competence Model for Design Managers: A Case Study of Middle Managers in Korea. *International Journal of Design, 9*(2), 109–127.
Kennedy, P. (1988). *The Rise and Fall of the Great Powers*. London: Fontana Press.
Landes, D. (1972). *The Unbound Prometheus*. Cambridge University Press.
Logevall, F. (2020). *JFK Volume 1*. Penguin Viking.
Maslow, A. (1943). *A Theory of Human Motivation*, 2016 Midwest Journal Press Edition
Mathias, P. (1969). *The First Industrial Nation*. Methuen and Co.
Mayo, M. (1933). *The Human Problems of an Industrial Civilization, 2003 Edition*. Routledge.
Mazali, T. (2018). From Industry 4.0 to Society 4.0, There and Back. *AI & Soc, 33*, 405–411. https://doi.org/10.1007/s00146-017-0792-6
McGregor, D. (1960). *The Human Side of Enterprise*, McGraw Hill, 2006 Edition
McWilliams, D. (2020). *We Are Living Through a 'Pandession'—Here's How We Escape*, http://www.davidmcwilliams.ie/we-are-living-through-a-pandession-heres-how-we-escape/
Meakin, A. (1928). *The New Industrial Revolution*. Victor Gollancz.
Mintzberg, H. (1973). *The Nature of Managerial Work*. Harper and Row.
Mintzberg, H. (1975). The Manager's Job, Folklore and Fact. *Harvard Business Review, 53*(4), 1.
Mintzberg, H. (2011). *Managing*. FT Prentice Hall.
Moingeon, B., & Edmondson, A. (1996). *Organisational learning and Competitive Advantage*. Sage Publications.
Mokyr, J. (2009). *The Enlightened Economy*. Penguin Books.
Mokyr, J., Vickers, C., & Ziebarth, N. L. (2015). The History of Technological Anxiety and the Future of Economic Growth: Is This Time Different? *Journal of Economic Perspectives, 29*(3), 31–50.

Morgan, J. (2019). Will We Work in Twenty-first Century Capitalism? A Critique of the Fourth Industrial Revolution Literature. *Economy and Society, 48*(3), 371–398.

Morris, B. (2017). The 'Human factor' in Business, https://www.cipd.co.uk/news-views/changing-work-views/future-work/thought-pieces/human-factor-business.

Muellerleile, C., & Robertson, S. L. (2018). Digital Weberianism: Bureaucracy, Information, and the Techno-rationality of Neoliberal Capitalism. *Indiana Journal of Global Legal Studies, 25*(1), 187.

Muldoon, J., Gould, A., & McMurray, A. (2020). *The Palgrave Handbook of Management History*. Springer International Publishing.

Nadworny, M. J. (1957). Frederick Taylor and Frank Gilbreth: Competition in Scientific Management, *Twentieth-Century Literary Criticism*, edited by Jennifer Gariepy, 76, Gale, 1998.

Naeem, M. (2020). Understanding the Role of Social Media in Organizational Change Implementation. *Management Research Review, 43*(9), 1097–1116.

Nicholas, T. (2010). The Role of Independent Invention in U.S. Technological Development, 1880–1930. *The Journal of Economic History, 70*(1), 57–82.

Nobre, F., Walker, D., & Brown, M. (2014). Ability Based View in Action; A Software Corporation Study. *Brazilian Administrative Review, 11*(2), 1.

Ouchi, W. (1981). *Theory Z: How American Business Can Meet the Japanese Challenge*. Basic Books.

Parker, L. D. (1984). Control in Organizational Life: The Contribution of Mary Parker Follett. *Academy of Management Review, 9*(4), 736–745.

Parker, L. D., & Ritson, P. (2005). Fads, Stereotypes and Management Gurus: Fayol and Follett Today. *Management Decision, 43*(10), 1335–1357.

Peters, T. J., & Waterman, R. H. (1982). *In Search of Excellence: Lessons from America's Best-run Companies*. Harper & Row.

Philbeck, T., & Davis, N. (2019). The Fourth Industrial Revolution : Shaping a New Era. *Journal of International Affairs, 72*(1), 17.

Poba-Nzaou, P., Lemieux, N., Beaupré, D., & Uwizeyemungu, S. (2016). Critical Challenges Associated with the Adoption of Social Media: A Delphi of a Panel of Canadian Human Resources Managers. *Journal of Business Research, 69*(10), 4011–4019.

Pollard, S. (1965). *The Genesis of Modern Management*. Penguin Books.

Porter, M. E. (1990). *The Competitive Advantage of Nations*. The Macmillan Press.

Prieto, L. T., & Phipps, S. T. A. (2019). African American Management History, Emerald Points, Emerald Publishing Limited

Rabeh, M., Husam, A., & Saeed, M. (2017). The Fourth Industrial Revolution (Industry 4.0): A Social Innovation Perspective. *Technology Innovation Management Review, 7*(11), 12–20.

Roulac, S. (2019). The Industrial Revolution Remembers. *Journal of Property Investment & Finance, 1*, 1463–578X.

Sanger, M. R., Nei, D. S., Ferrell, B. T., & Yang, F. (2017). Agency, Conscientiousness, and Leadership Emergence in Asia: How Managers in Countries with and without British Influence Differ from Each Other. *Consulting Psychology Journal: Practice & Research, 69*(4), 296–314.

Schawbel, D. (2019). How Artificial Intelligence Is Redefining the Role of Manager, World Economic Forum, https://www.weforum.org/agenda/2019/11/how-artificial-intelligence-is-redefining-the-role-of-manager/

Schwab, K. (2016). The Fourth Industrial Revolution: What It Means, How to Respond, World Economic Forum, https://www.weforum.org/agenda/2016/01/the-fourth-industrial-revolution-what-it-means-and-how-to-respond/

Scott, A. J., & Gratton, L. (2020). New Ways Of Living, *The Sunday Times*, May 24.

Sheldrake, J. (2003). *Management Theory*. Thomson.

Skilton, M., & Hovsepian, F. (2018). *The 4th Industrial Revolution*. Palgrave Macmillan.

Škrinjarić, B., & Domadenik, P. (2020). Examining the Role of Key Competences in Firm Performance. *International Journal of Manpower, 41*(4), 391.

Smith, A. (1776). *The Wealth of Nations, Penguin Books Edition, 1986*. England.

Sofer, C. (1972). *Organisations in Theory and Practice*. Heinemann.

Takeuchi, J. (1999). Human Resources Management Systems of Asian Companies. *Japanese Research Institute, 45*, 1. https://www.jri.co.jp/english/periodical/rim/1999/RIMc199904resource/

Taniguchi, N. (2004). *Industrial Revolution, 1899–1905. In Castle Valley America: Hard Land, Hard-won Home*. University Press of Colorado. https://doi.org/10.2307/j.ctt4cgp5n.1

Taylor, F. W. (1911). *The Principles of Scientific Management*, First World Library Edition 2005.

Temin, P. (1997). Two Views of the British Industrial Revolution. *The Journal of Economic History, 57*(1), 63–82.

Tengblad, S. (2012). *The Work of Managers*. Oxford University Press.

Thomas, K. J., & Akdere, M. (2013). Social Media as Collaborative Media in Workplace Learning. *Human Resource Development Review, 12*(3), 329–344.
Toda, A., Chuma, H., Hayashi, S., and Kume, K. (2017). Role of Managers in the Fourth Industrial Revolution: From the viewpoint of comparing Japan and the United States (Japanese), *Discussion Papers 17062*, Research Institute of Economy, Trade and Industry
Van Lent, W., & Durepos, G. (2019). Nurturing the Historic Turn: 'History as theory' Versus 'History as method'. *Journal of Management History, 25*(4), 429–443.
Watson, T. J. (1994). *In Search of Management*. Thomson Business Press.
Weber, M. (1920). *The Theory of Social and Economic Organisation, 1947 edition with an Introduction by Talcott Parsons*. The Free Press.
WEF. (2017). *Jobs and the Fourth Industrial Revolution*, https://www.weforum.org/about/jobs-and-the-fourth-industrial-revolution
WEF. (2019). *The 4 types of leader who will thrive in the Fourth Industrial Revolution*, https://www.weforum.org/agenda/2019/01/these-four-leadership-styles-are-key-to-success-in-the-fourth-industrial-revolution/
WEF. (2020). *Fourth Industrial Revolution*, https://www.weforum.org/focus/fourth-industrial-revolution
Wilson, J. F., & Thomson, A. (2009). *The Making of Modern Management*. Oxford University Press.
Yang, C.-C. (2015). The Integrated Model of Core Competence and Core Capability. *Total Quality Management & Business Excellence, 26*(1/2), 173–189.

2

Management During the First Industrial Revolution: European Pioneers—The Genesis of Modern Management

Strange and Interesting Things

Early industrial management evolved from a sequence of challenge and response.

From the mid-eighteenth to the mid-nineteenth century a combination of technological invention, innovation and improvement in multiple industries, underpinned by favourable institutional structures and processes, led to a transformation of the British economy and became known as the First Industrial Revolution. Mechanisation and the standardisation of systems and processes were at its heart, with dynamics that were mutually reinforcing across industrial, commercial and infrastructure sectors. Cotton, coal and iron output grew significantly; production per head more than doubled and there were major capital investments in metallurgy with larger organisations in the production process—a number of companies having 5000+ employees. The rate of growth in the economy was faster than in any preindustrial stage and involved qualitative structural and technical change, which gave Britain a comparative advantage in international trade and led to a decisive break in the history of technology and the economy (Pollard, 1965; Landes, 1972; Mitchell, 1975;

P. Turner, *The Making of the Modern Manager*,
https://doi.org/10.1007/978-3-030-81062-7_2

Jackson, 1992; Botticelli, 1997; Greasley & Oxley, 1997; Temin, 1997; Mokyr, 2009; Allen, 2011). There was an innovative zeal at this time that went beyond Hargreaves' spinning jenny and Arkwright's water frame. 'One must look at the full range over which entrepreneurs were seizing on and applying new inventive insights', including agriculture, road and canal building, iron manufacture and the steam engine as well as cotton textiles. The introduction of engines for converting heat into work provided the final and most decisive stage. 'By liberating it from its last shackles', steam enabled the immense and rapid development of large-scale industry to take place. The sheer diversity of manufactures was astounding—for example, hundreds of different types of hammer were produced in Birmingham—each adapted to a specific function (Mantoux, 1928; Landes, 1972; Rostow, 1978; Basalla, 1988; Kapas, 2008). At this point there was a break with a tradition of economic life, and a pace of change, which had existed for centuries and had been universal across all countries up to that time. The favourability of Britain's unique informal institutions—whereby business was undertaken based on informal codes; and its formal institutions—based on the fact that parliamentary control meant that the state was not predatory, and profits generated for entrepreneurs were not expropriated by the state; added to a formula for technological and economic progress. Innovations took place in an increasingly urban environment whose economy was heavily dependent upon factory-based manufacturing industry. The growth of cities, the increase in population, the rise in national income per head and the shift from farm to factory (Mathias, 1969; McCloskey, 1985; Kapas, 2008; Mays et al., 2008) had global repercussions. Even with tempering and revision of arguments which posit a less sequential approach (de Vries, 1994; Crafts, 1996), the fact that a series of transformational events took place, that these events were more readily observed in Britain before becoming evident in Continental Europe and the United States to varying degrees, and that these had a considerable impact on both the economies and the societies in which they took place, is a viable thesis. The consequences of change, particularly the introduction of machinery, were 'simply stupendous' (Kennedy, 1988). Furthermore, the financial infrastructure evolved in support of Britain's industrial economy (Garnett et al., 2017). Where technological change took place, commercial change soon followed.

Clear lines of demarcation between roles and descriptions of the authorities and responsibilities included in those roles, as represented by modern day organisation charts, were few and far between during the First Industrial Revolution. A range of possible managerial roles included owner, managing partner, agent, under-agent, foreman, manager, under-manager, underviewer, oversman, corporal and steward (British Government Commission, 1842; Williams, 1980; Van den Eeckhout, 2009). In this context, a business owner could be the only manager in the operation; or the owner would appoint an agent, overseer or foreman to take responsibility for day-to-day operations. As organisations grew in size and scope during the course of the late eighteenth and early nineteenth centuries, the personal form of management or family-based ownership and management existed alongside other forms (Wilson & Thomson, 2009). More under-managers or those in senior supervisory roles were appointed with multiple levels of management activity—owner/agent or overseer/senior supervisor. And then there were the many supervisors themselves, responsible for operational planning and organisation, workflow in small teams and providing the *unintermitting attention* described by Richard Gaskell in his survey of the manufacturing population (1833). The definition of manager during the First Industrial Revolution could apply to a multiplicity of different roles involved in planning, implementing new technology applications, organising work, employing and training a workforce, and ensuring that outputs were measured and consistent.

Management Challenges During the First Industrial Revolution

The production logic of the factory was irrefutable, how to achieve productivity was not and a complex mix of economic, technological, demographic and social factors brought challenges which were commercial—maximising the opportunity inherent in significant growth; technological—making the most of advanced industrial technologies and organisational—implementing new systems and processes or integrating aligned industries in the supply chain. There was also the cultural shift that came about as the products of many skilled craft workers were replaced by cheaper, simpler, ready-made products in large manufacturing operations with the necessity of recruiting and maintaining a vast new workforce of people whose previous lives had been on the land or in domestic workshops (Pollard, 1965; Donkin, 2001). The upshot was a level of direction and supervision and greater coordination of resources to determine the overall business direction. In the latter phase, production planning was paramount—forced by the need to secure capital; longer production runs and the detailed scheduling associated with them; in the former was workforce planning; how to recruit, motivate and direct the workforce whilst implementing hard and fast rules of performance, time-keeping and behaviour—'work started, meals were eaten and worked stopped at fixed hour, notified by the ringing of a bell. Within the factory, each had his allotted place and strictly defined and invariable duty. Everyone had to work steadily and without stopping under the vigilant eye of a foreman' (Mantoux, 1928). For some managers these challenges were faced without support or assistance; but others chose a complementary approach—in a London lace factory, 'like most men of great administrative talent, Mr Fisher gathered round him very active people to carry out his operations' (Felkin, 1867). Either as a single practitioner or as part of a management team, the prospect was sometimes daunting. The manager who in 1764 pleaded with the directors to 'give him directions in the company's affairs of which he at present stands much in need being harassed' (Malcolm, 1950, p. 51) or the manager at Kirkstall Forge opened in 1777 who complained that 'I begin to grow weary of having so much to do, for really, I cannot do what ought to be done and very important work is neglected every day for want of having proper assistance' reflect the level of activity and change that were taking place and are perhaps sentiments that have resonated amongst managers in the subsequent 200 years or so. They reinforce the point that it is not only technological innovation but the ability to incorporate such innovation into day-to-day production or service systems and processes that creates a successful management outcome. The environment in Germany, France and other European countries was no less challenging. A feature of all was that the industrial revolution was a process of interconnected changes which transformed the direction of working life. The changes brought with them new and progressively increasing standards of economic efficiency and productivity growth (Hoppit, 1990). Managerial attitudes, perceptions, competence and understanding of production and economic opportunities were central to success.

The advent of new industrial organisations, new ways of working in factories and increasing urbanisation created wealth for those industrialists willing to invest and irrevocably changed the lives of the workers who flocked to the new industrial towns and cities. Political commentators such as Friedrich Engels sought to politicise the harshness of the industrial capitalism by drawing attention to the difficulties faced in this new environment. Announcing Richard Arkwright as 'a barber from Preston' and Dr Cartwright as 'a country parson', Engels' analysis of *The Condition of the Working Class in England* (Engels, 1845), based in part on his experiences at his father's cotton mills in Manchester, England, painted a bleak picture. The causes of and solutions to these problems were discussed with a colleague, Karl Marx, in Paris in 1844. Regardless of the political inspiration behind the work, Engels drew attention to the often, horrific circumstances in which many workers in the new industrial factories lived. However, whilst it may seem somewhat at odds with the characterisation of life and work in the new industrial cities—the subject of health and well-being may have been a relatively low moral or social concern for many owners and managers—the availability of an able, well workforce was an economic consideration for the owners and managers of commercial enterprises. Social reformers and some factory owners such as Robert Owen and his New Lanark Mills, were very aware of the need to take care of their workforces if business enterprises were to be successful. Living conditions in the new industrial towns and cities mitigated against health and well-being and managers often found themselves up against labour shortages because of this. Frequent epidemics and pandemics contributed to the problem. Examples are numerous, including inter alia in 1784 in Manchester, where the Health Board decided that control of such epidemics would be best achieved by enforced social distancing in the form of isolation hospitals (Meiklejohn, 1959); in 1832 a cholera epidemic appeared in Nottingham which 'broke out with alarming violence' and killed hundreds of people (Field, 1884); and it didn't discriminate; as one contemporary noted in 1831, 'all parts of London, and most of the Suburbs, felt its influence: the city was severely visited; all ranks of life became affected' (Gilbert, 1998). A few years later, a further pandemic killed 23,000 of all ages. In the town of Gainsborough with a population of 8000, the deceased included millers, labourers, tailors, bricklayers and stocking-makers (Farr, 1852). The problems faced by managers of commercial enterprises in these communities were as nothing compared to the pain felt by the families of those affected. But decisions had to be made about how to ensure a healthy workforce in the face of epidemic or pandemic. In the first place there was recognition of the need for the improvement of environmental conditions in mills and factories, driven by local Health Boards with which industrial enterprises and their managers must abide. But it was on the shop floor of factories and other commercial enterprises that rapid adjustments had to be made because, as one factory manager commented: 'I have not half my people come in today and I have no great fascination at the prospect' (Pollard, 1963). Operational workforce planning was an important part of the role of the manager, whilst flexibility, adaptability and perhaps courage in the face of epidemic were equally so.

Take-up or Take-off—A Sequence of Challenge and Response in Technology

The first area for consideration was the replacement of artisan skills or individual knowhow with collective know how in high and rapid production methods and new forms of power-water mills and steam engines. A conventional historical interpretation is that development was linear. Hence, John Kay's Flying Shuttle of 1733 preceded James Hargreaves' spinning jenny of 1764 which were refined by Richard Arkwright in his 1771 mill at Cromford in Derbyshire. James Watt's steam engine of 1775 and Henry Cort's advanced methods in iron production added further technologies to the eighteenth-century mix and were inspirational in the same way as the creation of microprocessors, fibre optics and computer aided design centuries later. The interconnectedness meant that British

Inventors worked hand in glove with those who provided with tools and workmanship (Mokyr, 2009; Duarte et al., 2018) creating 'strange and interesting things to be seen in the busy hives of industry distributed throughout the kingdom' (Mayhew, 1865).

The economies of France, Germany (which became a centralised state in 1871) and others on the Continent grew during this period in response to endogenous pressures towards change in a similar way to Britain; and as a reaction to new methods which were being developed in Britain (Landes, 1972, p. 130). Whilst progress was slower and more sporadic, there were many examples of late eighteenth- and early nineteenth-century technological innovation and organisational adaptation. British ironmaster, William Wilkinson was brought over to France and advised on the design, specification and building of the coke smelter at Le Creusot in 1785; cylindrical carding machines were installed at Chateau de la Muette (which could do 24 times as much work as human labour) and in 1784, a version of Arkwright's spinning machine was set up in Amiens (Renard & Weulersse, 1926). Partnerships or *societies en commandite* were formed after 1815 to undertake the mass production of iron (Smith, 2005). Reaumur popularised producing new methods and the French iron and steel industries grew significantly from the 1820s; Clouet made cast steel, Jacquard invented a silk loom, Berthollet invented chlorine bleaching, Oberkampf and Widmer made a cloth producing cylinder and Leblanc produced artificial soda. There was a notable 'skill intensive' form of industrialisation in France which suited the craft traditions of French labour leading to a period of parallel development where modern techniques of production sat with more traditional ones (Heywood, 1992). In Germany Winterschmidt produced a water pressure engine; Diesbach and Barth came up with new dyes and technical education was encouraged in colleges and academies (Henderson, 1961). Regions such as Wurttemberg with 342 industrial plants of which 21 had 100 workers or more, benefitted significantly from the opportunity to trade—the German Customs Union (Zollverein) was put in place in 1834 and provided an impulse to the industrialisation process by creating a free-trade area throughout much of Germany (Braun & Franke, 2019). The interconnectedness of woollen cloth, coal mining and iron and steel in the region around Aachen, led to innovations—the use of steam engines in

1815 and the introduction of spinning and carding machines—such that by 1830 there were centralised factories and vertically integrated firms (Reckendrees, 2017). These regional innovations sat side by side with more traditional forms of production but laid the foundation for concentrated growth after the middle of the century. The expansion of German railways after 1840 though, proved to be the decisive turning point in the growth of the German Economy at this time as the country went from 469 kilometres of railway line in 1840 to 11,000 by 1860.

There were differences between the Continental experience and that of Britain. War and political obstacles obstructed industrialisation and even post Waterloo, Continental European countries found it hard to emulate the British experience. Nor was there (until later) the large-scale concentration of activity which would provide economies of scale and scope, a characteristic of British Industrialisation. Both France and Germany had dispersed textile production and it wasn't until the mid-nineteenth century that localisation of production took place—in France where progressive improvement in organisations in Alsace and in Germany where from the 1840s a new generation of entrepreneurs set up large-scale manufacturing from capital accessed by joint stock companies. Weulersse's early anecdotal presentation of the First Industrial Revolution in Europe (1926), only 100 years distant, noted pockets of industrialisation in France and Germany and other European countries. In Spain, for example, under the reign of Charles III, the 'cloth industry' was developing significantly in Guadalajara, the 'great' linen factory at San Ildefoso and the armoury at Toledo. Though the Spanish experience exemplified the challenge faced by all of converting scientific innovation to profitable output, the transfer of the spinning jenny to Barcelona in Spain did not lead to its large-scale take-up in 1784, though there was some diffusion in Catalonia. But the slower uptake of new technologies for a period gives support for the idea of continuity, rather than discontinuity between the eighteenth and late nineteenth centuries in parts of Europe such as Spain and Belgium. For many industries there was not 'a transformation of techniques … but a slow spasmodic diffusion of new methods alongside the old' (Landes, 1972; Thomson, 2003; Buyst, 2018). Nevertheless, the seeds of revolution in Continental Europe had been sown in certain regions, industries and certain industrial processes.

The dawn of American Industrialisation can also be traced back to the late eighteenth and early nineteenth centuries. Enhanced manufacturing capability prompted by war with Britain in 1812, permeated a number of industries (from guns to soap to candles) with an American model focussed on organisation and emerging from local to regional to national networks where New England and middle Atlantic states were 'hotbeds of industrialisation' from the 1820s fuelled by the 'American penchant for mechanised large-scale production' (Morris, 2012). In the United States at this time, most businesses were proprietorships or partnerships with a few incorporated as joint stock companies—mostly, but not all in the financial sector (e.g. Bank of New York appeared in the 1780s and the Insurance company of North America in the 1790s. The DuPont Chemical firm was founded in 1802.). Whilst it was really the Second Industrial Revolution at the end of the nineteenth century that saw the growth of the American economy to world dominance, evidence was there during the latter part of the eighteenth century when the 'American people enjoyed the best of both worlds. They fulfilled Thomas Jefferson's (1780) dream of a vast land populated by yeoman farmers. And they brought to fruition Alexander Hamilton's (1791) vision of a diversified economy that took full advantage of manufacturing and production by machine.' Statesman Henry Clay argued for infrastructure and encouragement of manufactures in what became known as 'The American System' (McCraw, 1997, pp. 309–312).

Single inventions or mechanical adaptations do not constitute a revolution. But the accumulation of inventions and improvements across Europe and a set of economic conditions that took advantage of these developments, at first in Britain and after the end of the Napoleonic Wars, in Continental Europe produced an environment of unprecedented economic and social transformation. The availability of technological innovation is one thing; its practical application is another. 'There is an important distinction between an invention incorporating a principle later proved viable and an invention refined to the point when production on a cost-effective basis can begin. Working out an invention almost always requires many hands and minds', which is a characteristic of the British experience (Rostow, 1978). However, and as discussed above, there was rarely an absolute cut off point between new and old technologies with a dependence on other factors across supply chains and the availability of a labour force. Hence 'the workplace during the transition to industrial society remains a largely mysterious place … and a number of critical questions remain unresolved' (Evans, 1998). The trials and tribulations facing managers as they tried to implement new technologies were many. William Topliss in Nottinghamshire and Derbyshire Mills, for example, having seen his Cuckney Mill burn down in 1792, took his next venture north of the town and soon faced both organisational and technological challenges. First there was that of integrated manufacture of spinning and weaving cotton and woollen goods. This failed because the organisation established to do so was too ambitious. The second was to install new machinery for combing wool which also faced problems such that; 'his ingenious contrivance did not obtain very wide acceptance, nor was Mr Topliss encouraged to make any attempt to improve his machine' (quoted in Chapman, 1965). These experiences of industrialisation raise the questions of what actions did managers take to ensure that the technological developments could be successfully integrated into a coherent and workable production plan? What knowledge and skills did they need to achieve this? And how was such knowledge acquired? These are important questions because the positive case studies that have informed the narrative of the First Industrial Revolution can mask the real problems faced by managers—experience of the introduction of the spinning jenny to Spain is an example and demonstrates that whilst there was a mastery of general manufacturing skills which existed already in the Barcelona region, the installation of the first machine in the 1780s was a 'tortuous' experience. In Germany, the strong craft tradition, whilst allowing for the swift transfer of new technical processes meant that most German factories remained collections of workshops—with technology transfer acceptable as long as it remained under the auspices of skilled craftsmen, at least in the early years. In Britain, the maximisation of opportunity through technology depended on its application to large-scale manufacturing operations—one of which, the Soho factory of Boulton and Fothergill, saw 'innumerable Pilgrims', as learning on the job provided effective means to productivity and innovation (Pollard, 1965; Fear, 1997; Thomson, 2003; Khan, 2018). If this is the case, then the competence of the managers in industrial enterprises was based on technical understanding, organisational capability and competence and resilience in the face of failures of experimentation. The practice of management was one not only of science, but also of art and craft.

The Challenge of the Free Movement of Labour

A corollary to the challenge of innovation was that of labour markets and the workforce. In addition to the intellectual dexterity required to convert scientific invention into practical application, those managing in the First Industrial Revolution needed to be adept at dealing with a scale of human resource management for which there was little precedent. Writing in 1776 Adam Smith noted that the success of an enterprise is regulated by the 'skill, dexterity and judgement with which its labour is generally applied' (Smith, 1776, p. 104). Investments in larger scale manufacturing operations and the relatively free movement of labour during the First Industrial Revolution brought with them a sharp increase in demand for these exceptional levels of skill, dexterity and judgement. How to make the new technology work depended on human resource which often led to 'paradigmatic partnerships' (e.g. Boulton and Watt), which became resonant 'of the marriage between manufacturing and science'. The Lunar Society in Birmingham and the Literary and Philosophical Society of Manchester (1781) became places that scientists and businessmen 'brushed shoulders and talked science, and of the which joined the intellectual curiosity and useful knowledge' (Ó Gráda, 2016). Theoretical ideas or hypothetical designs needed those with practice experience and understanding to make them work and organisations in which the concepts could be scaled to make them economically viable. As these organisations grew, amongst the practitioners were managers, engineers, machinists, accountants, foremen, mechanics, carpenters, boilermakers, blacksmiths, clerks and salespeople. In the cotton industry the significant change from the domestic to the factory system was that of a single set of machinery to work a large number of looms, with all the workers in one building. In steel mills or coal mines, the growth in scale meant new forms of organisation. And those providing services, new ways of monitoring or controlling the larger scale demands. These organisational changes increased the necessity for management exponentially. Specialisation and complexity in the production process, made coordination, monitoring and supervision extremely important.

At first, simple organisational structures with centralised decision-making, discipline, organisation of the flow of goods and quality control had the supervisor acting as 'undermanager' responsible for supervision and discipline (Kapas, 2008, p. 22), which in current terms would be within the boundaries of modern human resource management such as training, performance management, motivation and retention. The relative novelty of the new factory environment made the application of these concepts somewhat hit and miss. Wedgewood the potter found, for example, that when he tried to enforce a strictly regulated division of labour in his establishments, he had to fight against the hostility of the workforce in so doing. He was eventually successful and 'thus the manufacturer being at the same time a capitalist, a works manager and a merchant set a new pattern of the complete businessman' (Mantoux, 1928, p. 374). Robert Owen, cotton mill manufacturer in Manchester and, famously, New Lanark, was successful because of his people management skills, his organisational skills and technical awareness, but most importantly 'a careful selection and training of under managers' (Pollard, 1965, p. 293). In France as well, 'the great manufacturers had created beneath them a series of Directors, Inspectors and Controllers who stood between them and the nameless crowd of the ordinary workman' (Renard & Weulersse, 1926, p. 191) in an early form of hierarchical management structure; a point mirrored by the Anzin Coal Company after 1817. Here a radical shake up in administrative personnel and organisation saw tightening, clarification and regularisation of duties, with the creation of an hierarchy of officials and clear lines of authority; with a single General Agent, acting on the part of the owners combining both technical and business management responsibilities (Geiger, 1974). Each of these examples point to not only changes in the way in which goods and services were produced by new technologies, but changes in the way that production systems and processes were developed and the management philosophies behind them were articulated—the Scottish flax spinner

William Brown's systematic management included 'produce good quality yarn, make a large quantity, produce with as little waste as possible, keep costs as low as possible, consistent with the above; and keep the machinery in good working order'. At James Naysmith's engineering works, the foremen were expected to monitor quality as well as output and the reward system reflected both. Whilst at Josiah Wedgewood's Etruria pottery there was advanced organisation, a fine division of labour, supervisors on each shop who enforced strict factory discipline, quality inspectors and detailed work instructions (Geraghty, 2003, pp. 539–540).

So, it was not enough for the technology merely to exist. It was up to the managers to make it work in association with other factors—labour, supporting technologies, the integration of diverse activities and their own career aspirations. As one Manchester cotton manager noted in 1824, it would be difficult to use new technologies 'without having at hand people competent to its repair and management;' (Mokyr, 2009, p. 107) or government contractor Alexander Copeland who explained that he was only able to manage such large operations with success because he had 'able foremen who were accustomed to carry out large works at a rapid rate' (quoted in Pollard, 1965, p. 105); or by John Coltman a prominent Leicestershire hosier, who promoted among his workpeople 'a spirit of rising in the world and was the means of setting forward many a mechanic to become a master' (quoted in Chapman, 1965, p. 2).

Arkwright's Derwent Valley Mills in Britain provide a microcosm of the human resources challenges because as production in his mills became more specialised there was a need for different types of worker. In 1775, for example, a switch to calico production required a greater proportion of weavers; in 1782 a continued focus on yarn production meant more unskilled workers; in the early 1790s more skilled workers were needed to undertake the specialised finishing processes; and by the mid-1790s a mix of skilled and unskilled were required to manufacture different cotton threads. In order to address the needs for different types of skill across different operating sites the mill owners were faced with attracting not only new, unskilled workers but specialised workers as well, many of which came from beyond the local area. The mobility of some skilled workers showed the importance of human resources to the manager of the First Industrial Revolution organisation and where this went awry the possible impact. Shortages of skilled workers at Bassaleg forge in Monmouthshire led to the manager issuing a plea to an associate—'if you have anyone … to spare, please send us one' (quoted in Evans, 1998). Efficient *management* of the workforce was necessary to satisfy increasing demand for goods, which meant that a core of skilled workers sat alongside a large number of unskilled workers who were trained as quickly as possible in simple operational processes, meaning that organisational models of work were successfully applied together with mechanisation (Mellor, 2005; Cimatti & Campana, 2015; Lilley, 2017, p. 124). So, whilst innovative activity and the implementation of the outputs of that activity were economically significant determinants of per capita growth in the economy, these in turn were dependent on the application of specialised scientific knowledge, excellence in implementation and project skills and the acquisition of a significant operational workforce (Madsen et al., 2010; Khan, 2018). Human resources challenges were as much a feature of the First Industrial Revolution as technology ones.

A Note on the Shameful Practice of Child Labour

However, whilst these can be placed in the context of macro level technological change and significant economic opportunity, it is not possible to discuss the First Industrial Revolution without the subject of the horrific exploitation of child labour. Elizabeth Barratt Browning's 1843 poem *The Cry of the Children* described a shameful period where children were set to work from the earliest ages in mines and factories. Britain's role as prime mover during the First Industrial Revolution meant that it was also the first where the nature of children's work changed dramatically making it both a social problem and a subject for intense political enquiry. Evidence from parliamentary investigations showed that children were a substantial part of the labour force, particularly in the textile mills that were at the vanguard of the Revolution—there were 4000 children in the mills of Manchester, 1600 in Stockport, 1500 in Bolton and 1300 in

Hyde in 1833, for example (Tuttle, 1999). The question of child labour, in its relatively new industrial context, could not be ignored by the beginning of the nineteenth century. Bills were brought to the British parliament in 1801–1802 'for preserving the health and morals of apprentices in cotton mills', but it was later that the movement to change working conditions gathered momentum, with bills brought before parliament in 1819, 1820, 1825, 1829, 1832 and 1836. As a result of these, the British parliament passed numerous Acts (the Cotton Factories Regulation Act of 1819, the Regulation of Child Labour Act in 1833 and the Ten Hours Act in 1847), which sought to ameliorate working conditions. The Factory Acts prevented children under nine years old from working in the factories and limited their working hours. In addition, new documentation was required for each child with monitoring undertaken by external officials of government. Similar legislation (1842) was also introduced into the mining industry. The question of child labour during the First Industrial Revolution in France was addressed by Legislation in 1841 applying to factories and workshops setting a minimum age of employment at eight years old and limitations on working hours for those between 8 and 12 years old. Similar legislation was passed in the industrial regions of Prussia forbidding the employment of those younger than nine years of age in factories. More recently 'scholars have made an effort to distil a clearer and less politically charged picture from very partial records', and factors such as the choice between pauperism and vagrancy and factory work, the incidence of large numbers of children amongst the 'labouring poor' as a cause of poverty and work as its partial alleviation and the fact that child labour was a minority of children (Mokyr, 2009, p. 333) are put forward as trying to explain the system. But the only conclusion, even with these mitigating factors, is that it was a shameful event. Too often, 'men of station and property are to be found, and often occupying very large factories, who will at least shut their eyes and silently acquiesce in the oppressive treatment of children within their own premise' (British Parliamentary Papers, 1840).

Contextual Competences of Managers During the First Industrial Revolution—'Bricks and Mortals'

Writing at the apogee of Britain's dominant period as world leader in industry and commerce, Samuel Smiles, author of *Self Help*, encapsulated conventional popular thinking about what made for the good businessman and perhaps what made for the contextual competence during the First Industrial Revolution:

> *The path of success in business is usually the path of common sense. Patient labour and application are as necessary here as in the acquisition of knowledge or the pursuit of science ... to become an able man in any profession, three things are necessary—nature, study and practice.* (Smiles, 1859)

Patient labour was perhaps a luxury as the changes linked to growth in demand; the need to respond with output and productivity, and the integration of increased numbers in the workforce happened at a frenetic pace. Greater managerial supervision with centralised manufacturing processes and organisations became increasingly evident. The contextual competence was one of change and adaptability on the one hand and the ability to manage multiple operations simultaneously on the other. Some such as Betty Beecroft, who managed the Kirkstall Forge in Britain, had a broad range of responsibilities covering all business operations and wrote: 'I undertook the care of the trade and books, also the buying and selling and all the engagements of the men up to March 31, 1780' (letters and diaries from the Kirkstall Forge, Butler, 1945). In a different context, Sir Richard Arkwright dealt with cash flow—'if you can send a few bills in a short time it will be very acceptable as several matters has [*sic*] turned out different to expectations', stock control—'we have made an abatement in the price of our twist', the purchase of new equipment and general coaching on business practice—'this is my real opinion and I have often given it to you' (Arkwright-Oldknow Papers, 1783–1796). In some cases, the manager controlled all facets of the operation in others there was a greater division of managerial responsibilities, and with the increase in size of operations, 'more articulate management developed with a division of function' (Mathias, 1957). The management of an iron forge, for example, was by an agent (manager) under the auspices of the owner, who rode over on horseback once a week to check on progress and outstanding issues. A daily workbook was kept with two blank pages at the end of each week. One page was headed 'Proprietors Remarks', the other 'Agents Replies'. The forge had gone from a relatively simple system of management to possibly one of the earliest examples of a Performance Management Review. And things progressed even more by 1816 when three partners decided to define the management roles of each with more specificity with one attending 'to all the workmen employed in the Square, the Shovel Handle Shops, the Tilting Forges, the Fender Shops and Grinding Mill and see that every article manufactured therein be done in the best manner'. Adding an example of a job description to measures of performance. As the First Industrial Revolution gathered momentum the subject of management did also. To John Stuart Mill (1848) clear guidelines were important since 'the successful conduct of an industrial enterprise requires two quite distinct qualifications: fidelity, and zeal. The fidelity of the hired managers of a concern it is possible to secure. When their work admits of being reduced to a definite set of rules, the violation of these is a matter on which conscience cannot easily blind itself, and on which responsibility may be enforced.'

Attitudes towards the workforce were also articulated is more detail. There was come consensus along the theme of 'it is very important to keep the workmen under the continual necessity of working' (quoted in Renard & Weulersse, 1926). William Brown, a Dundee flax spinner whose East Mill managed in conjunction with his brother became something of a benchmark for others in the industry during the 1820s wrote, 'the first and great object to be aimed at by the Manager of East Mill is profit.' To do so, he noted, required establishing order and discipline amongst the workforce, and improvement and regularity in capital equipment (quoted in Pollard, 1965, p. 294). To deal with the greater complexity, entrepreneurs would take on partners to provide complementary technical/managerial experience in a particular industry or sector. In the case of the Staveley Ironworks, as it became a limited liability company in the mid-nineteenth century, the owner Richard Barrow partnered with an engineer, Charles Markham who provided technical and managerial skills as learned competences (Staveley Industries, 1988). Boulton and Watt's partnership, combining manufacturing and engineering skills formed the basis of production from 1800 for over a hundred years with discipline and supervision of the labour force providing competitive advantage through both cost reduction and productivity increase (Torrington & Weightman, 1985). In this case the managers would need the willingness and the ability to collaborate in the development of their businesses. Sir Robert Peel who contemplated in 1816 'it is impossible for a mill at any distance to be managed unless it is under the direction of a partner or superintendent who has an interest in the success of the business' (quoted in Pollard, 1965, p. 34). Engaging the managers was as much of a success factor as engaging the workforce.

Hence, the contextual competences in managers during the First Industrial Revolution could be influenced by prevailing social, political or religious factors. Attitudes to child labour, whilst abhorrent from the current age, were accepted and modified; Robert Owen's mills were a Utopian Socialist experiment and religious beliefs permeated many of not most of the industrial establishments of the time. History is more than a mere record of past events, since it is also necessary to extract meaning from the facts that are available (Grattan, 2008). Is it possible to do so in respect of those managers who crafted their way through the First Industrial Revolution?

Core Management Competences During the First Industrial Revolution

As the First Industrial Revolution gathered momentum, agents, general managers, under-managers and supervisors were involved in initiating new technology projects, implementing new systems and processes—and all whilst recruiting and training people to work in this new environment. Whereas once a craftsman would see a job through from start to finish, work in the new factories and workshops involved one or two processes repeated many times per hour (Henderson, 1961). In this context technical knowledge was important, but so were competences in change management, planning, execution and workforce management. Sources of knowledge of organisational or managerial best practice were in demand. There had been from about 1780 'a diffusion of knowledge among the body of the people the like of which had never been known'. And there was a clamour for education in commercial matters as well as industrial techniques by 'stockbrokers, cashiers, tax collectors, doctors, lawyers, manufacturers, mine owners and some craftsmen'. The 'new learning' was greatly influenced by the massive changes that were taking place. Academies had been established in London, York, Lancaster and Bristol and by the end of the eighteenth century, there were nearly 200 offering some commercial and technical training (Pollard, 1965, p. 135). However, formal management development continued to be a rarity and the main method to acquire management competence during much of the period continued to be on the job. Matthew Boulton, James Watt, Josiah Wedgewood each benefitted from learning their managerial competence on the shop floor of the various manufacturers to which they were seconded. Archibald Buchanan was trained by Richard Arkwright before returning to Scotland to set up a large spinning firm. David Dale sent those who had been instructed by him to manage several mills and 'Jedediah Strutt's sons were trained in the works from a tender age' (Pollard, 1965, p. 149). Edward Thomason (Knighted in 1832 by King William IV) was articled in his younger years to Boulton's Soho factory in Birmingham and later combined this practical day-to-day operational experience with exposure to new ideas and technologies once he was admitted into the Scientific School of Soho 'which induced in me a taste for mechanism' (Thomason, 1845). Thomason opened his factory in 1793 making buttons, tokens, medals, toys, chains and between 1802 and 1816, 120,000 patented corkscrews. John Smith a senior manager at the Butterley Park Colliery Company told the Parliamentary Commissioners in 1851 of his own path to management, from literally working at the coal face through to middle management positions of overman and agent (Mottram & Coote, 1950). The British-based Bryan Donkin company gave its contract to build a paper mill in St Petersburg in 1858, to Bryan Donkin Junior aged 24 (the grandson of the founder) whose education in engineering at University College London, was supplemented by time at the Ecole Centrale des Arts et Metiers in Paris and experience on the shop floor in the successful engineering works in Britain—a combination of the theoretical and practical (Donkin Jr was eventually made a partner in the company). The quest for rationality and efficiency was underpinned by serious attempts to measure human work and effort. In France, scientists such as Desaguliers, Coulcomb and de Borda 'repeatedly tried to measure the amount of work that people could perform'—an important management precursor to the work of F.W. Taylor over 100 years later (Mokyr, 2009, p. 42). In Britain, Charles Babbage, the Cambridge mathematician, produced a pioneering study of Industrial Management and concluded that there was still much to be done if the full advantage of the division of labour was to be realised (Sofer, 1972). It is possible to speculate that there were certain aspects of the managerial role that were core and within which the manager would need a combination of skills to be proficient.

The first of these core competences was *adapting to change*. Any of the milestones that have been indicated—whether these be technological developments or economic opportunities—required managers who were responsive to change. This was responsiveness to the external environment—demand and supply of raw materials and goods produced, responsive to new technologies, and responsive to the internal environment—needs of their growing, but often fledgling workforce. Change included both conceptual and practical elements because the innovation process of the First Industrial Revolution was multi-faceted. Scientists and entrepreneurs took the headlines, but it was operational managers and skilled artisans who realised their ideas, put them to work, maintained them and improved them. Without these skilled workers and managers 'the new insights might have ended up like Leonardo's wonderful machines, none of which were ever built' (Mokyr, 2009, p. 61). In Dr Cartwright's early venture into manufacturing in 1788 he envisaged a full-service factory which undertook all of the processes for converting raw wool and cotton into cloth. But after pressure from his shareholders and advice from James Watt to concentrate on a single process, rather than the full range, he wrote: 'I am this day returned from Doncaster and Retford. Upon further consideration of our experiments on wool spinning, that article, instead of being a secondary object, is now becoming the primary one, and the whole wing of the Retford Mill, already built is to be appropriated thereto' (Chapman, 1965, p. 104). He was aware not only of the opportunity that would arise from change, but also of the potential danger of not doing so.

Cartwright's decision was based on good advice rather than gut instinct and this leads to a second core competence—that of the *use of knowledge and information in decision-making.* All revolutions are unpredictable. There is an element of the unknown that precipitates reaction rather than pro-action, but as the First Industrial Revolution progressed, more information became available to help in decision-making. A core competence of the managers at this time was their ability to seek and use that information. A key aspect of this was the breadth and depth of technical knowledge needed to be successful, the breadth and depth of commercial knowledge and the balance between the two. The early narrative is replete with stories of inventor/entrepreneur/business owner. Arkwright, Boulton, Watt, Wedgewood are amongst those who successfully fill this mould. Each of these was influenced by a prevailing wisdom that emerged at the time, namely, the encouragement to acquire knowledge in an era of Industrial Enlightenment, 'whereby research was directed to areas where there was a high chance of solving practical problems—in medicine, manufacturing, navigation and so on'. The Industrial Enlightenment created a bridge between intellectuals and producers, between the savants and fabricants (Mokyr, 2009, pp. 40, 54). The *Gentleman's Magazine* in July 1820, railing against the use of 'things and facts hinted at in a mysterious manner', instead argued that 'an ordinary word ... from a man of extraordinary sense or knowledge of business has more weight than the most studied harangue of a mere rhetorician' ('Yorick' 1820). And the *Banker's Clerk* journal in 1843 emphasised attention to detail in its advice, noting that 'an officer in a bank ... can successfully aspire to the highest honours of the profession; and become himself a banker, or at least the manager of a joint-stock bank, if his talents and assiduity qualify him for the office' (*Banker's Clerk* 1843 quoted in Jeacle, 2010). The emphasis on assiduity or attention to detail being a constant feature of management activity over the centuries. Information was a valuable commodity, converting it into applicable knowledge was a core competence.

Hence, the First Industrial Revolution was not just about invention, although there was a good deal of that and many examples of inventors who turned into entrepreneurs and managers. But for many it was more about innovation and improvement. Managers had to be acutely aware of how to do both and their role was to take an invention and convert it into something practical. The effective use of knowledge 'required not only access and incentives to create and access new technology, but also the competence to make use of it and to carry out the instructions contained in the blueprint of the technique' (Mokyr, 2009, p. 107). For the industrialist, membership of one of the many philosophical societies was a way to access knowledge and information that might prove useful in managing the industrial or commercial process. Although any linear causality would be difficult to prove, the Birmingham Lunar Society, the Manchester Literary and Philosophical Society and the Royal Society, each gave the opportunity for those present to discuss technical and practical issues relating to the nature of their business and how to manage it.

> The original Lunarmen gathered together for lively dinner conversations, the journey back from their Birmingham meeting place lit by the full moon. They were led by the larger-than-life physician Erasmus Darwin, a man of extraordinary intellectual insight with his own pioneering ideas on evolution. Others included the flamboyant entrepreneur Matthew Boulton, the brilliantly perceptive engineer James Watt whose inventions harnessed the power of steam, the radical polymath Joseph Priestley who, among his wide-ranging achievements discovered oxygen, and the innovative potter and social reformer Josiah Wedgwood. Their debates brought together philosophy, arts, science and commerce, and as well as debating and discovering, the "Lunarticks" also built canals and factories, managed world-class businesses—and changed the face of Birmingham (The Lunar Society, 2019).

Converting ideas into practical action using knowledge obtained from a wide range of sources is perhaps one of the outstanding competences of managers at this time. Organisations such as the Lunar Society created channels through which useful knowledge could flow to productive methods (Ashworth, 2020). 'In consequence of the multiple means of instruction the man of science and the manufacturer are daily becoming more assimilated to each other' (Humphrey Davy 1802, quoted in Mokyr, 2009).

Once capital had been secured, the success of the venture depended on two important criteria. First that the person responsible for delivering the 'vision' of the organisation that had been funded (possibly also a partner) had enough technical knowledge of that business. The second was an understanding of the importance of implementation of new technologies, work systems and work processes to deliver a viable working business.

A key part of this was the *ability to motivate a workforce consisting of employees with different skill types and levels* and this again might be regarded as a core competence. In giving evidence to the Parliamentary Select Committee on Artisans and Machinery in 1824, a British factory owner stated that 'I would not have any one man in my manufactory that would not work with any other man I choose, or would not do anything I put him to; the consequence was the resentment of the men who left me. I lost many of them and I believe sustained considerable loss in my business in consequence of that resentment' (British Parliamentary Papers, 1824). The ability to motivate a workforce, whilst not a new requirement of managers, was brought into sharp perspective by the larger organisations that were springing up and the ability of members of the workforce to leave if working conditions were not right. John Taylor, a mine owner, commented that 'important as the improvements are, which we have contemplated in the in the instruments which the progress of physical science has placed in our hands, those which relate to the government of large bodies of workmen to the removal of difficulties in their way or of placing them in circumstances most favourable to effective exertion are even more important' (quoted in Burt, 1977). These are human resource challenges of individual motivation and engagement on the one hand, and as highlighted in the above quote, effective team working on the other. The same 1824 committee had heard of managers and employees who were dissatisfied, leaving England to work in France and taking key employees with them.

Some managers at this time had recognised this aspect as a critical factor in their success. John Watts' lecture about the industrialist and philanthropist Robert Owen, 'The Visionary', at the third anniversary of the opening of the Manchester Hall of Science in 1843, asked 'what power is that to which we owe all our improvements' and concluded as an homage to Owen 'to imagination we owe all and every improvement' because 'facts are but brute elements until systematized and put into shape' (Watts, 1843). He noted that Owen's visionary status was not because of some mastery of machine, but with his ability to deal with 'the complex subject of the human mind. Owen's imagination has culled the flowers, woven them into a wreath and adorned the brows of his own impersonation of man; the beautiful picture of the future is brought by him to us to view'. He had in fact taken 'the lever of human improvement in hand'. The lecture was of course based on Owen's reputation for management at his New Lanark Mills from 1800 with a philanthropic approach to the workforce with the undercurrent of Utopian Socialism. Other examples of enlightened motivational attitudes were those of Matthew Boulton's feast for 700 employees when his son came of age, Wedgewood's feast for 120 when he moved to a new factory and Heathcote's outing for 2300 workers from Tiverton. 600 workers sat down to a feast to celebrate the Duke of Bridgewater's new canal at Runcorn (Pollard, 1963). Nevertheless dismissal or the threat of dismissal remained the main force of discipline in the early factory environment. In a survey of 575 companies as part of the factories commission in 1833, 353 used dismissal as a form of discipline whilst 2 used 'kindness' and 9 'promotion' as a means to enforce 'obedience' (Pollard, 1963). First Industrial Revolution managers used far more sticks than carrots. Kindness was rarely used as a motivational tool, but workforce planning and management were high on the agenda.

The *ability to integrate multiple activities through effective organisation* also featured on the list of core management competences. Success did not come from any single activity or set of activities; instead, it came from the ability to integrate multiple innovations or improvements. Robert Owen's letters to James Craig about the operation of the Stanley Mills between 1802 and 1811 gives insight about the necessity of joining up production levels from new equipment and stock control thereof. 'In the context of the factory system, the new machine technologies of the Industrial Revolution were complementary with the organisational innovations of the full-fledged factory system, more intensive supervision, new compensation schemes based on time rates fines or bonuses, and disciplinary systems that attempted to balance worker incentives among multiple tasks—output, volume, quality and asset maintenance' (Cooke, 1979; Geraghty, 2003, p. 538). It was essential that the output of the factories achieve high levels of quality and workmanship. A factor in this was the ability of the manager to implement processes and new technologies whilst at the same time providing management to ensure quality and consistency from a motivated workforce. In short, this required competence in the ability to integrate multiple activities—some technological, some commercial and some human resource related. These assumptions applied in commerce to equal effect. The financial services sector, for example, also had the management challenge of integrating multiple activities as they structured organisations to ensure the appropriate levels of authority and accountability. Large Savings Banks had a senior manager in place under which would be employed assistants—cashiers, auditors, clerks and deposit receivers in a hierarchical formation whose roles and responsibilities were as clearly delineated as any Manchester factory. The ability to integrate aspects of the lending and borrowing process were facilitated by specialisation and authority levels (House of Commons, 1849). After 1836, British Building Societies were also required to follow rules around the responsibilities of full-time officers and managers, who would report into a management committee and trustees; and in Scotland, after 1824, a new system of organising in the banks meant that 'the executive powers of the treasurer were much enhanced. By the end of the mid-1830s the treasurer had assumed all the powers of a general manager.' Evidence given to the Select Committee on Joint Stock banks concluded that where 'competent directors' were able to have an overview of all the activities of the running of the bank there was more effective management. 'But when a bank has 40 or 50 establishments many perhaps not under the eye of competent directors, it is possible that the eagerness of partners to extend the business should be under prudent control' (British Parliamentary Papers, 1836; Bellman, 1950; Boot, 1991). The ability to integrate multiple activities was a factor in the management of a range of different organisations in different industry sectors. It was a core management competence that transcended any one type of business.

At the end of this period, Britain was in a dominant economic position that it had occupied for decades. The nation's first mover advantage had been solidified as, particularly the Continental countries, faced obstacles that inhibited growth. Britain's advantage had given the nation its position as world leader in industrialisation and trade with the apogee of this dominance coming at the Great Exhibition of 1851.

> If you took a bus past London's Hyde Park, in that summer, you would see an astonishing sight. Glittering among the trees was a palace made of glass, like something out of the Arabian Nights. This was the 'Crystal Palace', home to the Great Exhibition, an idea dreamt up by Queen Victoria's husband, Prince Albert, to display the wonders of industry and manufacturing from around the modern world. There were some 100,000 objects, shown along more than ten miles, by over 15,000 contributors. Each country displayed its finest achievements: there were steam engines and hydraulic machines that could add, print and build at unprecedented rates; there were fabrics, carriages, musical instruments and jewels; there were foldable pianos, 80-blade penknives and dioramas of stuffed kittens. Queen Victoria opened the Exhibition and became a frequent visitor. Over 6 million people visited the exhibition, and they came from all over the country and all walks of life: from aristocrats to factory workers, country villagers to schoolchildren. (British Library, 2020)

In trying to explain such as rise in fortunes, the chemist Humphry Davy began a series of lectures in January 1802 and argued that science would enable man to shape his future. 'It has bestowed upon him powers which may almost be called creative', he said, 'which have enabled him to modify and change the beings surrounding him and by his experiments to interrogate nature with power, not simply as a scholar … but rather as a master.' The challenge facing owners and managers at this time was to harness the potential of these technological developments. To do so, they needed to have competences that were particularly of their time and aligned to the political and social mores of this early period in Industrialisation. However, there were also competences, outlined above, that seemed to transcend any one historical period. The ability to deal with change, the ability to use knowledge and information in decision-making, the ability to integrate multiple activities and the ability to motivate a diverse workforce are four that may apply in any era.

The First Industrial Revolution provided a momentum that gathered pace towards the end of the nineteenth century and to a new stage of economic development.

References

Allen, R. C. (2011). Why the Industrial Revolution was British: Commerce, Induced Invention, and the Scientific Revolution. *The Economic History Review, 64*(2), 357–384.

Arkwright-Oldknow Papers. (1783–1796). Columbia Rare Book and Manuscript Library, Columbia University in the City of New York.

Ashworth, W. J. (2020). The British Industrial Revolution and the Ideological Revolution: Science, Neoliberalism and History. *History of Science, 52*(175), 178–199.

Basalla, G. (1988). *The Evolution of Technology*. Cambridge University Press.

Bellman, H. (1950). *Bricks and Mortals: A Study of the Building Society Movement*. Hutchinson and Co.

Boot, H. M. (1991). Salaries and Career Earnings in the Bank of Scotland 1730–1880. *Economic History Review, XLIV*, 629–653.

Botticelli, P. (1997). British Capitalism and the Three Industrial Revolutions. In T. McCraw (Ed.), *Creating Modern Capitalism*. Harvard University Press.

Braun, S. T., & Franke, R. (2019). *Railways, Growth, and Industrialisation in a Developing German Economy, 1829–1910*. MPRA Paper.

British Government Commission. (1842). *Condition and Treatment of the Children Employed in the Mines and Collieries*. William Strange.

British Library. (2020). *The Great Exhibition*. https://www.bl.uk/learning/timeline/item106129.html

British Parliamentary Papers. (1824). *Report of Minutes of Evidence from the Select Committee on Artisans and Machinery*. Irish University Press, British Parliamentary Papers (1968).

British Parliamentary Papers. (1836). *Report from the Select Committee on Joint Stock Banks*. Irish University Press, British Parliamentary Papers (1968).

British Parliamentary Papers. (1840). *Reports from Select Committees on the Act for the Regulation of Mills and Factories with the Minutes of Evidence*. Proceedings and Index, Irish University Press, British Parliamentary Papers (1968).

Burt, R. (1977). *John Taylor; Mining Entrepreneur and Engineer 1779–1863*. Moorland Publishing Company.

Butler, R. (1945). *The History of Kirkstall Forge*. The Ebor Press.

Buyst, E. (2018). The Causes of Growth during Belgium's Industrial Revolution. *Journal of Interdisciplinary History, 49*(1), 71–92.

Chapman, S. D. (1965). The Pioneers of Worsted Spinning by Power. *Business History, 7*(2), 97.
Cimatti, B., & Campana, G. (2015). The Value of Craftsmanship in Manufacturing and Related Organizational Models. *International Journal of Organisational Innovation, 7*(4), 7–16.
Cooke, A. J. (1979). Robert Owen and the Stanley Mills 1802–1811. *Business History, 21*(1), 107–111.
Crafts, N. F. R. (1996). The First Industrial Revolution: A Guided Tour for Growth Economists. *The American Economic Review, 86*(2), 197.
de Vries, J. (1994). The Industrial Revolution and the Industrious Revolution. *The Journal of Economic History, 54*(2). Papers presented at the Fifty-Third Annual Meeting of the Economic History Association, 249–270.
Donkin, R. (2001). *Blood Sweat and Tears*. New York, USA: Texere.
Duarte, A. Y. S., Sanches, R. A., & Dedini, F. G. (2018). Assessment and Technological Forecasting in the Textile Industry: From First Industrial Revolution to the Industry 4.0. *Strategic Design Research Journal, 11*(3), 193–202.
Engels, F. (1845). *The Condition of the Working Class in England*. Oxford World Classics Edition, 1999.
Evans, C. (1998). A Skilled Workforce during the Transition to Industrial Society: Forgemen in the British Iron Trade, 1500–1850. *Labour History Review, 63*(2), 143–159.
Farr, W. (1852). *Report on the Mortality of Cholera in England, 1848–49*. University of Nottingham, Medical Rare Books.
Fear, J. (1997). German Capitalism. In T. McCraw (Ed.), *Creating Modern Capitalism*. Harvard University Press.
Felkin, A. (1867). *History of the Machine Wrought Hosiery and Lace Manufacturers*. Reprinted by David and Charles, 1967.
Field, H. (1884). *The Date Book of Remarkable and Memorable Events Connected with Nottingham and its Neighbourhood, from Authentic Records. Part 2, 1750–1884*. University of Nottingham, East Midlands Collection Not 3.D14 FIE: Extracts from Henry Field.
Garnett, P., Mollan, S., & Bentley, R. A. (2017). Banks, Births, and Tipping Points in the Historical Demography of British Banking: A Response to J.J. Bissell. *Business History, 59*(5), 814–820.
Gaskell, R. (1833). *The Manufacturing Population of England*. Baldwin and Cradock.

Geiger, R. G. (1974). *The Anzin Coal Company, 1800–1833: Big Business in the Early Stages of the French Industrial Revolution*. Temple University Press.
Geraghty, T. M. (2003). Technology, Organization and Complementarity: The Factory System in the British Industrial Revolution. *The Journal of Economic History, 63*(2), 536.
Gilbert, P. K. (1998). A Sinful and Suffering Nation: Cholera and the Evolution of Medical and Religious Authority in Britain, 1832–1866. *Nineteenth-Century Prose, 25*(1).
Grattan, R. (2008). Crafting Management History. *Journal of Management History, 14*, 174–183. ISSN: 1751-1348.
Greasley, D., & Oxley, L. (1997). Endogenous Growth or Big Bang: Two Views of the First Industrial Revolution. *The Journal of Economic History, 57*(4), 935–949.
Henderson, W. O. (1961). *The Industrial Revolution on the Continent*. Reprinted by Routledge, 2006.
Heywood, C. (1992). *The Development of the French Economy 1750–1914*. Cambridge University Press.
Hoppit, J. (1990). Counting the Industrial Revolution. *The Economic History Review, 43*(2), 173–193.
House of Commons. (1849, March 5). *Abstract of Return to an Order of the Honourable*. The House of Commons.
Jackson, R. V. (1992). Rates of Industrial Growth during the Industrial Revolution. *Economic History Review, 45*(1), 1–23.
Jeacle, I. (2010). The Bank Clerk in Victorian Society: The Case of Hoare and Company. *Journal of Management History, 16*(3), 312–326.
Kapas, J. (2008). Industrial Revolutions and the Evolution of the Firm's Organisation. *Journal of Innovation Economics and Management, 2*, 15–33.
Kennedy, P. (1988). *The Rise and Fall of the Great Powers*. Fontana Press.
Khan, B. Z. (2018). Human Capital, Knowledge and Economic Development: Evidence from the British Industrial Revolution, 1750–1930. *Cliometrica, 12*(2), 313–341.
Landes, D. (1972). *The Unbound Prometheus*. Cambridge University Press.
Lilley, S. (2017). Stitching Together the Fabric of Industrial Houses: Investigating the Origins and Development of Cotton Workers' Accommodation in the Derwent Valley, Derbyshire. *Industrial Archaeology Review, 39*(2), 117–128.
Madsen, J. B., Ang, J. B., & Banerjee, R. (2010). Four Centuries of British Economic Growth: The Roles of Technology and Population. *Journal of Economic Growth, 15*(4), 263.

Malcolm, C. A. (1950). *The History of the British Linen Bank*. T & A Constable Ltd.
Mantoux, P. (1928). *The Industrial Revolution in the Eighteenth Century*. Harper Torch Books.
Mathias, P. (1957). *The Entrepreneur in Brewing 1700–1830*. Papers presented at the Annual Conference of the Economic History Society, Cambridge, UK.
Mathias, P. (1969). *The First Industrial Nation*. Methuen and Co.
Mayhew, H. (1865). *The Shops and Companies of London and the Trades and Manufactories of Great Britain*. Strand Printing.
Mays, S., Brickley, M., & Ives, R. (2008). Growth in an English Population from the Industrial Revolution. *American Journal of Physical Anthropology, 136*(1), 85–92.
McCloskey, D. (1985). The Industrial Revolution 1780–1860: A Survey. In J. Mokyr (Ed.), *The Economics of The Industrial Revolution*. Rowman & Littlefield.
McCraw, T. (1997). American Capitalism. In T. McCraw (Ed.), *Creating Modern Capitalism*. Harvard University Press.
Meiklejohn, A. (1959). Industrial Health—Meeting the Challenge. *British Journal of Industrial Medicine, 16*(1), 1.
Mellor, I. (2005). Space, Society and the Textile Mill. *Industrial Archaeology Review, 27*(1), 49–56.
Mill, J. S. (1848). *Principles of Political Economy with Some of Their Applications to Social Philosophy*. Edition used ed. W. J. Ashley. Longmans Green and Co., 1909.
Mitchell, B. R. (1975). *European Historical Statistics*. Macmillan Press.
Mokyr, J. (2009). *The Enlightened Economy*. Penguin Books.
Morris, R. C. (2012). *The Dawn of Innovation: The First American Industrial Revolution*. PublicAffairs.
Mottram, R. H., & Coote, C. (1950). *Through Five Generations, The History of the Butterley Company*. Faber and Faber.
Ó Gráda, C. (2016). Did Science Cause the Industrial Revolution? *Journal of Economic Literature, 54*(1), 224–239.
Pollard, S. (1963). Factory Discipline in the Industrial Revolution. *The Economic History Review, 16*(2), 254–271.
Pollard, S. (1965). *The Genesis of Modern Management*. Penguin Books.
Reckendrees, A. (2017). Dynamics of Overlapping Clusters: Industrial and Institutional Revolution in Industrial District of Aachen, 1800–1860. *Revista de Historia Industrial, 26*(66), 37–75.

Renard, G., & Weulersse, G. (1926). *Life and Work in Modern Europe.* Kegan Paul.
Rostow, W. W. (1978). No Random Walk: A Comment on Why was England First? *Economic History Review, 31*(4), 610–612.
Smiles, S. (1859). *Self Help*. Penguin Books Edition, 1986.
Smith, A. (1776). *The Wealth of Nations*. Penguin Books Edition, 1986.
Smith, M. M. (2005). *The Emergence of Modern Business Enterprise in France, 1800–1930.* Harvard University Press.
Sofer, C. (1972). *Organisations in Theory and Practice.* Heinemann Educational Books.
Staveley Industries. (1988). *Survival Against the Odds.* Company Publication.
Temin, P. (1997). Two Views of the British Industrial Revolution. *The Journal of Economic History, 57*(1), 63–82.
The Lunar Society. (2019). https://lunarsociety.org.uk/
Thomason, E. (1845). *Sir Edward Thomason's Memoirs during Half a Century.* Longman, Brown and Green.
Thomson, J. (2003). Transferring the Spinning Jenny to Barcelona: An Apprenticeship in the Technology of the Industrial Revolution. *Textile History, 34*(1), 21–46.
Torrington, D., & Weightman, J. (1985). *The Business of Management.* Prentice Hall International.
Tuttle, C. (1999). *Hard at Work in Factories and Mines: The Economics of Child Labour during the Industrial Revolution.* Westview Press.
Van den Eeckhout, P. (Ed.). (2009). *Supervision and Authority in Industry: Western European Experiences, 1830–1939.* Berghahn Books.
Watts, J. (1843). *Robert Owen—The Visionary, a Lecture on the Third Anniversary of the Opening of the Manchester Hall of Science.* Abel Heywood.
Williams, C. (1980). *National Union of Mineworkers.* NUM.
Wilson, J. F., & Thomson, A. (2009). *The Making of Modern Management.* Oxford University Press.

3

Management During the Second Industrial Revolution: American Gods and Scientific Management

The Decline of the Rich Old Firms

From the end of the nineteenth century, industrial development gathered pace worldwide and the application of scientific methods provided a step function for the management concept.

In 1915 Patrick Geddes coined a new historical term—the Second Industrial Revolution—to predict a phenomenon in which the 'palaeotechnic' economics 'of crowded and monotonous industrial towns' would be replaced with 'neotechnic' economics and 'the potentialities of wealth and leisure beyond past utopian dreams'. The features of these potentialities were new industries, new industrial processes and a revolution in ideas about how to deliver them. Technological developments bore out this optimism, including the internal combustion engine, the widespread deployment of electricity and innovation in communications. In 1876 Bell invented the telephone. Edison and Swan perfected the design of the light bulb in 1879. Then came automatic signals on railways, new processes in steel mills, the elevator and structural steel improvements which enabled the development of the first skyscrapers—the Chrysler Building was erected in 1930, the Empire State Building in 1931. It was

P. Turner, *The Making of the Modern Manager*,
https://doi.org/10.1007/978-3-030-81062-7_3

the age of motion pictures, the electric generator used in refrigerators and washing machines, the internal combustion engine for automobiles and the first airplane flight by the Wright brothers. The jet engine and electron microscope were invented in the 1930s. As were frozen foods and instant coffee. To top it all, the Macy's Thanksgiving Parade Day was inaugurated in 1924. The use of pure science by engineers in industries from bridge building to shipbuilding, applied science in business methods such as accounting and management, and an increase in competition with more companies in 'ever-widening markets' came together to bring about a reshaping of the world economic order (Jevons, 1931). Whilst each invention, each innovation or improvement was in theory available to business leaders in any of the early industrialising countries, over the course of the later years of the nineteenth and early years of the twentieth, it was predominantly the United States which maximised those opportunities. The signs were evident 20 years earlier.

From the 1850s onwards, the challenge to Britain's international supremacy became greater and as a result annual growth rates fell from around 3–4% in the late 1840s to 1.6% by the 1880s. Whilst there was an awareness of intensifying foreign competition, business leaders often struggled to respond. A visit by a group of them to the mechanised factories of the United States in the 1850s, for example, was overwhelming. The production of screws, files, clocks, watches and small arms using standardised interchangeable parts on workshop machinery came as a shock to those companies, many of which used tools and techniques that had been in place for 50 years or so. British manufacturers were forced to defend themselves against accusations of complacency, of resting on their oars or of indifference to the dissemination of technical information and the lack of a scientific approach to production. Economist Alfred Marshall criticised some British manufacturers because 'an unprecedented combination of advantages enabled businessmen to make money even when they were not throwing themselves with energy into that creative work by which industrial leadership is made and maintained' (quoted in Church, 1975, p. 49). The picture may be more nuanced than this. For example, there was a radical change in production methods with the formation of the Birmingham Small Arms Co. (BSA) in 1861 which 'initiated a transformation in the making of military small arms from a skilled handicraft to the factory production by machinery of weapons with interchangeable parts. The newly built Small Heath factory, where the first rifle was assembled in 1865, is notable as one of the very early examples in Great Britain of the 'American system of manufactures'. There were attempts at innovation and upgrading after World War I, including the Cadbury Conferences on the new post-war industrial and social order; the Rowntree Lecture Series, to bring together employers and employees to debate key issues confronting British industry; and Rowntree's idea for key industrialists to meet to debate and solve some of the intractable problems facing them (Lumley, 1989; Maclean et al., 2020). Nonetheless, the door to commercial dominance, that had been forced as Germany and France fought to catch up with Britain's position, was now wide open and the United States seized the opportunity with many hands. We can depict the Second Industrial Revolution as the move towards invention, innovation and large-scale mass production. It took place between 1870 and 1950 leading to the rise of the United States as the key player in international business. The horrors of slavery consigned to history after the brutal Civil War of 1861–1865 led to new social and economic infrastructures which helped in this shift of power.

The United States was well placed to take advantage of any new opportunities that came along. Abundant raw materials and being a country 'most open to entrepreneurial opportunity, the one whose laws best encouraged rapid economic growth' and the one most open to new ideas were a formula for great progress. American companies founded in the 1880s included Coca Cola, Westinghouse Electric, General Electric, PepsiCo, Goodyear Tyres, Ford Motor, Gillette, UPS and IBM, and in the 1920s Walt Disney, Delta and Northwest Airlines (McCraw, 1997; Magnusson, 2014). Notable African American business innovators prospered, including Charles Clinton Spaulding, who led the North Carolina Mutual Life Insurance Company, and Maggie Lena Walker, who became the first woman in the United States to charter a bank, the St. Luke Penny Savings Bank, in 1903 as well as being head of a mutual-aid society she ran for 35 years. Madame C.J. Walker was of course a notable pioneering business entrepreneur. Walker thought that it was important to motivate others to remain or become optimistic about their future. Her self-efficacy helped to create motivation at times of harsh and adverse situations. Booker T. Washington, a major proponent of African American businesses and advisor to multiple Presidents, debated the benefits or otherwise of embracing entrepreneurship and capitalist values with W.E.B. DuBois—although subsequent experience showed that many challenges remained in the quest for equality (Levenstein, 1995; Bussel, 1998; Prieto & Phipps, 2019; Hasan et al., 2020; Sharp, 2020). After 1870 the world order began to change, and the Second Industrial Revolution saw the baton being passed from the rich, old firms of the old world to the aspiring corporations of the new.

The Second Great Divergence

The ascendancy of the US economy had its roots between 1870 and 1914. Although Britain and Europe still commanded a share of some 70% of worldwide trade in manufactured goods, the United States' share of exports increased from 4% in 1876 to over 10% by 1913, with the country building surpluses as it expanded its sphere of trading influence and became less dependent on European markets. American political institutions provided an infrastructure for an American developmental state and this combination of technology and economics, a willingness to invest financial capital in new machinery or processes and intellectual capital in new management philosophies, meant that by 1899 the Second Industrial Revolution was in full swing. At the same time, science was beginning to have a significant effect on industry—such as organic chemistry and its influence on synthetic dyes and the nature of electricity and magnetism (Weber & Handfield-Jones, 1954; Kenwood & Lougheed, 1973; Basalla, 1988; Broadberry, 1994; van Driel et al., 2007; Link & Maggor, 2020). The impact on national income was soon felt. At $37 billion, it was far higher than any other of the industrialised countries, equating to $377 per capita compared with $244 in Britain, $184 in Germany, $153 in France and $108 in Italy. Japan's per capita income at this time was $36. The scale of its industrial production meant that by 1913 US energy consumption was equal to that of Britain, Germany, France, Russia and Austria Hungary combined. The use of electric motors expanded from around 5% of mechanical horsepower in manufacturing in 1899 to 90% by 1939. Labour productivity in the United States rose to and remained at levels at about twice that of Britain (Kennedy, 1989; Broadberry, 1994; Rosenberg, 1998). A further indicator of industrial and commercial development was the growth of towns and cities and between 1880 and 1920, as the percentage of urban population rose from 28.2 to 51.2. Cities grew at prodigious rates—linked as they were by telegraph and railroad—and became larger—from 41 cities with a population of 50,000 or more accounting for 14.3% of the population in 1880 to 144 cities with 31.0% of the population by 1920. Migration from Europe and beyond was significant at this time as was the 'Great Migration' of 1910 to 1920 which saw thousands of African Americans move to industrial cities to find work—and also fill labour shortages created by World War I. Large industrial cities became more specialised, such as those of Akron, Ohio, with rubber manufacturing, and Detroit with the automobile industry. The development of urban conglomerations of specialised industries was correlated with faster labour productivity growth (Friedman, 2020; Klein & Crafts, 2020). By the end of World War I, the United States was set up to capitalise on its position as one of the leading world economies and the development of American production capacity proceeded at pace overall, accompanied as it was by new approaches to organisation and management.

By 1929 the United States had 43% share of world manufacturing output (Kennedy, 1989; Atkeson & Kehoe, 2007; Magnusson, 2014). At this time, industrial production was driven by increased demand for inter alia, automobiles, radios and rayon, machine parts and equipment, petroleum, lacquer, paints, and solvents. Over 20 million automobiles were produced, with over 4 million automobiles in 1929 alone compared with 211,000 in France, 182,000 in Britain and 117,000 in Germany. The production of aluminium also increased which helped civil aviation from the mid-1920s (the first transatlantic crossing was conducted in 1927, by Charles Lindbergh flying the Spirit of Saint Louis). New levels of wealth saw ownership of cars, household appliances and new housing spread through the population. Undoubtedly, this period benefitted from transformative organisational and technological progress involving new products and a revolution in factory organisation and its design (Lorant, 1967; Field, 2011). But the boom was not destined to last. Worldwide economic crisis from 1929 to 1931 was devastating for large sectors of the US economy.

The US share of world trade fell from 43% in 1929, to 28% in 1938 forcing economic policy to become more introspective. The value of exports decreased from $5.24 billion to $1.61 billion and in the depths of the Great Depression real GNP fell by 31%, private investment levels collapsed, and unemployment reached 25% in 1933 (Paya et al., 2005; Beaudreau, 2017). The evidence of the dramatic and often traumatic impact of the depression on the US economy was there for all to see. But it was not a binary choice between success and failure and 'productivity advance between 1929 and 1941 was far stronger than has been traditionally appreciated' (Field, 2008). Some had faith in the longer-term prospects. At this time economist John Maynard Keynes began to purchase US investments which he thought would benefit from the recovery. He continued to buy US securities despite the banking crisis in 1933 and had increasingly large-scale dealings in 1934, through 1935, 1936 and early 1937. In the aftermath of the London World Economic Conference in 1933, for example, Keynes wrote, 'President Roosevelt Is Magnificently Right', and commented enthusiastically on Roosevelt's rejection of a scheme of rigid exchange stabilisation. His longest held shareholdings included those in American Power and Light, Central States Electric, Chicago Rock Island and Pacific Railway and Prudential Investment Corp out of a diverse portfolio of 79 companies. Whilst his praise waned in later years, Keynes maintained a sizeable portfolio of US shares (Cristiano et al., 2018). Some economists had faith in the American Economy even in the face of such testing times.

The final period of the Second Industrial Revolution coincided with the end of the Great Depression through the years of World War II to the 1950s. Writing in 1941, Theodore Krepps of Stanford University put forward the proposition that perhaps reflected the belief, enthusiasm and action that had led the United States to be the most powerful economic force in the world, 'opportunities for investment in 1940 are virtually unlimited—unlimited, that is, provided measures to expand the buying power of consumers are vigorously pushed forward' (Kreps et al., 1941). His argument was for greater capital investment in industry and greater innovation in products. Points borne out by his example of du Pont whose 1937 annual report had noted that articles not in production in 1928 accounted for 40% of total sales in 1937, including new products such as, Dulux enamels, neoprene, synthetic camphor, dyes, anhydrous ammonia, synthetic methanol, urea, titanium pigments and Cellophane. In 1927, the company had 10,700 workers making products like these; in 1937 there were about 18,000, a 70% increase in employment. And during this period the company's investment in manufacturing facilities increased from $63 million to $174 million. By 1940, he argued that the US economy was able to produce at better per capita levels than 1929. As things turned out underutilisation was soon reversed by enormous rearmament programmes (e.g. expenditure of $37 billion on arms production in 1943; and the production of over 96,000 aircraft in 1944 (Kennedy, 1989, p. 428)). The United States' manufacturing capability during this period was startling as commercial manufacturers converted their factories to war time production. Rock Ola a Chicago manufacturer of juke boxes started making rifles, Frigidaire switched from refrigerators to airplane propellers. And 'huge numbers of American factories, many of them in California, which saw its population increase by 14% in 1942, turned to manufacturing for the war'. Over the course of the war, US factories produced 300,000 airplanes, 102,000 armoured vehicles and 77,000 ships (Logevall, 2020). By 1945, the United States was in an 'extraordinarily favourable' economic and strategic position. Though figures vary, one estimate has put the total GNP of the United States by 1950 at $381 billion equating to $2536 per capita. Equivalent figures for the United Kingdom were $71 billion and $1393 per capita; for France $50 billion and $1172 and for Japan $32 billion and $382 (Kennedy, 1989, p. 474; Gordon, 2016).

As companies grew away from being single workshop, bank or transportation line, and grew into multi-unit, multi-product entities came the emergence of managers to monitor and coordinate work:

> *As it was vital to keep the expensive installations running at full speed, managers felt it necessary to co-ordinate the procurement of raw materials and the production and distribution of (semi)finished goods much more intensively than before and often even integrated these activities in one organisation. The*

large scale, horizontally and/or vertically integrated managerial firm was born. (Chandler, 1977; Magnusson, 2014)

Two management challenges stand out, that of growth and scale in production and that of workforce planning and deployment.

Management Challenges During the Second Industrial Revolution—The Challenge of Growth and Scale Production

Dexter S. Kimball, writing in 1929, noted that 'in addition to the more tangible and visible changes of industries and products, there has been a great advance in the last few years in what may be called the theoretical side of production'. Specifically, mass standardisation and production. The impetus to identify and install new technologies and develop new management techniques to ensure their effective implementation was strong. One of the most significant changes to business organisation was the professionalisation of management from a 'pragmatic organisational role ... to a career unto itself'. This was a response, as US business grew, to one of the biggest challenges—how to maintain continuous mass production both for national and for international markets (Friedman, 2020). This in turn stimulated innovation in organisations with the growth of new leading industries which transformed the entire US economy and society (Bodrožić & Adler, 2018). In electrical goods manufacturing, for example, operations with sales of $1.6 billion paved the way for wholesale change. The largest company, General Electric, created high-volume, high-quality appliance production lines for electric fans, heating and cooking devices and refrigerators. The emergence of GE's mechanical refrigerator in the 1900s itself revolutionised the preservation, transportation and refrigeration of food. Its mass production came about by standardising components, which in turn required investment in tools and equipment and a focus on technology to improve scale and quality so that manufactured items could move from factory to home directly, without any preinstallation services. The challenge to the company's managers was to upscale in the light of growing consumer demand whilst simultaneously reducing costs. Having done so, major retailers, such as Sears Roebuck, could market the efficient products without additional finishing (Tobey, 1997; Valli, 2018; Smiley, 2020). The Hoover Suction Sweeper Company of Ohio made vacuum cleaners in 1915 and were also faced with the challenge of mass production (to back up, from 1919, the advertisement 'It Beats ... as it Sweeps ... as it Cleans'); whilst Hotpoint mass-produced volume electric irons and electric cookers. Producing at scale in these companies allowed the supply of cost-effective new household appliances to be within the reach of many, which coupled with increasing demand, and outlets from which they could be purchased (J.C. Penney had 1000 stores by the end of the 1920s) ensured that unit cost and therefore unit price fell. The management challenge in these industries was not only to reduce unit cost by scale production but to do so whilst maintaining or improving quality. The same assumption was true in the chemicals industry where new products derived from petroleum and natural gas complemented American strengths in natural resources. A growing automobile industry created a large and expanding domestic market for chemical industry products, and innovation in research and manufacturing created a solid foundation for growth (Lesch, 2015). The pattern of installing new technologies and mass production methods to achieve scale and scope were also present in metalworking, the outputs of which provided form and structure to many end products. Here, the relative scarcity of suitably skilled labour in the United States in the later years of the nineteenth and early years of the twentieth century led to a higher capital intensity and from 'the late nineteenth century, the United States was credited with having pioneered a new type of mass production—"American" tools'. By 1930 the United States had 94,000 production grinders, 30,000 forging machines, 116,000 milling machines, 308,000 lathes and 174,000 presses. The adoption of new technologies in this case came about through labour scarcity which provided the impetus to mechanisation (Ristuccia & Tooze, 2013).

The glass industry also saw technological innovation such as that under the auspices of the American Window Glass Company, which developed a machine that could replicate the gathering and blowing operations previously performed by skilled workers; the creation of an automatic bottle-making machine—patented originally by the Owens Bottle Machine Company; and by the 1920s spawning a number of alternative fully automatic machines; and a way to manufacture window glass—sheet drawing—which by 1930 accounted for about 80% of domestic output (Lamoreaux & Sokoloff, 2000). As the number of glass industry establishments grew so did capitalisation reflecting higher levels of investment and larger organisations. Mass production was introduced into manufacturing everyday items—such as that at the Ball Brothers Glass Manufacturing Company, in Indiana which, with electric power in the early twentieth century used glass-blowing machines instead of manual processes. At this time the workforce in the glass industry consisted of recruits from the United States, England, Scotland, Ireland, Sweden, Switzerland, Belgium, France, Germany, Italy, Croatia, Greece, Hungary and Poland reflecting the large-scale labour movements to the United States (U.S. Immigration Commission, 1910). In Ford City Pennsylvania in 1895, the introduction of new technologies for glass-making meant the import of skilled workers from overseas because of the lack of experience in such new techniques in the United States; although after 1895, many employees were drawn away from the glass industry into the steel plants in and around Pittsburgh (U.S. Immigration Commission, 1910, p. 27).

In each of these examples, the pressure was on to keep the expensive manufacturing installations running at capacity whilst coordinating the procurement of raw materials and distribution of finished goods—'administrative co-ordination by and within these firms enabled them to profit from the 'economies of speed' of steady high-volume production: 'modern business enterprise appeared for the first time in history when the volume of economic activities reached a level that made administrative coordination more efficient and profitable than market coordination' (van Driel et al., 2007). The shift towards mass production through new technology and processes was instrumental to their competitiveness. But this was rarely a straightforward process.

After market testing the Model N, the Model R and the Model S, Henry Ford launched the Model T in 1908, a huge success which became the first car owned by many in the United States. Between 1908 and

1927 the Ford Motor Company produced more Model T's than all other American car-makers combined. To keep up with demand meant efficient and effective mass production techniques. Ford looked to both the armaments and meat manufacturing industries (in particular the Chicago meatpacking business) for best practice. Integrating the learning from these industries back into automobile factories mean that by 1927, the production of all Model T's was based on common platforms, sharing modules, components and manufacturing processes and services at the Highland Park Plant, bringing down the costs of a Model T. It involved the creation of large-scale design of machine tools, deployed in mass production assembly plants. The launch of the Model T and the subsequent increase in production volumes in 1908 led to Ford's market dominance and a decade of unequalled profitability (Langlois & Robertson, 1989). And of particular importance to this study, is the systemic nature of organisation and production planning. For these reasons Henry Ford's Highland Park and River Rouge plants became the world's most extensively studied factories because of the productivity impact of the moving assembly line; and information systems that paralleled and enabled mass production. Ford-style mass production emerged from the logic of management control at the point where the scientific management of F.W. Taylor met the shop floor of large-scale manufacturing with the resulting mass production providing the foundation for a new approach to organisation and work. On the one hand, this was 'a thoroughly Taylorised operation, in which white-collar engineers, ensconced in a planning office, laid out the subdivision of tasks and dictated the pace of production', but on the other, there were less structured elements. Indeed, sometimes Ford engineers had an 'ambiguous relationship with scientific management, aware of its meaning yet disdainful of its narrow focus on the task rather than total factory organisation'. This does not mean that the principles of scientific management weren't adopted; just that the process wasn't always neat and sequential. Undoubtedly Fords innovations in mass production were part of broader economic and social processes, including the professionalisation of American engineering and the rise of large-scale management, with the creation of distinctive language and practice in both areas. Efficiency, planning and systems became watchwords of scientific management

(Wilson & McKinlay, 2010; Link, 2018). The argument being that factory rationalisation wasn't possible without a clear chain of command and control. And even then, there were challenges in respect of how much to delegate and to whom. Alexander Graham Bell, as the largest shareholder, wrote to the Vice President of his company expressing his dismay at the perceived overstepping of authority by one of its managers. 'to decide at once whether he is a suitable person' (Bell, 1906). Growth was not always a straightforward affair.

The scientific approach to management went hand in hand with mass production and the 'tyranny of the production line'. But paradoxically, agility and flexibility were also necessary, especially during transition, because in many cases 'there was neither a blueprint of how this process was to be managed nor a bureaucratic system for compiling and assessing production knowledge'. Depending instead on the tacit knowledge of key managers or engineers until this was converted into explicit knowledge as best practice emerged. At Ford, foremen found themselves part of a complex hierarchy. Staff transfers and discharges remained the supervisor's domain but became subject to oversight by Ford's central personnel office with the observation that the extensive process of administrative innovation entailed a loss of managerial power and autonomy (Wilson & McKinlay, 2010). Expanded and accelerated information flows required by mass production also meant that managers had to be effective administrators. Over time Ford created a hierarchy of supervision and the ratio of supervisors to total factory employees rose to around 1:100. But there were also elements that were more crafted because moving to mass production was an organic process. Here was a distinction between Ford's system and Taylorism. 'Where Taylor focused on the task and physical measures to find the "one best way", the assembly line offered a more powerful mechanism for driving productivity.' Using descriptions from supervisors who worked on the implementation of the production lines at Ford it was very much an 'iterative learning process … once the broad principles of applying the moving assembly line were understood, and rudimentary timings established, the rest became a rapid, pragmatic process' (Wilson & McKinlay, 2010).

The challenge of growth and scale production therefore had elements of technology innovation, which required managers to be open to new ways and methods, new systems and processes. It had elements of technology improvement which by a sequence of challenge and response, managers were able to influence improvements in the new methods. It had elements of organisational transformation in which team working was replaced by long run processes with tasks identified for individuals. And it had elements of adhocracy, learning by doing and trial and error.

Management Challenges During the Second Industrial Revolution—The Human Challenge of Mass Production and Mechanisation

The impact of the transition to mass production is reflected in the statistic that for every 100 men required to fill the production line at Henry Ford's factories, scores of new recruits were needed, such was the turnover in reaction to these new, different and largely monotonous jobs. The restructuring of factories involved the transformation of the flow of work on the shop floor as well as social reorganisation, different work arrangements and 'new patterns of specialisation on the part of both workers and management', which took significant experimentation and learning (Rosenberg, 1998; Farber, 2002; Magnusson, 2014). Mass production technologies radically changed the world of jobs and occupations across the US economy. In the coal industry, for example, pick or hand miners were replaced by lesser skilled workers with the introduction of mining machinery; whilst in wool and cotton, skilled weavers were replaced by unskilled minders after the introduction of machinery; and further still, mechanisation of the boot and shoe Industry in New England and the Midwest was the highest development of the factory system; and in the iron and steel sector 'inventions have made it possible to operate the plants with a much smaller proportion of skilled and specialised employees than was previously the case'. The glass industry, which grew fourfold during the early years of the Second Industrial Revolution, provides some idea of the nature of this spectrum. As reported by the US Immigration Commission in 1910, the invention of machinery had made possible the extensive employment of unskilled labour, replacing the skilled workers who had previously been responsible for its production (U.S. Immigration Commission, 1910). In one Pennsylvania factory, for example, machinery was introduced in 1900 which displaced skilled workers, who went on strike, lost the dispute and left. Senior Managers then had the problem of replacing the skilled workers with practically a new workforce. The competition to do so was intense. In 1900 the plant manager was faced with the fact that change was taking place and that his plant faced competition from tin and steel mills as well as other glass plants in the labour market (U.S. Immigration Commission, 1910, p. 28). In 1903 new machinery was installed at a glass factory in Arnold Pennsylvania, resulting in a strike in 1904 and the replacement of the strikers with a non-unionised workforce again with the challenges of recruitment and training—in the immediate term of the transition to mechanisation and beyond. The human resource challenges for management were threefold around the loss of skilled workers and industrial memory; the employment of unskilled labour most of whom were new to the industry; third, retaining workers once employed because of the intensity of competition in the US labour market at this time of economic expansion. Furthermore, managers had a broad span of control in which to undertake their human resources challenges. In a single plate glass manufacturing plant in Pennsylvania the colouring department had 1 foreman for a team of 20 of multiple skills from cutters to labourers; the bricklaying department had 1 foreman to 31 bricklayers and helpers; other departments had ratios of between 1:20 and 1:40.

Once again, Ford and the automobile sector represent the human resource challenges across industry. For the company, the improvements in productivity were astonishing but at a cost for the workforce—in the early days of the new production techniques labour turnover was significant (Donkin, 2001; Alizon et al., 2009). On the one hand, the creation of production lines with rigid standards and targets conjure strict hierarchies and clear divisions of labour, power and authority. And there is some evidence of these being in place. If this were the only narrative, then outlining human resource management challenges would be planning and organising, motivating and workforce engagement. But things were not as straightforward. Indeed, there is some evidence that once Henry Ford regained control of the company from outside investors, he turned it into a mission as much as a process driven organisation in which administration was more informal and flexible than the rigours of Taylor would imply. And any attempt at codification was sometimes given short shrift. In 1919, a New York efficiency firm Thompson and Black were brought into the company to manage the buyout and produced a company-wide organisation chart. It was an attempt to 'make the company's flexible and informal administrative structures legible to the logic of systematic management'. In April 1920, Ford dismissed the chart because he believed it was too confusing or too military. Which begs the question how did Ford's managers actually manage? In the first place those on the shop floor 'relied on ingrained collective protocols and routines based on an intimate familiarity with the production process'. To do so required managers and supervisors who had cut their teeth in Ford. How else would they know about protocols without learned experience? In fact, much like the factories of the First Industrial Revolution, 'both on the shop floor and in the offices, Ford's staff consisted of men whose upward mobility depended on sustained work experience and continued allegiance to the company'. Management of the plant at shop floor level was the responsibility of foremen with a shared culture; and favoured continuous improvement based on practice experience. While other corporations increasingly put 'theoretically schooled engineers in charge of their shops and business school graduates into their boardrooms, promotion at Ford came through the ranks' (Link, 2018).

Whilst all of this human adaptation to the rigours of the new systems and processes that were being implemented across the large industrial complexes, was taking place, external factors and shocks often forced unexpected adjustments. In particular, the incidence of epidemics and pandemics not only brought untold sadness to individuals and their families but often had a significant impact on their workplaces and forced organisations to adapt rapidly. The 1918 influenza pandemic, for example, spread worldwide. It is estimated that about 500 million people or one-third of the world's population became infected with this virus. The number of deaths was estimated to be at least 50 million worldwide. In the United States, it was first identified in military personnel in spring of that year with about 675,000 occurring subsequently. The high mortality in healthy people, including those in the 20- to 40-year age group, was a unique feature of this pandemic and the one that had most of an impact on the workforce (CDC, 2019). The fact that the virus disproportionately affected young men, in combination with losses during World War I, created a shortage of labour. Organisations had to adapt their human resource practices considerably. Most notably the gaps left in the workforce enabled women to play a greater role in the workforce. After the end of World War I the number of women was 25% higher than it had been previously. By 1920 women made up 21% of the national workforce, including in manufacturing roles that were previously held by men. The upshot was that 'leadership positions within the workforce could now be occupied by women' (Blackburn et al., 2018).

In summary the management challenges facing those working in companies in the United States during the Second Industrial Revolution cover the whole gamut of human resource management practice. The first was how to deal with the human resource implications of the introduction of new technology. This demanded an approach to Industrial Relations at the time of intense labour market competition. There was little experience in this situation. Second, there was the daunting task of recruiting people to work in the new factories and industrial plants, although immigration at this time went some way to ameliorating the problem of labour shortages—between 1850 and 1930, 5 million Germans emigrated to the United States; over 5 million Italians between 1880 and 1920; 2 million from Central Europe and over 1.5 million Swedes and Norwegians. Third there was the challenge of training a workforce, often with little experience of the industry or the new methods of factory production. And fourth there was the challenge of retaining the workforce once the investment in training had taken place. So, what was required to undertake one of the thousands of new managerial jobs that sprang up? In the first place, there were contextual competences that were specific to the time and place of the Second Industrial Revolution in the United States.

Contextual Competences of Managers During the Second Industrial Revolution

As American organisations took advantage of their powerful economic position, their increasing scale and scope gave rise to historic changes in the structure of industries and historic changes in the way in which managers went about their business. Firstly, managerial roles were affected by macro-economic dynamics whereby the United States became the leading economy in the world after picking up the mantle previously held by Britain until the late nineteenth century. This context here is of significant economic growth in absolute terms and the adoption of invention and innovation across key industries from automobiles to iron and steel and sectors from electricity to railroads. Managers were faced with strategic choices in respect of markets and capital investment to follow the pattern of economic opportunity and development; and the success of their organisations often resided in their competence in making the right decisions. Secondly, having made such choices, American organisations of all sizes were faced with the challenge of implementing new technologies and systems. The third level of context came about with the growing separation of ownership and control, particularly in larger companies with the installation of a hierarchy of managers to ensure their smooth day to day operation with (theoretically) greater role clarity—senior managers should focus their attention on strategic issues such as raising funds and planning future capital expenditure, other managerial roles should be concerned with operational and administrative matters (Chandler & Salsbury, 1971). The professionalism of management gathered pace.

These influences had an impact on management practice and the competences required for its successful execution, management theory in response to the new environment and how the role of managers was perceived and ultimately on the contextual competences required to perform the role. In the early years, the ideas of Frederick Winslow Taylor, whose time and motion methods (based on his analysis of the efficiency of coal shovellers at the Pennsylvania Bethlehem Steel Corporation) and the creation of the concept of scientific management from his findings led to a greater understanding of managing and organising human work for maximum output. Undoubtedly the implementation of Taylor's methods went hand in hand with the mechanisation of production lines across multiple industries over many years and can be seen as a contributor to the contextual competence of managers who had to learn to work with this way of operating. The transition to new more efficient methods, however, was not always a smooth one for managers and the workforce alike leading to often high levels of labour turnover and industrial action creating the additional challenge of industrial relations in ways that were unprecedented. In response and soon after World War I, the more progressive thinkers in American management, such as Henry Dennison and the brothers Edward and Lincoln Filene, actively encouraged business leaders to meet and share knowledge. It is perhaps no coincidence that towards the end of a period a complementary approach to management began to emerge with recognition of human relations in management thinking—particularly through the work of those such as Mary Parker Follett and Chester Barnard (the latter being an Executive with New Jersey Bell, whose book *The Functions of the Executive* emphasised the importance of the 'softer' side of management such as communication), and Elton Mayo's famous studies at Western Electric's Hawthorne Plant. Dale Carnegie's *How to Win Friends and Influence People* was published in 1937 which quickly sold out its initial print run of 5000. It 'touched a nerve and filled a human need that was more than a faddish phenomenon of post-depression days'. Carnegie's own words perhaps explain the reason:

> *[A] man with 314 employees ... for years he had driven and criticised and condemned his employees without stint or discretion. Kindness, words of appreciation and encouragement were alien to his lips. After studying the principles in this book, this employer sharply altered his philosophy of life. His organisation now inspired with a new loyalty, a new enthusiasm, a new spirit of teamwork.* (Carnegie, 1937)

Contextual management competences in the Second Industrial Revolution were influenced by waves of technological change affecting the organisational paradigm and henceforth new management models. In the first place there was the contextual management competence of the ability to deal with rapid growth, change and transformation. The experience of the consolidation in the US chemical industry during the 1920s is one that was replicated elsewhere, creating larger organisations with new manufacturing systems and processes and large-scale continuous processing plants (Landau & Arora, 1999; Bodrožić & Adler, 2018). Each of which required new management methods. In this respect competences on the part of managers were polyvalent, that is, the ability to perform different tasks depending on the organisation's needs. On the one hand there was the rigour of the production line and it was expected that managers would achieve their targets by ensuring continuous and profitable production runs. But simultaneously, there was the requirement to spot opportunities for improvement and as Henry Ford noted of his own facilities 'everyone in the place has an open mind as to the way in which every job is being done' (Ford, 1922). Such an outlook was important because to create any long-term advantage, innovation does not only need to be on a new principle, but needs to be systemic, across a range of processes and methods, and to form part of an ongoing programme of where progress accumulates and compounds over time (Hamel, 2006). This required managers who could respond to the unpredictability of innovation by being flexible in how they approached their jobs. And whilst the systemisation of production led to the systematisation of management methods, managers still remained agile. Managers at the Ford Motor Company (Link, 2018) and General Motors (Wilson & McKinlay, 2010) had to function with the rigours of the production line—because of set production targets—whilst at the same time expected to spot opportunities to improve methods. The basis of this approach was pragmatism and executive persuasion in place of coercion. Henry Ford's mission driven organisation was an example and from 1920, Alfred Sloan who had transformed General Motors 'from the ramshackle collection of car manufacturing companies assembled by William Durant into the archetypical multidivisional form' introduced structural reforms which separated strategic and operational decision-making and 'combined robust, centralised financial control within an organisation geared to constructing consent'. An industry that was evolving at pace required managers who could keep up with technological development whilst demonstrating flexibility and agility regardless of the organisational forms in which they operated. The competences to do so were very much of their time.

In addition to the powerful contextual influence of technology, changes in the expectations of the workforce of the newly mechanised plants was also an important consideration. In particular, industrial relations and dealing with organised labour came to prominence, although the number of trade union members fluctuated. At the beginning of the period, strikes in industries such as glass-making were on occasion the result of introduction of machinery to replace both skilled and unskilled work. Installations often met with labour force resistance, strikes and industrial action. Similarly, in the automobile industry there were strikes and clashes with companies at production plants in 1933 and 1934, strikes at GM in 1936–1937 and the Ford strike in 1941 (Meyer, 2002). Union membership as a percentage of the workforce began to rise with the onset of the Great Depression and continued to do so until its peak in the early 1950s. The impact on management practice of these disruptions meant a transition from employee relations based on individual engagement to industrial relations based on dealing with blocs of organised workers. Umpires were employed at the Ford Plant to act as arbitrators to deal with any disputes between those in management positions and the workforce (Meyer, 2002). Large-scale industrial relations were a relatively new situation for managers.

There was also the challenge of different types of organisation structure. Some worked in hierarchies. But motivation through the hierarchical management structure was not the only model of engaging the workforce. Indeed, Henry Ford countered against this clarity of management roles through hierarchy instead advocating clarity of roles through recognition of specific circumstances, regarding rigid organisation as being counter to productivity and innovation. He viewed the 'great big chart' as being 'heavy with nice round berries' each of which bore the name of a man or an office. Ford's preferred point of view was of a more fluid structure of management and decision-making:

> *Now a business in my way of thinking is not a machine. It is a collection of people who are brought together to do work and not to write letters ... it is the business of those who plan the entire work to see that all of the departments are*

working properly toward the same end ... the sole object ought to be to get work done and get paid for it. (Ford, 1922)

Hence, two areas of competence stand out, the importance of which increased in the upwards climb of the United States from the late nineteenth to the mid-twentieth century. The first related to the competence of working with the uncertainties that came from innovation, particularly in technology but also in management methods. The second was the fundamental change in all aspects of human resource management. Whilst the approach of the managers was very much of their time and place, there were other competences can be identified as having relevance across time.

Core Competences of Managers During the Second Industrial Revolution

American organisations responded dynamically to the opportunities for growth that came about during the Second Industrial Revolution creating the world's foremost economy; and American managers were instrumental in both setting a strategic course and backing this with operational excellence. As they were faced with new circumstances—through innovative technology, economic opportunity or new forms of organisational structure—managers proved to be adaptable and willing to accept change. They were involved in evaluating and selecting machines for running the production lines, which they then requisitioned, and installed; achieving higher output targets as a result, and on top of this they implemented new ways of working in new types of organisation structure. As corporations grew, managers emerged as a new social and professional group. 'It became progressively more critical as more salaried managers, without being shareholders, were appointed to run businesses. Owner families often kept control of their companies ... but they progressively and massively recruited managers to run their companies' (Gospel, 1988; Segrestin et al., 2019). In some cases, managers worked directly to the owners; in others, managers would work through a hierarchy to a general manager. Managers crafted strategy; or Executive Committees were set up to take this role and managers would be responsible for operations. In some cases there was explicit knowledge of documented systems and processes; in others the tacit knowledge of the manager would craft production processes in response to learning on the job as production lines were installed. In some, management decision-making was informed by external parties—consensus standards committees of engineers in the railroad, steel and electrical industries, where cooperative networks sustained 'the American style of competitive managerial capitalism' (Russell, 2009). These considerations reflect the complex and fast-moving nature of the job of many managers. Not only did they have to deal with technological change but also with changes in workforce dynamics. Not only did they increasingly work in systematised production plants but also had to implement new production methods based on in-job learning. And through it all the principles of what managers should be capable of were evolving through development of new management theories. There was recognition of the idea of management as something primarily designed to operate objectively and instrumentally towards human resources (Dent & Bozeman, 2014).

Adaptability and agility were watchwords of the manager in the late nineteenth and early twentieth centuries. The ability perform in an environment of change and uncertainty was applied in the fast-moving environment of the new automobile factories or that of the machine tools, chemical or glass industry. It was a requirement that spanned most industries across many states. The seeds of change which had been sown during the latter years of the nineteenth century came to fruition in the early years of the twentieth and continued to blossom thereafter. Even during the periods of recession, change was present in some industries and they responded to the harsh environment with new products or services. Hence, *making change work effectively* is the first and one of the most fundamental of the core management competences of the Second Industrial Revolution. A willingness to adapt to new contexts and not accept the status quo ante were both vital; the knowledge and skills to do so and the attitudes and behaviours that would be the outward articulation of this were of great importance. The constituents were the acquisition of knowledge about change and its possibilities; and skills to plans and organise for change; and the skills to install new processes or systems effectively. There is a strong cognitive dimension to the core management competence of making change work effectively as witnessed by AT &T's decision to move to automatic switching in the US telecommunications market which didn't come about only because of market or financial forces but also through the intelligence and creativity of key individuals amongst its engineers and its managers (Nix & Gabel, 1996). In summary, the term change is often a cliché in studies of organisations and 'change is the norm' its mantra. But the ability to manage change and make it work effectively was not an abstract concept to the managers at Ford or GM, at Du Pont, GE, Hotpoint or Hoover at AT&T or the American Window Glass Company. It was a core management competence of the highest order.

Change was the precursor to the second core management competence of *seeking continuous improvement*—'everything can always be done better than it is being done' (Ford, 1922). The sheer scale of invention by US companies was matched only by the ability to build on its progress. In American steel, for example, technological innovation, intensified use of energy and plant design permitted a great increase in the volume and speed of throughput. But these would not have been successful without the improvement in overall management procedures. Indeed, the managerial revolution was not just about the separation of ownership from control but of significant organisational and processural transformation (Chandler, 1977, p. 269). Where companies adopted Taylor's scientific management there was, in his opinion, an inbuilt improvement mechanism. With standardisation came continuous improvement and as Taylor himself wrote 'you must have standards. We get some of our greatest improvements from the workmen in that way. The workmen, instead of holding back are eager to make suggestions ... in that way, we get the finest kind of teamwork, we have true cooperation, and our method ... leads on always to something better than *has been known before*' (Taylor, 1912 quoted in Boer et al., 2000). The challenge for the manager then was not only to adopt innovative machinery and techniques, not only to have the project management skills to install it, but also in the competence of delivering continuous improvement. One the one hand, the manager had to manage against strict deadlines and have an environment of efficiency in achieving targets, mostly driven by the speed of the production line; but on the other they had to create an environment where they or members of the workforce could identify improvements and act on them. An engineering view written in 1924 picked up on this essential competence—'variation is creative, it pioneers the advance; standardization is conservational, it seizes the advance and establishes it as an actual concrete fact … Standardization is thus the liberator that relegates the problems that have already been solved to their proper place, namely to the field of routine, and leaves the creative faculties free for the problems that are still unsolved. Standardization from this point of view is thus an indispensable ally of the creative genius' (Whitney, 1924 quoted in Russell, 2009). The message was that it was not enough to capture and cement the gains from innovation. Instead, these had to be built upon through continuous improvement—as characterised by a sustained and rich stream of suggestions supported by recognition, reward and both top-down and bottom-up systems (Boer et al., 2000). Henry Ford was constantly experimenting with ideas for improvement in production processes. 'Testing out the idea is very different from making a change in the car. Where most manufacturers find themselves quicker to make a change in the product than in the method of manufacturing—we follow exactly the opposite course' (Ford, 1922). A core competence of the manager during the Second Industrial Revolution was to make sure that the rich stream flowed after the initial investment in new technology. The manager who had the knowledge, skills, attitudes and behaviours to make change work effectively was an invaluable human asset. As Ford wrote of his manufacturing operations '*They never stand still*' (Ford, 1922). And neither did successful managers.

By their nature, invention and innovation inevitably produced uncertain outcomes and managers often had to make changes as they implemented new systems or processes. To do so required a good deal of tacit knowledge based on experience, but there was also the need for explicit knowledge, whether this was in relation to systems, processes or people. Managers needed both types of information to be effective and therefore the ability to *use information to support business decisions* was an essential attribute and may be seen as a core management competence.

On the one hand, the judicious 'strategic' use of management information systems allowed senior managers to monitor competitor pricing or new products; or to monitor the performance of business units or departments. At department level the information was concerned with operational performance of a newly installed production line or cost management in a team. AT&T in the 1920s used informational innovation for 'firm-specific learning'. Metrics were identified which corresponded to key business processes and these were integrated into operational plans (Chandar & Miranti, 2009). GM, whilst recognising the importance of production information and improvement in achieving effective cost management, used information explicitly in management decisions' (Hoskisson & Hitt, 1994, p. 30). To perfect this approach, Alfred Sloan of GM set up information sharing processes—such as the General Technical Committee of 1923—to coordinate information, and standardise systems and processes that would benefit all rather than one division or department (Sloan, 1963). By the end of the 1920s around one third of executives and managers in American rubber, chemical and electrical industries had college degrees. Information about management systems and processes was also available externally. By 1920, 65 American Business Schools awarded over 1500 business degrees annually; by 1950 over 600 American higher education institutions offered courses which were attended by over 370,000 students (Matthews et al., 1998).

The corollary for the above is then to convert the innovation in systems and the knowledge in how to make these work into wider progress for the company as a whole and a core management competence would be that of *delivering business results*. This competence covered the ability to meet challenging output targets set by the introduction of new technology or machinery or improvements to systems and processes. The Chair of the Board of General Electric outlined the responsibilities of his managers in 1922. He described management's sole purpose as to make the investors in the company and the workforce '*function together adequately to produce something that is of value—that is of real service to the world*' (Owen Young 1922 quoted in Schatz, 1983). GE brought management discipline to the chaotic process of scientific discovery and DuPont developed capital-budgeting techniques through return on investment calculations in 1903 (Hamel, 2006). In the Ford factories each department had its rate of production targets and the standing of the manager depended on reaching them—'every foreman checks his own department daily; he carries the figures always with him. The superintendent has a tabulation of all the scores. If there is something wrong in a department the output score shows it at once, the superintendent makes inquiries and the foreman looks alive .... The foreman need not be a cost accountant ... his charges are the machines and the human beings in his department. When they are working at their best, he has performed his service' (Ford, 1922). In 1912 Pierre du Pont prepared a detailed booklet that prescribed the duties of the Du Pont workforce (Chandler & Salsbury, 1971). Delivering business results was paramount.

None of the above would be possible without the human resources to do so. And so, the ability of *motivating and engaging a diverse workforce* during and after the transition to the new working environment becomes a core management competence. On the one hand it was concerned with balancing the needs the team or the plant as a whole. On the other hand, it was concerned with satisfying individual aspirations. For some, the company's ideology provided 'a set of values and principles infused by an organisation's history which inform and underpin its social and economic order in the present and future'. Procter and Gamble's strong workforce relationship came about through a long history of workforce improvement and when Cooper Procter became general manager in 1890 and later served as President (1907–1930) his enduring mark was to strengthen worker loyalty, 'persuading the partners to allow employees Saturday afternoons off and initiate a profit-sharing scheme to instil a sense of ownership. The profit scheme he launched placed the company at the forefront of 'welfare capitalism'. A sickness-disability programme was established in 1915, followed by an eight-hour working day in 1918 (Maclean et al., 2014, p. 552). Here, the managerial task of motivating and engaging the workforce was set into the company culture. Henry Ford also recognised that the economic fundamental was his labour force since 'labour is the human element which makes the fruitful seasons of the earth useful to men' (Ford, 1922). One of the original tenets of scientific management was to deal with members of the workforce on an individual basis. The argument being that labour and management had common interests (Braeman et al., 1968). But higher labour turnover as new systems and processes were installed, and an increase in Trade Union members prompted new approaches, including the concept of an employment manager, new hiring techniques—at GE Westinghouse these included preference for those applicants coming from more casual industries such as clothing or construction because they preferred steadier work, even though it may pay less—or the recognition that 'you've got to treat each workman as an individual' (Schatz, 1983). Sentiments that may have been displayed by managers in telecommunications who recognised 'the importance of generating greater efficiency by cultivating better human relations within the company culture;' (Russell, 2015) and the electronics industry (organisations in Boston and in Silicon Valley from the 1920s to the 1960s), who developed original human resources practices to deal with the problems of attracting and retaining a highly skilled workforce—'independently of the welfare capitalism plans of corporations such as Eastman Kodak and before the guru theorists and work empowerment programs of the 1960s' (Lecuyer, 2003). The ability to attract, motivate and engage a diverse workforce was a core management competence whether this was in the metalworking industry of the early or technology industry of the mid-twentieth century.

The growth in the size of companies and the demands for collective recognition in some was further complicated by the sheer diversity of the US workforce. Migration and mobility coupled with the absolute increase in numbers created one of the most significant challenges requiring a human resource competence on the part of managers for which there was little precedent. The diversity of the workforce in the glass industry, outlined in the US Immigration Commission reports, required knowing how to behave as well as know-how, by managers the demonstration of which could impact productivity or labour turnover. During the 1920s and 1930s the US automobile industry gathered together an industrial workforce of incredible cultural and social diversity 'creating an enormous social and cultural patchwork' (Meyer, 2002). Growth in employment in the electrical industry went from few in 1875 to over 300,000 in 1919 and half a million by the end of the period covered by the Second Industrial revolution. By 1930, some 20% of the workforce had been born outside of the United States and in the years before World War II over a quarter of the electrical workforce were women in the electrical factories making products such as light bulbs, radio tubes and telephones (Schatz, 1983).

By the end of the Second Industrial Revolution, the United States was the foremost industrialised country. The ability to implement mass production successfully, judicious investment in a range of industries throughout the period and enough government intervention to provide a foundation on which industrialists could build had enabled the country to reach a zenith of prosperity. By 1950 the American Dream was a reality and high pay for working people had created the world's first middle class society (Hoopes, 2011). With theoretical underpinnings from such as F.W. Taylor and practical application of new approaches to management on the part of Ford and Sloan amongst many others, business managers became 'ensconced in Western Society as professional, responsible and legitimate' (Gould et al., 2017). America's managers were instrumental in the creation of efficient productive corporations. From the end of the nineteenth century, they had demonstrated competence in the field of technology, its identification and implementation. They had shown ability in managing a growing and extremely diverse workforce, dealing with waves of human migration into and within the country and throughout, they continued to deliver the results required by owners and stockholders. These were people who got things done, achieved targets and installed new technologies. They dealt with people, persuading and cajoling, coaching and directing. All the time they had provided the testing ground for new theories of management based on scientific analysis at first and human relations later.

The Second Industrial Revolution was the age of the American Manager. From the 1950s the challenge was to continue the steep upwards trajectory.

References

Alizon, F., Shooter, S. B., & Simpson, T. W. (2009). Henry Ford and the Model T: Lessons for Product Platforming and Mass Customization. *Design Studies, 30*(5), 588–605.

Atkeson, A., & Kehoe, P. (2007). Modelling the Transition to a New Economy: Lessons from Two Technological Revolutions. *The American Economic Review, 97*(1), 64–88.
Basalla, G. (1988). *The Evolution of Technology*. Cambridge University Press.
Beaudreau, B. (2017). Electrification, the Smoot-Hawley Tariff Act and the Decline in Investment Expenditure in 1931–1932: Testing the Excess-Capacity Hypothesis. *International Advances in Economic Research, 23*(3), 295–308.
Bell, A. G. (1906). *Letter from Alexander Graham Bell to Edward J. Hall, March 7, 1906*. Library of Congress. https://tile.loc.gov/storage-services/service/mss/magbell/271/27100313/27100313.pdf
Blackburn, C. C., Parker, G. W., & Wendelbo, M. (2018). How the Devastating 1918 Flu Pandemic Helped Advance US Women's Rights. *The Conversation*. https://theconversation.com/how-the-devastating-1918-flu-pandemic-helped-advance-us-womens-rights-91045
Bodrožić, Z., & Adler, P. S. (2018). The Evolution of Management Models: A Neo-Schumpeterian Theory. *Administrative Science Quarterly, 63*(1), 85.
Boer, H., Berger, A., Chapman, R., & Gertsen, F. (2000). *CI Changes: From Suggestion Box to Organisational Learning*. Ashgate Publishing.
Braeman, J., Bremner, R. H., & Brody, D. (1968). *Change and Continuity in Twentieth Century America: The 1920's*. Ohio State University Press.
Broadberry, S. (1994). Technological Leadership and Productivity Leadership in Manufacturing since the Industrial Revolution: Implications for the Convergence Debate. *The Economic Journal, 104*(423), 291–302.
Bussel, R. (1998). "The Most Indispensable Man in His Community"; African-American Entrepreneurs in West Chester, Pennsylvania, 1865–1925. *Pennsylvania History: A Journal of Mid-Atlantic Studies, 65*(3), 324.
Carnegie, D. (1937). *How to Win Friends and Influence People*. Vermillion, 2006 edition.
CDC. (2019). *1918 Pandemic (H1N1 Virus)*. Centres for Disease Control and Prevention. https://www.cdc.gov/flu/pandemic-resources/1918-pandemic-h1n1.html
Chandar, N., & Miranti, P. J. (2009). Integrating Accounting and Statistics: Forecasting, Budgeting and Production Planning at the American Telephone and Telegraph Company during the 1920s. *Accounting and Business Research, 39*(4), 373–395.
Chandler, A. D. (1977). *The Visible Hand: The Managerial Revolution in American Business*. Harvard University Press.

Chandler, A. D., & Salsbury, S. (1971). *Pierre Du Pont and the Making of the Modern Corporation*. Beard Books, 2000 edition.

Church, R. A. (1975). *The Great Victorian Boom, 1850–1873*. Macmillan Press.

Cristiano, C., Marcuzzo, M. C., & Sanfilippo, E. (2018). Taming the Great Depression: Keynes's Personal Investments in the US Stock Market, 1931–1939. *Economia Politica, 35*(1), 13–40.

Dent, E. B., & Bozeman, P. (2014). Discovering the Foundational Philosophies, Practices, and Influences of Modern Management Theory. *Journal of Management History, 20*(2), 145–163.

Donkin, R. (2001). *Blood, Sweat and Tears*. Texere.

Farber, D. (2002). *Sloan Rules; Alfred P. Sloan and the Triumph of General Motors*. University of Chicago Press.

Field, A. J. (2008). The Impact of the Second World War on US Productivity Growth. *Economic History Review, 61*(3), 672–694.

Field, A. J. (2011). *The Great Leap Forward*. Yale University Press.

Ford, H. (1922). *My Life and Work*. Doubleday, Page and Company.

Friedman, W. (2020). *American Business History: A Very Short Introduction*. Oxford University Press.

Geddes, P. (1915). *Cities in Evolution*. Williams and Norgate.

Gordon, R. J. (2016). *The Rise and Fall of American Growth*. Princeton University Press.

Gospel, H. F. (1988). The Management of Labour: Great Britain, the US, and Japan. *Business History, 30*(1), 104–115.

Gould, A. M., Bourk, M. J., & Joullié, J.-E. (2017). From the Industrial Revolution to Trump: Six Periods of Changing Perceptions of American Business Managers. *Journal of Management History, 23*(4), 471–488.

Hamel, G. (2006). The Why, What, and How of Management Innovation. *Harvard Business Review*.

Hasan, M. K., Hayek, M. J., Williams, W. A. J., Pane-Haden, S., & Martinez Gelvez, M. P. (2020). Activist Identity Construction of Madam C.J. Walker. *Journal of Management History, 26*(3), 335–351.

Hoopes, J. (2011). *Corporate Dreams*. Rutgers University Press.

Hoskisson, R., & Hitt, M. A. (1994). *Downscoping: How to Tame the Diversified Firm*. Oxford University Press.

Jevons, H. S. (1931). The Second Industrial Revolution. *The Economic Journal, 41*(161), 1–18.

Kennedy, P. (1989). *The Rise and Fall of the Great Powers*. Fontana Press.

Kenwood, A. G., & Lougheed, A. L. (1973). *The Growth in The International Economy 1820–1960*. George Allen & Unwin.
Kimball, D. S. (1929). Changes in Old and New Industries. In *Prosperity and Thrift: The Coolidge Era and the Consumer Economy, 1921–1929*. Library of Congress.
Klein, A., & Crafts, N. (2020). Agglomeration Externalities and Productivity Growth: US Cities, 1880–1930. *The Economic History Review, 73*(1), 209.
Kreps, T. J., Bissell, R. M., Jr., & Altman, O. L. (1941). The Status and Role of Private Investment in the American Economy, 1940. *American Economic Review, 30*(5), 177–247.
Lamoreaux, N. R., & Sokoloff, K. L. (2000). The Geography of Invention in the American Glass Industry, 1870–1925. *The Journal of Economic History, 60*(3), 700.
Landau, R., & Arora, A. (1999). The Chemical Industry: From the 1850s until Today. *Business Economics, 34*(4), 7.
Langlois, R., & Robertson, P. (1989). Explaining Vertical Integration: Lessons from the American Automobile Industry. *The Journal of Economic History, 49*(2), 361–375.
Lecuyer, C. (2003). High Tech Corporatism: Management-Employee Relations in US Electronics Firms, 1920s–1960s. *Enterprise and Society, 4*(3), 502–520.
Lesch, J. E. (2015). Kathryn Steen. The American Synthetic Organic Chemicals Industry: War and Politics, 1910–1930. *American Historical Review, 4*, 1501.
Levenstein, M. (1995). African American Entrepreneurship: The View from the 1910 Census. *Business and Economic History, 24*(1). Papers presented at the forty-first annual meeting of the Business History Conference, 106–122.
Link, S. (2018). The Charismatic Corporation: Finance, Administration, and Shop Floor Management under Henry Ford. *Business History Review, 92*(1), 85–115.
Link, S., & Maggor, N. (2020). The United States as a Developing Nation: Revisiting the Peculiarities of American History. *Past & Present, 246*(1), 269–306.
Logevall, F. (2020). *JFK, Volume 1*. Viking.
Lorant, J. (1967). Technological Change in American Manufacturing during the 1920's. *The Journal of Economic History, 27*(2), 243–246.
Lumley, R. (1989). The American System of Manufacturers in Birmingham. *Business History, 31*(1), 29.

Maclean, M., Harvey, C., Sillince, J. A. A., & Golant, B. D. (2014). Living Up to the Past? Ideological Sensemaking in Organizational Transition. *Organization, 21*(4), 543.

Maclean, M., Shaw, G., Harvey, C., & Booth, A. (2020). Management Learning in Historical Perspective: Rediscovering Rowntree and the British Interwar Management Movement. *Academy of Management Learning and Education, 19*(1). https://doi.org/10.5465/Amle.2018.0301

Magnusson, L. (2014). Business History and the History of Work—A Contested Relationship. *Business History, 56*(1), 71–83.

Matthews, D., Anderson, M., & Edwards, J. R. (1998). *The Priesthood of Industry*. Oxford University Press.

McCraw, T. (1997). American Capitalism. In T. McCraw (Ed.), *Creating Modern Capitalism*. Harvard University Press.

Meyer, S. (2002). Rough Manhood: The Aggressive and Confrontational Shop Culture of U.S. Auto Workers during World War II. *Journal of Social History, 36*(1), 125.

Nix, J., & Gabel, D. (1996). The Introduction of Automatic Switching into the Bell System: Market versus Institutional Influences. *Journal of Economic Issues, 30*(3), 737–753.

Paya, I., Matthews, K., & Peel, D. (2005). The Term Spread and Real Economic Activity in the US Inter-war Period. *Journal of Macroeconomics, 27*(2), 331–343.

Prieto, L., & Phipps, S. (2019). *African American Management History* (Emerald Points). Emerald Publishing Limited.

Ristuccia, C. A., & Tooze, A. (2013). Machine Tools and Mass Production in the Armaments Boom: Germany and the United States, 1929–44. *The Economic History Review, 66*(4), 953.

Rosenberg, N. (1998). The Role of Electricity in Industrial Development. *Energy Journal, 19*(2), 7.

Russell, A. L. (2009). "Industrial Legislatures": Consensus Standardization in the Second and Third Industrial Revolutions. *Enterprise & Society, 10*(4), 661–674.

Russell, J. (2015). Organisation Men and Women: Making Managers at Bell Canada from the 1940s to the 1960s. *Management and Organisational History, 10*(3–4), 1–17. Review.

Schatz, R. W. (1983). *The Electrical Workers*. University of Illinois Press.

Segrestin, B., Johnston, A., & Hatchuel, A. (2019). The Separation of Directors and Managers: A Historical Examination of the Status of Managers. *Journal of Management History, 25*(2), 141–164.

Sharp, K. K. (2020). Current Trends in African American Business History of the Nineteenth and Twentieth Centuries: Recent Historiography and Applications of the Field. *History Compass, 18*(1), n.p.

Sloan, A. P. (1963). *My Years with General Motors*. eNet Press, 2015 edition.

Smiley, G. (2020). The US Economy in the 1920's. *EH.net*. https://eh.net/encyclopedia/the-u-s-economy-in-the-1920s/

Tobey, R. C. (1997). *Technology as Freedom: The New Deal and the Electrical Modernization of the American Home*. University of California Press.

U.S. Immigration Commission. (1910). *Report on Immigrants in Industries*. Government Printing Office.

Valli, V. (2018). *The American Economy from Roosevelt to Trump*. Palgrave Macmillan.

van Driel, H., de Goey, F., & van Gerwen, J. (2007). Testing the Chandler Thesis: Comparing Middle Management and Administrative Intensity in Dutch and US Industries, 1900–1950. *Business History, 49*(4), 439–463.

Weber, B., & Handfield-Jones, S. (1954). Variations in the Rate of Economic Growth in the U.S.A., 1869–1939. *Oxford Economic Papers, 6*(2), new series, 101–131.

Whitney, A. W. (1924). *The Place of Standardization in Modern Life*. Government Printing Office.

Wilson, J. M., & McKinlay, A. (2010). Rethinking the Assembly Line: Organisation, Performance and Productivity in Ford Motor Company, c. 1908–27. *Business History, 52*(5), 760–778.

4

Management During the Third Industrial Revolution: Asian Tigers and Global Players

Automation—'A Lot of Science Fiction'

Globalisation transformed both the structure and the management of organisations.

From the later years of the eighteenth century to those of the mid-nineteenth companies appointed managing partners, agents, foremen, under-agents, overmen, corporals, supervisors and stewards to take on managerial responsibilities. During this time, of which the Great Exhibition in London in 1851 was the apogee, Britain's industrial companies reigned supreme and their approaches to factory management were held as exemplars in organisation and efficiency. But the industrial powerhouses of Germany, France and other European countries began to close the gap on Britain's leading position. By the end of the nineteenth century, the door to industrial supremacy was ajar. However, whilst the opportunity was there for all, it was America's entrepreneurs who took full advantage. Their dynamism, combined with new technologies, new industries and a highly productive workforce, was enhanced by the development of scientific approaches to management, implemented with ultimate efficiency. Over a period of 50 or so years, the US economy

P. Turner, *The Making of the Modern Manager*,
https://doi.org/10.1007/978-3-030-81062-7_4

developed and exploited new technologies on an unprecedented scale. The internal combustion engine revolutionised travel, electricity revolutionised manufacturing and domestic living, and the invention of the telephone revolutionised communications. The elevator and the first skyscrapers appeared—the Chrysler Building in 1930, the Empire State Building in 1931; motion pictures and air travel; frozen foods and instant coffee all came out of this period. Companies which had their beginnings at this time included Coca Cola, PepsiCo, Westinghouse Electric, Goodyear Tyres, Ford Motor, GM, Gillette, UPS, IBM, Walt Disney, Delta and Northwest Airlines. The phenomenon brought with it the reshaping of the world economic order and by 1950 the United States was at its head.

It wasn't just the type of products, but how they were made that gave the country its competitive advantage. From early in the twentieth century, mass production in larger manufacturing units replaced relatively low-technology factories, artisan or craft methods. These more sophisticated factories required innovative approaches to planning and organising and with this scaling-up of production came the scaling-up of management practice. Each increase in organisational complexity—significant technology development, the creation of mass production lines and evolution in methods of financing and structuring companies—was a step towards the professionalism of management. Theories about its nature came out of the scientific analysis of work processes by Frederick Taylor to the behaviouralist, humanistic approaches of Mary Parker Follett and Chester Barnard. By 1920, 65 American business schools awarded over 1500 business degrees annually; by 1950 over 600 American higher education institutions offered courses which were attended by over 370,000 students. The Second Industrial Revolution saw the rise of American corporations and their business methods, and the ascendancy of American management thought. But developments in the decades after World War II would test this dominant position to the full. A new phase of technology and economic dynamics was imminent. Writing in 1954, Peter Drucker alerted the world to a new phenomenon:

> *Management faces the first great test of its competence and its hardest task in the imminent industrial revolution which we call 'Automation.' A lot of 'science*

> *fiction' is being written today about automation. It is no accident that so much of this speculation comes from the advocates of controlled economy and central planning. Yet every one of these assertions, conclusions and fears is the direct opposite of what the new technology really means. Automation is not 'technical' in character. Like every technology it is primarily a system of concepts, and its technical aspects are results rather than causes.* (Drucker, 1954)

Drucker argued that the anticipated automation would not make managers superfluous but would create a situation whereby new skills would be required to deal with the new age. Flexibility and autonomy were the watchwords and it remained to be seen whether the United States could rise to this challenge in the way that it had before.

The Second Wave of Fordist Development

The environment in which these influences took place was one of relative political stability. The United States was instrumental in stimulating global markets with new economic structures emerging such as the IMF, WTO, World Bank, NAFTA and the EEC. Global economic potential was translated into global economic reality. The annual growth rate of production of the world's manufacturing industries grew from 2% in 1938, to 4.1% in 1953, 5.3% in 1963 and 6.2% in 1973. By 1950 most European countries were at their pre-war levels against a series of indicators and between 1950 and 1970 European GDP grew on average at about 5.5% per annum. In parallel with this was the economic transformation of Japan—a spectacular example of sustained modernisation which outperformed nearly all other countries as a commercial and technological competitor. Nevertheless, for much of the 1950s and 1960s the United States continued to demonstrate its prowess in technological development and consumer prosperity as well as a 'vast outward surge' of investment across the world. Although US annual average rate of growth of output per capita between 1948 and 1962 was lower than the United Kingdom, the country retained its primacy (Kennedy, 1988; Seavoy, 2006) by fostering a second wave of the Fordist model of development. However, as the 1960s progressed, the United States, as had Britain a century earlier, found its position as the world's leading economy under increasing challenge. The envisaged benefits of the second wave didn't produce the dramatic results of the first because many of the industries to which this applied were already in stages of maturity compared with competitors elsewhere in the world. The US share of gross world product, which stood at 26% in 1960, fell to 21% by 1980. That of Europe fell from 26% to 22%. But that of Japan doubled. Of course, one of the reasons for the closing of the gap between the United States and the rest of the industrialised world was that the United States had already experienced large increases in productivity. There was an element of catch up during the 1950s (Kenwood & Lougheed, 1973; Kennedy, 1988; Valli, 2018). In spite of this, the United States experienced three remarkable decades of growth from the 1950s onwards and by 1979 the output of the civilian economy stood at $1.516 trillion dollars with the increase over 30 years about twice the rise over all preceding American history. Given the scope for development in other countries, though, there was an inevitability in the United States' dominance being challenged—even during the Pax Americana. Particularly from the end of World War II, the type of capitalism pioneered in the United States has strongly influenced the transformation of a number of national economies outside of the United States (Djelic & Amdam, 2007; Field, 2011; Jorgenson et al., 2016; Gordon, 2016).

The Third Industrial Revolution

As the US economy developed in the post-war period, new corporations of unprecedented size, complexity, breadth and international scope began to emerge. Oil and Automobile companies flourished—General Motors, Chrysler, Ford, Exxon, Standard and Amoco were amongst the largest by revenue in 1970; and companies such as IBM and ITT were two of several hundred United States-based corporations that became multinational with a significant proportion of their assets abroad. This trend 'marked the true beginning of The Third Industrial Revolution' (Leighton, 1970, p. 3). Such a point of view defined the revolution in terms of scale, geography and management systems; but later the role of Information

Technology on almost all aspects of the operation and management of business corporations was added to the mix such that the Third Industrial Revolution became increasingly known as the *information revolution* or the *digital revolution*. The coming together of various enabling technologies created 'informatisation' with the miniaturisation of electronics and the integration of telecommunications and computing. The shift involved microchips, computer-aided design and computer-aided manufacturing (CAD/CAM), fibre optics, lasers, holography, biogenetics, word processors, robotics, engineered materials and space exploration (Finkelstein & Newman, 1984; Fitzsimmons, 1994; Altenpohl, 2009; Economist, 2012; Stokes, 2014; Schwab, 2016; Taalbi, 2018; Philbeck & Davis, 2019; Pouspourika, 2019). It brought new products, processes and the development of new markets; new macro- and micro-economic structures and new flows of information. It was fundamentally shaped by the 'diffusion of pervasive and radical technologies', to an era of high-level of automation. Technology developments aggregated, sequences of challenge and response spread over time and economic trends ebbed and flowed. But from just after the end of World War II, there were fundamental shifts in technology as the Third Industrial Revolution gathered momentum. The concept—based on the twin pillars of the globalisation of trade and the revolution in multiple technologies—have for the purposes of this study been located from 1950 to the present day.

The Third Industrial Revolution was the harbinger of economic change and the globalisation of opportunity saw a steep trajectory in the economic fortunes of Asian economies, the companies of which achieved prominence in a multiplicity of industries and sectors. So, whilst the United States maintained its position as the largest economy in the world and continues to do so, there were notable economic performances from Japan, the rapid and significant economic growth in the economies of Singapore, Hong Kong, South Korea and Taiwan (growth rates of GDP in the period 1960–1995 of between 6% and 8% per annum) followed by Indonesia, Malaysia and Thailand (Davis & Gonzales, 2003; Rao et al., 2010); through to the incredible growth of the Chinese Economy as the second largest in the world and of India, which at $2.94 trillion GDP had become the fifth-largest economy by 2019. Outstanding economic performance was first identified in the so-called Dragons—Hong

Kong, Singapore, South Korea and Taiwan, followed by the so-called Tigers—Indonesia, Malaysia, Philippines and Thailand (Kozlova & Noguera-Santaella, 2019). For the purposes of this study, the evolution of countries or groups of country for consideration are Japan, China, the 'Asian Dragons' and 'Asian Tigers', and India. The objective is to identify the nature of contextual and core competences of the managers in each and the contribution to the making of the modern manager.

Asian Dragons, Asian Tigers and Global Players

The advent of the Third Industrial Revolution initiated waves of increased economic activity in countries across Asia with varying levels of government intervention. For some, this was the building of national competitive advantage; for others, incentives to be part of global value network or global value chain. For some, support and investment in structure and infrastructure; for others, a model of industrial development led by foreign direct investment (Nederveen Pieterse, 2015). How these macro-level national policies were translated into company-level management practice also varied.

There had been industrialisation in Japan before World War II and as the population grew from 34 million people in 1870 to over 60 million by 1930, economic activity increased accordingly. A strongly oligopolistic trend in Japanese industry at this time led to the establishment of conglomerate enterprises—the Zaibatsu ('well knit, tightly controlled relationships' amongst a series of affiliated organisations by means of holding companies, interlocking directorships and mutual shareholding)—into every area of industrial activity, shaping industries, their strategies and their development (Ranis, 1959; Yamamura, 1964). However, the events of World War II devastated the structural basis on which economic progress had been built, requiring a reconstruction strategy with the United States as its chief exponent. Hence from the mid-1950s through to the early 1970s, Japan enjoyed rapid growth of around 10% and significant industrialisation led by the manufacturing sector. By

1970, Japan became the second-largest economy in the world after the United States. During the period of growth, MITI (the Ministry of International Trade and Industry) played a role in guiding industrialisation through government intervention, including preferential taxes, subsidies, low-interest policy loans, R&D assistance and coordination of output, investment and exports; although some industries—consumer electronics, cameras, motorcycles, pianos, watches and calculators—needed less official promotion than others. With or without government intervention the goal was to improve productivity 'through investment in new technology and machinery and reorganizing production and management' (Ohno, 2006). Companies such as Honda, Matsushita—with brand names National and Panasonic—Toyota, Sumitomo, Mitsui, Mitsubishi and Sony achieved global success through their product design and development, manufacturing or service prowess and effective management aligned to international trade and globalisation. Geographically, Japan's markets came to be those that needed advanced industrial products and by 1970, around 30% of exports went to the United States. By the mid-1980s Japanese corporations had achieved 82% of the share of world exports in Motorcycles, 80% in TV image and sound recorders and 71% in calculating machines, as well as 51% of world export share in pianos and musical instruments, 45% of electric typewriters and 39% of metalworking lathes (Beasley, 1985; Porter, 1990; Ohno, 2006; Yoshino & Taghizadeh-Hesary, 2017). An additional aspect of the development of Japanese companies at this time was their contribution to the evolution of management theory and practice with knowledge acquisition and application, new methods and processes and additions to the language of management. Amongst these were total quality management (notwithstanding Deming and Juran's models of TQM), continuous improvement and just in time systems that gained traction not only in Japan but throughout the world. And towards the end of the period there was growing focus on core competences within companies (Hirasawa, 2014; Hout & Michael, 2014). But there was no standing still in the competitiveness of Asian corporations and Korean and Chinese electronics firms rapidly improved their organisational capabilities allowing them to catch up with Japanese competitors as the Third Industrial Revolution progressed (Nishizawa, 2014). In 2020 Japan remains one of the world's most successful economies. During the time that Japan progressed and gained growing economic influence and share of world markets, there was inevitable competitive friction with the United States, even as early as the 1960s; a situation that also occurred as the result of China's growing commercial might.

China's economic growth over the past 30 years has become a world changing economic event. Market oriented reforms in the 1980s, its open-door policy from the 1990s and entry into the World Trade Organisation in 2001 are milestones along the road to the creation of the world's second-largest economy by 2020. Average GDP growth of 9.4% between 1978 and 2004 are testament to China's industrialisation success. The nature of the economy has been referred to as 'formally centralised but in practice highly decentralised', with local governments having a high level of autonomy and the ability for significant local experimentation in production methods underpinned by huge investment in infrastructure by central government. Export oriented manufacturing gave a considerable fillip to economic growth. The internationalisation of product supply chains, the proximity to East Asian production chains and access to one of the world's great seaports in Hong Kong made China perfectly placed for a position as the world's largest outsourced manufacturer. By the end of 2014 China accounted for 12% of global exports and 18% of manufactured exports (Lin, 2006; Kroeber, 2016). By any measure, China has become one of the world's leading economies, its GDP is of the order of $19 trillion (in constant 2011 international dollars) and 36% of the cumulative global economic growth from 2007 to 2016 (Han, 2019; Li, 2020; Lu et al., 2020). Its banks, financial services and petrochemical companies are amongst the largest in the world and technology-based companies such as China Mobile, Tencent, Lenovo and Alibaba have become multi-billion-dollar corporations. A significant investment in education has contributed to this growth since in 1978, China produced almost no PhDs in science and engineering, but by 2010, they were producing significant numbers (Fernald & Jones, 2014).

For much of the period covered by the Third Industrial Revolution, the remarkable growth of the Chinese economy ran parallel to growth in another Asian phenomenon, collectively known as the Asian Dragons and Asian Tiger economies. These experienced rapid growth between the

1960s and the 1990s; but more recently the group comprises amongst others and to varying degrees of scale of Singapore, Hong Kong, South Korea, Taiwan, Indonesia, Malaysia, Vietnam, the Philippines and Thailand. From the beginning of the Third Industrial Revolution these economies achieved levels of growth of around 7% (with checks and balances such as during the mid-1980s) until the economic difficulties of the late 1990s. Real GDP in some accelerated dramatically—in Thailand between 1987 and 1990 by 40%; in Malaysia and Singapore by 30%. Per capita income in these economies also grew in a pronounced way from an average of $158 in 1970 to nearly $1400 by 2002. Development was the result of the changing nature of the economic structure of some, which saw the share of agricultural contribution fall in favour of services and manufacturing—in Indonesia and Malaysia the contribution of the industrial sector rose from around 20% to over 40% between 1970 and 2002. Much of this was export led industrialisation with the bulk of foreign investment going into manufacturing organisations (Daquila, 2007). By 2015 the Asia-Pacific region was home to three of the ten most competitive economies in the world, with a further three in the top 20' (WEF, 2015). By 2018 the combined economies of the Asian Tigers constituted nearly 4% of the world economy.

After the economic progress of Japan and China and the successes of both Asian Dragons and Asian Tigers, India has also experienced a spectacular rise in fortunes. From 1991 onwards liberalisation and globalisation has become a distinctive era of growth and prosperity. Liberalisation brought with it economic success and rapid growth, particularly in newer industries where higher levels of human capital were important (Masrani et al., 2021). By 2015 the World Economic Forum judged that 'the Indian Economic Tiger will roar' on the foundations of a stable government and positive trends in economic growth and in 2018 made up 15% of global growth, facilitated by political reform, foreign investment and strong domestic demand. India became one of the world's fastest-growing large economies and in 2020, India was the fifth largest in the world. The trajectory has been one of modest gains in the early years of the Third Industrial Revolution climbing rapidly in more recent periods. Whilst Indian GDP was $37 billion (current US$) in 1960; it grew to $186 billion in 1980; $468 billion in 2000; $1.7 trillion in 2010 and $2.7 trillion in 2018. From around 2004 the trajectory of the Indian economy has been sharply upwards—notably from 2015. The response of India to global industrial and commercial opportunities has been strategic in shaping a commercial environment conducive to efficient business operation and tactical in encouraging and supporting key industries in their development. Companies as diverse as Tata Steel and Motors, Reliance Industries, significant players in Coal and Oil and technology companies such as Infosys and HCL have responded in their respective markets to be amongst the world leaders. The World Economic Forum noted that India was 'a remarkable example of a country that has been able to accelerate on the pathway to innovation' (WEF, 2019). The growth in the economy was represented by a diverse set of organisations that demonstrated a diverse set of management styles ranging from paternalistic or nurturant task to integrated and internationalist, or a rich hybrid of Western and traditional Indian practices (Branine, 2011).

The emergence of countries across Asia as significant players on the world stage has been one of the stand-out features of the Third Industrial Revolution. In different ways the powerhouse economies of China and India have grown to be amongst the largest in the world competing with the United States on several levels. Japan, once the leading Asian nation before the bursting of the land and asset bubble has reclaimed its economic position. And the Dragon and Tiger economies of East Asia continue to build on their impressive rise to global economic success. Understanding the nature of the challenges that these countries faced in their growth periods will be useful in informing the question of the nature of both contextual and core management competence.

Management Challenges During the Third Industrial Revolution

The beginnings of the Third Industrial Revolution brought the potential of global opportunity to organisations in Asia. For some, post-war rebuilding meant regaining the industrial capability and infrastructure that had been lost. For others it was a transition to an industrialised society with the right levels of commercial and financial capability. For others still it was the opportunity to build almost a totally new commercial and industrial society. From the 1960s therefore the prime management challenges for many Asian countries were strategic. What long-term vision to pursue, what objectives to set to achieve the vision and what practical knowledge and skills were required to achieve both. As the debate about the answers to these questions filtered through to the micro-level economy, the organisations within those countries had their own strategic choices in how to achieve competitive advantage; in which markets; with what resources; how to upgrade factor advantages, including human resources and their management to a level that would ensure competitiveness on world markets. A range of solutions for strategy-making and hence the management competences to do so therefore, would be required (Li & Li, 2009). The sheer pace of change and scale of opportunity in a rapidly globalising world economy accentuated this challenge. Not least was the unpredictability of the environment and its impact on anticipating future demand and supply. Undoubtedly the opportunities were there. But organisational managers were unclear about how these would develop. Whilst long-range strategic planning remained an approach to inform both strategy and structure (Chandler, 1962), and indeed Ansoff's seminal work on strategic choice was itself published in 1965, applying rational premises to a logical and sequential planning methodology was not always possible. So, whilst the need for coherent strategic planning remained, managers often adopted a less rigid, more flexible approach. In this context the role of the manager itself was subject to adaptation and change (Simon, 1965; Finkelstein & Newman, 1984).

It's possible to see the management challenges of the Third Industrial Revolution at three levels. The first was on the scale of change. World Bank data shows that global GDP was $1.373 trillion (current US$) in 1960 and around $11 trillion in 1980. This had risen to over $22 trillion in 1990, to over $33 trillion in 2000 and to $86 trillion in 2018. Furthermore, it took around 20 years for global GDP to double starting in 1960; only a further six years to double again (World Bank, 2020). The challenge facing Asian organisations during this period was how to gain a foothold and then an advantage against well-established competitors in the United States and Europe. In this respect, the Third Industrial Revolution, with its significant global implications (globalisation came of age during this era) raised questions of which management competences were needed to compete in periods of growth and how to achieve the subsequent interconnectedness and interdependence on a global as opposed to local stage. For many, the export orientation meant that the scope of management was no longer confined to a single organisation in a single location but across borders to new sources of market opportunity, supply and support. The second related challenge was of the pace of change. The impact of the First Industrial Revolution was spread over a century; the Second Industrial Revolution a more rapid diffusion of technology and techniques with room for a short 'breath and second wind'. The impact of the Third Industrial Revolution, however, was rapid and overwhelming. The time available to adapt was dramatically compressed and as it was noted during the period in question, 'the pace of change threatens our capacities—individual and institutional—to cope with change' (Finkelstein & Newman, 1984). In this context, speed of recognising opportunity, speed of decision-making to take advantage of that opportunity and speed of output to deliver to the opportunity were paramount. In the case of Asian organisations looking to maximise potential revenues from markets in which they had previous limited access, speed at each of these scenarios became a potential source of competitive advantage. The third challenge was one of strategy, stewardship and the adaptability to change as raised by the necessity of being flexible and agile with questions about balancing short-term management actions against longer-term strategies. How could the two objectives be reconciled and how could the resultant decisions be converted into management practice? Flexibility and agility would be recognised by managers in contemporary organisations as desirable characteristics during times of unpredictability (the age of VUCA—volatility, uncertainty, complexity, ambiguity). But what did this mean in practice and how was this manifested by those managers in organisations that were established in countries which were Asian Dragons and Asian Tigers eager to take advantage of new opportunities. The first aspect was at senior management level and how the need for flexibility or patience could be presented to shareholders who required certainty in the direction of their investments. And at other levels in the organisation, how would managers interpret flexibility in terms of production runs or processes and how could they design systems to allow such stretch in capability? (McKenzie et al., 2019). The challenges of management during times of change were not straightforward. Some of these were generic that applied across most organisations as the tentacles of the Third Industrial Revolution spread around the world. Some were specific to the new rising economies of Asia and their leading companies.

A further consideration at this point is one that is episodic throughout the Three Industrial Revolutions that have been considered thus far. And that is the nature of short and immediate shocks that impact on society and the commercial organisations within them through the incidence of epidemic or pandemic illness that strike indiscriminately. In the First Industrial Revolution these were often around poor living or working conditions and included such disease as cholera; in the Second Industrial Revolution, such disease was still common, but it was the pandemic of the 1918 influenza outbreak that was most serious. And during the Third, two further pandemics had an impact on society and then commercial organisations. These were the influenza pandemics of 1957 and 1968 (both of which were responsible for millions of deaths) that swept the world with no predictable periodicity or pattern (Kilbourne, 2006). The 1957 pandemic, for example, closed factories, offices and mines; whilst the 1968 pandemic spread throughout China and Hong Kong, to India and Australia and then much further afield (Cockburn et al., 1969) contributing to a fall in the Dow Jones Index of over 20% in 1968. The management challenge was how to cope with relatively sudden shocks. Here it was pandemic, but the period also featured economic turmoil and discontinuity in technologies each of which demanded a management response with few recent best practices to fall back on.

The dynamic of the growth of the Asian Dragons and Tigers was predicated on exports contributing positively by, facilitating the exploitation of economies of scale, enhancing efficiency and ensuring the diffusion of technical knowledge through learning by doing. A challenge to managers at all levels was to convert this theoretical position into one of reality (Mahadevan & Suardi, 2008). In China's case, as in others, the export orientation necessitated constant upgrading of technology, supply chain control and critically, management techniques. Much of this was enabled internally, but there was also a strong willingness to gain knowledge from other countries in how to do so. China had the benefit of successful East Asian neighbours from which it was able to learn and gain ideas which could be integrated into its own methods. In particular the export-oriented manufacturing approach of such as Japan and South Korea (Kroeber, 2016). However, it's important to note that simple categorisations can be misleading because 'Asia is not at all a homogeneous entity—it is as heterogeneous as what is called the 'West' (Hofstede, 2007). So is it possible to reach any conclusions about core management competences from the diverse experiences of Asian organisations that can be transferred to other situations and times?

The Nature of Contextual and Core Competences in Asia

The Third Industrial Revolution brought significant technological change in a shorter time frame than had been witnessed in previous eras and the globalisation of economic opportunity that went beyond the traditional concept of bilateral international trade. National governments adjusted to this new environment with different levels of direction, policy and investment. In turn, corporations adjusted by assimilating the outcomes of government initiatives which cascaded down to business strategy and operations. Each of these took place with burgeoning economic opportunity as international trade became global trade. The context of management for Asian corporations was therefore bounded by three particular forces—namely government policy, corporate objectives and market opportunity. Managers were required to display the competences that were best fit to each of these realities. On the one hand translating government policy into corporate strategy and action in ways that could create competitive advantage. On the other ensuring that competence was identified and applied in a way that was best fit for their own individual corporations. Of course, such forces applied equally to organisations in the United States and Europe at this time, but the difference was starting point of development; caused by economic and structural damage during World War II in the case of Japan; being largely rural economies such as Thailand or at the early stages in the level of competitiveness against more advanced, market experienced competitors, as were China and India during the early part of the Third Industrial Revolution. These factors made the performance of Asian economies all the more remarkable. The Weberian thesis 'began to shake as East Asian nations, especially Japan, began to emerge in the 1970s ... the spirit of capitalism that Weber identified with the characteristics of individualism', was being superseded or at least challenged by alternative approaches to economic growth fostering a new type of entrepreneurial spirit and management style (Chen, 2004, p. 24). In part their success was achieved by the dynamism, innovation and entrepreneurialism of business owners and managers and in part by judicious government intervention. In some cases, strategic decision-making was informed by national policy which steered industries in the direction of realistic opportunity to achieve competitive advantage; companies responded by converting opportunity into products, systems and processes suited to their existing management competence, or in its absence by acquiring such competence. In others, the sheer dynamism of Asian companies and their managers were enough to set a course to take advantage of opportunity without undue government help.

But those searching for straightforward answers and binary choices as to how Asian managers contributed to these achievements in ways that were different to their Western counterparts will be disappointed. Instead of a 'homogenous' approach there is no equivalent of the 'American style of competitive managerial capitalism'. On the one hand, 'while it is generally accepted that there is indeed some influence of Chinese philosophies (including Confucianism and Taoism) on mediation and conciliation in business circles in the Far East, a comparison of modern-day Western generic business and corporate strategies with classical Chinese strategies indicated that there is really very little difference in strategic thinking between the East and the West' (Pheng & Leong, 2001, p. 128). On the other, differences between some of the principles, values and practices of Asian companies with their Western counterparts and of Asian approaches to management with Western management practice have been demonstrated. In Singapore, for example, management philosophies, management practices and management effectiveness between US subsidiaries and Singaporean firms yielding results that indicated significant differences with respect to the management variables (Low, 1984). Regardless, Singapore's achievement during this period has been remarkable. Its economy moving from labour intensive to skill intensive through capital, technology and ultimately to knowledge intensive. Its organisations adapted accordingly. The Japanese style of management *Nihonteki keiei* was itself seen by Japanese managers as being different to that in Western companies particularly in the area of group approaches to decision-making (Abbeglen & Stalk, 1990). Other differences include management practices 'in such areas as the training, background and orientation of leaders, group versus hierarchical style, the strength of individual initiative, the tools for decision-making, the nature of relationships with customers, the ability to co-ordinate across functions, the attitude towards international activities and the relationship between labour and management' (Porter, 1990, p. 109). The acquisition of knowledge—described as absorbing 'information into the head from the hands and feet' (Turner, 1994) was an important part of strategy setting and the management of implementation. The spectrum of opinion about what constitutes management practice in the region is broad though and lends support for the view that 'Asia seems to be particularly susceptible to oversimplification', when in fact there 'is no one single management culture that distinguishes the Asian countries from those of the rest of the world' (Sanger et al., 2017). Furthermore the influence on corporate strategy and decision-making attributed to management theorists in the West can equally be attributed to management and business practitioners in the East. For FW Taylor read Taiichi Ono of Toyota who is credited with developing the JIT (just-in-time) system in the 1950s and 1960s; for Peter Drucker read the successful business figures of Soichiro Honda, Zhang Ruimin, Lakshmi Mittal or Jack Ma. Ouchi's Theory Z (1981) drew on sources from both Eastern and Western experiences focusing on such aspects as consensual decision-making or individual responsibility. The reality is rather than a single prevailing point of view, perhaps inspired by one or two luminaries of management thinking, a rich canvass of Asian management styles and competences full of innovation begins to emerge and held up as exemplars for managing in a period of globalisation.

In practice it is possible to argue that 'the crucial elements of the management process show strong continuity over time' whilst recognising that there are differences from one country to another, possibly as a function of regional or local cultural influences (Hofstede, 2007). This means that whilst the underlying objectives of management in a particular organisation might be consistent, for example, shareholder or stakeholder value and the strategy to achieve them equally so, for example, low-cost manufacture or differentiation; there would be variations in the practice of management. Some Japanese companies will have different approaches to some American companies, but also to those in Singapore or Taiwan. Some Chinese companies had different practices to those in Europe but were also different to those in South Korea (Lee & Chung, 2015). That there are both commonalities and differences in management systems is an important part of the narrative about the strengths of management in Asia at this time (Chen, 2004). A common outcome though was that from the 1960s Asian companies were extremely successful in taking existing, tested approaches to management whilst at the same time applying new ones to meet the opportunities presented by both globalisation and the Third Industrial Revolution.

Contextual Competences During the Third Industrial Revolution

The effectiveness of managers in Asia, the contribution of management competences in achieving this success and the nature of management systems within which these were applied therefore are best evaluated in the context of a multitude of regional and national forces for economic development. Here, management can be seen as an intervening variable between a particular environment and the resultant level of business performance in which 'contextual skill' is critical (Takeuchi, 1999; Chen, 2004). In response, the idea of one best way, or a homogenous set of practices is difficult to envisage. Instead, different national and organisational cultures and subtle variations in practice give management in Asian organisations a richness and diversity that in itself has warranted recognition.

The first of these contextual competences was that of managers adapting to positive state intervention and crafting initiatives into the operations of their own organisations (Hout & Michael, 2014). At the most senior level, this was the ability to integrate national policy intervention into corporate strategy to maximise the opportunities in the longer term. In Japan, the role of MITI, whilst being of limited impact in some areas, did bring together the *keiretsu*, or groups of companies on technology development programmes in support of a series of research objectives. This was less about 'picking winners' and more about facilitating cooperation. It was still the role of the managers in each of the *kaisha*, with the relevant level of competence, to turn this facilitation into market relevant products achieved through efficient business processes. The same conclusion is evident in the context of Japanese government campaigns to improve the quality of products during the 1960s, which led to Japanese industries and their participating companies moving early and aggressively to confront quality issues with techniques and management approaches that were translated into international success (Porter, 1990). Organisations such as Toyota, integrated quality principles into *The Toyota Way* as part of longer-term strategy (Liker, 2004). And the proven outcome of quality circles, which organised the workforce to deal with operational problems in many Japanese corporations were emulated in Western organisations. More recently, alignment between organisational strategy and government initiative was a feature of the scaling-up of Indian organisations in industries as diverse as insurance; micro, small and medium Enterprises; chemicals; fertiliser; defence products; retail textiles and pharmaceuticals. A key growth area, the software industry, was facilitated by enlightened government policy. In all cases, success came about not just by government initiative, but by the ability of the organisations and their managers to turn such initiatives into meaningful practice. In China, 'firms are evolving from a simple familial model in which they are subcontractors to more complex network modes of organisation' and key to this is the employment of a growing 'stratum of professional middle managers'. Organisational response to national initiative or market change was not automatic but inspired by the ability of the managers of those organisations and their willingness to adapt to those changes. The Chinese government had been instrumental in supporting industrial development and 'is on all-out drive to move the country up the technological ladder. As the era of China as the world's low-cost manufacturer comes to an end, innovation has become the most important element in the state's development blueprint' (Lau et al., 2000; Khandwalla, 2002; Low & Cheng, 2006; Clegg et al., 2011; Gupta & Wang, 2016). In the Dragon and Tiger economies there was government intervention of differing types. The transition of Malaysia from an efficiency-driven economy towards an innovation-driven economy and the establishment of Thailand's status as an 'efficiency-driven economy' have both been facilitated by public financing policies which played an important role in technology transfer and commercialisation (Wonglimpiyarat, 2015). In all of these cases, the ability of the managers to harness the support given by government agencies was a contextual competence. For senior managers this would have been about explicit strategic knowledge possibly gathered from industrial and commercial networks as well as direct information; for managers at all levels explicit and tacit knowledge informed the implementation process inspired by government initiative. Knowledge of the opportunity, skill to harness the knowledge and make it work for the company, attitudes of openness and a willingness to adapt and learn, and a behaviour of dynamic interaction-adaptive translation were important aspects of the competence. But the management competence of identifying opportunity in the context of government initiative was not of itself a route to corporate success.

Hence, further contextual management competences relevant to all Asian companies seeking to take advantage of the global opportunities were those of strategic thinking and the ability to craft a strategy. In the *Mind of the Strategist*, Ohmae (1982) reinforced the principles and the strategic approach of a detailed understanding of markets and their needs and adapting the strategy accordingly became *de rigeur* as it was adopted by companies around the world. A corollary of this was the process of learning from experience that could be incorporated back into the organisation and the strategy amended. Whilst these competences were important in previous industrialising eras, they were particularly relevant because of two factors. First was the scale of the change as the opportunity for expansion became global. Second was the pace of change as the success of technological developments depended on the ability to implement them quickly. Strategic management, was most often couched in a competence requiring analysis, planning and systematising—such as using the Ansoff (1965) or later the Porter models of strategy (1980 and 1985)—or Sun Tzu's *The Art of War* (Lee et al., 1998; Zhang et al., 2016). Managers in Asian companies applied a variety of strategy methodologies; taking a longer-term view and planning accordingly but ensuring that they were able to adapt and move quickly should circumstances dictate. In some, whilst the competence of setting strategy was firmly rooted in the most senior levels, feedback was sought by senior managers from lower- and middle-level managers. Here the sources of strategic change were 'a continual, fluid, and usually systematic flow of information from bottom to top' (Fowler et al., 2018). In Japan, the inherent discipline in long-term organisational strategy did not prevent adaptation when necessary. In South Korea, the ability to take a long-term view went hand in hand with adapting to dynamic economic opportunities. Strategic focus and adept management led to successes in key industries. By 1985, South Korean companies had achieved a share of total world exports of 57% in iron, steel and wire, 52% in monochrome TV receivers and significant market shares in clothing (Porter, 1990, p. 454), although they were less concerned with being OEM oriented than companies in Hong Kong or Taiwan, for example. Undoubtedly the management competence, as well as government backed capital investment were features of their success.

The contextual competences were those that related to strategy setting in the unique context of globalisation, the technological revolution and potential national advantage. A convergence of these three forces created an environment of huge opportunity for companies across the region. How these were translated at company level and whether these could be regarded as relevant in a wider sphere is the basis of core competence.

Core Management Competences During the Third Industrial Revolution

In the mid-1990s when Asian economies were performing well, there was a good deal of interest in an 'Asian-style management'; an idea that proved to be attractive to those seeking a neat interpretation. But as was outlined above, the richness and diversity that was a feature of Asia mitigated against simple interpretations. Indeed, the financial crash towards the end of that decade saw a re-examination of what worked and what didn't (Takeuchi, 1999; Fowler et al., 2018). So, for example, adaptiveness, a market orientation and a willingness to take advantage of economic opportunity are perceived necessary characteristics at the time of the Third Industrial Revolution across Asia (Chen, 2004; Chen & Kimura, 2019) and informed the competences of managers at all levels in Asian organisations. But there are variations as to how these are converted into practical management actions. Whilst the competence might be, for example, 'effective decision-making', this may have different interpretations both nationally and organisationally. It will be impacted by both the core activities of the organisation and the social systems that are relevant to it. On the one hand it might require a senior management cadre able to make the right strategic decisions and are versed in the ways in which to do so. But it might depend on managers who are involved in everyday business activity also making effective operational decisions. There is evidence of the existence of each type, and also of the ability to combine both approaches simultaneously. The challenge, as outlined earlier is to identify such competences across the Asian experience of the Third Industrial Revolution without oversimplifying or presenting a stereotypical perspective. The facts are that Asian companies, beginning with Japan, working through the Dragon and Tiger economies and continuing with China and India have been remarkably successful in the period from 1960. Many are global leaders in their industries and exemplars in strategic decision-making. Some of this success has been built on management theory and practice that transcend both time and geography. and indeed, many management practices that have transferred successfully to Western organisations.

The first of these core management competences is that of *the ability to convert strategy into actionable plans and processes* and can best be exemplified by the experience of Japan whose organisations were faced with a shattered economy in the immediate post-war aftermath. The macroeconomic recommendation was to standardise, mass produce and focus intensely on product quality in order to climb out of the severely depressed state of the economy. To do so would require organisations that could produce volume effectively and secure market share—which Japanese organisations pursued relentlessly as the figures shown earlier in this chapter demonstrate. This was strategic thinking on the one hand but dynamism, rapid and continual innovation, and a relentless upgrading of competitive advantages on the other (Porter, 1990). Responding to external market forces went hand in hand with changes to internal systems and processes. Often this was through *translative adaptation* or the introduction of knowledge, ideas and systems from outside of the country not in their original form but 'with modifications to fit local needs' (Ohno, 2006). More recently, Chinese organisations have also been able to adopt this concept of translative adaptation to their own management systems and the speed with which Chinese companies are able to develop new products from existing technologies and ramp up large-scale production has been impressive. Chinese companies tend to acquire new technologies, but they keep the work of experimentation and production in-house (Hout & Michael, 2014).

Adopting new production methods, building on successes and learning from failures, ability to adapt to new methods and responsiveness in approach to changes in production runs or plans were contextual competences necessary for almost all of the countries and companies involved. As long ago as 1971 Peter Drucker drew attention to some of the observed principles of Japanese management style that would become influential over the coming decades and help in this process of rapid implementation and continuous improvement. Amongst his findings was the inclination to make decisions by consensus; the second was focusing on the problem before reaching a conclusion about what the answer to the problem is; the third area was that once a problem has been identified and a decision made as to its solution was to take action—this made for more effective decisions (Drucker, 1971). One of the most significant approaches to management and organisation was embodied by *The Toyota Way* (Liker, 2004). Fourteen principles were outlined which contributed to the importance of long-term management thinking; putting in place the right processes; developing people and partners and ensuring organisational learning by continuous improvement solving problems at their root cause. The implementation of these principles and the success of Toyota were important from the liberalisation of the Japanese economy during the mid-1960s. In this context Japanese carmakers established mass-production structures and strengthened their technology development capabilities. The company made significant contributions to management theory and practice and the Toyota Production System (TPS) introduced the core concepts of the just-in-time system; *jidoka* or 'automation with a human touch'; *kanban*, a production tool helping just-in-time production; and *poka yoke* or mistake proofing—concepts that were ingrained into management thought. In 1965 Toyota received the Deming Prize for quality and by 1975, Toyota overtook Volkswagen to become the leading import brand in the United States. Aligned with this competence was the need to ensure that the resulting strategy was inclusive. In all cases the commitment of the workforce to the goals, objectives and value of the company were of paramount importance and one of the key roles of the manager was to ensure that these criteria were in place in every part of the organisation. In some cases, management compensation was not tied to short-term results (Porter, 1990), which gave a further incentive to managers to do all in their power to secure a workforce committed to the longer-term vision. In addition to the usual market inspired approach to strategy it was also necessary (e.g. in China) to develop a nonmarket business strategy, including networking with government, business partners, suppliers, customers and other industry and public stakeholders. This idea of being able to work within a network of companies was as important as within one company and sophisticated groups of companies in territory, promulgated innovation and opportunity. These include the Japanese *keiretsu* and the South Korean *chaebol*, who supported the quest for competitiveness on world markets. If culture and environment are important management influencers (Chen, 2004; Lynton, 2013) then the ability to work within those cultures is a critical success factor and the ability to network extends from being a useful way of making contacts, an important aspect of any manager's job, to one of creating competitive advantage.

The second core competence is *the ability to adapt and change.* It was crucial that companies became agile and learning organisations able to reinvent themselves. In this area, Asian companies were once again adept. For some there was an element of improvisation, though the different types of structure could mitigate against this, especially in structures with high power distance (Zailani & Rajagopa, 2005; Hofstede, 2007). In China, adaptation was recognised as an ongoing activity on the part of its business managers and to achieve this companies created structures that gave business units some autonomy. Chinese companies have learned to manage differently over the past 30 years because they've had to cope with a turbulent environment. In so doing has developed an enormous and rapidly evolving ecosystem with '*bold experimentation and rapid iteration*—to create innovation opportunities (Child & Warner, 2003; Hout & Michael, 2014; Yip, 2016). So, the competence of adaptability is more nuanced than simply changing according to the environment. It requires particular skill recognising the unique circumstances within which the change takes place, the specific processes by which it should do so and respecting the organisation's internal dynamics. As in the First Industrial Revolution where management apprenticeship was often served at the ground floor level, so in the Third and 'three of China's legendary company founders—Haier's Zhang Ruimin, ZTE's Hou Weigui, and Wanxiang's Lu Guanqiu—all started on the factory floor' (Hout & Michael, 2014). Their understanding of the organisation's dynamics and the necessary processes required for change and adaptation were honed by this apprenticeship. A similar process of adaptation to the market environment and the skill to manage the process of change internally was found in the Japanese experience. Home market demand initially allowed corporations to invest aggressively in large, efficient facilities with the latest technology and management practices 'whilst US and European competitors were incrementally adding to existing, less efficient older plants' (Porter, 1990)—the second wave of Fordist development that had less of an impact than that of the first. In addition, the factor conditions of human resource investment reinforced these strategic approaches—through education and training and an inclination to group working and problem solving in organisations created favourable conditions to take advantage of the economic opportunities that were emerging on the world stage. Here are examples of management ability to take a long view of strategy whilst also achieving short-term tactical gains through the ability to adapt and change. Success in new production methods and approaches to product quality, both steered by managers aware of their importance was a national outlook that became a corporate competitive advantage. Japanese company success in industries as varied as sewing machines and shipbuilding are testament to management factors as well as any others. Throughout, there is an inherent inclination and skill to adapt (Fowler et al., 2018, p. 325).

The Third Industrial Revolution brought opportunity to those organisations that not only could adapt strategy and translate this into swift responsiveness but also were able to implement change accordingly. To do so required the core management competence of *cooperation and team working*. This is striking because 'the most evident difference between Asian countries on the one side and Western European and Anglo countries on the other relates to the dimension of Individualism versus Collectivism' (Hofstede, 2007). Consensus formation and cooperation are high priorities and the ability to achieve both is core to the success not only of Asian work systems but of the manager in the system. Collective strength gives a comparative advantage. In Japan, for example, 'cooperation, subordination of the individual to the group and ... the unique ability to coordinate across functions' were significant sources of competitive advantage. Group decision-making is often taken through a formalised process known as *nemawashi* characterised by horizontal organisation flows which facilitates integration and knowledge sharing (Porter, 1990; Calori, 1999; Chen, 2004). Whilst in China a management culture was identified as being quintessentially of a human orientation and behavioural cultivation by self-discipline. The engagement of the workforce was key to sustained productivity improvements and a competence of managers has been one of paying particular personal attention to staff and colleagues—'the best companies have a culture, set from the top, of working toward common goals in a spirit of mutual respect' (Su & He, 2001; Fryxell et al., 2004; Lynton, 2013). This required a willingness on the part of the manager to see their personal goals in the wider context, and where necessary, participate in projects that were set outside of the normal hierarchical structures. Cooperation and team working facilitate these requirements.

The fourth core competence was *using knowledge transfer and sharing in decision-making*. It has been noted that national and local governments in Asia played a significant and direct role in promoting knowledge transfer and innovation through government-corporation collaborations. This facilitated the modification, improvement and application of technologies (Lu et al., 2008). Strategic adaptation was enacted through the authority of the most senior managers but was informed by knowledge, feedback and information in response to market forces or industry trends (Fowler et al., 2018). The benefits ranged from rapid introduction of new products but also the continuous improvement of systems and processes. Collaborations between divisions, business units and departments were a source of advantage. The competence of the manager in ensuring that knowledge was transferred, but also that an environment in which it was possible to do so was core to success. Sustained organisational learning was one of the factors on the rise of Huawei as a formidable international organisation. Other studies have emphasised the importance of participatory motivation in this process and the particular orientation of the individual to the larger collective with recognition that knowledge is critical to informing adaptation and change (Lau et al., 2000; Hong & Snell, 2015; Chung-Hsuan & Ting-Ya, 2017).

At a time of fast-moving change organisations face an inevitable tension between the ideal or perfect and business pragmatism where there were gaps between the two. The question facing managers therefore is on what basis to make decisions in this type of environment since such decisions will have to be crafted with less than perfect background data. The competences outlined above informed effective decision-making. based on sharing of information and where this has been researched 'almost all reported a fluid process of inter-level communication as a major source of strategic change' (Fowler et al., 2018). Furthermore, in many cases, they also required the ability to move at pace. Tencent, China's leading Internet service portal, illustrates how companies gain an advantage by quickly rolling out new offerings (Hout & Michael, 2014). And in the case of Huawei, their dynamic capability allowed them to adapt to the changing environment 'through the seizing of opportunities, allocation of resources, sustained organisational learning and reconfiguration'. Asian companies could be exemplars for responsiveness, improvisation, flexibility and speed.

The rise to pre-eminence of economies from Japan, China, India and the Asian Dragons and Tigers is a remarkable success story. From the 1960s through to the present day, each area of the region has been held up at some point as an exemplar of national policy on the one hand and organisational effectiveness on the other. But there has been no single model of management or single path to management success. Contextual features have mitigated against homogeneity of approach. Nevertheless, the ability to develop a strategy to meet the opportunity of economic and technological development was common to all. And in so doing there were certain characteristics that featured in many Asian companies as the world economy moved to a new globally networked phase from the 1990s.

In the same way as Britain and Europe in the nineteenth and America in the twentieth, Asian countries became some of the most successful in the world and continue to do so as the Fourth Industrial Revolution begins to chart its course.

References

Abbeglen, J. C., & Stalk, G. (1990). *Kaisha; the Japanese Corporation*. Charles E. Tuttle Company.

Altenpohl, D. G. (2009). "Informatization" of Industry and Society: The Third Industrial Revolution. *International Journal of Technology Management*.

Ansoff, I. (1965). *Corporate Strategy: An Analytic Approach to Business Policy for Growth and Expansion*. McGraw Hill.

Beasley, W. G. (1985). *The Modern History of Japan*. Charles E. Tuttle Company.

Branine, M. (2011). *Managing across Cultures*. Sage.

Calori, R. (1999). National Administrative Heritages in Borderless Organisations. In R. H. Rosenfeld & D. C. Wilson, *Managing Organisations*. McGraw Hill Publishing, 2009.

Chandler, A. D. (1962). *Strategy and Structure*. MIT Press.

Chen, L., & Kimura, F. (2019). *Developing the Digital Economy in ASEAN*. Routledge.

Chen, M. (2004). *Asian Management Systems*. Thomson Learning.
Child, J., & Warner, M. (2003). Culture and Management in China. *Research Papers in Management Studies*. Judge Institute of Management Cambridge
Chung-Hsuan Yeh, & Ting-Ya Hsieh. (2017). A Study on the Management Styles and Job Satisfaction of Employees at Taiwan's Architectural Firms. *International Journal of Organizational Innovation, 10*(1), 185–204.
Clegg, S., Carter, C., Kornberger, M., & Schwitzer, J. (2011). *Strategy: Theory and Practice*. Sage.
Cockburn, W. C., Delon, P. J., & Ferreira, W. (1969). Origin and Progress of the 1968–69 Hong Kong Influenza Epidemic. *Bulletin of the World Health Organization, 41*(3), 345–348.
Daquila, T. C. (2007). *The Transformation of Southeast Asian Economies*. New Science Publishers Inc.
Davis, J. C., & Gonzales, J. G. (2003). Scholarly Journal Articles about the Asian Tiger Economies: Authors, Journals and Research Fields, 1986–2001. *Asian-Pacific Economic Literature, 17*(2), 51–61.
Djelic, M.-L., & Amdam, R. (2007). Americanization in Comparative Perspective: The Managerial Revolution in France and Norway, 1940–1990. *Business History, 49*(4), 483–505.
Drucker, P. (1954). *The Practice of Management*. Harper & Row, 1993 edition.
Drucker, P. (1971, March). What Can We Learn from Japanese Management. *Harvard Business Review*.
Economist. (2012). *The Third Industrial Revolution*. https://www.economist.com/leaders/2012/04/21/the-third-industrial-revolution
Fernald, J. G., & Jones, C. I. (2014). The Future of US Economic Growth. *The American Economic Review, 104*(5), 44.
Field, A. J. (2011). *The Great Leap Forward*. Yale University Press.
Finkelstein, J., & Newman, D. (1984). The Third Industrial Revolution: A Special Challenge to Managers. *Organizational Dynamics, 13*(1), 53–65.
Fitzsimmons, J. (1994). Information Technology and the Third Industrial Revolution. *Electronic Library, 12*(5), 295–297.
Fowler, R., Gajewska-De Mattos, H., & Chapman, M. (2018). Adapting Adaptation: Expanding Adaptive Strategy Theory to Account for the East Asian Business Context. *Journal of World Business, 53*(3), 323–336.
Fryxell, G. E., Dooley, R. S., & Li, W. (2004). The Role of Trustworthiness in Maintaining Employee Commitment During Restructuring in China. *Asia Pacific Journal of Management, 21*, 515–533.

Gordon, R. J. (2016). *The Rise and Fall of American Growth*. Princeton University Press.
Gupta, A., & Wang, H. (2016, November). How China's Government Helps—And Hinders—Innovation. *Harvard Business Review*. https://hbr.org/2016/11/how-chinas-government-helps-and-hinders-innovation
Han, Q. (2019). International Real Business Cycles of the Chinese Economy: Asymmetric Preference, Incomplete Financial Markets, and Terms of Trade Shocks. *Emerging Markets Finance & Trade, 55*(9), 1926–1953.
Hirasawa, T. (2014). Management Philosophy and Reforms in a Japanese Mid-Sized Enterprise Concerned about Regional Development. *Keiei Shigaku (Japan Business History Review), 49*(2), 2_28–2_50.
Hofstede, G. (2007). Asian Management in the 21st Century. *Asia Pacific Journal of Management, 24*, 411–420.
Hong, J. F. L., & Snell, R. S. (2015). Boundary-crossing and the Localization of Capabilities in a Japanese Multinational Firm. *Asia Pacific Business Review, 21*(3), 364–382.
Hout, T., & Michael, D. (2014, September). A Chinese Approach to Management. *Harvard Business Review*.
Jorgenson, D. W., Ho, M. S., & Samuels, J. D. (2016). The Impact of Information Technology on Postwar US Economic Growth. *Telecommunications Policy, 40*(5), 398–411.
Kennedy, P. (1988). *The Rise and Fall of the Great Powers*. Random House.
Kenwood, A. G., & Lougheed, A. L. (1973). *The Growth in The International Economy 1820–1960*. George Allen & Unwin.
Khandwalla, P. N. (2002). Effective Organisational Response by Corporates to India's Liberalisation and Globalisation. *Asia Pacific Journal of Management, 19*(2/3), 423.
Kilbourne, E. D. (2006). Influenza Pandemics of the 20th Century. *Emerging Infectious Diseases, 12*(1), 9–14. https://doi.org/10.3201/eid1201.051254
Kozlova, O., & Noguera-Santaella, J. (2019). Are Asian Dragons and Tigers Catching Up? *Empirical Economics: Journal of the Institute for Advanced Studies, Vienna, Austria, 57*(2), 589.
Kroeber, A. R. (2016). *China's Economy, What Everyone Needs to Know*. Oxford University Press.
Lau, C. M., Law, K. K. S., Tse, D. K., & Wong, C. S. (2000). *Asian Management Matters, Regional Relevance and Global Impact*. Imperial College Press.

Lee, B.-H., & Chung, S. (2015). *Diffusion of a Korean Labour–Management Partnership Model across Asia: The Case of LG Electronics*. Oxford University Press.

Lee, S., Roberts, P., Lau, W., & Bhattacharyya, S. (1998). Sun Tzu's The Art of War as Business and Management Strategies for World Class Business Excellence Evaluation under QFD Methodology. *Business Process Management Journal, 4*(2), 96–113.

Leighton, D. (1970). The Internationalization of American Business—The Third Industrial Revolution. *Journal of Marketing, 34*(3), 3.

Li, H., & Li, J. (2009). Top Management Team Conflict and Entrepreneurial Strategy Making in China. *Asia Pacific Journal of Management, 26*, 263–283.

Li, M. (2020). The Future of the Chinese Economy: Four Perspectives. *Journal of Contemporary Asia, 50*(2), 228–247.

Liker, J. K. (2004). *The Toyota Way*. McGraw Hill.

Lin, J. Y. (2006). Is China's Growth Real and Sustainable? In Y. Yao & L. Lueh (Eds.), *Globalisation and Economic Growth in China*. World Scientific Publishing.

Low, P. S. (1984). Singapore-based Subsidiaries of US Multinationals and Singaporean Firms: A Comparative Management Study. *Asia Pacific Journal of Management, 2*(1), 29–39.

Low, W.-S., & Cheng, S. M. (2006). A Comparison Study of Manufacturing Industry in Taiwan and China: Manager's Perceptions of Environment, Capability, Strategy and Performance. *Asia Pacific Business Review, 12*(1), 19–38.

Lu, S., Shen, J. H., Li, W., & Zhang, J. (2020). A Theory of Economic Development and Dynamics of Chinese Economy. *Economic Modelling, 86*, 69–87.

Lu, Y., Tsang, E. W. K., & Peng, M. (2008). Knowledge Management and Innovation Strategy in the Asia Pacific: Toward an Institution-based View. *Asia Pacific Journal of Management, 25*, 361–374.

Lynton, N. (2013). Managing the Chinese Way. *McKinsey Quarterly*. https://www.mckinsey.com/featured-insights/asia-pacific/managing-the-chinese-way

Mahadevan, R., & Suardi, S. (2008). A Dynamic Analysis of the Impact of Uncertainty on Import- and/or Export-led Growth: The Experience of Japan and the Asian Tigers. *Japan and the World Economy, 20*(2), 155–174.

Masrani, S. K., Morelli, C. J., & Bagchi, A. K. (2021). The Rise of Indian Business in the Global Context in the Twentieth Century: A Review and Introduction. *Business History, 63*(1), 1–17.

McKenzie, D., Bloom, N., Mahajan, A., & Roberts, J. (2019). *Do Management Interventions Last*. World Bank. https://microdata.worldbank.org/index.php/catalog/3545

Nederveen Pieterse, J. (2015). What Happened to the Miracle Eight? Looking East in the Twenty-First Century. *Canadian Journal of Development Studies, 36*(3), 263.

Nishizawa, Y. (2014). Forging Ahead and Falling Behind of the Japanese Electronics Firms. *Keiei Shigaku (Japan Business History Review), 49*(2), 2_3–2_27.

Ohmae, K. (1982). *The Mind of the Strategist*. McGraw Hill.

Ohno, K. (2006). *The Economic Development of Japan*. GRIPS Development Forum, Tokyo, Japan.

Ouchi, W. (1981). *Theory Z: How American Business Can Meet the Japanese Challenge*. Basic Books.

Pheng, L. S., & Leong, C. H. Y. (2001). Asian Management Style versus Western Management Theories: A Singapore Case Study in Construction Project Management. *Journal of Managerial Psychology, 2*, 127.

Philbeck, T., & Davis, N. (2019). The Fourth Industrial Revolution: Shaping a New Era. *Journal of International Affairs, 72*(1), 17.

Porter, M. E. (1980). *Competitive Strategy*. The Free Press.

Porter, M. E. (1985). *Competitive Advantage*. The Free Press.

Porter, M. E. (1990). *The Competitive Advantage of Nations*. The Macmillan Press.

Pouspourika, K. (2019). *The 4 Industrial Revolutions*. Institute of Entrepreneurship Development. https://ied.eu/research/

Ranis, G. (1959). The Financing of Japanese Economic Development. *The Economic History Review, 11*(3), 440.

Rao, B. B., Tamazian, A., & Singh, R. (2010). What is the Long Run Growth Rate of the East Asian Tigers? *Applied Economics Letters, 17*(12), 1205–1208.

Sanger, M. R., Nei, D. S., Ferrell, B. T., & Yang, F. (2017). Agency, Conscientiousness, and Leadership Emergence in Asia: How Managers in Countries with and without British Influence Differ from Each Other. *Consulting Psychology Journal: Practice & Research, 69*(4), 296–314.

Schwab, K. (2016). *The Fourth Industrial Revolution: What it Means, How to Respond*. World Economic Forum. https://www.weforum.org/agenda/2016/01/the-fourth-industrial-revolution-what-it-means-and-how-to-respond/

Seavoy, R. (2006). *An Economic History of the United States*. Taylor & Francis.

Simon, H. A. (1965). *The Shape of Automation for Men and Management*. Harper & Row.

Stokes, R. (2014). The Third Industrial Revolution in Global Business Giovanni Dosi Louis Galambos. *The Economic History Review, 67*(4), 1199.
Su, D., & He, Z. (2001). Management Revolution in the Age of the New Economy. *International Journal of Asian Management, 1*, 0015–0029.
Taalbi, J. (2018). Origins and Pathways of Innovation in the Third Industrial Revolution. *Industrial and Corporate Change, 28*(5), 1125–1148.
Takeuchi, J. (1999). *Human Resources Management Systems of Asian Companies*. Japanese Research Institute 45. https://www.jri.co.jp/english/periodical/rim/1999/RIMe199904resource/
Turner, P. A. (1994). Japanese Financial Services Organizations: Contrasting Market Experiences between 1985 and 1993. *International Journal of Bank Marketing, 12*(1), 3–8.
Valli, V. (2018). *The American Economy from Roosevelt to Trump*. Palgrave Macmillan.
Wonglimpiyarat, J. (2015). Case Studies of Technology Financing and Commercialization Programs—Asian Tigers. In *Technology Financing and Commercialization*. Palgrave Macmillan.
World Bank. (2020). *GDP (Current US $)*. https://data.worldbank.org/indicator/NY.GDP.MKTP.CD
World Economic Forum. (2015). *Top 10 Most Competitive Economies in Asia Pacific*. https://www.weforum.org/agenda/2014/09/top-10-competitive-economies-asia-pacific/
World Economic Forum. (2019). *7 Things to Know about India's Economy Today*. https://www.weforum.org/agenda/2019/10/india-economy-powerhouse-population-inequality/
Yamamura, K. (1964). Zaibatsu, Prewar and Zaibatsu, Postwar. *The Journal of Asian Studies, 23*(4), 539.
Yip, G. (2016, June). 5 Strategy Lessons Companies Can Learn From China. *Forbes*. https://www.forbes.com/sites/ceibs/2016/06/06/5-strategy-lessons-companies-can-learn-from-china/
Yoshino, N., & Taghizadeh-Hesary, F. (2017). *Japan's Lost Decade*. ADB Institute and Springer.
Zailani, S., & Rajagopa, P. (2005). Supply Chain Integration and Performance. *Supply Chain Management: An International Journal, 10*(5), 379–393.
Zhang, M., Gao, Q., Wheeler, J., & Kwon, J. (2016). Institutional Effect on Born Global Firms in China: The Role of Sun Tzu's The Art of War Strategies. *Journal of Asia Business Studies, 10*(1), 1–19.

5

The Fourth Industrial Revolution

Technology Innovation and Boundaryless Trade

There was no hiatus in the pace of industrial and commercial development as a new century dawned.

At 11.59 pm on 31 December 1999, Business Executives around the world waited for a call from IT managers with some trepidation. The cause of their anxiety was a software problem called the 'Y2K' or 'Millennium' Bug. Their concerns were predicated on the belief that an inbuilt fault in older computer systems meant that the systems would fail to recognise when the year 1999 became the year 2000 (because of the way that earlier software had been configured). In the worst-case scenario, the next date after 1999 would be 1900 and not 2000. If this happened there would be chaos in the world's banks and computer-controlled commercial and transport systems. From the time when the fault was identified, technology teams worked tirelessly to fix the problem with significant spend on information and communications technology (ICT) to do so. The result of their efforts was a successful transition. The crisis was averted, the year 2000 was welcomed in and there were celebrations

P. Turner, *The Making of the Modern Manager*,
https://doi.org/10.1007/978-3-030-81062-7_5

that the collective effort had worked. The consensus coming out of the exercise was that prosperity in the new millennium would depend on efficient, accurate, secure computer systems because of the impact they had on almost every aspect of the way people lived and worked.

The Y2K event happened during a 50-year cycle, referred to as the Third Industrial Revolution, which embraced not only an information revolution but also a period of sustained globalisation of industry and commerce. Its characteristics were the extensive use of microchips in such things as home computers and computer-aided design or computer-aided manufacturing (CAD/CAM) and innovations in fibre optics, lasers and robotics. Each of these developments took place at a time when trade was moving globally using complex networks of interrelated commercial activities. Global supply chains became global value chains and with each link adding invention, innovation and improvement, ICT grew in importance—worldwide spend was estimated at $3.7 trillion by 2019 (Gartner, 2019). The accumulation of technology and the knowledge surrounding its applications heralded even more potential change. By 2016 Klaus Schwab of the World Economic Forum could confidently state that the world was on the brink of a new technological revolution which would fundamentally alter the way people lived and worked and, in its scale, scope and complexity, was unlike anything humankind had experienced before. He also noted that 'we do not yet know just how it will unfold, but one thing is clear: the response to it must be integrated and comprehensive, involving all stakeholders of the global polity, from the public and private sectors to academia and civil society' (Schwab, 2016). This view of the future was couched in terms of societal change and economic growth in which technology would become a fundamental part of everyday life. The picture being painted was one of a new transformation—a Fourth Industrial Revolution. And whilst the technologies were different, the impact scenarios bore some resemblance to what had gone on before.

The First Industrial Revolution in the eighteenth and nineteenth centuries, for example, not only transformed industrial processes through technology but shaped the very societies within which those processes took place. It was a break with a 'tradition of economic life, and a pace of change in that life, which had lasted for centuries' (Mathias, 1969). The impact on work was significant—machines in factories made many traditional jobs redundant but hugely increased the productivity of labour and in turn created many new ones. More complex organisations, with work on a continuous basis, required coordination jobs which weren't there before in which work had to be monitored and secured in order to avoid any disruptions (Marengo, 2019). The social impact was as dramatic as the economic one as workers moved to the new factory towns away from their traditional agricultural surroundings and new forms of social and political organisation sprang up. With equally significant consequences, the Second Industrial Revolution in the late nineteenth and early twentieth centuries introduced mass production in large manufacturing units; which in turn led to the growth of urban living as populations moved to the new manufacturing centres; which again had a transformational effect on many aspects of society as people changed the way they lived and worked. It was seen to usher in a new economic order in which 'palaeotechnic' economics were replaced with 'neotechnic' economics 'bringing the potentialities of wealth and leisure beyond past utopian dreams' (Geddes, 1915). Technological change was the forebear of social change. The Third Industrial Revolution, from the 1950s onwards, saw the advent of the microchip with its effects being felt in all computer applications with once again the outcomes being significant for industry, commerce and public and private life (Finkelstein & Newman, 1984). It brought together remarkable new technologies and ways of applying those technologies in manufacturing and service delivery. The context for the way people lived and worked was now a global one facilitated by new ways of organising, producing, living and communicating.

With each revolution came social, political and economic change. And each change was considered to be more dramatic than the one that had gone before. With each revolution came new ways of living and new means to live. And with each revolution came new ways to work, with technology development being the common denominator underpinning each, from water-power to steam to electricity; from factories to mass production to robotics; from the telegraph to the telephone to mobile communications. And now, the world is on the brink of a further great transformation; Industry '4.0'—a term with its origins in Germany and also referred to as the 'Connected Enterprise', with a possible timeline for the confluence of the various new technologies reaching its apogee in around 2030. 'If we draw on the concept of a Kondratieff wave, it is in combination that the technologies create the potential for the entirety of economies and society to restructure' (Morgan, 2019; 375). But there is a view that the Fourth Industrial Revolution will be different from those that have gone before. Whereas mechanisations in the past substituted routine manual work, new automation will go further because it will involve sophisticated cognitive skills and learning—digital technologies. The Internet of Things (IoT)—a worldwide network of interconnected objects based on standard communication protocols—will create a dynamic and global infrastructure with huge potential (Atzori et al., 2010; Marengo, 2019; King, 2020). The prospects inspired by transformational developments in the application of new technologies, have been portrayed as exciting and significant. But how they would play out in practice has been increasingly the subject of analysis and debate.

Characteristics of the Fourth Industrial Revolution

Opinion influencers such as the World Economic Forum, academics in business, social science and technological subjects and management consultancies have been prolific in their projections and advice on how to prepare for this revolution where new technologies 'are forming a fertile layer of innovation resting upon digital foundations'. Robotics, advanced materials, genetic modifications, the Internet of Things, drones, neuro-technologies, autonomous vehicles, artificial intelligence and machine vision are becoming more integrated into our physical, social and political spaces, 'altering behaviours, relationships and meaning'. Fundamentally, it is a series of significant shifts in the way that economic, political and social value is created, exchanged and distributed. General Electric have called this transformation the Industrial Internet, others the Internet of Everything or simply Industry 4.0 (Gilchrist, 2016; Philbeck & Davis, 2019; 17; Koh et al., 2019; Mazali, 2018; Chou, 2019; Li et al., 2017). Governments around the world have echoed the views that it is of a scale and speed that will disrupt, creating new opportunities and challenges for people, places and businesses. Manufacturing, Professional Services, Wholesale and Retail, Information and Communication, Financial Services, Construction—Smart Construction and Building Information Modelling—and HealthCare will all be affected by change. Interconnected IT systems will support instrumentation, monitoring and analytics through concepts such as Cloud, Enabled or Intelligent manufacturing. The caveat is that these developments will need a commitment to innovation on the part of the organisation and the availability of a trained workforce to ensure their implementation. Private and public sectors are investing to anticipate developments with governments worldwide funding research into the implications (Gilchrist, 2016; Accenture, 2019; Kumar et al., 2019; Tien, 2019; UK Government, 2019; Kipper et al., 2020). The impact on individuals will be in the context of society as a whole and governments are already considering how technological innovation should be applied and regulated. To deal with these changes it is envisaged that social policy innovations will include new models incorporating changes to law, behaviour, service, perception and organisation—though the level and scope of intervention will be 'contingent and varying' (Rabeh et al., 2017; Morgan, 2019; UK Government, 2019). New technologies will be ubiquitous; they will converge in unprecedented ways and combinations and their reach will be global.

Translating its many facets into practical implications means that the potential of the Fourth Industrial Revolution can be mapped across *digital energy* which will use digital technologies to manage the generation and distribution of energy from traditional as well as renewable resources; *digital health*—digitisation will have a significant role in improving healthcare by comprehensive monitoring of health status, better preventive care, more accurate diagnosis and efficient delivery of treatment; *digital transportation* and autonomous vehicles; *digital communication*—using sophisticated wirelessly connected smartphones; e-commerce web services and image and voice recognition and chatbots; and *digital production*. The impact of any one of these technologically inspired developments would be significant. The impact of all of them simultaneously will create unprecedented change with a confluence of key technologies automating many aspects of work and life. The net effect will be effectively to 'create time' by reducing the time taken to perform mundane physical tasks that defined the past and will usher in improvements in productivity because of the increased output per unit of time worked. A positive outcome will be the creation of new industries and the improvement in productivity in existing ones. This will lead to new jobs and types of jobs, the development of new skills and radically different approaches to ways of working. Less positive is the forecast that digitisation will lead to the substitution of human labour, especially in those occupations involving routine tasks. In these cases, AI and robotics will substitute those that went before (Iraj et al., 2017; Fanafuthi et al., 2019; Koh et al., 2019). Whilst there is much agreement about the potential inputs to the transformation—mostly technology inspired—there is less 'confluence' and more debate about the outputs. The amount of philosophy and speculation has helped to inform an interesting and sometimes contentious narrative.

A Fundamental Change in the Way We Live

That the Fourth Industrial Revolution is characterised by the widespread application of cyber-physical systems and deep integration of intelligence and networking systems, has significant implications for the way people live. The 'new chapter' in human development is not just about economic change but about social change since many elements of the new paradigm are widespread in society at large. The technology diffusion inherent in the new environment requires innovative and sustainable approaches to the development of social systems. The outcome of what might be called Society 4.0—the merging of physical, digital and biological worlds will take place 'in ways that create both huge promise and potential peril. The speed, breadth and depth of this revolution is forcing us to rethink how countries develop, how organisations create value and even what it means to be human. The Fourth Industrial Revolution is an opportunity 'to harness converging technologies in order to create an inclusive, human-centred future' (Rabeh et al., 2017; Mazali, 2018; WEF, 2020a, b). New technological developments will include implantable technologies, wearable internet, ubiquitous computing, the connected home, smart cities, driverless cars, bitcoin and blockchain, 'designer beings' and neurotechnologies. AI and robotics will become commonplace in the living space and cognitive architecture will allow them to be tailored specifically to the needs of individuals. As Morgan (2019) so eloquently writes: 'as the increasing integration of technologies into the home indicates, the idea of a fourth industrial revolution is not just production-focused but also diffusely service-providing within what is implicitly conceived as a whole life system. And this readily extends to a whole life-maintenance system, a cradle to grave network. Consider how the health service of the near future could draw on household management AI through a health monitoring function to seamlessly integrate this monitoring into personal calendar-matched (and so not missed) doctor and hospital appointments ... and then follow through with treatments that extend from subtle dietary modifications, implemented seamlessly through changes to grocery orders, all the way to state-of-the-art surgical intervention.'

The impact then, will be in applications that span every facet of human existence from healthcare to creating a smart environment for homes and offices; and a revolution in access to social 'centres' such as smart museums or gyms; even greater social networking and changes in the way people go about their daily lives such as by smart cars or robot taxis (Schwab, 2016; Lampropoulos et al., 2019). Social and cultural change will accompany technological change along a spectrum of positivity. For every advance there will be questions of social organisation and process, security of information and the role of the individual. For many, this is an exciting, but uncertain, near future. At its best employees may get more leisure time and more fulfilling work. The impact of technologies from AI to 5G have the potential to create a social environment that is attractive and humane. The effects on work will be equally significant for individuals and organisations.

A Fundamental Change in the Way We Work

Emerging technologies will also have a transformational effect on the nature of work. On the one hand there will be some displacement of human workers as technologies and automation spread and affect business models, tools, tasks and ways of delivering. On the other hand, new jobs will be created in the associated new industries and new services. This is a revolution accelerated by radical automation and AI, focused on 're-gearing our societies—releasing the full creative, collaborative craft and caring capacities of our citizens' (Johar, 2017; Mazali, 2018; Johar, 2017; Morgan, 2019; BCG, 2020). It is anticipated that the impact of the transformation 'will increase productivity, shift economics, foster industrial growth and modify the profile of the workforce ultimately changing the competitiveness of companies and regions. And as the World Economic Forum's *Future of Jobs Report* (2016) noted, 'the debate on these transformations is often polarized between those who foresee limitless new opportunities and those that foresee massive dislocation of jobs.' Levels of impact will be national; followed by organisational; and finally at the individual or job-related level.

At national level the survival of whole industries will depend on how they adapt to the new technologically enhanced environment. In this respect Industry 4.0. has the potential to transform 'traditional industries into intelligent ones by incorporating innovative technologies', it 'enables physical assets to be integrated into intertwined digital and physical processes thus creating smart factories and intelligent manufacturing environments.' (McKinsey, 2018; Lampropoulos et al., 2019). In this environment, technology will shift how traditional businesses go about their work and in so doing it will increase the pace of change in both job destruction and job creation—including new forms of work— as well as skills churn within existing jobs. In anticipation of the possibility of significant impact at national-level governments the world over are creating policies to facilitate the transition to the new environment. Studies have taken place in economies as diverse as South Korea and Hungary; South Africa and the UAE. Its scope spans industries from manufacturing to gas production to maritime in large, global corporations and SME's. It crosses professions from health to engineering to computer science to architecture. The sheer scope of the Fourth Industrial Revolution and digitisation means that it has national implications such that its potential could transform Africa into a global powerhouse (WEF, 2017; Jang et al., 2018; Juhasz, 2018; Abdelhameed, 2019; Njuguna Ndung'u & Signe, 2020; Odhiambo, 2020; Sutherland, 2020; UAE, 2020). Few events in modern economic and social history can lay claim to such far reaching outcomes.

The Transformation of Organisations

Whilst the greatest amount of value during earlier industrial revolutions came about by upgrading physical production assets in individual locations—'80 to 90 percent in the shifts to both steam and automation—capex-intensive upgrades are expected to account for only half of that in Industry 4.0'. New technologies that are not necessarily aligned to major machinery upgrades will facilitate gains in productivity and prompt new business models. At the micro-economic, organisational level, smart workplaces are forecast where physical systems will cooperate and communicate not only with each other but with humans in real time, enabled by the Internet of Things. Industry 4.0. integrates production systems horizontally—for example, from supplier to customer—and vertically from the shop floor to enterprise resource planning in smart factories or in smart service provision (Mathivathanan, 2021). This means human-oriented interfaces for workers: process-oriented simulation and visualization; products and work for different type of skills and reforms in education, training and knowledge development, and different approaches for management. The application of new technologies will allow organisations to achieve cost savings by improvements to supply chains; time savings from real-time data; new product developments by using data in product design and productivity gains. These changes imply a progressive shift from traditional production systems to those incorporating intelligent solutions, which can support rapidly changing and highly flexible production environments. The Internet of Things 'facilitates the combination of intelligent machines, advanced predictive analytics and machine-human collaboration, aiming at promoting productivity, efficiency and reliability. It will support smart factories and offices through virtual networks whilst at the same time collecting real-time data (McKinsey, 2015; Rabeh et al., 2017; Koh et al., 2019; Mazali, 2018; Moueddene et al., 2019; Zunino et al., 2020). Organisational competitiveness will depend on the ability to integrate new technologies across the value chain from product design to sourcing of materials to manufacture to marketing.

The anticipated changes create the opportunity for those in the workforce to acquire new skills since, on average, a third of the skillsets required to perform today's jobs will be wholly new. Such positive outcomes have been forecast to bring about the end of tedious jobs and replace them with more fulfilling work. As a result, it is forecast that traditional career paths will be disrupted, as roles are increasingly automated. The idea of a job or career for life, is fading (WEF, 2017; Rabeh et al., 2017; Koh et al., 2019; Corfe, 2018). Other forecasts are increases in income and leisure time with the potential to make working life more enjoyable with fewer monotonous tasks. In this scenario people are at the centre of production in which skills such as dealing with other people, communicating, leadership, management or how to undertake change 'are people added values that go beyond technology'. The positive point of view creates people-centred culture with collaborating workers in 'co-responsibilisation practices' (Tong, 2017; Corfe, 2018; Mazali, 2018). With AI, more robots and smart machines in day to day operations the physical and virtual world will fuse together. Human-machine interface requires communication between smart machines, smart products and employees. There is a flip side to this positivity made stark by the forecast of the automation of low-skilled repetitive jobs resulting in millions of job losses worldwide. The new technologies will transform jobs and the required skills to do them. In all cases, there will be a management imperative to adapt to the new circumstances with a new management paradigm becoming a reality.

Management Challenges in the Fourth Industrial Revolution—Continuous, Disruptive Change

Success in the Fourth Industrial Revolution will come about when organisations 'master the profound technological challenges at work and transform them into opportunities' (WEF, 2019a, b, c). But to do so will require crafting a pathway through the potential complexities for organisational systems and processes implied by these technological advances and now, the potential disruption of the effects of COVID-19 on how organisations operate; in some cases to dramatic effect—Hitachi introduced a remote working initiative for its 80,000 employees; Unilever announced a trial of a four day working week in new Zealand. In the view of Linda Gratton (2021) 'time is up for grabs, not just place'. A combination of technological revolution, with demographic and social change and the effects of pandemic will have far-reaching implications on almost every aspect of daily life, affecting how individuals interact with technology and transforming where and how work is done—necessitating different approaches to address issues of automation and digitalisation. A critically important question facing business leaders in this dynamic environment is how to craft a strategy for their organisations to achieve competitive advantage, taking account of technological factors and the exciting possibilities of Industry 4.0 and the necessity to protect their workforces through effective health and well-being policies. This will involve negotiating a path through the demands of market pull with the dynamics of technology push. Digitalizing internal processes is one outcome but leveraging the benefits of these processes will be the way in which organisations achieve advantage. This means insights about the possibilities and collaboration with stakeholders in the organisation, suppliers, partners and distributors. Managers are faced with the challenge of setting a new vision for their organisation and then translating this into firstly, a business strategy that aligns the organisation to achieve both scale and scope, and secondly an operational model supported by efficient, sustainable systems and processes to make it work. Furthermore, technological change will only be achieved with the right amount of talent in the right place requiring a workforce with the skill sets that are appropriate to strategy and operations. The management of human resources changes from being that of a 'steward of employment' involving, recruiting, hiring, onboarding and training to becoming a 'steward of work', orchestrating how work is done, whether through a person in a job, a person augmented by a machine or flexible labour such as gig workers or employees of an outsourcing organisation (Deloitte, 2018; Daim & Faili, 2019; Hofmann et al., 2020; Ramirez, 2020).

The management challenges of the Fourth Industrial Revolution, therefore, span both technology and human resources in the context of profound social change and centre on the union of physical systems with virtual systems. In this new world, sensors capture and control information; there is the automation and virtualisation of processes, and an essential requirement on new knowledge for workers needed to implement the concepts of industry 4.0 (Kipper et al., 2020). These take place in a business environment characterised by pace and continuity of change, demanding flexibility and responsiveness and a newly skilled, re-skilled or upskilled, diverse and technologically competent workforce. Added to the contemporary mix is the use of social media applications across value creating activity from marketing to recruitment; from research to products or services; from knowledge creation to idea generation—social media as a strategic tool (Poba-Nzaou et al., 2016; Chung et al., 2017). A convergence or confluence of these many factors, mean that organisations will move to new ways of operating with the existence of 'interoperability, virtualization, decentralization, real-time capability, service orientation and modularity' across virtually any activity in the industrial or commercial context (Gera & Singh, 2019; Koh et al., 2019; Morgan, 2019; Wilkins, 2019; Benassi et al., 2020; Griffiths & Ooi, 2020). The advent of mass digitization will transform most organisations on a significant scale.

The Fourth Industrial Revolution will be a continuous sequence that is likely to last for years or even decades as the application of technological innovations continues to grow (Caruso, 2018). In response, agile governance—advocated by the World Economic Forum (2018) at government policymaking level which is 'adaptive, human-centred, inclusive and sustainable – will apply equally at to commercial organisations. Such an environment will present management challenges that are both strategic – influencing the nature of the business model to address a particular market or context – and operational influencing how such a business model is implemented. Some of these will be identifiable to any organisation that is going through transformation and the experiences of previous revolutions would form a parallel narrative in such cases – but some will be unique in the context of the 21st Century and 'Industry 4.0.' For some the challenge will be no less than reinventing the future of work which will require ideas and initiatives from every quarter (Reif, 2018; Zunino et al., 2020). It is likely that this reinvention will not be a single experience but one of continuous learning and hence continuous change. Managers in all organisations will be required to adapt and change effectively, consistently and continuously.

Visioning the Organisation of the Future

Hence, there is the need to build flexibility and responsiveness into organisational processes, not only because of possible market volatility—which relates to both challenge and opportunity, but also because of the requirement of shorter product lifecycles, possible higher product complexity and the necessity to work within dynamic supply or production chains (Rabeh et al., 2017). To this latter point, McKinsey (2018) highlighted the incidence of such things as wearables to facilitate access, supplies or messaging; work performance informed by real-time metrics and supported by machine learning for root cause problem-solving of issues; monitoring of equipment in real-time to predict faults and then allowing machines to learn from their own mistakes and adjust their settings to improve quality output. They will require 'leveraging the internal technology ecosystem within the company; using dedicated project teams and experts in operational environments and implementing technologies that adhere to strict protocols'. Not only are the technologies different but the management process for working with the technology is too. Success will be achieved by combining technology implementation with a human-centric focus on workforce development. This conceptual model will be brought to life by managers who recognise the advantages to the new technologies and are able to apply them efficiently. The ability of the organisation to respond in a flexible way to market opportunity will be facilitated by the ability of managers responding flexibly to the new technologies and their applications. The outcome will be what might be referred to as real-time capability—a possibility for operational processes once technologies of Industry 4.0 are in place.

This outline demonstrates the potential to integrate manufacturing and services in new forms of business model, creating 'smart firms' which deepen the integration of technologies with both product design and development and responsive production processes (Dean & Spoehr, 2018). But the impact of technology-enabled digital manufacturing or service delivery brings with it significant workforce challenges, including both the nature of the workforce—knowledge skills attitudes and behaviours—and how members of this workforce interact in a rapidly and continuously changing operational environment. Ghislieri et al.'s (2018) excellent analysis of workforce issues raised three important questions namely, how is the interaction between workers and technology changing; how do new kinds of technology affect people's well-being; and are automated systems supporting humans or taking over their jobs? Hence how to ensure the availability and engagement of a workforce, that has the right skills, in the right place, at the right time will be high amongst the concerns and challenges of managers. The digital revolution is also a human revolution—'it is people who will bring it to life in businesses' and they will play a strategic role on the one hand by determining the organisation's strategy, be responsible for implementing the strategy and monitor progress against this and where necessary intervening in 'the cyber-physical production system' (Ghislieri et al., 2018; WEF, 2019a, b, c).

The Impact of the Pandemic

An additional factor that was not included in the debate about the potential of the Fourth Industrial Revolution until December 2019 was the most traumatic and shocking event that many could remember. Towards the end of 2019, the World Health Organisation's China office drew attention to an outbreak of a disease of unknown causes in the city of Wuhan in Hubei province. By January, this was identified as a novel coronavirus named COVID-19 and it soon spread throughout Asia and then into the Middle East, Europe and the United States. On 4 March, the WHO announced that the situation was unprecedented as the world became engulfed in a pandemic of this deadly, highly contagious disease. Within weeks there were millions of cases and tens of thousands of deaths. Few countries, cities or towns were exempt as COVID-19 ravaged societies and economies. Whole nations went into lockdown as people were urged or forced to stay at home to curtail its spread. Personal tragedies of families and individuals were often borne in isolation as the cruel reality of social distancing and isolation were felt. And the economic cost was also of the harshest possible kind as demand plummeted, supply chains were ruptured and stock markets the world over fell at an unprecedented rate eclipsing even catastrophic events such as the Great Depression and the Financial crisis of 2008. Organisations were forced, in short order to adapt to the new circumstances if they were to remain afloat. Many governments stepped in to help businesses with furlough schemes or short-term loans, but there were few rules or best practices on how to structure. The challenges were twofold. First how to survive when consumer demand was seriously affected and routes to market limited. Second what business model to adopt as the organisation emerged gradually from enforced lockdown; what systems and processes could be put in place to comply with new, mandatory health guidelines. The response of many organisations to this unprecedented situation was remarkable in its innovation and creativity. COVID-19 featured in the short-term business planning of many. Whether and how it would impact on organisational strategy will though take time to assess. Though it is fair to say, and outlined in earlier chapters, that pandemics throughout history had been met successfully with adaptation in both social and business processes.

The device of synthesizing the many and complex issues facing managers as they navigate a path through the impact of the Fourth Industrial Revolution is a heuristic approach rather than one that is complete or optimal. The challenges bear some resemblance to what has happened in organisational life in previous eras. But the differentiator of the Fourth Industrial Revolution is its scale and scope—massive and global—the pace and continuity of change—dynamic and real time, and the sheer ubiquity of its many strands of change—vertical and horizontal applications. To deal with these, there will be competences that are specific to the phenomenon. These are concerned with adaptation and change. But there are also those that might be regarded as core, that is, relevant to managers wherever they work.

Contextual Management Competences During the Fourth Industrial Revolution

The nature of management challenges during this period requires particular skills concerned with the transition to new methods, systems and processes. In the first place there may be a rapid and total transition from legacy to new systems and the transformation of the organisation's business model. This radical approach will ask of managers that they apply agility and flexibility as they rapidly adjust to new ways of working and the capability to implement new systems. But not all organisations will move at this pace and for some there may be parallel running in which several types of systems are maintained with a phasing out of the legacy over time and more gradual (but nonetheless relatively rapid) change to systems and processes. In this second scenario, agility will be a contextual competence since managers may be involved in multiple sets of processes simultaneously (Hahn, 2020; Kipper et al., 2020). And finally, there may be a gradual drawing down of new technologies in specific processes or locations. Such a scenario will require the manager to be able to see a longer view and have the ability to integrate new systems where they are relevant or advantageous. In all cases, management competences will be particular to the context of transition. Four considerations will be important and these concern the structure of the working environment and the culture of decision making; secondly the ability to integrate new systems either in their totality or into a legacy of existing systems; third the necessity to consider the social impact of the transformation and finally the impact on the workforce of new business models, structures, systems and processes.

The first contextual competence required is the ability to structure a working environment that is conducive to the demands of the Industry 4.0. This goes beyond peripheral changes in decision making but to the heart of how organisations adapt to the new requirements. It will require strategy setting to be more inclusive when it was previously the domain of dedicated strategists or the most senior of business managers. It will require operational decision making to be more collaborative. And it will require processes that take account of the skills and contribution of a broader swathe of the workforce than was previously the case. The pervasiveness of technology applications and the amount of data that will be generated by their usage both demand and facilitate this approach. It involves greater understanding—throughout the organisation—of the impact of new technology on every aspect of stakeholder management whether this be customer interface, employment or social responsibility. More than ever an 'ethical understanding of the power of these new technologies that will allow for safe and efficient use' will be a requirement on the part of organisations and their managers—regardless of the industries or sectors in which they operate. Actions and policies about workforce issues—training, talent management and workforce planning are important considerations and 'a proactive position and participatory role also correspond to a process where responsibility is shared' encouraging a level of participation and co-responsibility for the outcomes of any decisions (Deloitte, 2018; Mazali, 2018; Simmons & McLean, 2020). Responsibility is likely to be more democratic which will lead to a different way in which organisations make and implement decisions and a restructuring of the work relationship. Inclusivity and collaboration are based on the principle that the workforce of the future will be more involved in knowledge creation as routine work is taken over or displaced by intelligent machines. Hence the competences that have been considered as important to date- including problem solving, creative thinking, emotional intelligence and effective people management—will still be relevant but the organisational context may change. There will be an expectation that the decisions in response to strategic or operational choices will not be in the hands of a single decision maker but will entail greater consensus from a greater number of people who have greater knowledge and information on which to base their positions. This is indeed a radical departure from the Weberian hierarchies that have dominated the organisational world for many decades.

The efficiency benefits of new digital technologies will come about once an organisation has undergone a 'comprehensive transformation' in both its processes and its workforce. But as organisations craft their transition to future—Industry 4.0—preparedness how to do so from existing processes and infrastructure will be an important consideration. The paradigm shift from mass production to customized production or service delivery will have implications for all stakeholders. This means the installation of intelligent machines and systems and their integration into production or service delivery processes for productivity efficiencies and product or service flexibility. The size of the challenge is reflected because of the 'development and adaptation of more – smart, more interconnected automation systems' expected to be operating across multiple domains and serving different specializations. The integration of artificial intelligence, the optimisation of processes and systems, the integration between devices and systems, will be underpinned by human factors, real-time decision making and communication platforms. The successful transition to this new, complex, interconnected state will therefore require the ability to integrate existing and legacy systems with new sensors and networks (Koleva, 2019; Zawra, 2019; Griffiths & Ooi, 2020; Kipper et al., 2020; Saniuk et al., 2020).

The third area of contextual competence is as a result of an increasing requirement to establish that their business model or activity builds in societal impact. Company culture and employee expectations complement external forces—customer, shareholder, policymakers—as powerful driving forces towards this goal (Deloitte, 2019). How to do so will depend not only on the final output (products or services) but also the production or operational systems behind these. Managers have a role to play in both and hence a contextual competence will be the ability to build sustainable production systems which maximise positive societal impact. There will be stronger integration of 'top floor and shop floor' and thus more intelligence and flexibility to production (Rabeh et al., 2017). The manager will need the competence to work in this type of environment. The top floor to shop floor consultations will also include how to build this sustainability in a way that is safe for those working in the new sustainable processes.

The fourth area of contextual competence will be in relation to the preparation of a workforce through a culture of reskilling, upskilling and lifelong learning (WEF, 2019a, b, c). This goes beyond traditional workforce activities because of the significance of anticipated changes in the nature of the workforce and indeed the nature of work. A contextual competence is concerned with transition. How to move the skills of those involved in Third Industrial Revolution roles and ways of working to new social and technical skills more relevant to the new environment. An essential competence to prepare the workforce for the new industrial paradigm (Koh et al., 2019; 823). The forecasts about the impact of technology on the workplace cover a broad spectrum—'some fear a robot apocalypse that will eat up all jobs, leaving mass unemployment in its wake. Others are techno optimists and see a future where advancing technologies will create more new jobs than they eliminate.' Whatever scenario plays out the effect of future technology innovation will be on how people work, the tasks that make up jobs and how individuals and groups or teams combine tasks into work systems (Kochan, 2019). Industry 4.0. will have a far reaching and profound effect.

The management challenges of the Fourth Industrial Revolution will span the application and integration of new technologies to the creation of new business models for efficiency and productivity. Having a workforce with the right level of skills in the right place at the right time will be an important objective for the manager; and having achieved this to ensure their engagement in the direction of the organisation and the methods by which it travels. The role of the manager will be critical to success as organisations craft their way from current state to future state and their contextual competences will range across technological application, change management and people engagement. The nature of the Fourth Industrial Revolution means that many of these experiences are unique to a specific time or place. However, there are also competences which are core to the role of the manager that may transcend the early days of Industry 4.0 and be applicable beyond.

Core Management Competences During the Fourth Industrial Revolution

Managers will not only be responsible for innovation outcomes (the 'what') but the innovation process (the 'how') as well as the corresponding determinants of innovation (the 'why'). The complexity of human resources interfaces will also require managers who 'know how to behave'. And so, whilst contextual competences during this period are those mostly concerned with transition, core management competences will be required to ensure that post-transition strategy and operations are effective. These will be made up of specific knowledge, skills, attitudes and behaviours relevant to the new management paradigm which will include 'comprehensive integration and information transparency; increasing automation of production systems; self-management and decision-making by objects; digital communication and interactive management functions.' In addition, the need to build flexible workforce planning systems is paramount. Furthermore, the success of any strategic or operational initiatives that concern for example, the introduction of new Industry 4.0. inspired technologies will benefit from the momentum and bottom-up ideas of employees whose 'highly specialized, sticky, and tacit knowledge offer potential.' This buy in will be dependent on how effective the manager can be at engaging the workforce affected by these developments and 'empirical evidence suggests that such buy-in cannot be taken for granted' (Lee et al., 2018; Ghislieri et al., 2018; Hahn, 2020; Schneider & Sting, 2020). This new environment will have implications for managers with the implementation of new technological systems and with the implementation of new human systems where at the centre of the creation of technology solutions are 'the aspirations, curiosity, creativity, competence, and passion of the people who have imagined, prototyped, and tested a technology' hence recognition of the centrality of people in organisational life (Lee et al., 2018). Core management competences will undoubtedly cover a broad spectrum of organisational activity.

In the first place there will be ability in *managing the integration of multiple technologies in the workplace.* To deliver this effectively will require explicit knowledge of integration tools and techniques (such as n step processes); explicit and tacit knowledge of the human factors of change; the ambidexterity to operate at multiple levels; and the ability to resolve any of the potential conflicts that arise from competing objectives of these systems—innovation will not only rely on analytics and 'smart things' but will also require smart people *technology* and the 'human-centric approach'. A key objective will be to achieve the optimal combination of human workforce and automation for a positive impact on the future of work (WEF, 2019a, b, c; Hahn, 2020; Kipper et al., 2020). The qualifications of the manager to deliver to this challenge will be agility and flexibility on the one hand and a willingness and skills to collaborate on the other; it will be a willingness to acquire knowledge (of systems, processes and people) and to disseminate that knowledge to facilitate the integration process; and it will require stakeholder management of the highest order to ensure that all of the affected people or parts of the organisation are able to relate to the implications of integration.

Integrating new technologies will involve restructuring and process reengineering, resulting in new distributed, networked or swarm organisational forms. The manager may be at the centre as a pivot for operations but may also be at the edge as a facilitator. Whilst decentralisation will facilitate innovation, managers will require a different outlook to the one which fared well in more defined, hierarchical types of organisation. Managing for change and adaptability is the underlying approach and this is manifested in such traits as intuition, collaboration and cooperation. These can be summarised in the competence *to manage in distributed or network organisational forms* and cultivate the culture within which such organisations and their workforces can thrive. The new forms of organisation will, from the perspective of intelligent and connected products, require capabilities in monitoring, controlling and systems optimisation on the one hand (Rosin et al., 2020); but the creation of shared values, employees with personal values that are aligned with organisational values and flexibility in respect of rules and regulations (Hlupic, 2014; Fatorachian & Kazemi, 2020). To do so will necessitate being able to manage in a multiplicity of circumstances, structures and processes.

In traditional transaction-based business architectures management control or activity was determined by a *product-centric approach and* a *service-centric approach* with a classical pipeline logic of linear business activities with a focus on resource control and internal optimisation. However, the advent of Industry 4.0 presents a third business architecture—a *platform-centric approach*, built around creating collaborative value. The approach is a more complex and dynamic environment which can change rapidly (Hahn, 2020). Hence managing in the new organisation will require the core competence of *agile governance* on the part of managers creating business responsiveness and the ability to initiate rapid response in the face of uncertainty (Nawaz, 2020). On the one hand this agile governance will be strategic and in response to the direction of the organisation and where it allocates its resources; and on the other agile governance in how operational decisions are made. This agility brings with it such approaches as the delegation of decision making to a wider group of employees and indeed, parallel decision making. Possible identified outcomes have been listed as improved performance because of shorter decision cycles (agility speeds up the process), improved quantity and quality of decisions and greater levels of organisational resilience (Hlupic, 2014; 115).

The new approaches to collaboration outlined above are marked by geographic diversity of participants, a cross-industry focus, shorter and more flexible deal structures and continuous value creation by and for members (WEF, 2019a, b, c). The interoperability and communication potential of new technologies should have the effect of eliminating the silos that have often been a feature of organisations in previous times. Indeed, digital communication technologies including social media, have irrevocably altered how people interact at work, 'relying on computer-mediated communication technologies is now a must, rather than an alternative' (Darics & Gatti, 2019). But this will only be the case if managers are able to use shared information effectively. In this respect the competence of *effectively managing internal and external collaborative networks* will be one that underpins the new ways of working and this will be facilitated by 'a technology ecosystem enables new levels of collaboration, facilitated by a digital infrastructure' (McKinsey, 2020). Where this has taken place (such as on open-source projects), 'internal *and* external social capital' *interact* in unique ways to influence success thereby reinforcing the importance of collaboration and management in a way that both encourages and facilitates such collaboration. To do so effectively will require emotional involvement as a means of developing empathy and in achieving productive cooperation and commitment 'based upon the shared belief that the team can succeed' (Daniel et al., 2018; Darics & Gatti, 2019; Kumar et al., 2020). Collaboration goes beyond sharing of information but instead reaches to the heart of the culture that prevails. Emotional intelligence, empathy and an understanding of the nature of collaboration will be important skill sets.

As organisations move to more open and inclusive models so will the way they develop business strategy, business operations and organisational structures. Bearing in mind the challenges discussed above and the need for greater inclusivity in direction setting, then an important role of the manager will be that of gaining the commitment of a diverse set of workforce members to whatever outcomes are decided. Amongst these members will be 'a curious workforce of builders and problem solvers .... in whole brain thinking organizations;' operations workers, technical or systems specialists, systems facilitators and work progressors. Success in the future of work may well depend 'on our ability to effectively prepare our workforce' (NESTA, 2017; Accenture, 2019; WEF, 2019a, b, c). Building this environment will depend largely on the competence of the managers and *the ability to motivate and engage a diverse, collaborative and empowered workforce* through enhancing the employee experience to providing skills development, building a personalized reward and learning culture (WEF, 2019a, b, c) to ensuring a safe and healthy workplace will be critical. The questions to be answered concern future interaction and communication; the organisation's structure and the nature of inclusivity in decision making (Flores et al., 2020). Just how much of a challenge envisaged by this aspect has been detailed by Vlatka Hlupic's concept of a 'management shift' and the belief that people have unlimited potential; that everyone is connected; that they are looking for opportunities for continuous self-development and personal growth or have a 'can do anything' attitude. In response, those leading or managing the organisation will see challenge as opportunity, are content to release control in favour of collaboration and are committed to 'emergent collective action' (Hlupic, 2014; 107). The response to the changed attitudes and behaviours of the workforce will be one of widespread cooperation and collaboration, with high levels of trust and a strong team culture. Managing the soft skills of personality types will be balanced against the hard skills of technical knowledge or capability. In all cases workforce engagement will require the alignment of individual goals with organisational ones. 'Industry 4.0 is imposing a paradigm-shift towards organisation structures and human roles and activities. The role of people needs 'to be placed in the centre as they are considered the leading component for a given revolutionary shift' (Flores et al., 2020). The role of the manager will be one of engagement, but the context of Industry 4.0 means that this takes place in complex networks with a renewed focus based on transparency, collaboration and inclusiveness.

The Fourth Industrial Revolution has been hailed as one of the most significant phenomena to emerge from the rapidity of technological developments that have emerged in recent times and continue at an unprecedented pace. But it isn't only the number of individual technological innovations that are creating the new environment but a combination or a confluence of inter alia, AI, the Internet of Things and mobile communications. The impact caused by the digital environment will impact on energy, health, transport and communication; it will affect all industries and commercial enterprises and will have global implications and its scale and scope. Organisations are therefore faced with a series of management challenges. The first concerns the transition to the new technologies overcoming such obstacles as the lack of expertise or skills shortages, inappropriate organisation design or a lack of methods and procedures (Moeuf et al., 2020). Since there are unlikely to be best practices, most organisations will have to adopt a best fit approach and craft their way through the choices in a way that suits their own culture (or competence). Managers will be required to adapt and change and build sustainable strategies, whilst at the same time ensuring continuity in business as the move from legacy to new processes takes place. The second aspect of Industry 4.0 will be for organisations to take full advantage of the opportunities that arise by maximising the impact of new technologies on their business operations once the transition has taken place. Once again, the role of the manager will be crucial and will be one of strategic choice and operational excellence. And there will be no one right way or practice. A manager with a strongly operational presence, for example, will balance resources to facilitate the realisation of an Industry 4.0 project. Or 'in the case of a manager with an 'early-adopter' profile, he will seek to quickly implement Industry 4.0 or any other technology that he thinks could have a positive impact on industrial performance' (Moeuf et al., 2020). Conversely, a manager who is more conservative will move at a different pace. Which technologies to apply and how; what is the scale and what is the scope of operation; and is this one of a global value chain or will the effects of pandemic force a rethink to more localised business operations are critical questions. The approach to management once decided will depend on contextual competences during any transitionary phase and core competences once this has taken place. And so, success during the Fourth Industrial Revolution will depend on 'the totality of its implementation' (Nawaz, 2020).

Effective agile governance, the ability to integrate systems into the new business model, collaboration in increasingly networked organisational structures and a focus on engaging a diverse workforce emerge as core management competences for a new age.

References

Abdelhameed, W. (2019). Industrial Revolution Effect on the Architectural Design. *International Conference on Fourth Industrial Revolution* (ICFIR) 1–6.

Accenture. (2019). *Beyond digital: Transcending status quo in Industry X.0*, https://www.accenture.com/gb-en/insights/strategy/digital-transformation-investment

Atzori, L., Iera, A., & Morabito, G. (2010). The Internet of Things: A Survey. *Computer Networks, 54*(15), 2787–2805.

BCG. (2020). *Embracing Industry 4.0 and Rediscovering Growth*, https://www.bcg.com/capabilities/operations/embracing-industry-4.0-rediscovering-growth.aspx

Benassi, M., Grinza, E., & Rentocchini, F. (2020). The Rush for Patents in the Fourth Industrial Revolution. *Journal of Industrial and Business Economics: Economia e Politica Industriale, 1*, 1.

Caruso, L. (2018). Digital Innovation and the Fourth Industrial Revolution: Epochal Social Changes? *AI & SOCIETY: Journal of Knowledge, Culture and Communication, 33*(3), 379.

Chou, S.-Y. (2019). The Fourth Industrial Revolution: Digital Fusion with Internet of Things. *Journal of International Affairs, 72*(1), 107.

Chung, A. Q. H., Andreev, P., Benyoucef, M., Duane, A., & O'Reilly, P. (2017). Managing an Organisation's Social Media Presence: An Empirical Stages of Growth Model. *International Journal of Information Management, 37*(1, Part A), 1.

Corfe, S. (2018). *4IR in the Workplace: Ensuring Employers and Employees Benefit*. The Social Market Foundation.

Daim, T. U., & Faili, Z. (2019). *Industry 4.0. Value Roadmap*. Springer.

Daniel, S., Midha, V., Bhattacherhjee, A., & Singh, S. P. (2018). Sourcing Knowledge in Open Source Software Projects: The Impacts of Internal and External Social Capital on Project Success. *Journal of Strategic Information Systems, 27*(3), 237.

Darics, E., & Gatti, M. C. (2019). Talking a Team Into Being in Online Workplace Collaborations: The Discourse of Virtual Work. *Discourse Studies: An Interdisciplinary Journal for the Study of Text and Talk, 21*(3), 237–257.

Dean, M., & Spoehr, J. (2018). The Fourth Industrial Revolution and the Future of Manufacturing Work in Australia: Challenges and Opportunities. *Labour & Industry, 28*(3), 166.

Deloitte. (2018). *Preparing Tomorrows Workforce for the Fourth Industrial Revolution,* https://www2.deloitte.com/content/dam/Deloitte/global/Documents/About-Deloitte/gx-preparing-tomorrow-workforce-for-4IR.pdf

Deloitte. (2019). Success Personified *in the Fourth Industrial Revolution*, https://www2.deloitte.com/content/dam/Deloitte/global/Documents/gx-davos-DI_Success-personified-fourth-industrial-revolution.pdf

Fanafuthi, M. M., Nyawo, J., & Mashau, P. (2019). Analysis of the Impact of Artificial Intelligence and Robotics on Human Labour. *Gender & Behaviour, 17*(3), 13877–13891.

Fatorachian, H., & Kazemi, H. (2020). *Impact of Industry 4.0 on supply chain performance*. ISBN 0953-7287

Finkelstein, J., & Newman, D. (1984). The Third Industrial Revolution: A Special Challenge to Managers. *Organizational Dynamics, 13*(1), 53–65.

Flores, E., Xu, X., & Lu, Y. (2020). Human Capital 4.0: A Workforce Competence Typology for Industry 4.0. *Journal of Manufacturing Technology Management.*

Gartner. (2019). *Gartner Says Global IT Spending to Grow 3.7% in 2020* www.gartner.com/en/newsroom/press-releases/2019-10-23-gartner-says-global-it-spending-to-grow-3point7-percent-in-2020

Geddes, P. (1915). *Cities in Evolution.* Williams and Norgate.

Gera, I., & Singh, S. (2019). A Critique of Economic Literature on Technology and Fourth Industrial Revolution: Employment and the Nature of Jobs. *Indian Journal of Labour Economics, 62*(4), 715.

Ghislieri, C., Molino, M., & Cortese, C. G. (2018). Work and Organizational Psychology Looks at the Fourth Industrial Revolution: How to Support Workers and Organizations? *Frontiers in Psychology, 9*, 1.

Gilchrist, A. (2016). *Industry 4.0. the Industrial Internet of Things*, Apress Publishers

Gratton, L. (2021). quoted in *Work*, Spring, CIPD, London, UK

Griffiths, F., & Ooi, M. (2020). The Fourth Industrial Revolution—Industry 4.0 and IoT. *IEEE Instrumentation & Measurement Magazine, 21*(6), 1.

Hahn, G. J. (2020). Industry 4.0: A Supply Chain Innovation Perspective. *International Journal of Production Research, 58*(5), 1425–1441.

Hlupic, V. (2014). *The Management Shift*. Palgrave Macmillan.

Hofmann, E., Selensky, S., & Kirstatter, N. (2020). Emerging Technologies and Supply Chain Management, in Machado, C. and Davim, J.P. (2020) *Industry 4.0.* CRC press, UK

Iraj, S., Kamat, S., Prakash, S., & Weldon, M. (2017). Will Productivity Growth Return in the New Digital Era? An Analysis of the Potential Impact on Productivity of the Fourth Industrial Revolution. *Bell Labs Technical Journal, 22*, 2–18.

Jang, K., Park, M., & Kim, W.-J. (2018). Topic Analysis for the fourth Industrial Revolution Using LDA and Centrality Analysis in Korea. 2018 *International Conference on Machine Learning and Data Engineering (ICMLDE), Machine Learning and Data Engineering (ICMLDE)* 103–107

Johar, I. (2017). *Robot Future Prompts Us to Rediscover What It Is To Be Human*, https://www.cipd.co.uk/news-views/changing-work-views/future-work/thought-pieces/human-response-rediscovery

Juhasz, L. (2018). *The Fourth Industrial Revolution in Hungary.* IEEE 18th International Symposium on Computational Intelligence and Informatics (CINTI), Computational Intelligence and Informatics (CINTI) 000167–000172

King, M. (2020). Coming Together. *The Wilson Quarterly, 44*(2), 1.

Kipper, L. M., Furstenau, L. B., Hoppe, D., Frozza, R., & Iepsen, S. (2020). Scopus Scientific Mapping Production in Industry 4.0 (2011–2018): A Bibliometric Analysis. *International Journal of Production Research, 58*(6), 1605–1627.

Kochan, T. A. (2019). Shaping the Future of Work: Challenges and Opportu nities for U.S. Labor Management Relations and Workplace Dispute Resolution. *Dispute Resolution Journal, 74*(1), 11–31.

Koh, L., Orzes, G., & Jia, F. (Jeff). (2019). The Fourth Industrial Revolution (Industry 4.0): Technologies Disruption on Operations and Supply Chain Management. *International Journal of Operations & Production Management,* 39(6/7/8), 817–828

Koleva, N. (2019). An Empirical Study on Human Resources' Attitude Towards Manufacturing Digitalization, 2019 *International Conference on Creative Business for Smart and Sustainable Growth (CREBUS)* 1-5

Kumar, K., Zindani, D., & Davim, J. P. (2019). *Industry 4.0.* Springer.

Kumar, S. H., Talasila, D., Gowrav, M. P., & Gangadharappa, H. V. (2020). Adaptations of Pharma 4.0 from Industry 4.0. *Drug Invention Today, 14*(3), 405–415.

Lampropoulos, G., Siakas, K., & Anastasiadis, T. (2019). Internet of Things in the Context of Industry 4.0: An Overview. *International Journal of Entrepreneurial Knowledge, 7*(1), 4–19.

Lee, M., Yun, J. J., Pyka, A., Won, D., Kodama, F., Schiuma, G., Park, H., Jeon, J., Park, K., Jung, K., Yan, M.-R., Lee, S., & Zhao, X. (2018). How to Respond to the Fourth Industrial Revolution, or the Second Information Technology Revolution? Dynamic New Combinations between Technology, Market, and Society through Open Innovation. *Journal of Open Innovation Technology, 4*(21), 1.

Li, G., Hou, Y., & Wu, A. (2017). Fourth Industrial Revolution: Technological Drivers, Impacts and Coping Methods. *Chinese Geographical Science, 27*(4), 626.

Marengo, L. (2019). Is This Time Different? A Note on Automation and Labour in the Fourth Industrial Revolution. *Journal of Industrial and Business Economics: Economia e Politica Industriale, 46*(3), 323.

Mathias, P. (1969). *The First Industrial Nation.* Methuen and Co.

Mathivathanan, D. (2021). Introduction and Evolution of Industry 4.0. in Jayakrishna, J. et al. (2021) *Sustainable Manufacturing for Industry 4.0.* CRC Press, UK

Mazali, T. (2018). From industry 4.0 to society 4.0, there and back. *AI & Soc, 33*, 405–411. https://doi.org/10.1007/s00146-017-0792-6

McKinsey & Company. (2018) *The Fourth Industrial Revolution and the factories of the future* https://www.mckinsey.com/business-functions/operations/our-insights/operations-blog/the-fourth-industrial-revolution-and-the-factories-of-the-future

McKinsey & Company. (2020). *Industry's fast mover advantage; Enterprise value from digital factories,* https://www.mckinsey.com/business-functions/operations/our-insights/industrys-fast-mover-advantage-enterprise-value-from-digital-factories

McKinsey Digital. (2015). Industry 4.0 How to Navigate Digitization of the Manufacturing Sector, https://www.mckinsey.com/media/Operations

Moeuf, A., Lamouri, S., Pellerin, R., Tamayo-Giraldo, S., Tobon-Valencia, E., & Eburdy, R. (2020). Identification of Critical Success Factors, Risks and Opportunities of Industry 4.0 in SMEs. *International Journal of Production Research, 58*(5), 1384–1400.

Morgan, J. (2019). Will We Work in Twenty-first Century Capitalism? A Critique of the Fourth Industrial Revolution Literature. *Economy and Society, 48*(3), 371–398.

Moueddene, K., Coppola, M., Wauters, P., Ivanova, M., Paquette, J., & Ansaloni, V. (2019). Expected Skills Needs for the Future of Work Understanding the Expectations of the European Workforce, *Deloitte Insights,* https://www2.deloitte.com/content/dam/insights/us/articles/22923_expected-skills-needs-for-the-future-of-work/DI_Expected-skills-needs-for-the-future-of-work.

Nawaz, S. S. (2020). Embracing Industry 4.0—Guidelines for Managers. *International Journal of Psychosocial Rehabilitation, 24*(2), 1436–1442.

NESTA. (2017). *Who'll win from the fourth industrial revolution*? https://www.nesta.org.uk/blog/wholl-win-from-the-fourth-industrial-revolution/?gclid=EAIaIQobChMI1biEgqi96QIVVe7tCh1tywzSEAAYBCAAEgJ9QfD_BwE

Njuguna Ndung'u, N., & Signe, L. (2020). *The Fourth Industrial Revolution and Digitisation Will Transform Africa into a Global Powerhouse,* Brookings Institute, https://www.brookings.edu/research/the-fourth-industrial-revolution-and-digitization-will-transform-africa-into-a-global-powerhouse/

Odhiambo, F. (2020). *The Awareness, Preparedness and Roles of the Workforce and Managers for the Fourth Industrial Revolution in Africa,* Consultancy Research Report.

Philbeck, T., & Davis, N. (2019). The Fourth Industrial Revolution : Shaping a New Era. *Journal of International Affairs, 72*(1), 17.

Poba-Nzaou, P., Lemieux, N., Beaupré, D., & Uwizeyemungu, S. (2016). Critical Challenges Associated with the Adoption of Social Media: A Delphi of a Panel of Canadian Human Resources Managers. *Journal of Business Research, 69*(10), 1.

Rabeh, M., Husam, A., & Saeed, M. (2017). The Fourth Industrial Revolution (Industry 4.0): A Social Innovation Perspective. *Technology Innovation Management Review, 7*(11), 12–20.

Ramirez, J. C. (2020). Fourth Industrial Revolution Brings Challenge and Opportunity, *H.R. Executive*, https://hrexecutive.com/fourth-industrial-revolution-brings-challenge-and-opportunity/

Reif, L. R. (2018). *A Survival Guide for The Fourth Industrial Revolution*, World Economic Forum Annual Meeting

Rosin, F., Forget, P., Lamouri, S., & Pellerin, R. (2020). Impacts of Industry 4.0 Technologies on Lean Principles. *International Journal of Production Research, 58*(6), 1644–1661.

Saniuk, S., Grabowska, S., & Gajdzik, B. (2020). Social Expectations and Market Changes in the Context of Developing the Industry 4.0 Concept. *Sustainability, 12*(4), 1.

Schneider, P., & Sting, F. J. (2020). Employees' Perspectives on Digitalization-Induced Change: Exploring Frames of Industry 4.0. *Academy of Management Discoveries, 6*(3), 406–435.

Schwab, K. (2016). *The Fourth Industrial Revolution: What It Means, How to Respond*. World Economic Forum.

Simmons, E., & McLean, G. (2020). Understanding the Paradigm Shift in Maritime Education: The Role of 4th Industrial Revolution Technologies: An Industry Perspective. *Worldwide Hospitality & Tourism Themes, 12*(1), 90–97.

Sutherland, E. (2020). The Fourth Industrial Revolution—The Case of South Africa. *Politikon*

Tien, J. M. (2019). Toward the Fourth Industrial Revolution on Real-Time Customization. *Journal of Systems Science and Systems Engineering, 1*, 1.

Tong, D. (2017). *Keeping It Human: Co-creating Our Future with the Machines*, https://www.cipd.co.uk/news-views/news-articles/keeping-future-human

UAE. (2020). *The UAE Strategy for the Fourth Industrial Revolution*, https://u.ae/en/about-the-uae/strategies-initiatives-and-awards/federal-governments-strategies-and-plans/the-uae-strategy-for-the-fourth-industrial-revolution

UK Government. (2019). *Regulation for the Fourth Industrial Revolution*, Department for Business, Energy and Industrial Strategy, Policy Paper, https://www.gov.uk/government/publications/regulation-for-the-fourth-industrial-revolution/regulation-for-the-fourth-industrial-revolution

Wilkins, J. (2019). Digitalization and Innovation Driving Manufacturing's Future: Manufacturing Is in the Midst of the Fourth Industrial Revolution--Known as Industrie 4.0--and Constant Plant-floor Changes Are Forcing Companies to Keep Up with the Rapid Pace or Risk Getting Lost and Falling Behind. *Control Engineering,* 1

World Economic Forum. (2016). *The Future of Jobs*, http://reports.weforum.org/future-of-jobs-2016/preface/

World Economic Forum. (2017). *Realising Human Potential in the Fourth Industrial Revolution*, http://www3.weforum.org/docs/WEF_EGW_Whitepaper.pdf

World Economic Forum. (2018). *How Can Policy Keep Pace with the Fourth Industrial Revolution*? https://www.weforum.org/agenda/2018/02/can-policy-keep-pace-with-fourth-industrial-revolution/

World Economic Forum. (2019a). *The Importance of Collaboration in a Connected World*, https://www.weforum.org/agenda/2019/01/how-collaboration-is-the-modern-company-s-secret-weapon/

World Economic Forum. (2019b). *HR4.0: Shaping People Strategies in the Fourth Industrial Revolution*, http://www3.weforum.org/docs/WEF_NES_Whitepaper_HR4.0.pdf

World Economic Forum. (2019c). *3 ways firms can master the digital challenges of the 4IR*, https://www.weforum.org/agenda/2019/04/3-ways-digital-challenges-fourth-industrial-revolution-cybersecurity-ai-artificial-intelligence/

World Economic Forum. (2020a). *Fourth Industrial Revolution*, https://www.weforum.org/focus/fourth-industrial-revolution

World Economic Forum. (2020b). *COVID-19: Emerging technologies are now critical infrastructure—what that means for governance,* https://www.weforum.org/agenda/2020/04/covid-19-emerging-technologies-are-now-critical-infrastructure-what-that-means-for-governance/

Zawra, L. M. (2019). Migration of Legacy Industrial Automation Systems in the Context of Industry 4.0 – A Comparative Study, *International Conference on Fourth Industrial Revolution* (ICFIR), Manama, Bahrain 1-7. https://doi.org/10.1109/ICFIR.2019.8894776

Zunino, C., Valenzano, A., Obermaisser, R., & Petersen, S. (2020). Factory Communications at the Dawn of the Fourth Industrial Revolution. *Computer Standards & Interfaces, 71*, 1.

6

Core Management Competences—Preparing for the Future

Infinite Possibilities and Profound Implications

Life appeared to be much simpler when managers faced one of two options—to be a Theory X type or a Theory Y type.

The attributes of each surfaced in Douglas McGregor's work *The Human Side of Enterprise* (McGregor, 1960), a seminal contribution to the human relations approach to management. Theory X managers were stereotypically authoritarian, unrelentingly results driven and intolerant of discussion or debate. Theory Y managers on the other hand relied on influence rather than coercion, encouraged active participation and favoured openness. Such stark alternatives were, of course, tempered by the reality of organisational life, in which choice was rarely binary. Management is contextual and has many facets. A conclusion that has been borne out over the past two centuries as the concept evolved. So, the belief in Adam Smith's theory of the benefits of the division of labour was important for managers in the First Industrial Revolution; there were more choices as the American way of management evolved in the Second with progression from F.W. Taylor's view of organisations and management's role in their efficient running to behavioural or humanistic

P. Turner, *The Making of the Modern Manager*,
https://doi.org/10.1007/978-3-030-81062-7_6

approaches, extended as Asian corporations dominated the Third, enhanced by innovation derived from new philosophies about how organisations should function. And now, the elements of context, richness and diversity have rarely been more relevant for the Fourth Industrial Revolution with new technologies impacting on almost every aspect of work as it brings the digital world into the physical world, and brings life-changing technologies to life in applications for health and well-being, transport and the home. Generations of managers have adapted successfully to deal with the implications in each of these dramatic developments, and management structures, processes and techniques have provided the basis for success in organisations and societies (McDonald, 2011; Mokyr, 2009; Schwab, 2016; Cummings et al., 2017; World Economic Forum, 2017; Philbeck & Davis, 2019).

The Fourth Industrial Revolution has infinite possibilities but also profound implications for polity and society—a whole life system—'a cradle to grave network' (Morgan, 2019). Given the scale and scope of changes, the social narrative is likely to be a stand-out feature of this coming transformation. But of critical importance to this book, the implications for the business world as the new paradigm of Industry 4.0 rapidly spreads worldwide offering a platform where new technologies become pervasive. Amongst the developments are the virtualisation of work, open-source work practices, the decline of organisational hierarchy, changes in social values and business sustainability. (McDonald, 2011; Flores et al., 2020). Technological advances in artificial intelligence, robotics, machine learning, cloud computing, nanotechnology and the Internet of Things bring boundless and boundaryless possibilities for the way organisations structure and operate. Underlying these important considerations are two other factors. Firstly, there is a reset of the balance between work and home. Established during the time of the First Industrial Revolution, traditional working patterns of behaviour are changing and becoming more flexible in time given to family and work responsibilities; and secondly, the impact of COVID-19. The rapidly developing capabilities brought about by enforced lock down have raised questions about just how effective previous ways of interacting in the working environment were. Notwithstanding this, the confluence of the dynamics of technology innovation, social and behavioural change and virtuality, come together to fuel the debate not only about the nature of work, the working environment, organisational structures and processes, but also about where and how value chain activity takes place—will localism or nationalism replace globalism because of the perceived fragility of global supply and markets—has the pandemic 'put the brakes on globalisation (Arlidge, 2020)?

Disruptive Change and Developing Ideas

Is it possible to learn from experiences of disruptive change that characterised previous eras without falling into the trap of hindsight bias or the 'illusion of retrospective determinism' and to extend the narrative beyond the 'one dimensional, uni-cultural' approach?' There are some common challenges. To begin with, a feature of the Four Industrial Revolutions to date was the challenge of invention and innovation in technology and the response of new organisational types and modes of production. The commercial and industrial organisations of the First Industrial Revolution in the eighteenth century, for example, faced disruptive change caused by the introduction of new types of equipment in new types of industrial organisation; and having installed such equipment, the need to recruit and train a workforce to operate advanced industrial machinery in ways that were different to previous working methods. Adaptation and resilience were amongst the many competences that were needed to manage in one of Europe's larger and more mechanised industrial concerns. In all cases, managers had to be sufficiently adaptable to catch the wave of opportunity. In the early stages, working conditions could be brutal and it was not difficult to see how images of *Dark Satanic Mills* were formed. To the managers of the time, human resources could be little more than cogs in a great industrial wheel. But this too evolved and the business case for better working practices, such as those instigated by Robert Owen at the famous New Lanark Mills provided an alternative to the harshness of early factory life. There was, for some, recognition of the words of the industrialist Seebohm Rowntree that 'the factory is not just a soulless organisation for turning out cocoa and chocolate' (Morris, 2017). The seeds of a more humane management style with greater attention shown to the workforce were sown in this type of institution, but it would be many years before these practices became widespread.

A Second Industrial Revolution from the end of the nineteenth century saw the climb of the United States to the peak of the world's economic powers. By the early years of the twentieth century—the 'American Century'—the United States was the leading world economy. Mass production and management practices inspired initially by the scientific approach of F.W. Taylor, shaped American organisations until the United States' industrial and commercial performance outstripped that of its rivals. Companies which came out of this period of American dominance included those competing in the consumer market such as Coca Cola and PepsiCo to those succeeding in the automobile market such as Goodyear Tyres, Ford Motor and GM. A Third Industrial Revolution, from the 1950s once again based on technology developments for which the invention and application of the microchip played a significant role, created a new competitive landscape. The rapid rise of Japan in the immediate post-World War II period followed by the Dragon and Tiger economies of Southeast Asia and more latterly the remarkable performances of China and India brought a new level of economic competitiveness to the world in which Samsung, Toyota, Sony and Panasonic became household names. By the twenty-first century, corporate strategy took place in a global arena and competitive advantage was often gained through a combination of technological innovation, excellence in application and responsive organisational structures. Now, a Fourth Industrial Revolution has brought these requirements to the fore; but, unlike others, technology in this case can also be a great leveller. Not only was it the established large organisations that could be successful through the globalisation of opportunity but newer, agile, technologically adept, ones too. Corporations such as Apple and Google founded in 1998; Facebook, launched in 2004 (with 2.5 billion users) and Chinese company Alibaba founded in 1999, worth close to or into the trillions; were able to apply technologies with new management and organisational formats that saw them grow to be amongst the largest companies in the world. Amazon—whose business model, already a benchmark for the application of Industry 4.0 technologies—was bolstered by its remarkable adaptation to COVID-19's far-reaching implications, has become one of the world's most valuable companies; and in 2021 the Tesla and SpaceX companies reached an astonishing market value. Each industrial revolution brought the opportunity for value and wealth creation to those organisations that had the foresight, entrepreneurial drive and preparedness to risk capital investment. Each one of these organisations also had the need for managers to take key decisions about strategy or direction, and managers to take responsibility for implementation and application.

Management Challenges and Contextual Competences from the Four Industrial Revolutions

The emergence of new technologies has generally brought opportunities for entrepreneurs to invest capital in new machinery or new techniques; and economic history is replete with examples of individuals who did so from Matthew Boulton to Nicolas Leblanc (whose plant for the production of sodium carbonate was seized by French Revolutionaries of the political kind in 1794 before being returned to its owner by Napoleon in 1801); from Henry Ford to Sochiro Honda; from Jeff Bezos to Jack Ma to Elon Musk. So, each revolution had innovation from new enterprises, early movers to new methods from already established organisations and laggards who only came to the new revolutionary techniques after the trials and errors of others. Hence the nature of management challenges over the Four Industrial Revolutions beginning in 1750 covers a wide range of issues from start up to catch up; from innovation to adaptation. The range of experiences included some management challenges that were contextual such as the installation during the eighteenth century of water power to run new types of cotton-making machinery in a small, rural Derbyshire village in Britain; or the adaptation of systems and processes from the armaments and meat manufacturing industries (in particular the Chicago meatpacking business) to a new automobile factory at the Highland Park Plant in Michigan, the United States in 1927; or the application of robotics and artificial intelligence in commercial and industrial organisations in South Korea and Singapore in the twenty-first century. These specific challenges were relevant at a point in time when viewed through the prism of history. But some management challenges transcended any one era—such as ensuring the supply of raw materials across a supply chain whether this was local or global; planning a workforce to ensure full staffing for a shift or working day; or preserving cash flow which has been the bane of managers in businesses for centuries, perhaps represented by the note from the manager of the eighteenth-century manufacturing to request *'a few more bills in a short time … as several matters has turned out different to his expectations'* (Sir Richard Arkwright to Samuel Oldknow c., 1783), a sentiment that could be replicated in many growing businesses even to this day. Additionally, the need to deliver results in the face of operational pressures is something that every manager in every era would recognise and perhaps sympathise with the manager in 1777 who commented on his huge workload—'I begin to grow weary of having so much to do, for really, I cannot do what ought to be done and very important work is neglected every day for want of having proper assistance' (Butler, 1945). And there is the fundamental question of whether to adopt a new technology and how to make it work—as narrated by Henry Ford in 1922—'an idea is just an idea. Almost anyone can think up an idea. The thing that counts is developing it into a practical product.' Hence, whilst many of the challenges evaporated as time passed (such as the best source of water to drive a water mill) some can be identified as being relevant across the ages and it is worthwhile reflecting on these as the world moves into Industry 4.0.

In the first place, since all of the revolutions to date have been based on the application of new technology, the question of how to get the most out of the opportunity of economic growth depended upon *selecting and applying advanced industrial technologies.* With the advent of the First Industrial Revolution, the production logic of the new type of factory that was springing up was irrefutable. But making the transition from traditional methods to the new was not always straightforward because new technologies could be expensive and require new investment, a new type of workforce had to be recruited and trained and new management approaches were necessary to deal with the repetitive, time-controlled nature of production shifts. New processes based on the division of labour into simple routine tasks was something that required elaborate supervision at first as the new workforce was brought in and had to get used to a regime in which 'work started, meals were eaten and worked stopped at fixed hour, notified by the ringing of a bell' (Mantoux, 1928). The scale, scope and application of the new technology caused one observer at the time to comment on 'strange and interesting things to be seen in the busy hives of industry distributed throughout the kingdom' (Mayhew, 1865). Strange and interesting things were not confined to the eighteenth century. Indeed, Bill Gates founder of Microsoft reflected over 100 years later, 'how can technology help run your business better, how will technology transform business how can technology help make you a winner five or ten years from now' (Gates, 1999). Such a question was at the heart of those organisations facing the dilemma of deciding upon how to acquire and install new technology applications. An exemplar in this particular aspect of challenge was Toyota and their application of fourteen operational principles based on not only choosing the right systems or processes but continuously improving them once in place (Liker, 2004). The conversion of these principles into effective management practice enabled Toyota and other Japanese companies at this time to establish mass-production systems and thereby strengthen their technology development capabilities. In addition to new technologies for production processes, social media has transformed the way organisations gather and disseminate knowledge, engage both clients and members of the workforce and communicate key messages, with business advantages of faster access to knowledge, a reduction in communication costs; and a faster access to internal experts. Its platforms are connectivity-enabled applications that facilitate interaction, exchange and communication of information. They are 'expansive, dynamic and enable the sharing of several types of content' with three technological features, which are intermediation of the content generated by users; interactivity among users and direct contact with online content; and interconnection of individuals with other users on a network (Anthony, 2012; Poba-Nzaou et al., 2016; Chung et al., 2017; Ruparel et al., 2020). In every age, the ability to select and apply new technologies is one of the cornerstones on which effective management can be built.

Secondly, an important decision had to be made concerning *transitioning to new systems, structures and processes.* The choices ranged from being an innovator, to first mover, fast follower or laggard. In some industries there was a dynamic mix of business model from start-ups to established firms, each of which sought to maximise the opportunity from new technology. But making the most of new technologies during each of the industrial revolutions has not normally been through a well-travelled playbook. Instead, it was often messy and unpredictable. And even with the benefit of history organisations use advanced technologies either to protect their business or to drive disruption (HBR, 2019). There are no easy answers to the question of whether and when and how to adopt during times of revolutionary change. For some, this was conscious thought and based on deliberate management decisions. Richard Arkwright, for example, was a barber first, a publican second and an inventor third. It was increasingly towards the latter that he gravitated from the middle of the eighteenth century. Having taken a half-worked idea for a cotton-rolling/spinning machine (Fitton, 1989). Arkwright was able, with the assistance of two 'joint adventurers and partners' to develop a process that would change not only cotton manufacture but the nature of industrial society itself. Deliberate management decisions, during the Second Industrial Revolution, underpinned Ford's strategy when having market tested the Model N, the Model R and the Model S, Henry Ford was faced with the transition in manufacturing techniques and methods to launch the Model T and Ford sought best practices from elsewhere to do so. The new president of US corporation G.E. in 1922, made the decision to take the company into high-quality appliance lines, starting with refrigerators (Tobey, 1997). And organisations in Asia during the Third Industrial Revolution making strategic decisions on which industries to focus and operational ones in how to gain advantage—the success of which was shown by the remarkable Japanese performance by the mid-1980s of 82% of the share of world exports in Motorcycles, 80% in TVs, 71% in calculating machines and 51% of world export share in pianos and musical instruments (Porter, 1990). The contextual competence was perhaps exemplified by the experiences of Asian companies as they sought competitive advantage from the burgeoning global opportunities that arose in the immediate post Second World War period and did so by being flexible enough to craft a strategy as production experience, market conditions or market opportunities changed; and having new management practices to deliver world class operations to take advantage of them. The principle of *translative adaptation*—the introduction of ideas and systems from outside of the country not in their original form but 'with modifications to fit local needs' (Ohno, 2006)—was a feature of this.

Thirdly, the application of technology required *establishing new types of organisational structures and new systems and processes* if full advantage was to be gained. It is argued that the Fourth Industrial revolution will bring about a new generation of businesses which will upend entire industries by 'leveraging connectivity and automation in ways that have forced incumbent business leaders, regulators and the global workforce to rethink everything they once believed to be sacred' (Peccarelli, 2020). But to do so will mean the establishment of organisational structures and approaches that are relevant to the new context and this presents a particular management challenge that has been faced before. For example, during the eighteenth century, the production logic of the factory demanded new types of organisation to deliver the new methods. During the Second Industrial Revolution, mass production methods that were applied in several industries meant that 'it was vital to keep the expensive installations running at maximum capacity' necessitating that the manager's role ranged from the procurement of raw materials through to the production and distribution of the end product in a way that was more intense, required more integration and to maximise the 'economies of speed' of high-volume production. And during the Third Industrial Revolution from the 1960s Japanese organisations were faced with the challenge of organisation against well-established competitors in the United States and Europe. In this context strategic questions were faced in respect of how to achieve competitive advantage in which markets. But there was also the issue of upgrading factor advantages such as human resources and their management to a level that would ensure competitiveness on world markets (van Driel et al., 2007; Li & Li, 2009; Hout and Michael, 2014). This particular issue brought with it that of organisation. Would this be the planned and systematic type that characterised the mass production in Ford factories or would there be additional organisational types that could give the competitive edge. There were choices including the response do things differently and hence revolutionise manufacturing organisation by such methods as the Toyota Production

System (TPS) with its core concepts of just-in-time systems; *jidoka,* or 'automation with a human touch'; *kanban,* a production tool helping just-in-time production; and *poka yoke* or mistake proofing. In all cases, an understanding of the implications of management decision-making through insight or sweating the details—advocated by Indra Nooyi of PepsiCo—is a critical success factor. The contextual competences in relation to this are twofold. Firstly, the ability to take operational decisions in the context of wider strategy and secondly to be able to adapt the organisation to dynamic economic opportunities.

An additional factor was the *recruitment, training, engagement and retention of a workforce that was best fit to the new systems and processes.* Adam Smith noted in 1776 when he wrote that the success of an enterprise was regulated by the 'skill, dexterity and judgement with which its labour is generally applied' (Smith, 1776; 104). In the first place there was a need for a strong management culture with capable managers such as those in the eighteenth-century London lace factory—where the owner 'gathered round him very active people to carry out his operations' (Felkin, 1867). Then there was the challenge of putting in place a workforce in all operational and administrative areas. For those during the First Industrial Revolution the particular shift was cultural and came about as skilled craft workers were replaced by machine operators for the cheaper, simpler, ready-made products in large manufacturing operations (Pollard, 1965). Likewise, when Henry Ford set up his moving assembly line in 1913, individual workers had an input into just one part of the process. For the company, the improvements in productivity were remarkable but in the early days of the new production techniques labour turnover was over 300% (Donkin, 2001). Irrespective of technology, irrespective of the era in which the technology was applied, the presence of a trained, competent, adaptable workforce could be the difference between success or failure. And in this same area, the management challenges were related not only to technology or organisation but also to health and well-being issues. Great epidemics occurred in the nineteenth and twentieth centuries had devastating consequences in the same way as COVID-19 has in contemporary society. And with each came adaptation as societies and organisations found ways to ameliorate their worst effects and were able to respond with some vigour over time.

An important conclusion from these is that effective strategic and operational decisions whilst at the same time developing and protecting their workforces through effective health and well-being policies, depended on having an efficient, motivated, qualified, competent group of managers. On the one hand they were involved in setting a vision for their organisation, translating this into a business strategy that aligned the operations and resource allocation of the organisation to this vision (Deloitte, 2018). Then they were responsible for building and implementing an operational model supported by efficient, sustainable systems and an engaged competent workforce to deliver it.

Success Depends on the Sum Total of the Core Competences of Individuals

The nature and structure of organisations and the work that goes on inside them as Industry 4.0. evolves, remain open to interpretation. Each of the industrial revolutions discussed in preceding chapters has precipitated such a debate. A common outcome is that technological change invariably leads to the decline of traditional types of industry, work, careers or jobs. But at the same time generates new industries, growth in new commercial activities and opportunities for organisations to create wealth. In fact, each revolution has created more economic value than the one that has gone on before and the creation of this value has been by people applying entrepreneurial nous and management competence to new situations. A further conclusion, one that forms the basis of this review of management competence, is that all change has had a human dimension at its heart and a human dimension at its success. If these assumptions hold true then any meaningful future will also depend on a human dimension in which technology, rather than replacing, increases human capabilities. The words of Adam Smith in the eighteenth century about the potential of human beings; of Henry Ford in the twentieth about converting ideas into action; of Bill Gates in the twenty-first about the digital nervous system coming from individuals within the organisation; or of Sheryl Sandberg's observation that if we tapped the entire pool of human resources and talent, our collective performance would improve, resonate as the Fourth Industrial Revolution gathers pace. Kichiro Toyoda, urging his employees to *genchi genbutsu*—'go and see' and use knowledge to help in decisions; assumes a new meaningfulness in the context of Industry 4.0. Where organisations can make it possible for individuals to achieve the highest level of contribution through their confidence, creativity and innovativeness, then there is a foundation on which to combine technological advancement and human achievement. Success depends on the organisation's ability to exploit its core competences to the full recognising that this is based on the sum total of the core competences of individuals. Industry 4.0 will be 'a socio-technical system that contains social (human-related) and technical (non-human) aspects which will interact to pursue a common goal' (Kak, 2011; Sandberg, 2013; Sony & Naik, 2020). Understanding core competences in the achievement of that goal is therefore an important factor.

Core competences are relevant at both the organisational level and the individual level. In the former, core competences refer to the effective integration of technologies, specialised knowledge, skills, techniques and experiences in a way that delivers differentiated advantage against competitor organisations. It is a 'company's collective knowledge about how to coordinate diverse production skills and technologies', or 'a harmonized combination of multiple resources and skills that distinguish a firm in the marketplace'. Organisations build their core competence by strategic decision-making in respect of chosen markets or product/service areas and by applying business improvement methods such as total quality management, business process reengineering, six sigma improvement programmes or the principles of the Toyota production system with a view to delivering a business proposition—innovative products, services or business models, that will create value for their stakeholders. Successful organisations with the advent of Industry 4.0 will try to achieve core competence through the application of big data and knowledge management technology in the creation of uniqueness leading to competitive advantage. Knowledge will become one of the most important resources and harnessing it is both a feature of core competence and a means of developing it (Prahalad & Hamel, 1990; Le Deist & Winterton, 2005; Yang, 2015; Yin et al., 2020).

In this respect, the core competence of the organisation is made up of the sum total of the core competences of individual members of the workforce. Such core competences can be based on their contributions to organisational technology systems and processes—through their knowledge and skills—or effective interfaces with the organisation's structure, dynamics or culture—through their attitudes and behaviour. The core competence of the individual can therefore be defined as a 'specific, identifiable, definable, and measurable knowledge, skill, ability, and/or other deployment related characteristic (e.g., attitude, behaviour, physical ability), which a human resource may possess, and which is necessary for, or material to, the performance of an activity within a specific business context'. In contemporary organisations it is the result of a combination of cognition, intuition and emotional intelligence (Sparrow, 2000; Stepanenko & Kashevnik, 2017). The success of the application of this competence will be effective performance within a domain through the application of knowledge, skill, attitude and ability. As the requirements of the new environment begin to be articulated, a range of competence attributes of managers to ensure that those of the organisation and individuals are maximised, include social skills and emotional intelligence because technical skills will need to be supplemented with strong social and collaboration skills.

However, the subject of management competence is not a new one and points of view have evolved over time. John Gibbons, writing in 1844 on the subject of managing a forge or a mill, noted that 'character, capacity and technical knowledge ... are the three essentials, and I have placed them in the order of their importance ... character is the first requisite, cleverness and skill in his craft the second' (Pollard, 1965 105, 293, 294). Whilst 100 years later Mr Join Lambert, president of the Third International Thrift Congress in Paris in 1935, noted about the competences of two of the congress managers, that 'one is very calm, very methodical. The other, though methodical has a very ardent temperament ... through a union of this sort it has been possible to drive terribly powerful machinery' (Third International Thrift Congress, Paris, 1935). Certainly Sir Robert Peel's 1816 perspective that 'it is impossible for a mill at any distance to be managed unless it is under the direction of a partner or superintendent who has an interest in the success of the business' (Pollard, 1965 34) would resonate with Professor Tony Watson's findings during his sociological study of management during the 1990s in which one of his interviewees noted of the ZTC Ryland business, 'it is an absolute priority for us to get managers thinking of themselves as business managers. They must think first and foremost about how they and their people are contributing to the business' (Watson, 1994; 38). Most recently, priorities have changed and the World Economic Forum (2016) listed ten key skills as Complex Problem Solving, Critical Thinking, Creativity, People Management, Coordinating with Others, Emotional Intelligence, Judgement and Decision-Making, Service Orientation, Negotiation and Cognitive Flexibility. Whilst there are differences in management competence in language and style tempered by the era in which they were applied, there are nevertheless similarities in expectation. Looking forward, management competence in the world of Industry 4.0 will require a level of systems intelligence or intelligent behaviour in the complex systems that will be a feature of organisations (Hamalainen et al., 2018) that was also a feature of previous eras. Such competence has commonly been as much of a requirement as technical skills or qualifications.

The role of human resource as a foundation on which the core competence of the corporation is built has thus been recognised at every stage of the evolution of industrial and commercial organisations since the beginnings of the modern capitalist system. The factory owners of the First Industrial Revolution asked the same fundamental questions as the start up in the financial services sector of the Fourth. How can I maximise the contribution of new technology to creating value for my stakeholders? One of the answers to this question was to ensure that the competence of individuals was aligned to the competence of the organisation as a whole. And having recognised this to ensure that managers themselves had the core competences needed to deliver these objectives (Flores et al., 2020).

Core Management Competences During the Four Industrial Revolutions

Competences are characteristics that enable one to perform a job. They consist of numerous forms and combinations of knowledge, skills, abilities, motives and traits (2016, p. 423). Competences are qualities the individual can use to perform activities in an exemplary and successful manner. Competences are those characteristics that enable a manager to perform a role effectively. They consist of combinations of knowledge, skills, attitudes and behaviours and are used by individuals to perform their jobs in a way that supports the achievement of the organisation's goals. 'They provide that individual with an indication or map of the behaviours and actions that will be valued, recognised and in some organisations rewarded. Competences can represent the language of performance management in an organisation' (CIPD, 2020). But one size does not fit all and subgroups of competence have also been identified including cognitive competence or know what and know why, functional competence or the skills and abilities an individual should possess when working in a specific area—know-how, social competence—know-how to behave, and 'meta-competence' or the ability to acquire and learn new competences, and includes reflection and self-awareness—know thyself (Le Deist & Winterton, 2005; Cha & Maytorena-Sanchez, 2019; 962).

The analysis of the evolution of management as a concept, the various challenges faced by managers during the Four Industrial Revolutions to date and their responses to these were presented in previous chapters. Competence was highlighted as either contextual, that is, relating to a specific series of events during a particular time period, or core, which seemed to have resonance across more than one period. Contextual competences ranged from transitioning to new systems and processes to recruiting and engaging a workforce. Managers in each of the revolutions applied their skills to variations of these dependent upon their specific circumstance and whilst there was undoubted overlap, the context was sufficiently differentiated to view these as additional to what might be referred to as core competences. In the latter case, core competences go to the heart of a manager's role irrespective of the date or location of the industrial or commercial change that was taking place. Table 6.1. shows core competences against each of the revolutions. Five particular areas of managerial activity stand out from this analysis. In the first place, managers in each of the revolutions would have to draw on their change management capabilities if they were to be successful. For some this would involve identifying the need to change for others the need to initiate change. For all it would require managers to have a willingness to change

Table 6.1 Features of core management competences during the Four Industrial Revolutions

First Industrial Revolution	Second Industrial Revolution	Third Industrial Revolution	Fourth Industrial Revolution
Adapting to change—from artisan to factory; from human power to water and steam power; from ad hoc production methods to planned and systematic processes; rise of European industrial organisations; introduction of science into management	*Making change work effectively*—shift to mass production and electric power; faster pace of economic and social development; adopting new technologies and integrating them into new environments; rise of the United States as leading economic power; resilience during economic extremes—growth and recession, peace and war; scientific management	*The ability to adapt and change*; microprocessors in all forms of equipment; convergence of telecommunications and computing; automation of production using robotics; globalisation of value chains; responding to global competitors; rise of Japan, Asian Tigers, China and India; new management methods, behavioural and humanistic; agile learning organisations	*Agile governance*—AI and the Internet of Things; implementing fluid approaches to organisation structure; adaptive managers able to absorb significant change; change not bound by rigid organisational structures; internal *and* external social capital *interaction*
The use of knowledge and information in decision-making; sourcing from external scientific societies; internal challenge and response improvements to technology; collaboration of partners; documentation and systematic approach to management	*Use information to support business decisions*—work study and development of Taylor's approach using information to design and improve processes; learning from practice; hierarchical organisations with clearer boundaries of authority	*Using knowledge transfer and sharing in decision-making*; total quality management based on production analysis; continuous improvement methods; quality circles and inclusive approaches to problem solving; managing in a global context; the rise of long-term strategic planning;	*Effectively managing internal and external collaborative networks;* a technology ecosystem enables new levels of collaboration, facilitated by a digital infrastructure; manage in distributed or networked organisational forms

(*continued*)

Table 6.1 (continued)

First Industrial Revolution	Second Industrial Revolution	Third Industrial Revolution	Fourth Industrial Revolution
The ability to motivate a workforce consisting of employees with different skill types and levels; integrating unskilled rural workforce into new factories; training in new skills; maintaining discipline to production levels and processes; retaining key workers	*Motivating and engaging a diverse workforce;* scientific management; integrating multi-cultural workforce into new production operations; adapting from Taylor and Ford to humanistic methods of workforce management; workforce planning	*Cooperation and team working*; quality circles; group decision-making; *nemawashi*; participatory motivation; individual as part of a group collective; humanistic and behavioural management	*The ability to motivate and engage a diverse, collaborative and empowered workforce*; create and deliver shared values; demonstrates emotional intelligence, empathy and an understanding of the nature of collaboration
The ability to integrate multiple activities through effective organisation; managers responsible for multiple functions; introduction of formal organisational structures	*The ability to work in new forms of business organisation;* vertical integration; *function together adequately to produce something that is of value;* adapting to mass production organisation	*Seeking continuous improvement;* translating national policies into local actions; automation with a human touch; go and see philosophy, TQM	*Managing the integration of multiple technologies in the workplace,* horizontal integration across geographically diverse participants, adapting to the Internet of Things

(*continued*)

Table 6.1 (continued)

First Industrial Revolution	Second Industrial Revolution	Third Industrial Revolution	Fourth Industrial Revolution
Focus on production levels; managers judged on performance against output targets; maintaining continuous shift production	*Delivering business results;* performance management in mass production systems; role and goal clarity through bureaucratic processes	*Converting strategy into actionable plans and processes;* planned and systematic approach to strategy; emphasis on alignment between strategy and operations	*Managing in distributed or network organisational forms;* create business responsiveness and entails proficiency in dealing with external uncertainty with rapid responses; shared goals; from hierarchy to network to swarm

and the adaptability or agility to do so. The London, UK, lace manufacturer seeing and then adopting new manufacturing techniques in the eighteenth century; managers of new glass-making technologies in Ford City, Pennsylvania, USA, in the nineteenth, or the those in new production facilities for the manufacture of consumer electronics, cameras, motorcycles, pianos, watches and calculators in Japan in the twentieth were each faced with the problematic process that is known as change management in the organisation as a whole and adapting to change on the part of the individual manager. In later analysis the competence of the ability to adapt to change was often complemented by the need to be 'agile' in addressing both external and internal challenges.

Hence agility, the ability to adapt and then to make change work effectively was the first of the core competences of managers that seemed to span the generations. Often, but not always, because change is rarely neat and sequential, knowledge and information can be critical to helping management decision-making. Hence a second core management competence that appears throughout the Four Industrial Revolutions is the ability to acquire and use knowledge. This could refer to gaining knowledge of scientific techniques though attendance at events designed to bring together enlightened scientists and practitioners under the same roof—such as the Birmingham, UK, Lunar Society, the 'meeting of a few fertile minds' which change an age; or through collaboration and knowledge sharing within the organisation—the 'go and see' of Kichiro Toyoda during the twentieth. Thirdly, the success of all managers has involved the ability to maximise the output of a human workforce. In some cases, this was through rigorous approaches to scientific management as exemplified by F.W. Taylor or Henri Fayol in the early part of the twentieth century or more recently by using development in behavioural science to a more people rather than process centric approach.

The ability to recruit, train and motivate or engage a workforce is a core management competence that spans the centuries regardless of whatever technique is used to do so. Fourthly, the ability to integrate several types of system or different processes into a coherent whole was a characteristic that emerged in organisations as more complex machinery was used in manufacturing or more complex supply chains in an age of globalisation. As industrial and commercial organisations adapted and changed to new environments then the role of the manager did also. The ability to bring together systems with different moving parts into an end product or service was therefore instrumental to the success of both the manager and the organisation in which they worked. But this was only one aspect. A corollary was to improve the systems and processes and increasingly to make improvement a continuous cycle. And finally, management competences and the actions that resulted from their application were all geared to delivering results. In this respect, objectives are the abstract, results are the concrete and the ability to deliver both is the competence.

Core Management Competences of the Past; Core Management Competences of the Future?

The question remains, whether it is possible to project the conclusions reached about management competence of the past into the scenarios or contexts of the Fourth Industrial Revolution? Whilst it would be a mistake to oversimplify the findings of such an analysis; of being wary of 'the little pieces of the past' that can be 'distilled into inevitable certainties', there is merit in looking at how the introduction of systematic processes were reconciled with individuality in members of the workforce (Hanlon, 2016; Mollan, 2019). This is common practice at organisational level since Jim Collins famously stated that 'good is the enemy of great' in his milestone study of what factors led to good companies becoming great ones and then followed this up by raising the question of the factors that made companies 'built to last' (Collins, 2001; Collins & Porras, 2011). The conclusion was that lessons could be learned about strategy, management and leadership from the performance over time of companies that included General Electric, 3M, Merck, Wal-Mart, Hewlett-Packard, Walt Disney, Philip Morris, Procter & Gamble, Motorola and Boeing. Stadler's *Enduring Success* (Stadler, 2011) also addressed the question of how companies could succeed over time, concluding that 'the greatest companies' are ones that adapt to a constantly changing environment (by being intelligently conservative). Some analyses of anticipated competences for the next generation of manager and worker would certainly resonate across time. For example, understanding technology and technical competence would be important, as would creativity, problem solving, conflict solving, decision-making and efficiency orientation. Personal competences, including flexibility, ambiguity tolerance, motivation to learn and ability to work under pressure, would also feature. And the ability to communicate and to transfer knowledge equally so (Fitsilis et al., 2018). And so, the presentation of competences is intended, rather than as definitive statement more as a thought piece. There is evidence to support the conclusion, but there is also conjecture based on interpretation, particularly the further back in time the study goes. The language of competence was rarely present in early industrial times though the sentiment was always so.

But if the traditional management functions of planning, organising, controlling, delegating, coordinating, forecasting and so on are taken out of the manager's hands by virtue of automation technologies (Sony & Naik, 2020) then what remains for the role? In response to this question, Table 6.1 highlights common areas of core management competence derived from analysis of each of the Four Industrial Revolutions that may be relevant into the future. The challenge of multi-faceted change has been a constant factor and the competence to deal with it effectively was critical to managers in industrial and commercial organisations. 'Know thyself' was rarely more apposite than the manager faced with the challenge of change in which self-confidence in adapting to new circumstances and an outlook of agility to make it happen bore down on day to day operational goals. In contemporary contexts, the capacity to learn from workplace experiences, apply this to the knowledge of the business and adopt attitudes and behaviours that are organisationally and culturally relevant is an important management capability (Leslie et al., 2002). Industrial revolutions were rarely single-issue affairs and whilst the inventions of scientists and entrepreneurs are the events that are remembered it was their operationalisation that gave them form. Managers realised ideas and put them to work often through a sequence of challenge and response, adapting the approach or design as learning of its operation accumulated. Cartwright's ability to change his plans from a full-service factory in 1788 to concentrating on a single process after advice from James Watt is an example of the willingness to adapt and change that was a feature of early industrial managers. As the Second Industrial revolution gathered pace, led by the United States, this ability was once again at the forefront of management competence. As mass production and the management principles of FW Taylor gained traction, managers had to evaluate new technologies, put in new machinery to achieve higher productivity and implement new ways of working in new types of organisation structure. In the early stages there were few guidelines of how to do so and so the ability, once again to adapt working processes and methods was high on the capability agenda. Learning on the job as production lines were installed—for example, at Ford and GM—and adapting as learning improved knowledge was the norm. The dynamism of the US economy during this time required managers who were able to operate in a complex and fast-moving environment. Agility, adaptability and resilience went hand in hand and were paramount to success. The managers in the factories and offices during each of these transformations needed the attitude of willingness to adapt and the skill to do so. In applying these assumptions to a management competence that is relevant to today's environment, the term agility has been used and once adapted this might be termed as agile governance. Agile governance means that the manager as well as being able to adapt their own performance to changing circumstances, is also able to influence the organisation of work in a way that is fitting to any change. For top management teams this will depend on its 'absorptive capacity' (Bui et al., 2019), that is, its ability to take on change and adapt accordingly; for others it will mean the ability to both influence change and be agile enough to implement it accordingly. It is a personal agility and an organisational agility. In this respect the management competence might be articulated as 'demonstrates agile governance and adaptability to make change work effectively—'know thyself'. Figure 6.1 has this as the first of the adapted core management competences. The emphasis here is on agile governance which means not just being able to change but to influence the way in which change is managed.

What informed the need to change? Why were managers forced into a position of change? And what were the best practices for change are three questions that stand out when looking at the managerial experience throughout the Four Industrial Revolutions. The answers to these questions reside within the parameters of the second of the core management competences that have been identified which could be articulated as *collaborates to create and share knowledge and information—'know why'.* During the First Industrial Revolution entrepreneurs, scientists, engineers and technicians used both explicit and tacit knowledge as the basis for transformation and complemented this by increasing explicit knowledge through codifying practice after learning on the job. A combination of semi-formal and informal ways of acquiring and using knowledge and information helped in promoting 'creativity, flexibility, and the ability to make incremental adjustments' that transformed technologies into inventions and innovations (Khan, 2018). Hence knowledge did not reside with any one individual and when the members of the Lunar Society in Birmingham, UK, during the eighteenth century met, their goal was to share and seek information that would lead to progress not only in scientific method but in value creation through good practice (converting tacit to explicit)—though their language may have been couched in different terms. The most effective managers have traditionally been ones who are not afraid to seek knowledge and information to improve their own and their organisation's effectiveness. Alfred P. Sloan junior became President

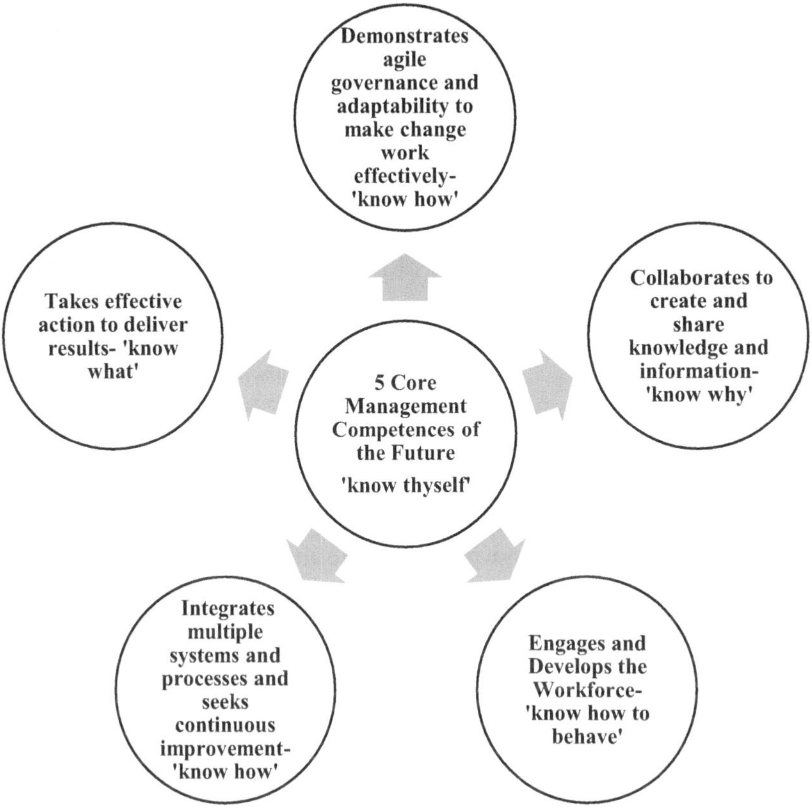

Fig. 6.1 Five core management competences

of General Motors in 1923 bringing the 'clear eyed approach of an engineer' to his job. In making and implementing policy he was mindful of the need to get both shareholders and senior managers onside—'while policy may originate anywhere, it must be appraised and approved by committees before being administered by individuals. In other words, General Motors has been a Group Management comprised of very competent individuals. And so I shall often say 'we' instead of 'I' and sometimes when I say 'I' I mean 'we' (Sloan, 1963). Now, whilst the process of committees may be anathema to the contemporary fast moving start up, and the mindset could be inward-looking, the sentiment of collaboration and inclusivity was not. The management competence of acquiring knowledge and information is a foundation on which other areas of competence can be built. Increasingly this will come about through collaboration within an organisation and collaboration without. Taiichi Ohno, architect of Toyota's Lean production systems perhaps summarises this collaboration when citing the need to work closely with engineers, 'you've got to remember that the purpose of automation is to raise profitability for the company, not to make things look pretty' (Interview with Taiichi Ohno, in Shimokwa & Fijumoto, 2009), an aphorism that accentuates the importance of knowledge sharing and collaboration to the management process. The trend from an industrial to a knowledge-based economy, means that wealth is created by developing and managing knowledge (Francioli & Albanese, 2017).

Each of the industrial revolutions has had technology as the harbinger of change, but each has had people as the initiators of change and the instruments of its delivery. Poor human resource management can damage competitive advantage by inhibiting the exploitation of existing competences or preventing the emergence of new ones (Lindgren et al., 2004; Flores et al., 2020). In Industry 4.0 the work force will be creative, resourceful and have interdisciplinary knowledge. How managers deal with workforce issues in this environment will therefore be important to success. *Engaging and developing the workforce* will therefore be core to the manager's role. There are some commonalities with earlier times. For example, Adam Smith believed that, in the right environment, an individual was 'continually exerting … to find the most advantageous employment for whatever capital' they could command (Smith, 1778). Something that would resonate in later periods. In early industrial organisations, however, the interpretation of how labour should be managed to create 'this most advantageous employment' was far from liberal—it was reported of John Marshall's flax mills in 1821 that if an overseer (line manager) was found talking to any person on the shop floor he was to be dismissed immediately. 'Everyone, manager, overseers, mechanics, oilers, spreaders, spinners and reelers, have their particular duty pointed out to them. If they transgress, they are instantly turned off as unfit for their situation' (Pollard, 1965; 216). Put in those terms, human resources were seen as expendable factors. Such a situation was common but not exclusive. As managerial pay increased so did the expectations placed on managers and out of this came the need for more effective practices and some formalisation of management principles.

Robert Owen was paid £1000 per annum in 1800, as was Joseph Dawson of Carron; Robert Stagg, general agent of the London Lead Company, £500 per annum. These were substantial salaries (the wage of a skilled spinner would be around £100 per annum) and many of those on the receiving end realised that their success would require more than brutal human resource practice. Hence for some managers their 'capital' in Adam Smith's terms, was based on their competence to manage a workforce to make and deliver products and services to a rapidly growing economy. One aspect of this was the systematising of management practice recognising that order, systems and cleanliness in the workplace and fairness of treatment of the workforce could lead to 'good effects on the habits of the people. Being obliged to be more regular in their attendance on their work, they became more orderly in their conduct' (Pollard, 1965; 302). During this time, workforce management in some organisations made the transition from applying ruthless discipline in a most uncaring manner to one more concerned with order and stability, both of which were essential for productivity in eighteenth- and nineteenth-century manufacturing operations. Looking back through the prism of history it is difficult not to regard some of the management practices in respect of the industrial workforce as horrendous. But this was very much an evolving story. The effectiveness of the human element of work output depended on that human element being able to function in clean and safe environments with recognition of individual needs. Whilst this was very much a formative idea, those managers who accepted it fared better than those who didn't over time. Maximising the output of the workforce could only come about by managers engaging (albeit in a different way with a different language than managers today) with them. The seeds of a core management competence that was workforce related were sown. They grew over time. Whilst theoretical considerations of whether Taylor's bottom-up work study approach to management was better than Fayol's top-down organisational one, was brought into reality once Henry Ford was faced with high labour turnover early in his factories' evolution. Such experiences demanded responses that are based on human intervention rather than technological ones. Some 250 years after the first, early steps towards more systematic management, technology giant Google regarded areas such as coaching, communicating and being productive, characteristics that would have been relevant in earlier periods; but also empowerment and 'not micromanaging' that would not (Thomson, 2015). So, managers have always had to ensure that the workforce under their area of responsibility delivered the requirements of the businesses in which they worked. How they did so changed from cajoling to controlling, to directing, to coaching and engaging, always with the same desired output. In this respect the core management competence to do so might be articulated as 'engages and develops the workforce—'know how to behave'. Beginning with clarity of purpose and contribution to that purpose—as exemplified by Mary Barra's interventions at General Motors, which ensured consistency in approach to the communication of performance, the result that her actions 'got white collar workers as well as factory staff to focus on business results and how their jobs contributed to them' (Colby, 2015) through to performance management in the contemporary way through coaching and developing. For one group 'Human Capital 4.0' was the nomenclature that could be attached to these new methods, and in their excellent summary of the characteristics of this competence, Flores et al. (2020) highlight soft and hard workforce competences; cognitive workforce competence; emotional intelligence workforce competence; and digital workforce competence, each of which will be discussed in later chapters. This resonates even more so after the trauma of the COVID-19 pandemic acted as an accelerant to remote working through virtual media and the consequence for managing in this new environment.

Having proven adaptability, agile governance capability, multiple sources of knowledge and information through collaboration and an understanding of how to engage a workforce, the foundations are laid for core management competences in the context of the advent of new technologies and the necessity for ensuring that maximum value is extracted from their installation. Output depends on ensuring that multiple characteristics run smoothly by interfacing with each other at each step of the process and are improved where circumstances allow. The processes adopted by many organisations as they negotiated the Four Industrial

Revolutions involved changes in key characteristics as new equipment was installed or new processes introduced. Furthermore, the processes were often complex and multi-faceted requiring significant management nous in ensuring that such characteristics were dealt with efficiently. The assumption is relevant whether upgrading manufacturing capability in the consumer goods industry in the early twentieth century or the aerospace industry of the twenty-first (Estrada et al., 2018; Smiley, 2020). The core management competence that represents this part of the role is 'integrates multiple systems and processes and seeks continuous improvement—'know how'. Contemporary accounts have referred to this as 'total innovation management' which is the reinvention and *management* of a value network that integrates strategy, technology, structure, process, culture and people at all levels of organisation to enhance the innovation competence of the organisation thereby creating value for stakeholders (Sazonova & Kolishchak, 2004). But earlier accounts also draw attention to the importance of this area. Robert Owen's letters concerning the Stanley Mills in Scotland in the early years of the nineteenth century emphasise the importance of this integration because of the 'multiple tasks—output, volume, quality and asset maintenance' required to deliver the output of the mills (Cooke, 1979). In this environment, a single task had knock on effects on others because of the interdependence of the new methods. Systems were both technological and human, and the integration of one with the other was a critical part of the management function. This competence was relevant in the iron forge of the eighteenth century in Britain, where a multitude of management activities needed coordination (as noted by Betty Beecroft its manager in 1780 [letters and diaries from the Kirkstall Forge, Butler, 1945]) to the Toyota factory in Japan during the 1960s. As Taiichi Ohno, one of the designers of the new management production systems, noted, 'we prefer multiprocess handling' (Interview with Taiichi Ohno, in Shimokwa & Fijumoto, 2009) and expected managers to fulfil their roles in this context and also to deal with continuous improvement in a planned and systematic way 'the quality commitment that they demonstrate in their work will spread naturally to their team members' to contemporary software production which relies on 'implementing process improvement methods to advance quality, productivity, and predictability of their development and maintenance efforts' (Al-Baik & Miller, 2019). Integration and improvement resonate as core management competences over time. Managerial know how in this process was instrumental to success.

The final core management competence for consideration concerns not input to the role of the manager but output from it and has been fundamental in which ever historical period they operated. Hence the manager *takes effective action to deliver results—the ability to convert strategy into actionable plans and outcomes—'know what'.* In conventional wisdom, successful managers adhere to establishing priorities, delivering their objectives in a targeted way (arising from years of performance management) managing their time and overcoming obstacles through the human competences of motivation and dealing with counterproductive behaviour (Wilson & Dobson, 2008). In previous eras achieving objectives as a manager tended to be less structured, though the objectives couldn't have been painted in starker terms and as stated by William Brown, a Dundee flax spinner during the 1820s, 'the first and great object to be aimed at by the Manager of East Mill is profit'. Whilst Sir Robert Peel, writing in 1816 believed in the clear direction of the manager towards the outputs of the business was an important step to the success of that business (Pollard, 1965). Henry Ford (1922) simplified management objectives with the working assumption that 'the quality of the article produced will be high and that the price will be low', actions to which would underpin every aspect of the objectives of the managers in his factories to deliver such results. Taiichi Ohno of Toyota wanted to make sure that the managers had clear objectives to make sure that 'the front end processes delivered consistently high quality work to the following processes', a role that was due to both systematisation of production and role clarity and empowerment of managers to intervene if these objectives weren't being delivered—so much so that 'we are prepared to accept idle machines … in exchange for using our human resources fully' (Interview with Taiichi Ohno, in Shimokwa & Fijumoto, 2009). Managers are bound by responsibility for accounting for their actions whereby such actions are set in the context of the business objectives of the organisations in which they work. To do so requires the 'interests of decision-makers in organisations should be aligned with the organisation's objectives through the design of (economic) structures of responsibility … to correlate with different contingencies, meaning that decision rights and economic accountability should be designed and changed in accordance with changes in these environmental conditions (contingencies) (Lennon, 2020). It has been argued that 'non-philosophers define business management self-evidently in terms of managerial power and mechanism of control' (Blok, 2019), and this is nowhere truer than in the competence of delivering the results of a business operation. However, the term 'mechanism of control' should not have a pejorative interpretation. Management as a mechanism of control in the contemporary organisation has different connotations to that of early industrial organisations. Control now is not by force but by persuasion. It doesn't relate to the control of the human resource but the inclusion and direction of that resource.

The locus of management is often at the point where the supply of unpredictability meets the demand for sureness or certainty—there is a 'basic need of humans to create a sense of order to help them manage their existence' (Watson, 1994). This basic need was a constant during the first Three Industrial Revolutions and has not diminished as the Fourth gathers momentum. Hence, core management competences are those that transcend any one historical time period. They consist of the knowledge, skills, attitudes and behaviours that managers display in order to deliver their objectives and roles effectively. They will require excellent judgement, decision-making ability and the ability to choose and employ talent; or relate to specific problems or issues (Partington et al, 2005; Cheng, 2014). For those at the most senior level, this will be a display in the context of strategy, policy or stewardship; for managers in operational or delivery roles these will be the translation of strategy into actions; for all this will require the engagement of a workforce in whatever outcomes are required—whether these be corporate objectives such as shareholder value or departmental objectives such as the delivery of a product or service to an end-user. The competences are relevant to the manager of a software development company or the manager of a goods shipping warehouse. As they stand, the core management competences outlined above are statements of intent.

References

Al-Baik, O., & Miller, J. (2019). Integrative Double Kaizen Loop (IDKL): Towards a Culture of Continuous Learning and Sustainable Improvements for Software Organizations. *IEEE Transactions on Software Engineering, 45*(12), 1189–1210.

Anthony, S. D. (2012). First Mover or Fast Follower, *Harvard Business Review*, https://hbr.org/2012/06/first-mover-or-fast-follower

Sir Richard Arkwright to Samuel Oldknow—written by J. Fletcher for Richard Arkwright. (Arkwright-Oldknow Papers (1783-1796), Columbia Rare Book and Manuscript Library, Columbia University in the City of New York)

Arlidge, J. (2020). *Project reboot*, The Sunday Times, May 24.

Blok, V. (2019). What Is (*Business) Management? Laying the Ground for a Philosophy of Management. Philosophy* of Management, 1.

Bui, A. T., Liao, Y., Nguyen, P. T., & Chang, C. F. (2019). Acquiring Top Management Team, Core Competence through Absorptive Capacity and Entrepreneurial Orientation. *Academy of Entrepreneurship Journal, 1*, 1a.

Butler, R. (1945). *The History of Kirkstall Forge*. The Ebor Press.

Cha, J., & Maytorena-Sanchez, E. (2019). Prioritising Project Management Competences Across the Software Project Life Cycle. *International Journal of Managing Projects in Business, 12*(4), 961–978.

Cheng, H. (2014). Analysis of the Three Core Competences the Enterprise Managers Should Improve. *Value Engineering, 26*, 182.

Chung, A. Q. H., Andreev, P., Benyoucef, M., Duane, A., & O'Reilly, P. (2017). Managing an Organisation's Social Media Presence: An Empirical Stages of Growth Model. *International Journal of Information Management, 37*(1, Part A), 1405–1417.

CIPD. (2020). *Competence and Competency Frameworks*, www.cipd.co.uk/knowledge/fundamentals/people/performance/competency-factsheet

Colby, L. (2015). *Road to Power*. John Wiley and Sons.

Collins, J. (2001). *Good to Great*. Random House.

Collins, J., & Porras, J. I. (2011). *Built to Last*. Harper Business.

Cooke, A. J. (1979). Robert Owen and the Stanley Mills 1802-1811. *Business History, 21*(1).

Cummings, S., Bridgman, T., Hassard, J., & Rowlinson, M. (2017). *A New History of Management*. Cambridge University Press. https://doi.org/10.1017/9781316481202

Deloitte. (2018). *Preparing Tomorrows Workforce for the Fourth Industrial Revolution*, https://www2.deloitte.com/content/dam/Deloitte/global/Documents/About-Deloitte/gx-preparing-tomorrow-workforce-for-4IR.pdf

Donkin, R. (2001). *Blood, Sweat and Tears*. Texere.

Estrada, G., Shunk, D. L., & Ju, F. (2018). Systematic Continuous Improvement Model for Variation Management of Key Characteristics Running with Low Capability. *International Journal of Production Research, 56*(6), 2370–2387.

Felkin, A. (1867). *History of the Machine Wrought Hosiery and Lace Manufacturers*, reprinted by David and Charles, Newton Abbot, UK 1967

Fitsilis, P., Tsoutsa, P., & Gerogiannis, V. (2018). Industry 4.0: Required Personnel Competences. *International Scientific Journal "Industry 4.0", 3*, 130–133.

Fitton, R. S. (1989). *The Arkwrights, Spinners of Fortune*. Manchester University press.

Flores, E., Xu, X., & Yuqian, L. (2020). Human Capital 4.0: A Workforce Competence Typology for Industry 4.0. *Journal of Manufacturing Technology Management, 31*(4), 687–703.

Ford, H. (1922). *My Life and Work*. Doubleday, Page and Company.

Francioli, F., & Albanese, M. (2017). The Evaluation of Core Competencies in Networks: The Network Competence Report. *Journal of Intellectual Capital, 18*(1), 189–216.

Gates, B. (1999). *Business @ The Speed of Thought*. Penguin Books.

Hamalainen, R. P., Saarinen, E., & Tormanen, J. (2018). Systems Intelligence: A Core Competence for Next-Generation Engineers? *IEEE International Conference on Teaching, Assessment, and Learning for Engineering (TALE)* 641–644.

Hanlon, G. (2016). *The Dark Side of Management*. Routledge.

HBR. (2019). How Leaders are Navigating the Fourth Industrial Revolution, *Harvard Business Review*, Sponsor content from Deloitte, https://hbr.org/sponsored/2019/03/how-leaders-are-navigating-the-fourth-industrial-revolution

Hout, T., & Michael, D. (2014). A Chinese approach to Management, *Harvard Business Review*, September

International Thrift Institute. (1937). *Minutes of the Third International Thrift Congress, Paris, 1935* published by the International Thrift Institute, Milan 1937

Kak, A. (2011). People and Core Competence in Relation with Organizational Excellence. *Values-Based Management, 1*(2), 107–118.

Khan, B. Z. (2018). Human Capital, Knowledge, and Economic Development: Evidence from the British Industrial Revolution, 1750-1930. *Cliometrica, 12*(2), 313–341.

Le Deist, F. D., & Winterton, J. (2005). What Is Competence? *Human Resource Development International, 8*(1), 27–46.

Lennon, N. J. (2020). Responsibility Accounting, Managerial Action and "a counter-ability": Relating the Physical and Virtual Spaces of Decision-making. *Scandinavian Journal of Management, 35*(3), 1.

Leslie, J. B., Dalton, M., Ernst, C., & Deal, J. (2002). *Managerial Effectiveness in a Global Context*. Centre for Creative Leadership.

Li, H., & Li, J. (2009). Top Management Team Conflict and Entrepreneurial Strategy Making in China. *Asia Pacific Journal of Management, 26*, 263–283.

Liker, J. K. (2004). *The Toyota Way*. McGraw Hill.

Lindgren, R., Henfridsson, O., & Schultze, U. (2004). Design Principles for Competence Management Systems: A Synthesis of an Action Research Study. *MIS Quarterly, 28*(3), 435.

Mantoux, P. (1928). *The Industrial Revolution in England*

Mayhew, H. (1865). *The Shops and Companies of London and the Trades and Manufactories of Great Britain*. Strand Printing.

McDonald, P. (2011). It's Time for Management Version 2.0: Six Forces Redefining the Future of Modern Management. *Futures, 43*(8), 797–808.

McGregor, D. (1960). *The Human Side of Enterprise*, McGraw Hill, 2006 Edition

Mokyr, J. (2009). *The Enlightened Economy*. Penguin Books.

Mollan, S. (2019). Management's Troubling Past and Management Studies' Troubling Present: Reflections on A New History of Management and The Dark Side of Management: A Secret History of Management Theory. *Academy of Management Learning & Education, 18*(3), 517–521.

Morgan, J. (2019). Will We Work in Twenty-first Century Capitalism? A Critique of the Fourth Industrial Revolution Literature. *Economy and Society, 48*(3), 371–398.

Morris, B. (2017). *The 'human factor' in business*, https://www.cipd.co.uk/news-views/changing-work-views/future-work/thought-pieces/human-factor-business

Ohno, K. (2006). *The Economic Development of Japan*. GRIPS Development Forum.

Partington, D., Pellegrinelli, S., & Young, M. (2005). Attributes and levels of programme management competence: an interpretive study. *International Journal of Project Management, 23*(2), 87–95.

Peccarelli, B. (2020). *Bend, Don't Break: How to Thrive in the Fourth Industrial Revolution*, World Economic Forum, https://www.weforum.org/agenda/2020/01/the-fourth-industrial-revolution-is-changing-all-the-rules/

Philbeck, T., & Davis, N. (2019). The Fourth Industrial Revolution : Shaping a New Era. *Journal of International Affairs, 72*(1), 17.

Poba-Nzaou, P., Lemieux, N., Beaupré, D., & Uwizeyemungu, S. (2016). Critical Challenges Associated with the Adoption of Social Media: A Delphi of a Panel of Canadian Human Resources Managers. *Journal of Business Research, 69*(10), 4011–4019.

Prahalad, C. K., & Hamel, G. (1990). *The Core Competence of the Corporation*, Harvard Business Review

Pollard, S. (1965). *The Genesis of Modern Management*. Penguin Books.

Porter, M. E. (1990). *The Competitive Advantage of Nations*. The Macmillan Press.

Ruparel, N., Dhir, A., Tandon, A., Kaur, P., & Islam, J. U. (2020). The Influence of Online Professional Social Media in Human Resource Management: A Systematic Literature Review. *Technology in Society, 63*, 1.

Sandberg, S. (2013). *Lean In, Women, Work and the Will to Lead*, W.H. Allen, Random House Group

Sazonova, G. A., & Kolishchak, A. N. (2004). Management of Technological Changes and Innovations as a Core Competence, *IEEE 2004 International Engineering Management Conference (Innovation and Entrepreneurship for Sustainable Development*)

Schwab, K. (2016). *The Fourth Industrial Revolution: what it means, how to respond*, World Economic Forum, https://www.weforum.org/agenda/2016/01/the-fourth-industrial-revolution-what-it-means-and-how-to-respond/

Shimokwa, K., & Fijumoto, T. (2009). *The Birth of Lean*. The Lean Enterprise Institute.

Sloan, A. P. (1963). *My Years with General Motors, USA*

Smiley, G. (2020). *The US Economy in the 1920s* , EH.net, https://eh.net/encyclopedia/the-u-s-economy-in-the-1920s/

Smith, A. (1776). *The Wealth of Nations, Penguin Books Edition, 1986*. England.

Smith, A. (1778). *An Inquiry into the Nature and Causes of the Wealth of Nations, Volume 2*. Strahan.

Sony, M., & Naik, S. (2020). Industry 4.0 Integration with Socio-technical Systems Theory: A Systematic Review and Proposed Theoretical Model. *Technology in Society, 61*, 1.

Sparrow, P. R. (2000). Strategic Management in a World Turned Upside Down: The Role of Cognition, Intuition and Emotional Intelligence in Flood. In T. Dromgoole, S. J. Carroll, & L. Gorman (Eds.), *Managing Strategy Implementation*. Blackwell.

Stadler, C. (2011). *Enduring Success*. Stanford University Press.

Stepanenko, V., & Kashevnik, A. (2017). Competence Management Systems in Organisations: A Literature Review. *Proceedings of the XXth Conference of Open Innovations Association FRUCT, 776*(20), 427–433.

Thomson, S. (2015). *8 skills Google looks for in its managers*—World Economic Forum. https://assets.weforum.org/wp-content/uploads/2015/11/Google-managers.png1.

Tobey, R. C. (1997). *Technology as Freedom the New Deal and the Electrical Modernization of the American Home*. University of California Press.

van Driel, H., de Goey, F., & van Gerwen, J. (2007). Testing the Chandler Thesis: Comparing Middle Management and Administrative Intensity in Dutch and US Industries, 1900–1950. *Business History, 49*(4), 439–463.

Watson, T. J. (1994). *In Search of Management*. Thomson Business Press.

Wilson, S. B., & Dobson, M. S. (2008). *Goal Setting*. American Management Association.

World Economic Forum. (2016). *The Future of Jobs*, http://reports.weforum.org/future-of-jobs-2016/preface/

World Economic Forum. (2017). *Jobs and the Fourth Industrial Revolution*, https://www.weforum.org/about/jobs-and-the-fourth-industrial-revolution

Yang, C.-C. (2015). The Integrated Model of Core Competence and Core Capability. *Total Quality Management & Business Excellence, 26*(1/2), 173–189.

Yin, X., Chen, J., & Zhao, C. (2020). Double Screen Innovation: Building Sustainable Core Competence through Knowledge Management. *Sustainability, 11*(16), 1.

7

Management Competence for the Fourth Industrial Revolution—Demonstrates Agile Governance and Adaptability to Make Change Work Effectively

'Willingness to Change Is a Strength'

It was a perfect storm. The unknowable collided head on with the unthinkable. Organisations that had prepared for the rough seas of disruption had no idea they were facing a pandession (McWilliams, 2020) as COVID-19 tore through the world's economies and societies. It happened during already significant social and demographic change as portrayed in Gratton and Scott's *The 100 Year Life* (Gratton & Scott, 2016). Their comments seem not only prescient but prophetic: 'we are in the midst of an extraordinary transition that few of us are prepared for.' And yet, in the absence of a blueprint for how to deal with this confluence of forces, many organisations proved agile and resilient. The early part of the 2020s demonstrated that the ability to build and maintain a sustainable business depended on the ability to adapt to external disruptions or discontinuity. New business models, using new technologies and new ways of working, emerged much faster than anticipated. Managers, once again at the heart of change, rose to the many challenges with entrepreneurial spirit and skills in agile governance. A combination of factors—some of

P. Turner, *The Making of the Modern Manager*,
https://doi.org/10.1007/978-3-030-81062-7_7

which were utterly tragic—inadvertently brought forward the changes that were envisaged by the Fourth Industrial Revolution.

But this was not the first time that multiple, dramatic forces had created uncertainty for business organisations. During the First Industrial Revolution, for example, centred mainly in Europe, the challenge was how to deal with the transition from artisan or small workshop production methods, which had been in place for hundreds of years to those of the factories that sprang up around fast-flowing rivers used to power new machines, and then with the advent of steam power became concentrated in large urban environments. It meant recruiting and training a whole new workforce to operate new technologies in new types of organisation. It also meant dealing with the pandemics and health crises that blighted industrial towns and devastated the communities that provided the workers for these institutions. Change was of historic proportions and affected not only production methods but workforce practices that became widespread across international borders. Successful organisations were ones that recognised the opportunity that was afoot and responded accordingly. A similar pattern of challenge and response occurred during the Second Industrial Revolution from the end of the nineteenth century, which saw an acceleration of change with the introduction of mass production, powered by electricity and a flow of goods and services for a booming consumer market from new, larger factories. Scientific management techniques accompanied large-scale industrial development primarily across the North American continent—not only in the automobile industry, but in electric motors, aluminium, synthetic materials and a proliferation of consumer goods. By the late 1920s the United States produced about half of the world's industrial goods and was the leading exporter. More than anything, the United States' economic prowess challenged the global power balance (Logevall, 2020). But technology was not the only dynamic. Wars, a global pandemic, social change and the migration of people to work in the new industrial establishments and the cities that surrounded them contributed to a transformative environment. American organisations responded with dynamism and a fierce determination to succeed. The Third Industrial Revolution, during the twentieth century, with its epicentre in Asia beginning with Japan, through the Tiger and Dragon economies and then in China and India, incorporated new technologies from the microchip through to robotics, new business processes, new production methods and the globalisation of supply chains, value chains and end-user markets. Total quality management and a culture, 'set from the top, of working toward common goals in a spirit of mutual respect' set Asian companies apart in their journey to global success. Now, a boundaryless Fourth Industrial Revolution is being hailed as the most transformative of all with the Internet of Things and AI facilitating unprecedented combinations of technologies in both creation and manufacture of goods and services. The experience of managers over time can be particularly important for understanding the whys and 'hows' of change and indeed, 'discussing change requires a historical perspective as change by definition only can be seen by comparing to different points in time' (Brunninge, 2009).

In each of these periods, organisations were forced to adapt their structures, systems and processes to achieve competitive advantage (Kruchten, 2013; Luna et al., 2013; Luna et al., 2020; Maisiri et al., 2019). And throughout, the ability of the organisations' managers to deal with such disruption was a critical factor to success. The solution could be through clear systems and structures (the organisation chart) to prevent relationships becoming entangled; (Steiner & Root, 1959; Tsaklanganos, 1973) or through less formal and rigid organisation structure and managerial agility. The manager's orientation or approach to governance was and will be an important antecedent of both strategic renewal and corporate longevity. Exploiting the opportunities of Industry 4.0. will require a rapid and flexible response to changes in markets and technologies, using both trans-organisation and trans-industry cooperation. These considerations accentuate the core management competence of 'demonstrates agile governance and adaptability to make change work effectively' (Kwee et al., 2011; Teece et al., 2016; Raman & Bharadwaj, 2017; Tatsuo Sato, 2019; Yin et al., 2018; Belinski et al., 2020; Penttilä et al., 2020). The competence constitutes the know-how of management and features in the overall core management competence framework shown in Fig. 7.1. Agile governance can be both strategic—relating to long-term objectives and direction—or operational relating to resource allocation and decision-making 'authority'. It can be a framework which includes both narrow and broad change management and a mindset—the willingness and

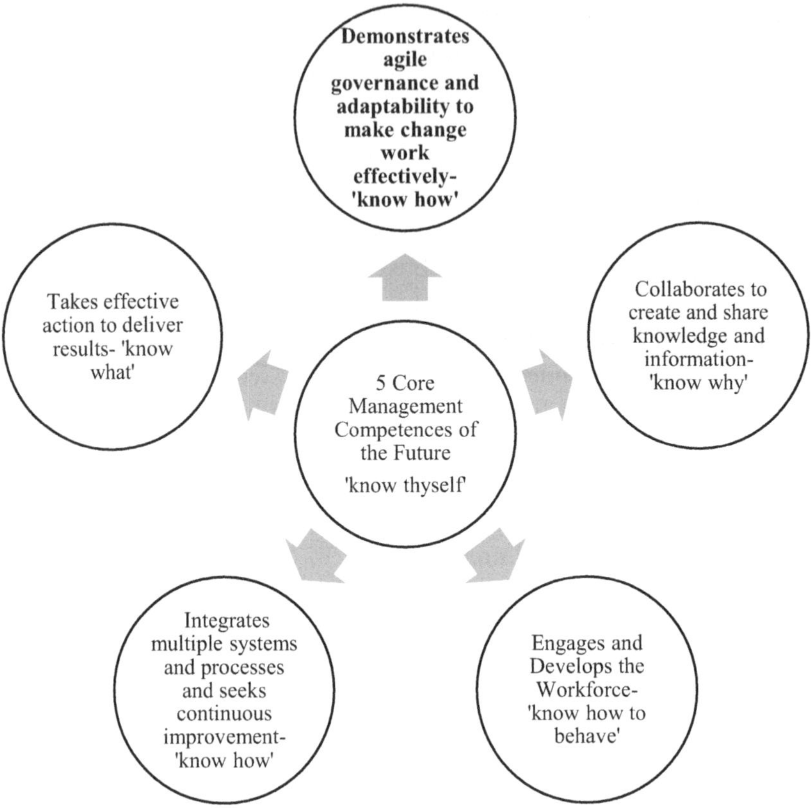

Fig. 7.1 Core management competences

capability to change. Whereas in more traditional hierarchical structures, change may have been a discrete activity relevant to a department or business unit, the ubiquity and reach of Industry 4.0. technology applications spread both the opportunity and challenge. Agile governance may therefore be defined as:

> the ability to respond to change in a dynamic and flexible way; aligning change methodologies to the needs of the unit; whilst identifying the ramifications of change for areas outside of the unit and influencing or shaping the organisation and its processes accordingly.

Business objectives are the drivers; change management is the process and agile governance is the enabler.

The competence refers to initiating change through invention, adapting the outputs of change through innovation and then improving these outputs on a continuous basis. If core management competences were articulated in each of the periods in question, the word 'change' would be prevalent. But, and to prevent such a term becoming a clichéd catch-all, it had different connotations and methods in each of the contexts of the Four Industrial Revolutions. Sometimes its cause could be anticipated, allowing change to be planned and systematic and cascaded through hierarchical organisation structures. Sometimes it came about because of disruption, forced or unplanned and the response was the use of more ad hoc change management techniques. And sometimes it was brought about by discontinuity, making existing business models redundant. The manager was likely to be at the heart of each of these scenarios and bearing responsibility for their outcomes. In the contemporary fast paced and dynamic environment, the modern manager will not only display the core competence of adapting to and managing change but also be required to display agile governance in how they go about it. The cascading of change through *n*-step processes is a starting not an end position.

'*N*-Step' Concept of Change Management

Organisational changes occur in response to disruption or opportunity in that organisation's external environment—such as macro-economic factors, evolving consumer or end-user demands, positive new market opportunities, threats from competitor activity or the incidence of unforeseen events—for example, pandemics. Additionally, change could be necessitated by internal dynamics such as the introduction of new technology, new operating systems, new operating processes or new management personnel and ideas. In all cases the objective of adaptation is to ensure that the organisation becomes fit for purpose to deal with any opportunity or threat because 'the organisation itself must change in order to produce the external change represented by innovation—the Model T wasn't achievable without the assembly line' (Gobble, 2013).

Hence, the importance of effective change management has grown over time, with the many challenges being addressed by models of theory and practice, mostly based on rational orthodoxy with '*n*-step' methodologies. Amongst the most prominent of the rational approaches is that articulated by Kurt Lewin (1947), who, writing at the cusp of the Third Industrial Revolution, believed that 'the practical task of social management' required insight into the desire for and resistance to change and therefore an understanding of the social forces for change. In approaching a key aspect of organisational dynamics in this way, he was able to set the benchmark for subsequent models. His view was that change was delivered to best effect by three steps which he termed as unfreezing, moving and freezing of group standards. Lewin postulated that individual behaviour was a function of the group environment and therefore to bring about change depended on group acceptance of change. Subsequent methodologies advocated a planned and systematic approach often involving a number of critical, sequential and interlinked steps (Lewin, 1947; 34-36; Burnes, 1996; Rosenbaum et al., 2018; Chinoperekweyi, 2020). Other processes included those by Nadler and Tushman (1980), with diagnosis, preparation, implementing change, consolidating change and sustaining change as the key steps; Bullock and Batten (1985), with an integrated four phased model embracing change phases and change processes; and Prosci's ADKAR model, which proposed that the process should include awareness, the desire to change, knowledge of how to change, the ability to implement change and reinforcement or how to sustain the change once effected (Hiatt, 2006). An *n*-step approach was proposed by Kotter whose model was based firstly on creating an urgency for change; secondly to form a powerful coalition; thirdly to create a vision and then to communicate that vision. Once these steps are in place then the process of implementation will follow by removing the obstacles to change and creating short-term wins as a result. The final two steps are to build on the change and then to anchor this into a new corporate culture (Kotter, 1996). And McKinsey consultants Tom Peters and Robert Waterman put forward a systematic process with the McKinsey 7S model which involved paying attention to and formulating plans for Strategy, Systems, Structure, Staff, Style, Skills and Shared Values, which in turn became one of the most utilised approaches to managing change.

Additional research has shown that the factors that impact on success included the will to change, intrinsic motivation and ability, capability and capacity as well as a 'mandate to change, governance, and the courage to change'. Most recently social media applications have proved to be beneficial during change processes—particularly through enhancing effective communication, increasing the level of trust and participation in decision-making and decreasing the level of resistance to change. Also, it can enhance the level of support for change acceptance in the workplace and 'foster informal, constructive and relevant discussion' (Năstase et al., 2012; Bierwolf & Frijns, 2019; Naeem, 2020). The subject of change management is rich in research, models, methodologies and advice at organisational level and the proliferation for such models reflects the demand for approaches that are translatable to the practice environment. Indeed, change management became a core service offering of consultancies around the world. Change at organisational level goes hand in hand with and is dependent on change at individual level because 'individual change is at the heart of everything that is achieved in organisations' (Lewin, 1947; Cameron & Green, 2004). Two interlinked factors are important. The first is the capacity for an individual member of the workforce to change their own behaviour or practice to align themselves with whatever changes have taken place at group, department, unit or organisational level. And secondly there is the capability of the manager in the implementation of organisational change. The questions to be addressed are what is the nature of individual response to organisational change and what can be done to facilitate this in a positive way? Managers are in a position to address both.

Individual Change and the Role of the Manager

The most notable contribution to understanding the dynamics of individual change was the work of the Swiss American psychiatrist Elizabeth Kubler-Ross (1969), which was adapted from the clinical setting to that of the world of business. The 'Kubler Ross change curve' or adaptations of it have become ubiquitous both as a way of explaining emotions and ways of dealing with them; 'there is a clear similarity between these stages and the stages individuals experience when dealing with organisational change' (McGuire et al., 2007). The original work was intended to challenge the 'authoritarian decorum and puritanism' of the day in its clinical setting but also the prevailing assumptions and expectations about change in a wider social and business setting. 'We cannot distinguish between a wish and a deed' (Kubler-Ross, 1969; 3) helped to inform the very practical necessity for individual recognition of the impact of change and that doing so would involve a model involving five stages—these being denial, anger, bargaining, depression and acceptance. But, accepting the role of group dynamics on individual behaviour, the ideal for individual change would be in a wider context of group change which in itself resides in an even wider context of organisational change. The process advocates aligning organisational and group or individual objectives; by consulting and engaging individuals and their peers in change processes alongside clarity of objectives, whilst setting milestones in its achievements and a preparedness to adapt once the practicalities become evident. The alignment of all organisational stakeholders with interlinked and interdependent objectives is a desired outcome for all.

The second aspect of change concerns the capability of the manager in its design and delivery. Indeed because of complexity and uncertainty this was seen as a particular managerial problem because it was assumed that change would be resisted, meaning that the human element would have to be managed as carefully as technical or organisational structural aspects. Amongst the factors that would get in the way were too much complacency and not enough urgency, failing to create a powerful coalition of those who were committed and could steer the change through. This assumption—that change would be difficult to implement—brought with it a range of possible solutions that the manager could implement from clear definition of what change entailed and its potential benefits, a strong commitment to consultation and communication with plenty of feedback loops as the change progressed, aligning with the values and ideals of those affected with the aim of reaching a consensual group decision. In response, factors such as a clear strategic vision, top management commitment and backing up the change with modifications to structure, human resource systems, information and control systems were considered as important (Huczynski & Buchanan, 1991; 537; Burnes, 1996; Kotter, 1996). The management of change became one of the most highlighted management competences during the period of the Third Industrial Revolution with the emphasis on 'responsiveness, adaptability and flexibility' which led to a surge in literature on change management and its techniques—with a growing acknowledgement of democratic and humanistic values (Bennis, 1969, 50; Huczynski & Buchanan, 1991). These considerations concluded that change management in organisations was most effective when it happened in a holistic way and took account of those factors that were intrinsic to change (*n*-step models) as well as those extrinsic—the context.

There is an abundance of explicit knowledge and information about change management on which to draw—academic publications, management practice guidelines and consultancy models and for some time the change management competence has featured high on the list of desirable attributes. And yet the success rate for change management programmes appears to remain low (Gibbons, 2015). Amongst the usual suspects for failure are a lack of commitment, poor project management, lack of employee engagement or a lack of skills. However, there is a further area that is particularly relevant in the context of Industry 4.0. This is the argument that structured, planned and systematic implementation processes as part of change management—such as those outlined above—can be counterproductive. The argument goes that 'rather than treat implementation as a complex and ongoing series of choices and activities that unfold in unexpected ways, some believe they can control a change effort by simply following a protocol and 'correcting the known difficulties'. This assumes that the difference between effective and ineffective change management is whether people comply or do not comply with the expectations of a given process (Cohen, 2019). The implications of this are that the core management competence associated with change in future will include the ability to manage step processes efficiently. The pace, frequency and unpredictability of change, the absence of hierarchical organisational structures within which the change may take place, the networked, collaborative nature of knowledge management and the sheer diversity of the members of the workforce with different expectations will be important influencers on how change takes place. In future therefore it may be necessary to adapt both the shape of change and the process of change. It is at this point that change management and agile governance converge into a core management competence.

Business Objectives Are the Drivers, Change Management Is the Process and Agile Governance Is the Enabler

As markets become increasingly volatile and heterogeneous because of constantly evolving customer expectations and needs—such as customised products on demand—then an organisation's governance, reflected in both its structure and management, may need to change to align to smarter production or output systems. Relating strategy to supply chain management and executing both effectively underpins fast moving retailers such as H&M, ZARA or UNI QLO and are a significant factor in their success. Trends such as the mass customisation of products and services are based on the 'dynamic adaptation of the processes that produce them. Effectively dealing with external events in business operation, such as fast market developments and unanticipated technology adoption, implies being able to deviate from previously set execution plans' (Huang, 2010; Hecklau et al., 2016; Grefen et al., 2018). The apparent absence of an economic or managerial blueprint for change that is fit for the current circumstances means that whilst some existing approaches to change management will continue to be relevant as the implications of Industry 4.0 unfolds, the scale and scope of change will require additional perspectives on the part of the organisation and its managers. And so, the 'ability to integrate, build, and reconfigure internal and external competencies to address rapidly changing environments' will impact on every aspect of business organisation with new levels of management competence if they are to be achieved. The causes of change are complex, multi-faceted and multi-dimensional and so the responses to change will therefore need to be agile taking account of both culture and process (Fountaine et al., 2019; Luna et al., 2020). In the first place, organisations will progressively move from an environment of siloed, fixed location work to one of interdisciplinary, inter-organisational collaboration, often virtual always transparent. Second the managerial approach will move from 'experience-based, leader-driven decision-making' to one that is more dependent on consultation on the one hand and evidence on the other; and third, organisations will move from being 'rigid and risk-averse to agile, experimental, and adaptable'. Managerial competence will be critical to each of these three requirements. That of agile governance particularly so. In this respect, change will be driven by not only processes, but organisational structure, organisational characteristics and an understanding of the organisation's readiness to leverage new technologies (Cohen, 2019; Cimini et al., 2020). Agile governance means adapting the organisation to the change as well as adapting the change to the organisation. It is both a framework for delivering an organisation's business (whereby authority is delegated through organisational levels or across organisational matrices and networks) and a mindset or culture that prevails in which managers are confident and empowered to make decisions in response to opportunity or threat.

At a strategic level, the concept of governance relates to the process of corporate decision-making for strategic planning and alignment—its strategy and policy—and controls to establish the strategic plan through the allocation of resources. At managerial level governance means the ability and authority to react to changes in the environment, empowerment to coordinate actions and empowerment to ensure that the organisation adapts to the implications of this change—whether this is structural or relating to resource allocation. For it to be effective, agile governance occurs when there is a level of awareness and practice that allows managers and teams to respond with dynamic capabilities. The manager facilitates awareness of the need to sense, adapt and respond to change in a coordinated and sustainable way. Competences on the part of managers will be simultaneously polyvalent and specialised; where polyvalence is the ability to perform different tasks depending on the organisation's needs and specialisation is based on knowledge that is unique to a particular area or function. This rests on an organisation developing 'a stimulating and compromise-generating environment, fostering a systemic and result-oriented team to validate the company's mission and vision of the future' (Lopes et al., 2016; Bui et al., 2019; Cimini et al., 2020; Luna et al., 2020). In practice this means that managers are able to influence the organisation as the change progresses and can take account of circumstances specific to that change regardless of whether such circumstances were factored into the step change model. 'Rather than expect the organisation and staff to conform to the model's protocol, the change agent acclimates to the twists and turns of managing change without losing sight of the desired endpoint.' In this context, managers should be versatile, flexible and 'dexterous with an array of tools and models in the event the change effort runs into problems or breakdowns'. The creation of flexible and reconfigurable organisational systems will require an agility on the part of the manager that goes beyond *n*-step processes. So, the challenge for managers will be to capitalise on the many opportunities that will be presented during Industry 4.0 dynamics by converting enabling technologies, capabilities of human resource, levels of capital allocation, organisational structure and culture into advantage. It 'creates a new level of interaction between actors and resources' (Cohen, 2019; Li et al., 2019; Madsen, 2020) and how to achieve this will require a focus on the knowledge, skills, attitudes and behaviours that constitute the core management competence of 'demonstrates agile governance and adaptability to make change work effectively'. As the organisation becomes a single entity at the virtual level with commonality of organisational culture the way it adapts and survives is by 'combining real and virtual global information and IT management knowledge' into a unified whole with the agility and flexibility to respond to change' (Liboni et al., 2019). In essence this is agility in the management of change at the interfaces between cyber-physical and socio-technical systems.

Knowledge and Skills for the Core Management Competence of 'Demonstrates Agile Governance and Adaptability to Make Change Work Effectively'

If the future belongs to people endowed with knowledge, then the future of management depends on managers who are able to use that knowledge to its maximum effect. It is based not only on explicit knowledge (that which is available to everyone), but on tacit knowledge (that which is highly personal and hard to formalise). Whilst explicit knowledge can be processed by computer, tacit knowledge is far harder to verbalise, systematise or communicate. But it is in the very act of so doing that the manager in Industry 4.0 will help to turn the organisation from 'a machine into a living organism…sharing an understanding of what the company stands for, where it is going what kind of world it wants to live in' (Nonaka & Takeuchi, 1995, 9; Nonaka et al., 1996). How to make that world a reality is the outcome and being agile in the process is the method. Hence change management is part of a 'fundamental field' or the 'imperative resource which causes the firm to create the drivers of change' (Yang, 2015). Agile governance will be one manifestation of this craft as organisations respond to external forces; a craft which rests on knowledge creation, knowledge retention, knowledge transfer and knowledge application. So, what type of knowledge and what level of skills will constitute the core management competence that is addressed by this point. The following are some of the constituent parts:

- Knowledge, its acquisition, its dissemination and its application are fundamental to the competence of agile governance and change. To managers in the era of Industry 4.0 this means knowledge of what the organisation stands for and where it wants to go; knowledge of technology and how it will help to deliver these aspirations, knowledge of markets or environments in which their organisations operate, the external forces that might precipitate change (political, economic, social and demographic and legislative change) and knowledge of the effect on people and organisational dynamics as a result of the change. A combination of management insight and technology understanding create 'professional credibility' which will be a source of legitimacy to undertake the complex task of change management. The extent of this knowledge will inform the first aspect of agile governance which is *defines and prioritises what is crucial to do* (Luna et al., 2020). It will differentiate between important and essential; between the nice to and must do. On the one hand it will be concerned with ensuring that the continuity of a unit's operations is maintained, whether this is a flow line in manufacturing or a link in the software development process or a node in the supply chain. The second is concerned with making priority decisions in the interests of the wider organisation; a point of view supported by a recent *Accenture* report (2020), which found that 'champion' companies prioritised the work that generated value for the broader organisation as well as stimulating collaboration between functions. Decisions will come about by knowledge of the environment, the competitive position of the organisation in that environment, the specific nature of the change and its probable impact and the strength of the organisation in dealing with it. Defining and prioritising will result in the manager directing time and resource to challenges or opportunities and ensuring that their own efforts are aligned with these. This is the agility in the allocation of personal resources and agility in the allocation of the organisation's resources.

- But agility doesn't mean diversion and so associated with this aspect of competence is *maintains course and manoeuvrability*. The ability to 'embed rapid and nimble decision-making into company cultures' whilst maintaining the course of the organisation to its objectives is an important characteristic of core management competence. It is being able to establish a focus on what needs to be done over the medium-to-long term whilst simultaneously undertaking change management (Cohen, 2019; Luna et al., 2020; Renjen, 2020). The achievement of such goals will be based on the application of well-grounded judgement in decision-making—'human decision-making will become more complex in the future workplace.' While machines and data can process information and provide insights that would be impossible for people, ultimately, a manager will need to make the decision against its broader implications. 'As technology takes away more menial and mundane tasks, it will leave humans to do more higher-level decision-making' (Marr, 2019). The manager will be clear in the outcomes and agree targets to achieve them, will have good judgement on any issues and choices and will capitalise on opportunities where they are identified. Paying attention to detail will highlight any possible variations to 'the course' and setting realistic objectives in the light of these will ensure that the direction towards the goal is maintained. There is a polyvalence about agile governance in management where different demands require multiple, sometimes contradictory responses—such as instigate change whilst at the same time maintaining course; promote flexibility without diverting from the objective. And to complicate things further, managers will have to demonstrate proficiency across disciplines which leads to the third aspect of competence.

- Hence, in future, change will span managerial and technological logics; require decisions that are relevant to people and technological systems and will require judgement to balance the demands of both. This doesn't mean that the manager is expert in technology and systems but sufficiently knowledgeable to understand their impact in the wider organisational context. In the same way as in the clinical profession, a 'purely mechanical, rational and predictable approach…is impracticable because the pluralistic nature of organisations' which demands 'organisational knowledge, professional legitimacy and an abundance of social capital' (Turner, 2018). Professional legitimacy emanates from knowledge which will form the basis of a further aspect of the competence of agile governance—*aligns the technological domain with the organisation's objectives.* The manager has sufficient knowledge of both the technology and the organisation to make effective decisions relating to both as independent entities and both as interrelated entities. Such knowledge will facilitate effective task-oriented behaviours to improve business or operational processes; change-oriented behaviours as a response to external forces and relations-oriented behaviours to deal with the engagement and direction of people (Yukl, 2010). The features of this competence are an understanding of technologies and the ability to adapt to the needs of technological change or the opportunities presented by technological change.
- The manager will learn from opportunities that are inherent in change but at the same time will want to ensure that resources are allocated to achieve objectives within given timescales. An aspect of this core management competence will be *implements* n*-step process change management in complex environments.* For some this might be regarded as a 'threshold' competence, that is, generic knowledge or skill which is essential for all managers' (Boyatzis, 1982). Achieving objectives is the priority; how to do so will be through change processes with knowledge of the business model and organisational dynamics essential in this mix. Where the organisation is built on decentralisation, flat hier-

archy, structural openness, high flexibility, empowerment, low formalisation and collaboration, the change process will be of a particular type; however, a swarm organisation, in which every level will be characterised by 'structural openness' and high flexibility' (Cimini et al., 2020) might be another—hierarchy, matrix and team-based structures may also have different levels of receptivity to change. In all cases a manager who applies agile governance will be able to adapt processes to a specific organisational context-shaping change—but will also be able to influence the organisational structure-shaping organisation. The features of this competence are an understanding of change processes, an ability to communicate elements of change and the ability to engage the workforce and the wider stakeholder base in the process of change. The manager will seek to establish priorities and their associated tasks or schedules in line with the anticipated change.

- Accompanying any process will be 'methodological' aspect of the competence, which is *handles situations and problems through conflict solving, creativity and decision-making. Workplace conflict* is an almost inevitable consequence of change. It can be caused by the opposition of needs, values and interests; between formal authority and power and those individuals and groups affected by change; about resource allocation, the nature of work or 'boundary' disagreements between individuals. There are also subtler forms of *conflict* which might be 'rivalries, jealousies, personality clashes, role definitions, and struggles for power and favour' (Karthikeyan & Thomas, 2017). On the one hand the solution will be by a rational process of problem solving often built into *n*-step change processes, but on the other, an agile form of conflict resolution will be based on the ability of the manager to encourage and explore issues and alternatives. Analytical (critical) thinking will satisfy the former because a manager with critical thinking skills can suggest innovative solutions and ideas, solve complex problems using reasoning and logic and evaluate arguments…after observing, someone who is a strong analytical thinker will rely on logical reasoning rather than emotion, collect the pros/cons of a situation and be open-minded to the best possible solution. People with strong analytic thinking will be needed to navigate 'the human/machine division of labour'. Agile governance can be used to deal with the latter.

Deciding and initiating action and taking responsibility for those actions to ensure that the process is not impeded by prevarication will be consistent to both (Marr, 2019; Cimini et al., 2020; Prifti et al., 2017). The features of this competence are problem solving skills, resilience and the ability to 'bounce back' when problems occur.

- In some cases, the need for change may be confined to a particular unit or department (such as new product development or manufacturing process) but in others they may have organisation-wide implications (such as the introduction of ERP systems). Hence managers may be called upon to manage change in three types of cross-boundary working—intra-organisational, inter-organisational and trans-organisational, often with challenges during the transition from one type of working to another. These three types of cross-boundary working interact with the traditional organisation, with the result of multiple layers of work organisation in a single context (Kinnie & Swart, 2019). Hence, *influences change across elements of the whole system regardless of system boundaries* is important as agile governance in practice. A requirement for conceptual ability and conceptual thinking as a way of seeing the whole system is an antecedent for the manager being able to influence beyond their own shores, to have the ability to demonstrate agile governance as a way of dealing with cross organisation change. Working in interdisciplinary environments and an awareness of intercultural needs and objectives will be elements of agile governance. The features of this competence are influencing skills, engagement skills and the ability to communicate across a broad section of the organisation. In any organisation, 'socially constructed, historical patterns of practices, beliefs, values and rules' will often determine reaction to change or transition. Where change has been implemented well, new initiatives may be embraced enthusiastically, where change has gone awry, less so. The challenge to managers is to deal effectively with institutional tensions and the dynamics of transition. How to do so may reside in knowledge of the functions, systems, values and culture that prevail (Bogel et al., 2019). Some of this knowledge will be processual—dealing with organisational culture, organisational values, enhancing change competences, explaining economic benefits, diagnostic capability. As well as identifying and removing any barriers to the operation of the system as a whole. This means applying understanding of technology and organisation in anticipating where problems or bottlenecks might occur. Agile governance and change management will facilitate the transition. On the one hand this will require digital capabilities such as knowledge of technology and a level of technical skills, but also a knowledge of processes and systems and organisational dynamics (Hecklau et al., 2016). The level of knowledge will inform predictive capability; and predictive capability will inform action. The features of this competence are foresight, anticipation and the ability to communicate and engage.

- The potential of the change—improving performance by methods such as data sharing, accessing real-time information and making real-time decisions—will materialise by the excellence of change management on the key elements of process, people, technology and ensuring the flow of data among them. Clarification and understanding of business processes and the impact on them is important and the manager will act as 'the process owner' seeking to work with others to ensure collaboration and so reshapes processes forms part of knowledge and skills (Hammer & Champy, 1993; Javidroozi et al., 2019; Maisiri et al., 2019). Management commitment; managing the risks; and dealing with culture will be important, ensuring that maintaining course goes hand in hand with manoeuvrability as outlined above. In addition, where the organisational shape or structure inhibit change, identifying the underlying causes and offering practical ways in which to flex structure will be important. The manager will think laterally to identify structural as well as process solutions to any challenges faced. To some extent this is business process reengineering along planned and systematic lines, but it is also the agile governance which recognises the need to go beyond the boundaries originally highlighted if this proves necessary or indeed an opportunity once the process has commenced. The core management competence means understanding and being able to navigate the organisation but then it is about being able to steer and shape the organisation. A requirement of agile governance at organisational level is the ability to respond that is informed by knowledge that is in turn informed by managers in their knowledge acquiring and disseminating role. Its features are an understanding of organisational dynamics and an ability to engage others.

- A further aspect of competence in this area concerns that of being able to deliver projects and keep them on track and might be articulated as *optimises resource deployment through effective project management.* This will require technical knowledge such as project management skills, behavioural knowledge in respect of attitudes and approach and contextual knowledge with respect to adapting to and being able to manage across the organisation through effective relationships with other key stakeholders. The manager will plan and coordinate resource allocation to achieve objectives or milestones. This will allow the change to be aligned with organisational elements such as the strategic plan. An understanding of the meso-level organisation and its macro (the socio-technical system) and micro levels (individuals) will facilitate where and how resource should be deployed as part of the overall project of transition (Lopes et al., 2016; Bogel et al., 2019). The features of this competence are an understanding of project management techniques, the ability to engage others in change and the ability to resolve conflicts (e.g. competing resource demands).

The knowledge and skills of the manager form the basis of organisational and professional credibility. They offer the manager the platform for facilitating change that goes beyond any positional authority. But knowledge or skill will not be effective unless they are accompanied by attitudes and behaviours that are appropriate for the organisational or cultural environment and aligned to the changes that are envisaged.

Attitudes and Behaviours for the Core Management Competence of 'Demonstrates Agile Governance and Adaptability to Make Change Work Effectively'

The managerial playbook for the new hyperconnected environment will include not only technology or digital knowledge but behavioural skills—personal and interpersonal competence—articulated in terms of actions and intent (Boyatzis, 2011; Ibarra & Hansen, 2011; Kirby, 2020). Emotional and social intelligence are therefore substantial and important in predicting or understanding agility or change management performance. The characteristics are the ability to embrace change enthusiastically; and have an agile outlook to make it work regardless of the circumstances (i.e. it may be heterogeneous and so each time may require a different approach). The skill requirements for success as a manager go beyond domain knowledge and 'the new paradigm cannot be merely considered a technological tsunami, but it is made by heterogeneous elements and may have heterogeneous consequences also from managerial point of view' (Boyatzis, 2011; Hecklau et al., 2016; Maisiri et al., 2019; Cimini et al., 2020; Fareri et al., 2020). Notwithstanding these perspectives, the reality in contemporary organisations means it is unlikely there will be a single change incidence and hence response. Programmatic change sits alongside non programmatic; managers will encounter centrally driven organisational change and that which they had initiated themselves in response to either external or internal forces. And on top of all of this they will be expected continuously to improve their own performance, develop their team members, improve processes, build new relationships, network and then deal with incoming change from other areas or departments (Gibbons, 2015). To deal with often complex layer upon layer of change, the manager will require a positivity of attitudes and behaviours:

- Given the importance of context to the subject and the necessity for agile governance it is important that the manager understands the impact they have on individuals and groups going through the process. Too forceful or too liberal; too focused on a particular culture or way of doing things and too reluctant to acknowledge issues may have an adverse effect on the change process. Hence the importance of the first aspect of the competence (relevant to each of the competences that will be covered later) is that the manager *has knowledge of and demonstrates self-awareness* which can be articulated as 'knowing one's internal states, preferences, resources, and intuitions' and will depend on the level of emotional self-awareness which is 'recognizing one's emotions and their effects' (Boyatzis, 1982; Boyatzis, 2011; Hlupic, 2014). This would include the characteristics of self-control as well as concern with close relationships and the impact of individual behaviour on these. Awareness of the importance of behaviour on workforce engagement, awareness of the impact of behaviour on nourishing a positive culture and an awareness of the approach to power and decision-making and to make both more inclusive will be positive outputs from this self-awareness—complemented by self-management and emotional self-control.

- Amongst the most important attitudes will be that the manager *focuses on outcomes*. They will not only apply skill and knowledge to achieve a goal but redirect their own time and resources to ensure that this is met. A combination of the above attributes of competence will unleash purpose through collaboration and enthusiasm, but it is the direction to which such forces move that will determine how successful this has been. A focus on the purpose and objectives of the organisation will provide such direction. This is not management by edict which produces a culture of activity (Connors & Smith, 2011; Hlupic, 2014; Cohen, 2019) but management by a focus on outcomes with flexibility recognising that options or alternative pathways will be available—an approach that has been shown to give product flexibility, capacity flexibility and operational flexibility. Where this is effective then direction, rather than being imposed, may emerge from both knowledge and networking activity. In part this will be brought about by the high-level social exchange relationship between employees and their organisations; in part by the managers who act as change agents. Top-down influences on social exchange will occur between a particular individual and the organisation through the individual's interactions with managers in which reciprocity is based on the particular employee's experiences of the exchange relationship with the organisation. Bottom up influences will include shared individual experiences and interpretations. In both cases a combination of focus and flexibility will be instrumental in determining whether these social exchanges are positive (Georgoulias et al., 2008; Zhang, 2020). Attitudes and behaviours that respect and value the focus on objectives, balanced by the ability to act on other points of view and a flexibility in approach as to how those alternatives are tested and implemented are key to agile governance.
- Learning from interaction and two-way communication flows provide the evidence and the narrative; whilst codifying knowledge, its analysis

and manipulation form the basis of organisational action (Haeckel, 1999; Gothelf & Seiden, 2017; Bogel et al., 2019). Agile governance *involves a sense-and-respond mindset*, in which the manager has an instinctive ability to sense and react and a presence to take action in the face of external forces on the one hand—new competitors, changes in market situations, the availability of new technologies—and shape this into appropriate organisational responses. Seeing change as an opportunity and not as a threat, making efforts to understand it and maintaining personal energy are features of this aspect of competence. It is about real-time sensors to discover, on a continuous basis, what customers need, for example, and to respond accordingly, but it is also about 'dynamic resource allocation and execution', to ensure the organisation is able to deliver. The attitude of sensing and responding is one of the most important ways in which organisations can 'create and capture' value in the age of Industry 4.0 (Bradley & Nolan, 1998; Cimini et al., 2020; Luna et al., 2020). It involves the willingness to transfer knowledge which will come about with a sense and respond mind-set and a systemic vision of situations; to support strategic as well as operational change.

- On the cusp of the Third Industrial Revolution, Norman Vincent Peale articulated a mantra that was taken up by millions around the world—'believe in yourself, have faith in your abilities. Without a humble but resourceful confidence in your own powers you cannot be successful or happy.' Amongst his remedies against negativity were to create a mental picture of succeeding and using positive thoughts to cancel negative ones. Other recommendations may not have universal relevance but the overall benefits of the *Power of Positive Thinking* (Peale, 1952) resonated over many years. And more than that it spawned a self-help industry with positivity as its basis with the belief that 'every adversity has the seed of an equivalent or greater benefit' (Hill & Stone, 1960). But the concept of positivity is one that has, rightly, endured with the understanding that 'effectiveness, efficiency, profitability and sustainability can be linked to the use of positive techniques' on the part of the manager. Hence, *adopts a positive attitude* can create favourable conditions for reaching positive outcomes. Such an attribute will come about if the manager is able to be flexible, tolerates ambiguity and is able to work under pressure (Walters, 2010; Boyatzis, 2011; Hecklau et al., 2016; Hlupic, 2014; Cimini et al., 2020; Luna et al., 2020). A rider to this aspect of competence is that positivity should be based on reality; which in turn should be based on knowledge; which in turn should be accessed from multiple sources.

- Building collaborative relationships and creating a sense of community are important in both hierarchical and networked organisations will be important. In the first instance such an attitude can overcome siloed mentality; in the second it can foster an environment of teamwork. To do so will require interpersonal competences, the ability to communicate and cooperate with others and networking skills (Bogel et al., 2019; Cimini et al., 2020), each of which is particularly relevant to an aspect of competence which is *recognises the importance of teams and teamwork*. The characteristics are an understanding of team dynamics, an ability to resolve conflicting demands or needs within a team, the use of encouragement rather than criticism and building trust within a group. The manager will be adept at engaging members of the workforce and responding to their suggestions as recognition of the potential contribution to the creation of knowledge and problem solving. In the connected environment this will go beyond traditionally organised and predefined teams—which remain the core of the manager's responsibility—but also necessitate engaging talented people throughout to create wider group synergy in pursuing collective goals (Boyatzis, 2011; Ibarra & Hansen, 2011; Hlupic, 2014). Each example will be enhanced by a deep understanding of the context, the place of a particular part of the organisation (unit, department, team, individual) and its importance to the whole. This area of competence recognises that teams may be *inter*-organisational as well as *intra*-organisational. The manager will seek to maximise the good use of the talent wherever it resides.
- Change management is both interdisciplinary and inter-functional. Firstly, the concept is related to both the psychology of work and the sociology of work. Second, it will require managers to be adept at the organisation of work (Turner, 2020). It is this latter point that accentuates the need for the manager to *develop effective relationships* across the organisation and manage those with skill. Modifying positions to

ensure a win-win, taking questions and challenges without defensive behaviour and acting as a role model for cooperation are all part of the competence. The networked, swarm or matrix organisation mean that the lines of authority and decision-making are less clear than those of a hierarchy. The manager will therefore have to 'induce desirable responses' from others whether they are in the direct line of authority or not, whether they are within or without the team. Relationships with people who may reside outside of the immediate 'line' are important for progress. Amongst the skills are those of 'sensing others' needs; guiding individuals and groups using effective persuasion and resolving any disagreements (Boyatzis, 2011). Effective relationships can be built out of shared values, knowledge and experience; they can be built by recognising the points of view of others and they can be built by encouraging the contributions of others.

- Workforce demographics, their level of knowledge, as well as attitudes and behaviours have changed dramatically in recent years and so to be successful the manager will have to cater to the diverse nature of that workforce. An organisation's culture will determine how it reacts to and adapts to change. Culture is the tacit social order of the organisation. It will be based on history and experience and articulated by habits of thinking, mental models, linguistic paradigms, shared meanings or 'integrating' symbols. Culture is what stands behind and guides behaviour. Addressing issues of compatibility between the culture and the objectives will therefore be an important management role (Kotter, 1996; Sinclair, 2005; Alvesson & Sveningsson, 2016; Schein, 2017). To this end, agility and change management will be involved not only in tasks but also in emotions. Since culture can evolve flexibly there is the opportunity, actually necessity, to ensure that it does so positively if it is to contribute positively to the achievement of results and may be regarded as a core management competence (Connors & Smith, 2011; Groysberg et al., 2020). Often this means reaching across the organisation where different cultures will be encountered and so, *works effectively in multicultural environments* becomes not only desirable but essential. This is an aspect of competence which is associated with 'interaction of cultural backgrounds and the reflective outputs ' that allows them to better serve the diverse nature of their team or organisation and will be essential given the diverse nature of Industry 4.0 organisations. The ability to 'exhibit empathy and become attuned to others' moods' is a function not only of emotional intelligence but of social intelligence, 'a set of interpersonal competences built on specific neural circuits that inspire others to be effective' (Goleman & Boyatzis, 2008; Hecklau et al., 2016; Kirby, 2020; Knox & Haupt, 2020).

- Change will occur when individuals accept its necessity, understand their role and embrace its implementation. In traditional forms of organisation this was undertaken through cascade communication in which large groups would hear communications at the same time and with the same message. Where this process is done well, then feedback loops allow the opportunity for questions and the importance of standard responses to those questions was built into the process. In contemporary organisations this may or may not be the best method and the role of the manager will be to sense and respond what the most appropriate ways of so doing are for that organisation in that specific context. One approach is to ensure that individuals are taken through the change as regards its impact on them in particular and *coaches for change* therefore becomes complementary to mass communication. The manager who actively looks for opportunities to help others through the change, ensuring that personal values are as closely aligned to organisational values as possible and where agile governance pertains, shaping organisational values to those of employees where these are more appropriate (based on the knowledge and experience of the employee rather than all of this residing in the single figure of the manager). This coaching for change will involve 'positive and invigorating energy' with the objective of building a 'resonant relationship' through 'coaching for compassion' rather than 'coaching for compliance' (Hlupic, 2014; Boyatzis et al., 2019). The manager will commit time and will relate the coaching to specific work or wider organisational requirements.

- Change is a human process. In this, both the collective voice of workforce members during periods of change and the individual voice—for self-determination—are important. Hence, there is a social role associated with the competence of agile governance and change and that is related to *adjusts social behaviour to a level that is 'appropriate and functional' to context and purpose of change.* This represents social skills and abilities to communicate and cooperate with others (Boyatzis, 1982; Barry & Wilkinson, 2016; Cimini et al., 2020). It represents a willingness to understand others' points of view or positions and in many cases, it represents unconditional positive regard for such views as famously articulated by Rogers (1957). In so doing, the manager will generate social capital—'the relationships of trust and co-operation that provide a foundation for effective action within social groups. Social capital can be defined as 'the goodwill that is engendered by the fabric of social relations and that can be mobilized to facilitate action' (Hodson, 2005). The objective for the manager is to encourage creativity and problem solving by engaging, through social behaviour, in a way that is right for the context of the change.

Industry 4.0 will bring about organisation-wide changes in socio-technical systems—the technological system and the human operating system (Liboni et al., 2019). Maximising the benefits of these changes to the organisation's competitive position will require management competences of the highest order, including agility on the part of the manager and agile governance in how they go about their roles. Managers will have to get to grips with new ways of production, operations and service whereby traditional roles are taken on by automated systems using AI, amongst other technologies. In addition, they will be required to keep costs low whilst customising products to the needs of a broader range of customer groupings. The modern manager will be adept at change management, whether this is through *n*-step models or not, and at the same time have agility in the way they make the transitions of which there will be many.

Agility and adaptability have proven to be essential in the competence set of managers over time.

References

Accenture. (2020). Together Makes Better; How To Drive Cross-Function Collaboration, https://www.accenture.com/gb-en/insights/industry-x-0/cross-functional-collaboration

Alvesson, M., & Sveningsson, S. (2016). *Changing Organisational Culture.* Routledge.

Barry, M., & Wilkinson, A. (2016). Pro-social or Pro-management? A Critique of the Conception of Employee Voice as a Pro-Social Behaviour within Organizational Behaviour, *British Journal of Industrial Relations*

Belinski, R., Peixe, A. M. M., Frederico, G. F., & Garza-Reyes, J. A. (2020). Organizational Learning and Industry 4.0: Findings from a Systematic Literature Review and Research Agenda. *Benchmarking: An International Journal, 27*(8), 2435–2457.

Bennis, W. (1969). *Organisation Development.* Addison Wesley.

Bierwolf, R. E., & Frijns, P. (2019). Consciousness, Competence, and Organizational Change. *IEEE Engineering Management Review, 47*(4), 32–38.

Bogel, P., Pereverza, K., Upham, P., & Kordas, O. (2019). Linking Socio-technical Transition Studies and Organisational Change Management: Steps Towards an Integrative, Multi-scale Heuristic. *Journal of Cleaner Production, 1*, 359–368.

Boyatzis, R. E. (1982). *The Competent Manager.* John Wiley and Sons.

Boyatzis, R. E. (2011). Managerial and Leadership Competencies: A Behavioural Approach to Emotional. *Social and Cognitive Intelligence, Vision (09722629), 15*(2), 91–100.

Boyatzis, R. E., Smith, M., & van Oosten, E. (2019). *Helping People Change.* Harvard Business School Press.

Bradley, S. P., & Nolan, R. L. (1998). *Sense and Respond.* Harvard Business School Press.

Brunninge, O. (2009). Using History in Organizations; How Managers Make Purposeful Reference to History in Strategy Processes. *Journal of Organizational Change Management, 22*(1), 8–26.

Bui, A. T., Liao, Y., Nguyen, P. T., & Chang, C. F. (2019). Acquiring Top Management Team, Core Competence through Absorptive Capacity and Entrepreneurial Orientation. *Academy of Entrepreneurship Journal, 1*, 1a.

Bullock, R. J., & Batten, D. (1985). It's Just a Phase We're Going Through: A Review and Synthesis of OD Phase Analysis. *Group and Organisation Studies, 10*(4), 383–412.

Burnes, B. (1996). *Managing Change.* Pitman Publishing.
Cameron, E., & Green, M. (2004). *Making Sense of Change Management.* Kogan Page.
Chinoperekweyi, J. (2020). Exploring Philosophical Proclivity of Change Management Articles: Technical-rational Perspective versus Other Change Philosophies. *Organization Development Journal, 38*(2), 15–26.
Cimini, C., Boffelli, A., Lagorio, A., Kalchschmidt, M., & Pinto, R. (2020). How Do Industry 4.0 Technologies Influence Organisational Change? An Empirical Analysis of Italian SMEs. *Journal of Manufacturing Technology Management.*
Cohen, H. (2019). The Change Management Fallacies. *SAM Advanced Management Journal (07497075), 84*(1), 4–15.
Connors, R., & Smith, T. (2011). *Change the Culture. Change the Game.*
Fareri, S., Fantoni, G., Chiarello, F., Coli, E., & Binda, A. (2020). Estimating Industry 4.0 Impact on Job Profiles and Skills Using Text Mining. *Computers in Industry, 118*, 1.
Fountaine, T., McCarthy, B., & Saleh, T. (2019). Building the AI-powered Organization: Technology Isn't the Biggest Challenge. *Harvard Business Review, 97*(4), 62.
Georgoulias, K., Papakostas, N., Chryssolouris, G., Stanev, S., Krappe, H., & Ovtcharova, J. (2008). Evaluation of Flexibility for the Effective Change Management of Manufacturing Organizations *Flexible Automation and Intelligent Manufacturing*, FAIM2008, Skövde, Sweden.
Gibbons, P. (2015). *The Science of Successful Organisational Change.* Pearson Education.
Gobble, M. M. (2013). Creating Change. *Research Technology Management, 56*(5), 62–64.
Goleman, D., & Boyatzis, R. (2008). Social Intelligence and the Biology of Leadership, *Harvard Business Review*
Gothelf, J., & Seiden, J. (2017). *Sense and Respond.* Harvard Business School Press.
Gratton, L., & Scott, A. (2016). *The 100-Year Life.* Bloomsbury.
Grefen, P., Rinderle-Ma, S., Dustdar, S., Fdhila, W., Mending, J., & Schulte, S. (2018). Charting Process-Based Collaboration Support in Agile Business Networks: Aligning the Need for a Dynamic Internet of Processes from Industry and Research Perspectives. *IEEE Internet Computing, 22*(3), 48–57.
Groysberg, B., Lee, J., Price, J., & Yo-Jud Cheng, J. (2020). *The Leader's Guide to Corporate Culture*, in HBR's Ten Must reads on Corporate Culture, Harvard Business School Publishing

Haeckel, S. H. (1999). *Adaptive Enterprise.* Harvard Business School Press.
Hammer, M., & Champy, J. (1993). *Reengineering the Corporation.* Harper Business.
Hecklau, F., Galeitzke, M., Flachs, S., & Kohl, H. (2016). Holistic Approach for Human Resource Management in Industry 4.0. *Procedia CIRP, 54*, 1–6.
Hiatt, J. M. (2006). *ADKAR: A Model for Change in Business, Government and our Community, How to Implement a Successful Change in Our Personal Lives and Professional Careers.* Prosci Learning Centre Publications CO.
Hill, N., & Stone, W. C. (1960). *Success Through a Positive Mental Attitude.* Prentice Hall.
Hlupic, V. (2014). *The Management Shift.* Palgrave Macmillan.
Hodson, R. (2005). Management Behaviour as Social Capital: A Systematic Analysis of Organizational Ethnographies. *British Journal of Industrial Relations, 43*(1), 41–46.
Huang. J. (2010). The Study of SCM Strategy and Business Model of Fast Fashion Enterprises, *International Conference on E-Business and E-Government*, ICEE, DOI: https://doi.org/10.1109/ICEE.2010.872
Huczynski, A. A., & Buchanan, D. A. (1991). *Organisational Behaviour.* Prentice Hall.
Ibarra, H., & Hansen, M. T. (2011). Are You a Collaborative Leader? *Harvard Business Review*
Javidroozi, V., Shah, H., & Feldman, G. (2019). A Framework for Addressing the Challenges of Business Process Change During Enterprise Systems Integration. *Business Process Management Journal, 26*(2), 463–488.
Karthikeyan, C., & Thomas, P. (2017). Evaluative Study on Workplace Conflict Resolution Strategies: A Leadership Perspective. *International Journal of Management, IT and Engineering, 7*(7), 198–217.
Kinnie, N., & Swart, J. (2019). Cross-boundary Working: Implications for HRM Theory, Methods, and Practice. *Human Resource Management Journal, 30*(1), 86–99.
Kirby, S. (2020). *5 ways COVID-19 has changed workforce management*, World Economic Forum, https://www.weforum.org/agenda /2020/06/covid-homeworking-symptom-of-changing-face-of-workforce-management/
Knox, C. C., & Haupt, B. (Eds.). (2020). *Cultural Competency for Emergency and Crisis Management: Concepts, Theories.* Routledge.
Kotter, J. (1996). *Leading Change.* Harvard Business School Press.
Kruchten, P. (2013). Contextualizing Agile Software Development. *Journal of Software: Evolution and Process, 25*, 351–361.

Kubler-Ross, E. (1969). *On Death and Dying, 50th Anniversary Edition*. Scribner.

Kwee, Z., Van den Bosch, F. A. J., & Volberda, H. W. (2011). The Influence of Top Management Team's Corporate Governance Orientation on Strategic Renewal Trajectories: A Longitudinal Analysis of Royal Dutch Shell plc, 1907-2004. *Journal of Management Studies, 48*, 984.

Lewin, K. (1947). Frontiers in Group Dynamics: Concept, Method and Reality in Social Science; Social Equilibria and Social Change. *Human Relations, 1*(1), 1.

Li, D., Fast-Berglund, A., & Paulin, D. (2019). Current and Future Industry 4.0 Capabilities for Information and Knowledge Sharing. *Strategies for Global Monitoring, International Journal of Advanced Manufacturing Technology, 105*(9), 3951–3963.

Liboni, L. B., Cezarino, L. O., Jabbour, C. J. C., Oliveira, B. G., & Stefanelli, N. O. (2019). Smart Industry and the Pathways to HRM 4.0: Implications for SCM. *Supply Chain Management: An International Journal, 24*(1), 124–146.

Logevall, F. (2020). *JFK Volume 1*. Penguin Viking.

Lopes, R., de, O. A., Sbragia, R., & Qualharini, E. L. (2016). The Psychological Contract and Project Management as a Core Competence of the Organization. *Procedia—Social and Behavioural Sciences, 226*, 148–155.

Luna, A. J. H de O., Kruchten, P., & de Moura, H. P. (2013). GAME: Governance for Agile Management of Enterprises: A Management Model for Agile Governance. *IEEE 8th International Conference on Global Software Engineering Workshops, Global Software Engineering Workshops (ICGSEW)*

Luna, A. J. H. d. O., Marinho, M. L. M., Kruchten, P., & de Moura, H. P. (2020). Agile Governance Theory: Operationalization. *Innovations in Systems and Software Engineering: A NASA Journal, 16*(1), 3.

Madsen, D. O. (2020). The Evolutionary Trajectory of the Agile Concept Viewed from a Management Fashion Perspective. *Social Sciences, 9*(69), 69.

Maisiri, W., Darwish, H., & van Dyk, L. (2019). An Investigation of Industry 4.0 Skills Requirements. *South African Journal of Industrial Engineering, 30*(3), 90–15.

Marr, B. (2019). The 10 Vital Skills You Will Need For The Future Of Work, *Forbes*, https://www.forbes.com/sites/bernardmarr/2019/04/29/the-10-vital-skills-you-will-need-for-the-future-of-work/#52b6cb8e3f5b

McGuire, D., By, R. T., & Hutchings, K. (2007). Towards a Model of Human Resource Solutions for Achieving Intergenerational Interaction in Organisations. *Journal of European Industrial Training, 31*(8), 592–608.

McWilliams, D. (2020). *We Are Living Through a 'Pandession'—Here's How We Escape*, http://www.davidmcwilliams.ie/we-are-living-through-a-pandession-heres-how-we-escape/

Nadler, D., & Tushman, M. (1980). A Model for Diagnosing Organizational Behaviour. *Organizational Dynamics, 9*(2), 35–51.

Naeem, M. (2020). Understanding the Role of Social Media in Organizational Change Implementation. *Management Research Review, 43*(9), 1097–1116.

Năstase, M., Giuclea, M., & Bold, O. (2012). The Impact of Change Management in Organizations—a Survey of Methods and Techniques for a Successful Change. *Review of International Comparative Management / Revista de Management Comparat International, 13*(1), 5–16.

Nonaka, L., Takeuchi, H., & Umemoto, K. (1996). A Theory of Organizational Knowledge Creation. *International Journal of Technology Management, 11*(7), 833–845.

Nonaka, L., & Takeuchi, H. (1995). *The Knowledge Creating Company*. Oxford University Press.

Peale, N. V. (1952). *The Power of Positive Thinking*. General Press.

Penttilä, K., Ravald, A., Dahl, J., & Björk, P. (2020). Managerial Sensemaking in a Transforming Business Ecosystem: Conditioning Forces, Moderating Frames, and Strategizing Options. *Industrial Marketing Management, 91*, 209–222.

Prifti, L., Knigge, M., Kiennegger, H., & Krcmar, H. (2017). A Competency Model for "Industrie 4.0" Employees, 13th International Conference on Wirtschaftsinformatik, February 12-15, 2017, St. Gallen, Switzerland

Raman, A., & Bharadwaj, S. S. (2017). Dynamic Service Capabilities Enabling Agile Services : Scale Development and Initial Validation in Indian Services Industry. *Journal of Enterprise Information Management, 30*(1), 166–187.

Renjen, P. (2020). COVID-19: How Leaders Can Create a New and Better Normal, World Economic Forum, https://www.weforum.org/agenda/2020/05/leaders-should-use-their-vision-and-trust-to-create-a-new-and-better-normal/

Rogers, C. R. (1957). The Necessary and Sufficient Conditions of Therapeutic Personality Change. *Journal of Consulting Psychology, 21*(2), 95–103.

Rosenbaum, D., More, E., & Steane, P. (2018). Planned Organisational Change Management. *Journal of Organizational Change Management, 31*(2), 286.

Tatsuo Sato, T. (2019). Agile Program Management for Chemical Engineering and the IOT. *Journal of Chemical Engineering of Japan, 51*(9).

Schein, E. H. (2017). *Organisational Culture and Leadership*. Wiley.

Sinclair, A. (2005). *Doing Leadership Differently*. Melbourne University Press.
Steiner, G. A., & Root, L. E. (1959). Linear Organization Charts. *California Management Review, 1*(2), 11–19.
Teece, D., Peteraf, M., & Leih, S. (2016) Dynamic Capabilities and Organizational Agility: Risk, Uncertainty, and Strategy in the Innovation Economy 2016.
Tsaklanganos, A. A. (1973). The Organization Chart: A Managerial Myth. *SAM Advanced Management Journal (00360805), 38*(2), 53.
Turner, P. A. (2018). *Leadership in Healthcare*. Palgrave Macmillan.
Turner, P. A. (2020). *Employee Engagement*. Palgrave Macmillan.
Walters, J. H. (2010). *Positive Management; Increasing Employee Productivity*. Business Expert Press.
Yang, C.-C. (2015). The Integrated Model of Core Competence and Core Capability. *Total Quality Management and Business Excellence, 26*(1/2), 173–189.
Yin, Y., Stecke, K. E., & Li, D. (2018). The Evolution of Production Systems from Industry 2.0 Through Industry 4.0. *International Journal of Production Research, 56*(1/2), 848–861.
Yukl, G. (2010). *Leadership in Organisations*. Pearson.
Zhang, B. (2020). Human Resource Change-agent Role, State Ownership, and Employee Behavioural Flexibility. *Asia Pacific Journal of Human Resources, 58*(2), 268–288.

8

Management Competence for the Fourth Industrial Revolution: Collaborates to Create and Share Knowledge and Information

Convergence and the Unknown Unknowns

The creation and application of knowledge will be mission critical to Fourth Industrial Revolution organisations.

How an organisation uses knowledge—made up of data, information, intelligence and insight—will contribute to how that organisation performs in its chosen markets. Through interactivity and the promotion of knowledge flow and integration, an organisation's core competence can be strengthened. Key to this is collaboration and cooperation, whereby members of the workforce share through formal channels such as strategic projects or business improvement schemes as well as outside of any structured or curated interactions (Wang et al., 2004; Deiser, 2009; Chaudhuri & Boer, 2016; Syed, 2020). In the words of Charles Clinton Spaulding, leader of the North Carolina Mutual Life Insurance Company during the peak of the Second Industrial Revolution, 'if I were asked to name the one fundamental necessity in the administration of big business, I would answer immediately that a thorough-going cooperation is essential' (Prieto & Phipps, 2016). These sentiments continue to resonate, and the manager has a significant role to play in 'thorough-going

P. Turner, *The Making of the Modern Manager*,
https://doi.org/10.1007/978-3-030-81062-7_8

cooperation' as the Fourth Industrial Revolution gathers momentum. It is on these assumptions that the second core management competence is based—'collaborates to create and share knowledge and information'—and its place in the overall core management competence schema is shown in Fig. 8.1. A working definition is as follows:

> *[T]he ability to disseminate knowledge by connecting individuals and teams and inspire them to collaborate in working towards common goals.*

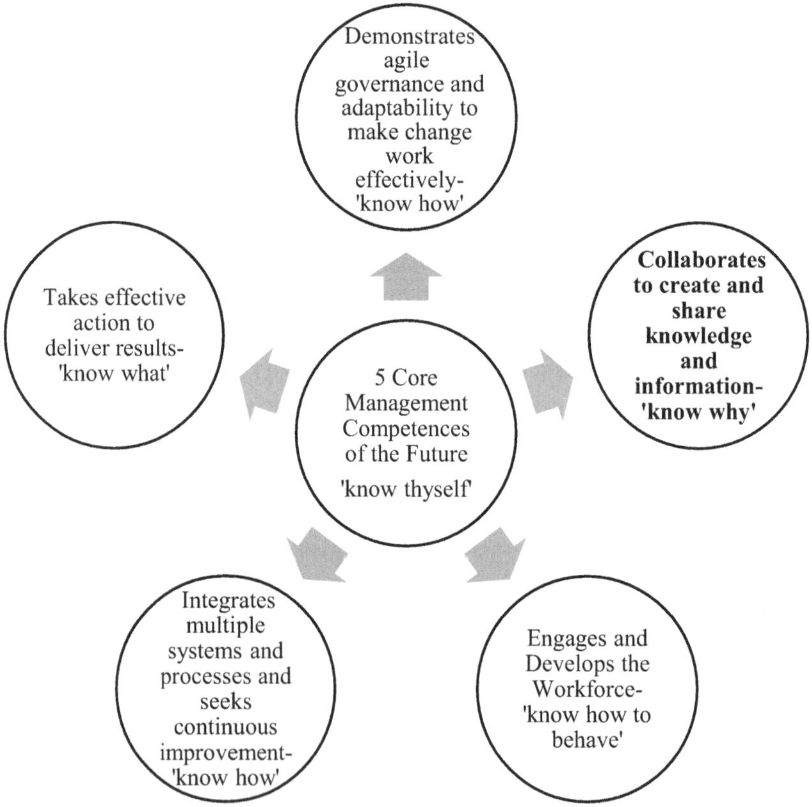

Fig. 8.1 Core management competences

The context in which this takes place is the convergence of powerful technological developments bringing unprecedented change to society—known as Society 4.0—and commerce—known as Industry 4.0. New technologies will be integrated into all work, physical, social and political spaces using advanced robotics, artificial intelligence and the Internet of Things producing applications for, inter alia, digital energy, digital health, digital transportation, digital communication and digital production. Automation and a digital culture will introduce new knowledge-based systems giving process flexibility and adaptability for business models, with significant shifts in the way that value is created, exchanged and distributed—in smart physical and virtual spaces with higher efficiency, higher productivity and radically altered processes across all aspects of the value chain. Agile governance will be necessary to respond in a way that allows the organisation to take advantage of the opportunity. But knowledge and collaboration will inform the practical implications of agility as they pertain to economies of scale or flexible specialisation, more efficient, extended supply chains and 'ephemeral organisation structures' (Wilson & Thomson, 2009; Iraj et al., 2017; Mazali, 2018; Koh et al., 2019; Philbeck & Davis, 2019; Accenture, 2019; Colman, 2020; Lepore et al., 2021; Salvadorinho & Teixeira, 2021). Collaboration becomes an imperative for introducing 4.0 technologies and, when combined with knowledge sharing, has implications for 'the more agile accommodation of artificial intelligence techniques'.

The speculators and philosophers—to use Adam Smith's words—who observe industrial revolutions have made bold forecasts for the Fourth. We are living in a world of interconnectedness that has permeated almost every aspect of life and work and for Klaus Schwab, Founder and Executive Chairman of the World Economic Forum, the Fourth Industrial Revolution will fundamentally change the way we live, work and relate to one another. The management of ideas will come of age, knowledge and innovation are key differentiators and new social collaboration tools will allow organisations to quantify and measure all aspects of innovation. Knowledge and its application will be mission critical for most. Indeed, as organisations transition from competing in the industrial economy to the new challenges of the digital or information economy, there will be a shift in focus from the physical to the application of intellectual resources

(Schwab, 2016; Easen, 2020; Kašćelan et al., 2020). But the events anticipated by Industry 4.0—have more recently been made even more complex by 'unknown unknowns' which have disrupted well laid plans. As outlined in previous chapters, during the early 2020s the unknowable collided head on with the unthinkable, succinctly articulated by David McWilliams as a 'pandession' that was unlike anything that has gone before (2020). When combined with Lynda Gratton and Andrew Scott's forecast that we are in the midst of an 'extraordinary transition' of demographic and social change (2016), the challenges become accentuated. Organisations strive for a blueprint that would allow them to face up to these events in a way that would secure and sustain their prosperity. Already, their actions have demonstrated that when faced with rapid, unexpected change, they can be remarkably innovative and resilient. Lessons have been learned about the requirements for agile governance and adaptability. Applying new knowledge is one of them.

Knowledge Is the Answer, Collaboration Is the Key

The creation of knowledge depends on collaboration 'to facilitate the working together of groups of people toward definite ends', maximising its value by making it available wherever and whenever it is needed (Barnard, 1948; Peng, 2011; Wang et al., 2019). During the First Industrial Revolution, for example, those organisations that could acquire and harness knowledge about the new mechanised manufacturing techniques and machinery were more likely to be successful than those weighed down by commitments to older ways of production. Entrepreneurs of the eighteenth and nineteenth centuries sought to acquire knowledge that would help them to establish strong competitive positions—the installation and management of a Boulton and Watt Steam Engine for Josiah Wedgewood came with instructions and training (Boulton, Watt and Co, 1802). Externally, sources of knowledge came from networking at such organisations as the Birmingham Lunar Society or the Literary and Philosophical Society in Manchester where scientists brushed shoulders with business people. Recognition of the importance of knowledge continued and became an essential feature in the development of mass production during the Second Industrial Revolution. Knowledge transfer about production methods from applications in Chicago's meat packing factories to Ford's motor production facilities in Detroit enabled the latter to run manufacturing processes that became benchmarks for modern factories; and the many business schools in the United States by the mid-1930s disseminated knowledge and best practice to their eager students facilitating the advent of the 'American Century'. Further instances of the power of knowledge in business processes, global market trends or innovative manufacturing or service methods were evident during the Third Industrial Revolution. The increased use of computer-generated information in support of managers was highlighted in Unilever's, 1968 Report and Accounts, which noted that computer-based 'tools of modern management' were being used in project control, forward planning, order processing, sales accounting and in the control of production, distribution and stocks because they provided 'management with the full and accurate information needed in running a complex world-wide business'. A major educational effort was put in hand to ensure that managers at all levels and of all nationalities became aware of the potential of computers in the future (Unilever, 1968). And the Indian economy prospered during the Third Industrial Revolution because they were able to use collaborative experiences drawn from 'global relationships of exchange, and transfer of knowledge, know-how and competences within the world economy' throughout the twentieth century—it was the ability to embed this knowledge and know-how into Indian business that was important to the success of these transfers (Masrani et al., 2021). The techniques of quality management, continuous improvement and just in time systems that gained traction in Japan, across Asia and then the world, were based on the efficacious use of internal knowledge. Where organisations could foster *kakushin, kaihatsu and kaizen (3 K)*, collaboration would create 'an enabling environment for innovation' (Shigaki & Koshijima, 2016). It's fair to assume that knowledge has been at the forefront of competitive success for over 200 years. And now, digital technologies have overturned the logic of protecting knowledge within organisations. In particular, social media tools are increasingly used—as 'collaborative media', which facilitates employee-to-employee interaction, allowing employees to co-create knowledge and hence additional intellectual property (Thomas & Akdere, 2013; Arjomandy, 2016; Lemmetty et al., 2020; Mukherjee, 2020; Namisango et al., 2020). There is much to support the argument that those organisations which have knowledge capabilities have the opportunity to create advantages in their competitive sphere. Understanding the nature, location and occurrence of knowledge and how collaboration can enhance its production and accessibility are therefore of utmost importance to the role of the manager.

Explicit and Tacit Knowledge

Knowledge can be explicit, that is, available to everyone and readily processed, or tacit, that is, knowledge that is personal to an individual member of the workforce, subjective, experiential, hard to formalise and rooted in action. Knowledge can be declarative—domain-related facts and concepts; procedural—to solve a problem or learn an implicit task; contextual—which defines an outcome using all available and relevant knowledge and somatic-sensory information (Samiotis & Poulymenakou, 2002; Bakken & Dobbs, 2016). Hence explicit knowledge (declarative or procedural) might be market research or customer data, supply chain information, manufacturing process data or HR policies and procedures. Tacit knowledge (contextual or somatic) might be concerned with knowledge of innovation or improvement that resides in an individual, or an employee's intuition about a product design based on customer feedback. If tacit knowledge can be turned in to explicit knowledge then the organisation may become 'a living organism' able to adapt to changing circumstances, whatever they may be, rather than a static bureaucratic machine. The role of the manager in creating an environment of freedom and trust will be paramount. 'Goodwill trust affects information sharing, while competence trust affects both information sharing and joint planning' (Nonaka, 1994; Nonaka et al., 1996; Cai & Yang, 2017; Adi & Sukmawati, 2020). Capturing knowledge, transforming it and converting it to commercial advantage is the desired state. The role of the manager will be to facilitate its absorption and application through cooperation and collaboration. It is in this absorptive capacity—the organisation's ability to recognise the value of knowledge, assimilate it and apply it through knowledge exploration and knowledge exploitation—where the manager can make a difference (Nahapiet & Ghoshal, 1998; Bapuji et al., 2011; Peng, 2011; Randhawa et al., 2017). If knowledge is the answer, then collaboration is the key and has the potential across the value chain from identifying market opportunities to boosting innovation (Shamsuzzoha et al., 2010). The role of the manager will be to engage members of the workforce in the importance of collaboration, ensure that there is a culture of collaboration, a process to maximise collaboration, systems for capturing knowledge as a result and a workforce where 'employees have the relevant data, information and knowledge necessary to make well-informed decisions' and are able to use that knowledge to its full potential (Li et al., 2019).

'Loosening Control Without Losing Control'

The 'shape' of the organisation will have an important part to play in both knowledge creation and collaboration. There was until more recent times, a certain homogeneity in organisation structure and style approximating to the traditional organisational hierarchy. Elliot Jacques' seminal article perhaps summarised the reasons why such a type of structure had endured. The proposal was that a managerial hierarchy was the most efficient, the hardiest and the most natural structure to put in place in business organisations. It could release energy and creativity, rationalise productivity and improve morale (Jacques, 1990). Praise of hierarchy was based on its essential qualities consisting of role clarity, enabling the clarity of objectives, reinforcing clarity of accountability and confirming clarity of authority through articulated policies and procedures. It was not hard to see why such a structure had endured, with variation and modification, through the Three Industrial Revolutions. In such organisations, knowledge was generated within clearly defined business units or departments that were in a largely vertical structure and as they evolved through to M-form structures with the larger, divisional units, the hierarchy was preserved. The most efficient hierarchical organisations with explicit knowledge gathering processes would have mechanisms by which the knowledge could be disseminated horizontally to other areas. However, the least efficient would have business units or departments erecting barriers that prevented transfer, the infamous silos which management theorists, consultants and practitioners have tried to dismantle over many years. In response to some of these limitations came more fluid structures, matrices and networks and swarms intended to overcome any silo mentality by spreading management authority across the organisation. Nevertheless 'despite the advantages that properly-managed institutional knowledge brings to organisations, impediments still remain in knowledge supply where there is a limited inclination to share because it is seen as exclusive personal property, in competitive and hierarchical settings … this reticence can be substantial' (Argyris & Ransbotham, 2020). The question that faces organisations is how to 'loosen control without losing control' in order to create a collaborative atmosphere. The challenge facing the manager is to maintain a level of control over direction and output whilst simultaneously creating an environment of empowerment and creativity. If this apparent paradox can be overcome, it may lead to 'an environment that is rich with information and motivates employees to take action in purposeful, directed ways. This environment facilitates employees' perception that they have the ability to take actions, make decisions, and produce novel ideas' (Spekle et al., 2017). The knowledge, skills, attitudes and behaviours of managers will be critical in this desired outcome. In some cases, agile governance will allow the manager to influence or shape the organisation—structure, systems and processes—to optimise knowledge creation and utilisation; in others the manager will require competence to work in more formal hierarchical structures where a more nuanced approach will be required. The principles of collaboration may be in a forthright, 'command and control' manner or at the other extreme based on consensus—in mixed or small groups and collaborative in dispersed, cross organisational networks. To be effective, the manager in the context of Industry 4.0, will respond to whatever the organisational form exists and act as a 'connector'. They will encourage knowledge sharing without abrogating the authority to make decisions—collaboration does not mean consensus (Ibarra & Hansen, 2011); and all of this whilst remaining focussed on key objectives. Hence the manager will be required to exert control to achieve objectives on the one hand, and yet give freedom of expression on the other—a hard-balancing act (Faßauer, 2018). The management competence of collaboration requires a broad range of characteristics and these are discussed in more detail below.

Knowledge and Skills for the Core Management Competence of 'Collaborates to Create and Share Knowledge and Information'

The sum total of knowledge created by the whole workforce if applied in a coherent and strategic way adds to the strength of the organisation in its market position and ultimately produces competitive advantage. Amongst the ways in which this can be achieved is that of the manager establishing or facilitating an environment within which knowledge can be created and processes by which knowledge can be codified and turned into profitable outcomes whether these be products or services on the one hand or intangible assets such as intellectual property, patents or copyrights on the other. The ability to do so is embodied within the core management competence of collaboration, creating and sharing—where competence is an antecedent of organisational success and comprises the level of 'fit' between ability requirements and abilities possessed. Each manager will display such competence at the nexus between people management, organisational dynamics and business strategy (Brinkmann, 2006; Boyatzis, 2011; Alshanty & Emeagwali, 2019; Törngren et al., 2019). Competence is made up of knowledge—facts and information, intuition, awareness or understanding acquired through experience or learning; skills—the ability to perform well in a job; attitudes—emotions or beliefs and behaviours, including social and personal skills—emotional and social intelligence, change receptiveness and an agile outlook. Here, knowledge and skills on the part of managers are manifested as abilities to undertake a role in pursuit of goals or objectives. Competence in respect of collaboration and knowledge sharing will help to foster inter and intra organisational learning.

There are a number of attributes of knowledge and skill in this competence area:

- The perception of the value of knowledge, its acquisition and dispersion will depend on members of the workforce having a positive disposition towards it either from previous experiences with successful outcomes or from understanding the reason for and purpose of, knowledge-related activity. Knowledge sharing is a contributor to the achievement of strategic objectives—towards cost-competitive products or services, or a differentiated market position, for example, and is a strong predictor of internal process performance. Knowledge absorption is 'pivotal' to a range of performance outcomes such as customer satisfaction or non-financial benefits on learning and growth and internal process improvement (Peng, 2011; Lin, 2015; Antunes & Pinheiro, 2020). In this respect it is important that the manager *facilitates a knowledge management orientation*, and this is the first aspect of core management competence. Knowledge management orientation may be defined as the organisation's propensity to 'build on its achieved wisdom (organisational memory) as well as the propensity to share (knowledge sharing), assimilate (knowledge absorption), and be receptive to new wisdom (knowledge receptivity)'. How these will be achieved depends on the culture of the organisation, its structure and its business model. In all cases, competence stems from understanding technology applications, the ability to think conceptually in how these applications will add value and how knowledge will contribute, the ability to sense the organisation's dynamics, the ability to manage people and projects towards identified goals, and the ability to communicate and engage effectively in the process. Managers will act as advocates of the benefits of knowledge and collaboration—first by demonstrating links between knowledge and successful outcomes on process or business measures; second by developing networks of individuals to share and disseminate knowledge and to establish systems and processes to do so. The success of the manager will be evident when there is a 'tendency and behaviour' which facilitates the management of knowledge and where knowledge is readily and perceptibly accumulated (Migdadi, 2016; Atthawej et al., 2020) systematically on an organisation-wide basis, with knowledge sharing, application and continuous new learning in evidence.

- However, since knowledge can come from a multitude of sources and in different forms, it is important that the manager *acts as knowledge seeker*. The role of the manager will be to ensure that knowledge, embedded in routines, processes and systems, is captured, continuously improved, organised and retained. As a contribution to this the manager will seek and identify the knowledge that is present in both individuals ('without a solid and diverse stock of individual knowledge, firms would not be able to find basic knowledge to combine or integrate to create new firm knowledge') and teams. This will be complemented by seeking and identifying relational capital—for example, knowledge that organisations receive from customers or from personal contact with peer groups—known as *ego networks*. Knowledge will be accumulated through formal organisational processes with the manager at the hub or through informal networks or communities of practice with the manager as coach or facilitator of people working together by interacting and exchanging ideas (Guechtouli & Guechtouli, 2009; Fallatah, 2018; Atthawej et al., 2020; Kashyap, 2020). The manager is in a unique position to act as knowledge seeker in each of these scenarios. The features of this competence are an open mind, an understanding of organisational dynamics and the ability to persuade others to impart knowledge to a wider audience.
- An important objective is for the manager to clarify not only who knows what, or where knowledge resides, but also who needs what and how to apply the knowledge to its best effect. This requires the manager to have a predisposition to sharing learning and knowledge, a sense of timing about when and where it needs to go and the ability to ensure that this happens effectively. So, *acts as knowledge disseminator* is a further aspect of core management competence. Such dissemination is an interactive process of communicating in a comprehensible way to relevant audiences. 'Dissemination is a core responsibility of

any organisation tasked with generating and sharing knowledge products, especially of new kinds of unique (and uniquely valuable) content that are as usable and accessible as possible. Dissemination of knowledge is just as important as its production' (Ordoñez & Serrat, 2017). It will require the manager to demonstrate how knowledge can contribute to the achievement of the organisation's visions or goals; and how it can be used in any change or transition. It is 'the transfer of wisdom, skills, and technology' between individuals and organisational subunits (Peng, 2011). Amongst these transactions are the promotion of new ideas and the effective acquisition and sharing of good practices. Self-efficacy and self-motivation are essential to convey confidence that dissemination throughout the organisation will have benefits. These will be intrinsic—the sense of belonging, community identity and community satisfaction in creating and providing knowledge for others—or extrinsic—because there are positive relationships between financial performance and collaboration behaviour. The manager assumes the role of connector in the dissemination process (Fallatah, 2018; Osinski & Rummel, 2019; Bitkowska, 2020). The features of this competence are communication, the ability to engage peers, the ability to engage the workforce at several levels and the ability to convert ideas into business propositions through communication and analytical skills.

- A knowledge management orientation create a positive environment and the skills of the manager and will be instrumental in bringing this about. The purpose is to reach innovative and value adding outcomes through collaboration using the entire spectrum of information distributed among team members. The challenge, much like converting data into information and insight is to synthesise the various way points into new knowledge (Claus & Wiese, 2019; Osinski & Rummel, 2019). The process by which this takes place might be referred to as collaborative sense-making and described as *integrates diverse bodies of knowledge into a coherent whole.* Deciding on where to focus, which aspect has priority, and when to act will be considerations to identify opportunities for the application of knowledge balancing the types of information or intelligence that are relevant; trying to avoid too much or little weight given to prior knowledge; too much or too little weight given to new evidence (Kahneman & Tversky, 1973; Simon, 1979). In the quest to integrate diverse knowledge into a coherent plan the manager will apply their own tacit knowledge, intuition, judgement and confidence on the body of knowledge at their disposal trying to navigate a path between the status quo and a desired alternative—the challenge here is that 'once a theory is well entrenched, it will survive many assaults of empirical evidence that purports to refute it unless an alternative theory, consistent with the evidence, stands ready to replace it' (Simon, 1979). The aspect of core management competence that relates to cohesion is concerned with planning and control; meeting deadlines on the one hand and developing options on the other; and about the balance between unbridled creativity and bridled financial constraints. The features of this competence are the analytical skills, the ability to prioritise and the ability to communicate and engage with others.

- The premise on which interest in knowledge is based is that its combination and integration will produce profitable outputs. But to do so will require cooperation and coordination among involved units and individuals. *Implements collaborative processes* is therefore essential and this addresses the issues of how to create an environment in which individual tacit knowledge becomes explicit knowledge. This can be through effective communication or by day-to-day collaborative activity or through agile networks that are dynamic and cross-organisational so that opportunity can be realised. A feature of Japanese corporations during the Third Industrial Revolution was ensuring that everyone on a project or business opportunity was brought up to date by the exchange of information, a characteristic that may be relevant to organisations into the Fourth (Wingrove, 1995). The objective behind each of these alternatives is collaboration in an efficient, effective and trustworthy manner. Where there is a collaborative environment, the benefits of knowledge creation and transfer will accumulate—'collaborative process competence mediates the relationship between absorptive capacity and collaborative engagement, and positively influences both operational and relational outcomes' (Meijer, 2000; Zacharia et al., 2011; Verdouw et al., 2014; Fallatah, 2018; Grefen et al., 2018). In the first place the need to develop trust and a strong level of communication infrastructure (formal and informal) between those involved in the collaboration is important to ensure 'meaningful, timely and useable information' The process for collaboration has elements of building, qualifying its efficacy once in place, implementation and assessment. to shape better knowledge management and organisational learning (Kyeongrim et al., 2005; Shamsuzzoha et al., 2010).

- The more people know about what knowledge exists and what is available, the more accessible it will be; and the more accessible it is the more people can add to it making the overall body of knowledge grow in value over time (Kashyap, 2020). *Uses knowledge to create value for stakeholders* therefore becomes an important part of core management competence by relating knowledge and collaboration to performance. On the one hand value can be created for the organisation as a whole and might include the development of new products or services or the increase in the value of intellectual capital, (intangible assets such as corporate reputation, patents or copyrights), which for many organisations will form the bulk of their value; or it can be value through non-financial benefits such as team performance and relationships (Meijer, 2000; Törngren et al., 2019; Atthawej et al., 2020; Özlen & Handzic, 2020). The strategic importance of this is that organisations which have high value knowledge will see improved returns in their financial performance. Knowledge will have an impact on 'vertical' applications (from research to product) and 'horizontal' applications (research to research, department to department). This is one explanation as to why organisations spend huge amounts on knowledge acquisition either through knowledge creation or through purchasing knowledge already created—by corporate acquisition. Hence there are several broad categories of business value that can arise, ranging from minimising risk to improving efficiency and effectiveness to enabling innovation. Some of these are important for short-term survival, whilst knowledge management for innovation underpins long-term economic success. The returns on investment come about in commercialised products or licensing or selling knowledge to others (Fallatah, 2018; Ganguly et al., 2020). The features of this competence are analytical skills to prepare a business case, understanding organisational dynamics and engagement skills to persuade others as to the value of the case once identified.

- Whilst an organisation's culture will be a strong determinant of the level of collaboration in creating and sharing knowledge, its structure will also have an important part to play. The hierarchical organisation, for example, provided (theoretical) formal routes by which these activities could take place, but the complexity and rich interconnectivity of contemporary organisations add an extra dimension to the challenge. The effectiveness of the manager on this aspect of competence will influence the level to which they are able to navigate through the various organisational checks and balances (strategy, stewardship and policy). And therefore, *understands organisational dynamics* becomes an important aspect of competence. The dynamics are the forces which influence how an organisation operates and responds to opportunity or threat; and which are determined by history, culture, language, politics and process (Uhl-Bien & Arena, 2017; Baskaran, 2018; Turner, 2019). Here, different modus operandi will require awareness on the part of the manager about the factors that will enhance the creation and dissemination of knowledge and the collaborative efforts to do so—and what obstacles might be present. Different environmental situations and contexts will require different management perspectives with responses contingent on specific circumstances (Kilburg & Donohue, 2011; Reichenpfader et al., 2015; Turner, 2019). The features of this competence are an understanding of the psychology of work and the sociology of work and how these impact on the organisation. Understanding different architectures and their attributes, as well as political and change management skills are important.
- The adoption of positive attitudes towards collaboration depends on how the organisation is able 'to build on its achieved wisdom … and be receptive to new wisdom' (Peng, 2011; Freeburg, 2019). How to do both will depend on collaborative processes leading to the maximisation of the value of knowledge, which will in turn be dependent on effective interpersonal skills and judgement on the part of the manager and *political skills to secure commitment to collaboration.* This aspect of competence requires further explanation since politics are often presented in a pejorative sense and of a destructive nature. But politics can also be described as a source of influence in both strategic (demand-side) and operational (supply-side) decisions. In this respect politics

means an ability to understand others at work, and to use such knowledge to influence others to act in ways that enhance organisational objectives. Political skill derives from social relationships and an understanding of those relationships in organisational decision-making such that 'individuals with high political skill utilise interpersonal skills to effectively influence others; are characterised by their sincerity and an engaging manner and are proficient in persuasion, negotiation, networking and mediation.' They are characterised by making a concerted effort to understand differing viewpoints then persuading others of the value of knowledge to these viewpoints and the benefits of collaboration in the achievement of knowledge creation (Gerow et al., 2017). The features of this competence are communication skills, the ability to engage with others at all levels and trustworthiness.

- Knowledge has a positive effect on performance when the organisation has 'absorptive capacity' to use that knowledge (Bapuji et al., 2011). It is one of the roles of the manager to ensure that decisions about how and where knowledge is applied are made with insight and reason. Hence an important factor associated with this competence is that the manager *makes rational decisions.* This means using information and facts, that take account of others' input or feelings and seeking out their opinions on immediate business or longer-term issues. In Weberian terms (Weber, 1920) an action is rational if it is oriented to a clearly formulated unambiguous goal or to a set of values which are clearly formulated and logically consistent. The challenge is to enable appropriate levels of 'control' whilst facilitating flexibility (Heinicke et al., 2016). Values embraced in the organisational culture support this process. Perceptions of a manager's rational decision-making style can be positively associated with a perception of the manager's openness to alternative perspectives, receptivity to new ideas and suggestions from others—each of which will facilitate the acquisition and dissemination of knowledge and these factors will increase the chances of collaboration being successful. In turn, perceptions of a manager's decision-making may increase a perceiver's mutual collaboration with that manager. 'Research has demonstrated that people prefer to collaborate with others who have a reputation for being competent'

(Tsai et al., 2020). The economist Herbert Simon, in his classic essay on the subject of decision theory concluded that 'decision makers can satisfice either by finding optimum solutions for a simplified world, or by finding satisfactory solutions for a more realistic world'. For the practising manager both co-exist in strategic decision-making and day-to-day operations, 'formidable and often intolerable computational burdens for their solution' (Simon, 1979). Those intolerable computational burdens are the bread and butter of business management and the ability to execute them in a way that is as rational as possible is one of the aspects of the core management competence. Bounded rationality is not omniscience, but knowledge combined with judgement. The features of this competence are analytical skills, the ability to take a balanced approach and commitment once a decision had been made.

Organisations will thrive when supply push factors such as sufficient resources, a positive culture and worthwhile jobs outweigh demand pull factors such as a lack of control, a poor working environment or poor communication. The role of the manager is to apply their knowledge and skills across the organisation to ensure that supply push factors continue to predominate. Knowledge management is one of those factors and the above section has outlined some of the knowledge and skills to produce an environment in which knowledge production flourishes through collaboration.

Attitudes and Behaviours for the Core Management Competence of 'Collaborates to Create and Share Knowledge and Information'

Attitudes and behaviours are the social manifestations of how a manager undertakes a role and are critical elements of competence necessary for the performance of an activity. In contemporary organisations different attitudes and behaviours will emerge from a combination of cognition, intuition and emotional intelligence and are derived from self-awareness and a sense and response mindset; each of which are relevant across the core management competence framework. However, there are aspects that are particularly relevant to the competence based on collaboration and knowledge creation:

- For example, critical to success will be the ability to engage others in both commitment and process through the language of collaboration on the one hand and the practice of collaboration on the other—that is, success will be based on more than just verbal communication or a statement of intent. Studies in France, Switzerland and Germany, for example, concluded that higher levels of knowledge-oriented leadership and management, trust and readiness to share knowledge, and a cultural environment that strongly supports interaction between stakeholders, enhanced knowledge management capability and had an impact on innovation (Minonne, 2007; Frey et al., 2009; Naqshbandi & Jasimuddin, 2018). It is to this area of practice that *acts a role model for collaboration* applies. This is the manager's demonstrated, positive, collaborative and open attitude towards colleagues within their own teams, colleagues in other areas, towards managers from different functions and towards those outside of the organisation on whom value creation may depend—partners or suppliers, for example. In being a role model the manager will apply rules consistently and subject their own ideas to the same tests as those that apply to others—intellectual humility (Meijer, 2000; Schierjott et al., 2020; Thomke, 2020). And given the fluidity of structures in many modern organisations, (networks, matrices, swarms) this means being a role model within a single team; across several teams; at multiple levels; across the organisation and across partner organisations. The role has evolved from one of control to one of empowerment and being seen as both enthusiastic and comfortable with the implications of this transition will go some way to deciding how other parts of the organisation respond to requests for collaboration or knowledge sharing.
- The cause of knowledge and its dissemination will be enhanced if the manager actively *promotes a collaborative environment*—collaborating within units or teams and 'teaming up' with others to deliver innova-

tive ideas by using open innovation approaches. A collaborative environment is no longer held within the confines of any one team, unit or organisation with cross fertilisation both within and without the organisation an integral part of modern collaborative relationships. The objective is to facilitate the opportunity for those who have value generating knowledge that will enhance the competitive position of the organisation to build on their knowledge. In so doing the manager will attempt to create an environment that respects initiative; that is positive and encouraging to ideas and innovation; that is non-judgemental with a working atmosphere of openness and cooperation. One in which new ideas are openly shared and discussed, in which trial and experimentation are encouraged and in which the allocation of work is done in a way that stimulates and challenges (Bellandi et al., 2013; Hashimoto & Nassif, 2014). The manager will seek to eliminate or reduce barriers that get in the way of initiative, and as outlined above will ensure that communications are transparent and value adding.

- Collaboration is not an end in itself. It is a means to an end and that end is the creation and application of knowledge. Knowledge to inform strategy, knowledge to create products and services, knowledge of customers, knowledge to solve problems, knowledge to ensure workforce engagement and knowledge of business processes; all of which will support the development of a learning organisation. The rationale for this is that knowledge awareness, knowledge availability and knowledge dissemination are directly related to performance outcomes. And so, *communicates the value of knowledge* may be seen as an important part of core management competence (Taweel et al., 2009; Baskaran, 2018; Pour et al., 2019). First, knowledge dissemination is essential to the achievement of long-term goals; second, knowledge value is important for operational improvements—efficiency, communication and decision-making by increasing buy-in from stakeholders and helping to solve problems (Li, 2010). A combination of these two factors and a knowledge 'business case' are critical to securing the support of the Board and shareholders, building a consensus amongst the Executives about direction and resource allocation, gaining the buy in of the workforce and engaging external suppliers or partners in the strategy. The role of the manager will be to communicate the value of knowledge to achieving the organisation's aims—factual information about the effectiveness of knowledge-based activity and achievements; or that related to goal attainment or specific business processes (Applen, 2002; Wingate et al., 2018). Decision-making in a multitude of business scenarios will be enhanced through knowledge, made up of data, information, intelligence and insight. Ensuring acceptance of the value of knowledge will therefore be key; to collaboration and ultimately to the achievement of business goals.

- Having communicated the benefits of collaboration, and the value of knowledge, the role will then be to *engage stakeholders in knowledge creation and dissemination* with individual members of the workforce, with teams, with peers and with other stakeholders. There are considerable advantages in so doing. For example, if members of the workforce are engaged in the aims of the organisation and are able to create and contribute knowledge to the achievement of those aims, then it will add to wider benefits of engagement such as shareholder returns, income, revenue growth, profitability and customer or client satisfaction. In this respect, engagement as the simultaneous employment and expression of a person's 'preferred self in task behaviours that promote connections to work and to others, personal presence (physical, cognitive, and emotional), and active, full role performance' (Saks, 2006, 2017; Schwarz, 2012; Meyer, 2013, 2017; Bakker, 2017) will add to the willingness to engage. This in turn will add to knowledge sharing and collaboration both of which are largely discretionary acts. The more engaged an employee is, the greater the chances of collaboration leading to a 'mutual investment approach' (Goleman & Boyatzis, 2008; Hui-Ru et al., 2016; Baskaran, 2018; Törngren et al., 2019; Gerpott et al., 2020).
- The optimal utilisation of knowledge depends on effective networking and a coherent relationship between technology, management systems, engagement of the workforce, a collaborative culture and a willingness to share. The creation, codification and transfer of knowledge will be facilitated when there is this cohesion. Where knowledge is embedded and situated in practice, it becomes a valuable, dynamic asset. However, advances in technology alone, with open systems that encourage

collaboration and knowledge sharing will not, by themselves, be enough to succeed, particularly in the instance of tacit knowledge. In this respect a key aspect of the role of the manager will be to make connections across the organisation to ensure that the value of the knowledge is maximised by enhancing the organisation's 'absorptive capacity'—fundamental learning processes about the ability to acquire and disseminate knowledge and belief that once gained it will be applied effectively (Bapuji et al., 2011; Baskaran, 2018; Bitkowska, 2020). It is this that requires a positive, outreaching attitude and hence *uses judgement in connecting sources of knowledge* (based on business needs and priorities as well as fairness, building trust and acknowledging credit) is an important factor in management competence. How and where to connect, what value will be created in what way and what are the implications across the organisation, its workforce and other stakeholders are key questions. A facet of knowledge management that might be applicable here is the 'Knowing Model', the objective of which is 'informed and targeted dissemination of information to spark emergent behaviour change in a specific area' (Freeburg, 2019). This means using knowledge of successes and experiences in connecting originators of sources of ideas and suggestions with others, networking with peers to gain knowledge of experiences and networking outside of the organisation for knowledge about environmental trends. It means communicating across as well as up and down the organisation and it means exercising judgements that are based on human as well as business criteria. If this is done effectively it will have both business and 'socio-emotional' benefits (Ibarra & Hansen, 2011; Teoh et al., 2016). Judgement will be based not only on business or technology knowledge, but also on an understanding of human resources and the importance of an attitude of equity and trust and actions of equity and trust. Indeed, the effectiveness of judgement will depend on the perception of the manager as a trusted and reliable receiver of knowledge and an efficient distributor of knowledge. Once both of these are in place then the role of 'connector' can be fulfilled.

- At a macro level, knowledge creation involves interactions between individuals, processes, the environment, technology and organisational strategy (Sundiman et al., 2019). However, at a micro level, knowledge and knowledge sharing behaviour are highly subjective to the individual and depend on willingness to participate in such behaviour. Not only is it important that the manager acts as advocate for knowledge sharing and its benefits to the organisation as a whole, but also that they *help others to learn* about how to do so. This behaviour will come about from understanding work characteristics and job design which give insights not only about the likelihood of both explicit and tacit knowledge (Goh & Lim, 2014; Gressgård & Nesheim, 2018), but also about human behaviour in organisations and how to engage the workforce in the tasks of knowledge. An important benefit of collaboration is the learning that results, where organisational learning is the willingness to apply new knowledge to decision-making and influencing others to use the knowledge in delivering the organisation's objectives. If managers have a positive attitude towards the use of knowledge in the learning process then it will increase receptivity and, with resource allocation, absorptive capacity. 'Organizational learning is both a function of access to new knowledge and the capabilities for using and building on such knowledge' (Srivastava & Frankwick, 2011).

- The final area of attitude and behaviour that forms the basis of this core management competence is that the manager has the attitude and behaviour that *keeps teams from being mired in debate* (Ibarra & Hansen, 2011). This is management in its most traditional form and whilst this is true its impact is no less. The disruption of Industry 4.0. technology with its multiple benefits does not mean the abrogation of organisational responsibility for the achievement of goals and objectives. The knowledge creation and collaboration in its application is rarely a linear process. There will inevitably be tensions based on business issues—such as on priorities or resource allocation—and between functions as specialists and generalists combine in their efforts to secure competitive advantage through knowledge. The role of the manager will be to act as facilitator and ultimately as arbiter as choices or options are evaluated. It will encompass a range of behavioural activities from enabling participation to conflict resolution. Two guiding criteria for decision-making in this context were identified by Accenture (2019) as prioritising projects that generate value for the broader organisation and that stimulate collaboration between functions; and investing in and rapidly scaling platforms that empower continuous collaboration thereby solving the problem of 'island isolation' that may be a feature of debate. There is a balance to be made and this aspect of behaviour leans towards value.

New technologies, including 'expeditious data processing models, configurable platforms, networking and the Internet', have raised the profile of knowledge and knowledge management as sources of competitive advantage, prompting organisations to maximise the sources of knowledge available to them. Managers *in* organisations recognised that the management *of* organisations could create and disseminate knowledge which would mean 'achieving higher efficiency, effectiveness, better quality of services and minimisation of costs' but also lead to the creation of unique products or services for external clients or customers. The second of the core management competences therefore concerned collaboration in the quest to create and share knowledge and information. Its importance was based on the assumption that knowledge management was possibly the most important antecedent of success and that collaborating with others and compromising to gain overall progress were keys to unlocking its potential. These held true whether the organisation had a hierarchical structure or was networked with non-hierarchical forms of management. Furthermore, any cultural differences disappear in knowledge intensive organisations (Dana et al., 2001; Migdadi & Abu Zaid, 2016; Prifti et al., 2017). A broad range of attributes were identified across the competence definition of knowledge, skills, attitudes and behaviours. Their understanding of the importance of collaboration and ability to navigate organisational dynamics in knowledge creation and dissemination; acting as knowledge seeker and disseminator in a collaborative environment; and having the political skills to navigate whatever structures were in place. In addition, attitudes of positivity and the ability to create a supportive and constructive environment in which members of the workforce could create ideas, (Unler & Caliskan, 2019) and acting as role model would complement knowledge and skills.

The conclusions about the importance of collaboration and knowledge creation have recently been reinforced by practice-based points of view—based on the experiences of management during the pandemic as well as the dynamics of Industry 4.0—including one from the World Economic Forum that is particularly relevant to the competence of collaboration—'it is unprecedented to have a large cohort of people, all over the world, start working remotely at once. The events as they have unfolded have shown how fast we can adapt though and have demonstrated that we can move faster and act in more agile ways than we thought. Business leaders now have, in some sense, been gifted with a better idea of what can and cannot be done outside their companies' traditional processes, and COVID-19 is forcing both the pace and the scale of workplace innovation. Many are finding simpler, faster and less expensive ways to operate' (Kirby, 2020). The core management competence of *collaborates to create and share knowledge and information* has rarely been more apposite.

References

Accenture. (2019). Beyond Digital: Transcending Status Quo in Industry X.0. https://www.accenture.com/gb-en/insights/strategy/digital-transformation-investment

Adi, M. P. H., & Sukmawati, A. (2020). The Effect of Levers of Control and Leadership Style on Creativity. *Journal of Indonesian Economy and Business, 35*(3), 236–256.

Alshanty, A. M., & Emeagwali, O. L. (2019). Market-Sensing Capability, Knowledge Creation and Innovation: The Moderating Role of Entrepreneurial-Orientation. *Journal of Innovation & Knowledge, 4*(3), 171–178.

Antunes, H. de J. G, & Pinheiro, P. G. (2020). Linking Knowledge Management, Organizational Learning and Memory. *Journal of Innovation & Knowledge, 5*(2), 140–149.

Applen, J. D. (2002). Technical Communication, Knowledge Management, and XML. *Technical Communication, 49*(3), 301.

Argyris, Y. "Anna", & Ransbotham, S. (2020). Knowledge Entrepreneurship: Institutionalising Wiki-Based Knowledge-Management Processes in Competitive and Hierarchical Organisations. *Journal of Information Technology, 31*(2), 226–239.

Arjomandy, D. (2016). Social Media Integration in Electronic Human Resource Management: Development of a Social eHRM Framework. *Canadian Journal of Administrative Sciences, 2*, 108.

Atthawej, T., Ueasangkomsate, P., & Sudharatana, Y. (2020). A Literature Review and Future Research on Knowledge Management Orientation in Organizations. *2020 Joint International Conference on Digital Arts, Media and Technology*.

Bakken, R., & Dobbs, J. (2016). The Relevance of Four Types of Knowledge for Leader Preparation in Radically Different Settings: Reflections on Data from a Case Study in Qatar and Teaching at a United States Military Academy. *Creighton Journal of Interdisciplinary Leadership, 2*(2), 17–23.

Bakker, A. (2017). Strategic and Proactive Approaches to Work Engagement. *Special Issue: Employee Engagement, Organizational Dynamics, 46*(2), 67–75.

Bapuji, H., Loree, D., & Crossan, M. (2011). Connecting External Knowledge Usage and Firm Performance: An Empirical Analysis. *Journal of Engineering and Technology Management, 28*(4), 215–231.

Barnard, C. I. (1948). *The Early Sociology of Management and Organisations* (2014 edition). Routledge.

Baskaran, S. (2018). Mediation Effect of Knowledge Management Enablers on the Relationship between Organizational Characteristics and Entrepreneurial Orientation. *Gadjah Mada International Journal of Business, 20*(1), 1–32.

Bellandi, V., Ceravolo, P., Damiani, E., Frati, F., Cota, G. L., & Maggesi, J. (2013). Boosting the Innovation Process in Collaborative Environments. *IEEE International Conference on Systems, Man, and Cybernetics, Systems, Man, and Cybernetics (SMC)*.

Bitkowska, A. (2020). The Relationship between Business Process Management and Knowledge Management—Selected Aspects from a Study of Companies in Poland. *Journal of Entrepreneurship, Management and Innovation, 1*, 169.

Boulton, Watt and Co. (1802). *Steam Engine Affairs, Letter Held at the Wedgewood Museum*. Stoke on Trent.

Boyatzis, R. E. (2011). Managerial and Leadership Competencies: A Behavioural Approach to Emotional, Social and Cognitive Intelligence. *Vision (09722629), 15*(2), 91–100.

Brinkmann, J. (2006). *Competence of Top Management Teams*. Deutsche Universitats Verlag.

Cai, S., & Yang, Z. (2017). Trust, Information Integration, and Coordination Costs: An Integrative Model. *Asian Journal of Business Research, 7*(1), 79.

Hui-Ru Cai, Min Li, & Pian-Pian Guan. (2016). Fostering Managers' Knowledge-Sharing Behaviour: The Impact of the Employee-Organization Relationship. *Social Behaviour & Personality: An International Journal, 44*(4), 669–678.

Chaudhuri, A., & Boer, H. (2016). The Impact of Product-Process Complexity and New Product Development Order Winners on New Product Development Performance: The Mediating Role of Collaborative Competence. *Journal of Engineering and Technology Management, 42*, 65–80.

Claus, A. M., & Wiese, B. S. (2019). Development and Test of a Model of Interdisciplinary Competencies. *European Journal of Work and Organizational Psychology, 28*(2), 191–205.

Colman, H. L. (2020). Facilitating Integration and Maintaining Autonomy: The Role of Managerial Action and Interaction in Post-Acquisition Capability Transfer. *Journal of Business Research, 109*, 148–160.

Dana, L.-P., Korot, L., & Tovstiga, G. (2001). Convergence vs. Divergence: A Comparative Analysis of Singapore versus Silicon Valley Knowledge Management Practices. *Journal of Enterprising Culture, 9*(1). https://doi.org/10.1142/S0218495801000031

Deiser, R. (2009). *Designing the Smart Organisation*. Jossey Bass.

Easen, N. (2020, July 27). Management of Ideas Comes of Age. *The Times*.

Fallatah, M. I. (2018). Does Value Matter? An Examination of the Impact of Knowledge Value on Firm Performance and the Moderating Role of Knowledge Breadth. *Journal of Knowledge Management, 22*(3), 678–695.

Faßauer, G. (2018). Linking Deviation with Innovation: Behavioural Effects of Management Control through the Lens of a Theory of Deviance. *Journal of Management Control, 29*(3–4), 275.

Freeburg, D. (2019). The Knowing Model: Facilitating Behaviour Change in Organisations. *Journal of Information & Knowledge Management, 18*(4). https://doi.org/10.1142/s0219649219500400

Frey, P., Lindner, F., Muller, A., & Wald, A. (2009). Project Knowledge Management Organizational Design and Success Factors—An Empirical Study in Germany. *42nd Hawaii International Conference on System Sciences,*

Ganguly, A., Kumar, C., Saxena, G., & Talukdar, A. (2020). Firms' Reputation for Innovation: Role of Marketing Capability, Innovation Capability, and Knowledge Sharing. *Journal of Information & Knowledge Management, 19*(2), 2050004.

Gerow, J. E., Grover, V., & Thatcher, J. B. (2017). Can Political Skill Enhance Business and IT Knowledge? *Information Systems Management, 34*(2), 157–171.

Gerpott, F. H., Fasbender, U., & Burmeister, A. (2020). Respectful Leadership and Followers' Knowledge Sharing: A Social Mindfulness Lens. *Human Relations, 73*(6), 789.

Goh, S.-K., & Lim, K.-Y. (2014). Perceived Creativity: The Role of Emotional Intelligence and Knowledge Sharing Behaviour. *Journal of Information & Knowledge Management, 13*(4), 1.

Goleman, D., & Boyatzis, R. (2008). Social Intelligence and the Biology of Leadership. *Harvard Business Review*, Published in *On Collaboration*, Harvard Business Review Press.

Gratton, L., & Scott, A. (2016). *The 100-Year Life*. Bloomsbury.

Grefen, P., Rinderle-Ma, S., Dustdar, S., Fdhila, W., Mending, J., & Schulte, S. (2018). Charting Process-Based Collaboration Support in Agile Business Networks: Aligning the Need for a Dynamic Internet of Processes from Industry and Research Perspectives. *IEEE Internet Computing, 22*(3), 48–57.

Gressgård, L. J., & Nesheim, T. (2018). Knowledge Management Systems and Work Improvements: The Moderating Effects of Work Characteristics. *Journal of Information & Knowledge Management, 17*(4), 1850042.

Guechtouli, M., & Guechtouli, W. (2009). Information Technologies' Impact on Individual Learning Process: The Case of a Community of Practice. In *Handbook of Research on E-Transformation and Human Resources Management Technologies: Organizational Outcomes and Challenges*. IGI Global.

Hashimoto, M., & Nassif, V. M. J. (2014). Inhibition and Encouragement of Entrepreneurial Behaviour: Antecedents Analysis from Managers' Perspectives. *BAR—Brazilian Administration Review, 11*(4), 385–406.

Heinicke, A., Guenther, T. W., & Widener, S. K. (2016). An Examination of the Relationship Between The Extent of a Flexible Culture and the Levers of Control System: The Key Role of Beliefs Control. *Management Accounting Research, 33*, 25–41.

Ibarra, H., & Hansen, M. T. (2011). Are You a Collaborative Leader. *Harvard Business Review*, Published in *On Collaboration*, Harvard Business Review Press.

Iraj, S., Kamat, S., Prakash, S., & Weldon, M. (2017). Will Productivity Growth Return in the New Digital Era? An Analysis of the Potential Impact on Productivity of the Fourth Industrial Revolution. *Bell Labs Technical Journal, 22*, 2–18.

Jacques, E. (1990). In Praise of Hierarchy. *Harvard Business Review*, January–February.

Kahneman, D., & Tversky, A. (1973). On the Psychology of Prediction. *Psychological Review, 80*(4), 237–251.

Kašćelan, L., Pejić Bach, M., Rondović, B., & Đuričković, T. (2020). The Interaction Between Social Media, Knowledge Management and Service Quality: A Decision Tree Analysis. *PloS One, 15*(8), e0236735.
Kashyap, R. (2020). The Economics of Enlightenment: Time Value of Knowledge and the Net Present Value (NPV) of Knowledge Machines, A Proposed Approach Adapted from Finance. B.E. *Journal of Economic Analysis & Policy, 20*(2), 1–23.
Kilburg, R. R., & Donohue, M. D. (2011). Toward a 'Grand Unifying Theory' of Leadership: Implications for Consulting Psychology. *Consulting Psychology Journal: Practice and Research, 63*(1), 6–25. https://doi.org/10.1037/A0023053
Kirby, S. (2020). *5 Ways COVID-19 Has Changed Workforce Management*. World Economic Forum. https://www.weforum.org/agenda/2020/06/covid-homeworking-symptom-of-changing-face-of-workforce-management/
Koh, L., Orzes, G., & Jia, F. (Jeff). (2019). The Fourth Industrial Revolution (Industry 4.0): Technologies Disruption on Operations and Supply Chain Management. *International Journal of Operations & Production Management, 39* (6/7/8), 817–828.
Kyeongrim, A., Hyuncheol, K., & Jinwook Chung. (2005). Cooperative Business Collaboration Business Process Modeling Using UN/CEFACT UMM. *Proceedings of the Ninth International Conference on Computer Supported Cooperative Work in Design, 2*, 950.
Lemmetty, S., Glăveanu, V. P., Collin, K., & Forsman, P. (2020). (Un)Sustainable Creativity? Different Manager-Employee Perspectives in the Finnish Technology Sector. *Sustainability, 12* (3605).
Lepore, D., Dubbini, S., Micozzi, A., & Spigarelli, F. (2021). Knowledge Sharing Opportunities for Industry 4.0 Firms. *Journal of the Knowledge Economy, 1*. https://doi.org/10.1007/s13132-021-00750-9
Li, C. (2010). *Open Leadership*. Jossey Bass.
Li, D., Landstrom, A., Fast-Berglund, A., & Alstrom, P. (2019). Human-Centred Dissemination of Data, Information and Knowledge in Industry 4.0. SMART PM—Sustainable Manufacturing by Automated Real-Time Performance Management Demonstration—Och Testbädd Inom Smart Digitalisering För Automation Med Människan i *Centrum Procedia CIRP, 84*, 380–386.
Lin, H. F. (2015). Linking Knowledge Management Orientation to Balanced Scorecard Outcomes. *Journal of Knowledge Management, 19*(6), 1224–1249.
Masrani, S. K., Morelli, C. J., & Bagchi, A. K. (2021). The Rise of Indian Business in the Global Context in the Twentieth Century: A Review and Introduction. *Business History, 63*(1), 1–17.

Mazali, T. (2018). From Industry 4.0 to Society 4.0, There and Back. *AI & Soc, 33*, 405–411. https://doi.org/10.1007/s00146-017-0792-6
McWilliams, D. (2020). *We Are Living through a 'Pandession'—Here's How We Escape*. http://www.davidmcwilliams.ie/we-are-living-through-a-pandession-heres-how-we-escape/
Meijer, B. R. (2000). A Management Attitude Towards Knowledge Fusion and Innovation. *Proceedings of the 2000 IEEE Engineering Management Society. EMS—2000 (Cat. No.00CH37139)*.
Meyer, J. P. (2013). The Science–Practice Gap and Employee Engagement: It's a Matter of Principle. *Canadian Psychology/Psychologie Canadienne, 54*(4), 235–245.
Meyer, J. P. (2017). Has Engagement Had Its Day: What's Next and Does It Matter? *Organizational Dynamics, 46*(2), 87–95.
Migdadi, M. M. (2016). The Role of Effective Chief Knowledge Officer in Facilitating Knowledge Management. *Journal of Information & Knowledge Management, 15*(4), 1.
Migdadi, M. M., & Abu Zaid, M. K. S. (2016). An Empirical Investigation of Knowledge Management Competence for Enterprise Resource Planning Systems Success: Insights from Jordan. *International Journal of Production Research, 54*(18), 5480.
Minonne, C. (2007). Towards an Integrative Approach for Managing Implicit and Explicit Knowledge: An Exploratory Study in Switzerland. *Proceedings of ECKM 2007 8th European Conference on Knowledge Management*.
Mukherjee, A. S. (2020). 5 Musts for Next Gen Leaders. *MIT Sloan Management Review, 61*(3), 1–4.
Nahapiet, J., & Ghoshal, S. (1998). Social Capital, Intellectual Capital, and the Organisational Advantage. In I. Nonaka (Ed.), *Knowledge Management*. Routledge.
Namisango, F., Kafuko, M. M., & Byomire, G. (2020). Orchestrating Enterprise Social Media for Knowledge Co-creation: An Interactionist Perspective. *VINE: The Journal of Information & Knowledge Management Systems, 50*(1), 57–74.
Naqshbandi, M. M., & Jasimuddin, S. M. (2018). Knowledge-Oriented Leadership and Open Innovation: Role of Knowledge Management Capability in France-Based Multinationals. *International Business Review, 27*(3), 701–713.
Nonaka, I. (1994). A Dynamic Theory of Organizational Knowledge Creation. *Organisation Science, 5*(1), 14–37.

Nonaka, L., Takeuchi, H., & Umemoto, K. (1996). A Theory of Organizational Knowledge Creation. *International Journal of Technology Management, 11*(7), 833–845.

Ordonez, M. and Serrat, O. (2017). Disseminating Knolwedge Products, *Knowledge Solutions*, 871.

Osinski, M., & Rummel, N. (2019). Towards Successful Knowledge Integration in Online Collaboration: An Experiment on the Role of Meta-Knowledge. *Proceedings of the ACM on Human-Computer Interaction, CSCW, 1*.

Özlen, M. K., & Handzic, M. (2020). Ambidextrous Organisations from the Perspective of Employed Knowledge Management Strategies: Evidence from Turkey. *Journal of Information & Knowledge Management, 19*(2), 1–15.

Peng Du. (2011). *An Empirical Study on the Relationships of Knowledge Management Orientation, Market Orientation, and Firm Performance.* International Conference on Management and Service Science, Management and Service Science (MASS).

Philbeck, T., & Davis, N. (2019). The Fourth Industrial Revolution: Shaping a New Era. *Journal of International Affairs, 72*(1), 17.

Pour, M. J., Matin, H. Z., Yazdani, H. R., & Zadeh, Z. K. (2019). A Comprehensive Investigation of the Critical Factors Influencing Knowledge Management Strategic Alignment. *Knowledge Management & E-Learning, 11*(2), 215–232.

Prieto, L. C., & Phipps, S. T. A. (2016). Rediscovering Charles Clinton Spaulding's the Administration of Big Business. *Journal of Management History, 22*(1), 73–90.

Prifti, L., Knigge, M., Kiennegger, H., & Krcmar, H. (2017). A Competency Model for 'Industrie 4.0' Employees. *13th International Conference on Wirtschaftsinformatik*, February 12–15, 2017, St. Gallen, Switzerland.

Randhawa, K., Josserand, E., Schweitzer, J., & Logue, D. (2017). Knowledge Collaboration between Organizations and Online Communities: The Role of Open Innovation Intermediaries. *Journal of Knowledge Management, 21*(6), 1293–1318.

Reichenpfader, U., Carlfjord, S., & Nilsen, P. (2015). Leadership in Evidence-Based Practice: A Systematic Review. *Leadership in Health Services, 28*(4), 298–316.

Saks, A. M. (2006). Antecedents and Consequences of Employee Engagement. *Journal of Managerial Psychology, 21*(7), 600–619. https://doi.org/10.1108/02683940610690169

Saks, A. M. (2017). Translating Employee Engagement Research into Practice. *Organizational Dynamics, 46*, 76–86.

Salvadorinho, J., & Teixeira, L. (2021). Organizational Knowledge in the I4.0 Using BPMN: A Case Study. *Procedia Computer Science, 181*, 981–988.

Samiotis, K., & Poulymenakou, A. (2002). Knowledge Management in E-Banking: A Competence-Based Perspective. *Journal of Computer Information Systems, 42*(5), 102–109.

Schierjott, I., Brennecke, J., & Rank, O. N. (2020). Entrepreneurial Attitudes as Drivers of Managers' Boundary-Spanning Knowledge Ties in the Context of High-Tech Clusters. *Journal of Small Business Management, 56*, 108–131.

Schwab, K. (2016). *The Fourth Industrial Revolution: What It Means, How to Respond.* World Economic Forum. https://www.weforum.org/agenda/2016/01/the-fourth-industrial-revolution-what-it-means-and-how-to-respond/

Schwarz, T. (2012). New Research: How Employee Engagement Hits the Bottom Line. *Harvard Business Review.* https://hbr.org/2012/11/creating-sustainable-employee.html

Shamsuzzoha, A., Kankaanpää, T., Carneiro, L., & Helo, P. T. (2010). Implementation Framework for Collaboration in a Non-hierarchical Business Network. *IEEE International Conference on Industrial Engineering and Engineering Management*, 2254–2258.

Shigaki, J. S., & Koshijima, I. (2016). 3K Catalyst for P2M Management. *Proceedings of International Association of P2M.* https://www.jstage.jst.go.jp/article/iappmproc/2016

Simon, H. (1979). Rational Decision Making in Business Organisations. *American Economic Review, 69*(4), 493–513.

Spekle, R. F., van Elten, H. J., & Widener, S. K. (2017). Creativity and Control: A Paradox – Evidence from the Levers of Control Framework. *Behavioural Research in Accounting, 29*(2), 73–96.

Srivastava, P., & Frankwick, G. L. (2011). Environment, Management Attitude, and Organizational Learning in Alliances. *Management Decision, 49*(1), 156–166.

Sundiman, D., Wu, C. H., Mursidi, A., & Ting, I.-H. (2019). Task-Individual-Social Software Fit in Knowledge Creation Performance. *International Journal of Knowledge Management, 15*(2), 36.

Syed, M. (2020, October 25). Economies Thrive When We Work Together and Play Together. *Sunday Times.*

Taweel, A., Delaney, B., Arvanitis, T. N., & Lei Zhao. (2009). Communication, Knowledge and Co-ordination Management in Globally Distributed Software Development: Informed by a scientific Software Engineering Case Study. 2009 *Fourth IEEE International Conference on Global Software Engineering, Global Software Engineering*, 370–375.

Teoh, K. R.-H., Coyne, I., Devonish, D., Leather, P., & Zarola, A. (2016). The Interaction between Supportive and Unsupportive Manager Behaviours on Employee Work Attitudes. *Personnel Review, 45*(6), 1386–1402.

Thomas, K. J., & Akdere, M. (2013). Social Media as Collaborative Media in Workplace Learning. *Human Resource Development Review, 12*(3), 329–344.

Thomke, S. (2020). Building a Culture of Experimentation: It Takes More Than Good Tools. It Takes a Complete Change of Attitude. *Harvard Business Review, 98*(2), 40–48.

Törngren, M., Asplund, F., Ericson, T., Granbom, C., Herzog, E., Lu, Z., Magnusson, M., Mansson, M., Norrwing, S., Olsson, J., & Öberg, J. (2019). Competence Networks in the Era of CPS; Lessons Learnt in the ICES Cross-Disciplinary and Multi-domain Center. In R. Chamberlain, M. E. Grimheden, & W. Taha (Eds.), *Proceedings of the International Workshop on Design, Modeling, and Evaluation of Cyber Physical Systems, CyPhy 2019: Workshop on Embedded Systems and Cyber-Physical Systems Education* (Vol. 11971, pp. 264–283). Cham.

Tsai, M.-H., Hinsz, V. B., & Melia, N. V. (2020). The Effects of Perceived Decision-Making Styles on Evaluations of Openness and Competence That Elicit Collaboration. *Personality & Social Psychology Bulletin, 1*, 124.

Turner, P. A. (2019). *Leadership in Healthcare.* Palgrave Macmillan.

Uhl-Bien, M., & Arena, M. (2017). Complexity Leadership: Enabling People and Organizations for Adaptability. *Organizational Dynamics, 46*, 9–20.

Unilever. (1968). *Annual Report and Accounts.* https://www.unilever.com/Images/1968-annual-report-and-accounts_tcm244-509311_1_en.pdf

Unler, E., & Caliskan, S. (2019). Individual and Managerial Predictors of the Different Forms of Employee Voice. *Journal of Management Development, 38*(7), 582.

Verdouw, C., Beulens, A., & Wolfert, S. (2014). *Towards Software Mass Customization for Business Collaboration.* Annual SRII Global Conference, Global Conference (SRII) 106–115

Wang, Jun, Ruilin Zhang, Jin-Xing Hao, & Xuanyi Chen. (2019). Motivation Factors of Knowledge Collaboration in Virtual Communities of Practice: A

Perspective from System Dynamics. *Journal of Knowledge Management, 23*(3), 466–488.

Wang, L., Kameoka, A., Ikawa, Y., & Li, M. (2004). 2G14 Roadmapping: A Promising Practice for Developing Core Competence through Collective Learning. *Proceedings of the Annual Conference of the Japan Society for Research Policy and Innovation Management, 19*(19), 634–637.

Weber, M. (1920). *The Theory of Social and Economic Organisation*, 1947 Edition with an Introduction by Talcott Parsons. The Free Press.

Wilson, J. F., & Thomson, A. (2009). *The Making of Modern Management.* Oxford University Press.

Wingate, L. A., Smith, N. L., & Perk, E. (2018). The Project Vita: A Dynamic Knowledge Management Tool. *Evaluation & Program Planning, 71*, 22–27.

Wingrove, T. L. (1995). Japanese Management Style and How to Work with It. *Cross Cultural Management, 2*(2), 42–48.

Zacharia, Z. G., Nix, N. W., & Lusch, R. F. (2011). Capabilities That Enhance Outcomes of an Episodic Supply Chain Collaboration. *Journal of Operations Management, 29*(6), 591–603.

9

Management Competence for the Fourth Industrial Revolution: Engages and Develops the Workforce

Insight, Intuition and Hunch

People issues are business issues.

The performance of the workforce will be a strong determinant of both operational and strategic outcomes. This assumption provides the rationale attached to the importance of employee engagement, accentuated by people management challenges of massive technology change and the global pandemic as organisations implement new business models, change the type of work available, add new skills and adopt innovative approaches to organisation, interaction and communication. Recruiting, developing, motivating and retaining employees with the right level of skill in the right place at the right time therefore remain priorities for managers as they have in each of the Four Industrial Revolutions to date. Adam Smith's (1776) conclusion that the success of an organisation was dependent upon the 'skill, dexterity and judgement with which its labour is generally applied' is a sentiment that has endured.

For example, a people management priority was to attract and train a workforce for the new water powered mills in rural Derbyshire, England, in the mid-eighteenth century; and equally to the effective deployment of

P. Turner, *The Making of the Modern Manager*,
https://doi.org/10.1007/978-3-030-81062-7_9

64,000 workers from Scotland, Ireland, Sweden, Switzerland, Belgium, France, Germany, Italy, Croatia, Greece, Hungary and Poland in the US glass industry during the Second Industrial Revolution in the nineteenth (U.S. Immigration Commission, 1910), as well as instilling a culture, 'set from the top, of working toward common goals in a spirit of mutual respect', and competence in 'Perceptive Ability, Self-Restraint, Social Appropriateness, Interpersonal Sensitivity and Tolerance for Ambiguity' in Japanese organisations during the Third Industrial Revolution in the twentieth. Effective people management will be high on the list of managerial skills and judgement in the 'application of labour' as the Fourth Industrial Revolution gathers momentum. Dealing with the interaction between people and technology, deciding on how automated systems might best support a highly skilled human workforce, and how best to protect and reengage employees in the fall-out of the pandemic of 2020–2021 will prove to be as much of a challenge as any that have gone before (Takai & Ota, 1993; Garratt, 2000; Romani et al., 2018; Ghislieri et al., 2018; Nienaber & Martins, 2020; Kucharčíková et al., 2021). Employee engagement is influenced not only by a conducive work environment and prevailing culture but by the nature of the new jobs that appear from transformation, the opportunity to develop, build positive relationships with working colleagues and team members, and the vision and purpose of the organisation. These considerations are in the context of worldwide talent shortages and greater competition for skills, significant demographic change, and different attitudes, behaviours and expectations about work.

The core message about people management resonates such that across the continents 'well educated citizens' supported by scientific advances, technology developments and innovation hold the key (Odhiambo, 2020). This means maximising the contribution of a workforce that is au fait with and skilled in the job at hand, that utilises both explicit and tacit knowledge, and that leverages knowledge into business processes and new products or services. Enhancing performance by capturing knowledge in the form of insights, intuitions and 'hunches' and converting those into something that could be used by the organisation as a whole are essential business drivers (Nonaka et al., 1996; Nonaka & Hirotaka, 2008). Managerial skills needed to be a 'steward of employment' involving, recruiting, hiring, onboarding and training will be complemented by those of being a 'steward of work', orchestrating how work is done, whether through a person in a job, a person augmented by a machine or flexible labour such as gig workers or employees of an outsourcing organisation (Ramirez, 2020). Either way, Sheryl Sandberg's (2013) words resonate and tapping the entire pool of talent would improve collective performance. A combination of more traditional approaches and new requirements will reinforce the core management competence—'engages and develops the workforce', and its place in the overall schema shown in Fig. 9.1. The definition of this competence is as follows:

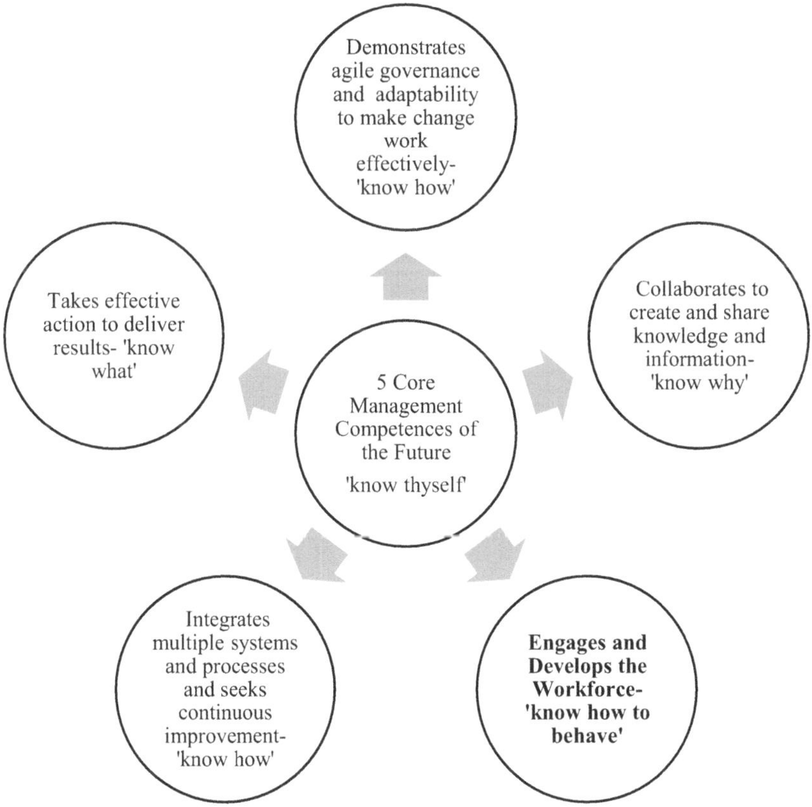

Fig. 9.1 Core management competences

> *[T]he ability to create a positive working environment and inspire individuals to apply themselves with intelligence, energy, resilience, enthusiasm and concentration; whilst providing the means for their personal and professional development.*

The modern manager will apply this competence to motivation, goal achievement and high performance on the one hand and security of the workplace, and workforce well-being on the other because employee productivity is not purely due to technology but to the positivity in the total employee experience. For an organisation to gain and keep competitive advantage human capital investment becomes as important as IT investment (Black, 2008; Bajorek, 2020; Cunha et al., 2020). The manager's understanding of technology will give professional credibility. Their understanding of the nature of employee engagement and developing the workforce will give them management credibility. It is therefore important to look at the subjects of employee engagement and employee development in a holistic way because of the interplay between them in determining the strength in which individuals are committed and able to deliver personal and organisational objectives.

Employee Engagement: Vigour, Dedication and Absorption

Employee engagement is a complex, multi-faceted concept. Its importance is reflected in the amount of interest that has been shown in the subject over the years and there is considerable evidence from which to draw good practice. The research findings of Elton Mayo at his study at the Western Electric Company's Hawthorne Works in Chicago during the early part of the twentieth century provided a foundation grounded in industrial psychology, adapted, amended or built upon by notable contributions to the science of management by inter alia Kurt Lewin and Mary Parker Follet, which brought a much greater emphasis on the human aspect of organisation, the nature of workforce performance and the competences of managers (Sofer, 1972). The question of why employees are enthusiastic and will engage with their job, team or organisation is one that has exercised academics and practitioners over time, although the language of engagement is a feature of more recent decades. A contribution to this conundrum was offered in ground-breaking research which articulated the concept of employee engagement as how employees 'harnessed' themselves and their roles through the application of their physical, cognitive and emotional resources whilst they were at the place of work (Kahn, 1990). In subsequent years the meaning of the concept, its antecedents, and its importance have been refined. Schaufeli and Bakker (2004), for example, conceptualised engagement as a positive work-related state characterised by vigour, dedication and absorption—where vigour concerns energy and resilience, dedication is about enthusiasm and being inspired, and absorption is the intense concentration in the work being undertaken. Engagement was the simultaneous employment and expression of a person's 'preferred self' in task behaviours that promote connections to work and to others, personal presence (physical, cognitive and emotional) and active, full role performance (Saks, 2006, 2017). Variations around the theme include organisational engagement—the level of employee commitment to the organisation; work engagement—a positive, fulfilling, work—related state of mind; job engagement—the level of commitment to the job or role. Further additions to the canon of engagement include cognitive engagement—how an employee understands their job; physical or behavioural engagement—effort, performance or productivity; personal engagement—the harnessing of self to work roles; and social engagement or how engaged individuals interact with colleagues and co-workers to propose and implement new ideas (Turner, 2020). Amongst the ideas that have traversed multiple definitions is the Jobs-Demand-Resources theory which brings together many of the concepts as it models all working environments or job characteristics on two categories, namely job demands—physical, psychological, social or organisational aspects of the job that require sustained physical or psychological effort; and job resources—physical, psychological, social or organisational aspects of the job that are functional in achieving work goals; reduce job demands or stimulate personal growth, learning and development (Bakker & Demerouti, 2014). In drawing together the various strands of research the Chartered Institute of Personnel and Development (CIPD) concluded that idea of employee engagement was one that focused on 'mutual gains in employment relationships, seeking the good of employees (well-being, job satisfaction etc.) and the good of the organisation they work for (performance, commitment etc.). Engagement included a variety of concepts, including work motivation, organisational commitment, job satisfaction, passion and enthusiasm, identifying with one's work, playing to one's strengths, absorption and energy in doing work, citizenship behaviour, and shared purpose or alignment to strategy (CIPD, 2019).

The attributed benefits that accrue to those organisations and individuals where engagement is high are increased shareholder returns, operating income, revenue growth, profit margins, creativity and innovation and customer or client satisfaction for the organisation and satisfaction and well-being for employees (Saks, 2006, 2017; Schwarz, 2012; Meyer, 2017; Bakker, 2017). Such was its value that the United States-based Society for Human Resource Management (SHRM) argued: 'employees who are engaged in their work and committed to their organisations give companies crucial competitive advantages—including higher productivity and lower employee turnover' (Vance, SHRM, 2006). Employee engagement is a high priority for many organisations and the demands of Industry 4.0 will continue to see this level of attention. New technologies and new business models have the potential for the workforce to 'express their talents, focusing their energies where they could add value'. For this to take place they will need to be engaged with the role, the team and the organisation as well as having the skills relevant to the work that is required; to be resilient and to tap into their emotional strength on the one hand and to employ their best skills on the other. It will require positive attitudes and behaviours towards organisational strategy and implementation, organisational commitment and team commitment. In conclusion, employee engagement is influenced by both individual and circumstantial elements (Davies et al., 2018; Sharafizad et al., 2019; Khodakarami & Dirani, 2020; Fareri et al., 2020; Molino et al., 2020; Kwon & Kim, 2020; Nienaber & Martins, 2020).

Employee engagement takes place at three levels. First, in the psychology of work which will include meaning at work, no fear or blame, emotional presence, emotional intelligence and positive mutual regard. Second, the sociology of work will include organisational climate and culture, work demand and resource supply, health and well-being and the physical work environment. Whilst third, the organisation of work will include the structure, organisational dynamics and the impact of technology. Managers are influential in each of these (Turner, 2020). It will be part of their role to encourage and facilitate active participation in change and adaptation through effective engagement.

Employee Development: A Whole Workforce Approach

A workforce that is engaged with and energised towards the organisation's goals or objectives, is one part of the human resource challenge; one that is appropriately trained is the second. In this respect, strategies for learning, training and development have taken on a more inclusive hue in recent times, in which a whole workforce approach is as much of a priority as that towards 'top talent'—inclusivity is considered an as essential antecedent of employee engagement and thereby organisational performance. A possible cause of this is the recognition of the value of whole workforce training and development to business innovation. Improvements in on-the-job productivity; improvement in customer satisfaction; reduced time away from the job; and greater levels of engagement are the result of the offer of training and career progress (CIPD, 2016). The effective transfer of training to improve performance or behavioural outcomes has been accentuated by the advent of the 'knowledge economy' and the experiences of organisations during the pandemic of 2020. This elevation means training and development for operational teams with knowledge and skills for specific roles or tasks; specialists in particular areas of the value chain—sales, marketing, procurement, finance or HR—and architects able to negotiate complex social, economic and political environments through innovation, the application of knowledge and problem analysis and solving. As a result, 'progressive' organisations are continuously seeking ways to increase effectiveness through development of the workforce and the transfer of training through rapid digital adoption and different modalities and content. In the contemporary context this has meant an increase in online delivery, a growing focus on training for workplace performance and an increase in social and collaborative learning (CIPD, 2016; Greenan et al., 2017; Qin & Xiao, 2017; Turner, 2018). A likely outcome of these trends will be that heterogeneity of approach—individual learning needs, individual learning packages, will be offered as well as homogeneity—groups of learners receiving the same information with the same methods of transfer. There is recognition that individuals have different levels of emotional intelligence, stages of learning, preferred ways of learning and different levels of competence. A combination of these will influence the level and types of training required and can inform subsequent programmes for individual learners (Shekar, 2015). The outcome will be flexibility through blended learning—where the employee controls the learning process and where 'learning lies in problem-based and real-world tasks', the learning environment is flexible and the goals are set by the learner. In addition, informal learning offers the opportunity to amass shared information and improve communication (Ha, 2015; Al-Mannaee & Ryan, 2018; Park et al., 2018; Moica et al., 2019; Popkova & Zmiyak, 2019; Howlett, 2020; Molino et al., 2020). Investing in the development of the workforce is a business imperative.

It is critical to ensure the right level of knowledge and skills required to navigate the challenging, dynamic environment of the Fourth Industrial Revolution as it unfolds in unpredictable ways. Those organisations that can do both to good effect improve their prospects of converting tacit knowledge into explicit knowledge, and then into progression and competitive advantage. Creating a positive environment will connect the dots between the individual and wider organisational transformation. To do so rests on leaders and managers 'who take interest in the perspectives of their employees, provide opportunities for choice and input, encourage self-initiation, and avoid the use of external rewards or sanctions to motivate behaviour' (Slemp et al., 2018; CIPD, 2020a). As with the case of employee engagement, managers will be instrumental in this process as they apply their own knowledge, skills, attitudes and behaviours to building a workforce that is fit for purpose. Figure 9.1 shows where this management competence fits in the overall framework.

Knowledge and Skills for the Core Management Competence of 'Engages and Develops the Workforce'

Employee engagement and a learning culture will come about when there are supportive organisational systems and processes—organisational competence and managers who have identifiable, definable and measurable knowledge, skills, attitudes and behaviours to their achievement—core management competence (Chrupała-Pniak et al., 2017; Krishnaveni & Monica, 2018; Nawangsari & Sutawidjaya, 2019). Amongst the requirements are cognitive competences such as systems thinking and pattern recognition; emotional intelligence competences—self-awareness and self-management competences—emotional self-control; as well as social intelligence competences, including social awareness and relationship management (Boyatzis, 1982, 2011; Stepanenko & Kashevnik, 2017).

A combination of these will coalesce to create a manager who is competent in engaging and developing the workforce for which they have responsibility:

- In the first place, it is important to address the 'why' of work or the purpose of an individual and their role in the organisation. In the management philosophy of Steve Jobs of Apple, 'everything starts with an inspiring vision' and 'defining its purpose and choosing which strategy will be more successful quickly is of the utmost importance for a company that wishes to adopt Industry 4.0' (Ulrich & Ulrich, 2011; Elliot, 2012; Cunha et al., 2020). It is the manager's role to inspire unity of purpose. On the one hand they will give clarity through formal definition of the goals and objectives; on the other hand, they will give stimuli, responses and 'environmental reinforcers' through positive management practice. It is to the latter that the aspect of competence—*articulates the why of work*—applies and is intended to create shared meaning for both individuals and teams, cooperation among members of the workforce around a common goal, a comprehensible end objective, a direction or pathway and an image of how the organisation will look on its achievement. If 'why' is the most powerful of the six forms of question, the why of work will produce the most powerful of answers. But it goes further than the why of work for the organisation. For many, 'work is who you are'. As a statement of the present and a vision of the future it is 'a vivid, detailed, and inspiring description' of what will be seen, heard and felt that will contribute to a positive relationship which in turn will lead to workforce engagement and ultimately organisational performance (Garratt, 2000; Rapaille, 2006; Williams et al., 2014; Ciampa, 2017; Kuntonbutr et al., 2017; Jøranli, 2018; Allahar, 2019; Toh et al., 2019). It will address the questions, what does the future look like for the organisation and where do individuals fit in to this future? This aspect of competence is relevant at all levels through operations—'managing is controlling and doing and dealing and thinking and leading and deciding and more;' and commitment—'conviction, intention, or a strong attitude toward pursuing a goal' (Mintzberg, 2011; Williams et al., 2014). Articulating the why of work aligns actions and commitment with the organisation's wider intentions and the ambition that is shown will be influential in employee engagement. It will be the role of the manager to identify and communicate key concepts behind the vision so that individuals understand the part they play in its achievement. The features of the competence are strategic orientation, communication skills, listening skills and an empathetic approach. They will help to influence by relating the vison to organisational need; and foster team working by communicating goals in a motivational and engaging way.

- For an environment of clarity about the why of work to be seen as achievable a further consideration is related to *the focus on output.* Employee engagement has multiple objectives. On the one hand it is intended to contribute to a psychologically safe and socially constructive organisation that can be achieved by considerations of the care and well-being of individuals, their aspirations and personal objectives. And as noted earlier people are an end in themselves rather than adjuncts to business objectives. On the other, the organisation's business objectives are critical to opportunities for personal learning and development on the part of members of the workforce. There is an alignment between business success and individual success and the challenge throughout the employee engagement competence is to ensure that this is recognised. Where there is convergence between what is being provided by the organisation and what the individual employee is prepared to offer, then there are two foundations from which employee engagement can flourish. The role of the manager as outlined above ranges from visioneer to objective setter; from awareness of culture to acting as learning coach; from welfare officer to resource manager. Each of these roles will require a manager who is adaptable and able to work in multi-cultural, multi-generational environments. To do so will require a sophisticated application of several facets of this competence. However, there is a further underlying purpose, and this concerns the organisation's dynamics with a focus on creating an engagement culture and converting this into meaningful outputs.

- Articulation of the why of work will provide a cognitive foundation and the basis for a shared, common picture of behaviours, systems and processes needed on which to base a strategy. It will give members of the workforce an understanding of where the organisation desires to be in future as well as the development needed to get there. However, its success will depend on how the vision of the why of work is converted to action (Williams et al., 2014; Ciampa, 2017; Nienaber & Martins, 2020). The focus on output provides the foundation for this and implementation planning to convert plans into action are therefore important. The third aspect of this competence is that the manager, using the why of work as a platform, *translates the vision into actionable plans*. This means providing straightforward, comprehensible rules and layered goals and the actions that result from the vision should be articulated in ways that follow these principles. The manager will transform values into actions, visions into realities, obstacles into innovations and risks into rewards whilst at the same time creating an environment and culture in which people can contribute to opportunity, problem solving and direction. The manager will ensure that there is a convergence of personal responsibility and that of organisational goals (Garratt, 2000; Kouzes & Posner, 2007; Bridger, 2014; Davies et al., 2017; Barry & Hunt Davis, 2020). The features of the competence are an action orientation, understanding organisational systems and processes, project management skills and communication skills. Establishing priorities and relating actions to these and ensuring that resources are aligned accordingly will be in support of this aspect of competence. All of these desirable outcomes will benefit from firstly an engagement culture—to embrace the vision—and secondly a learning culture—to enact the vision. Each of which will make the why of work sustainable.

- How to ensure that members of the workforce continue to be energised in the face of significant change will require managers who are able to 'cultivate a positive, engaged environment for employees while understanding how certain job changes, might have both positive and negative effects on an individual's ability to adapt'. Recognition that people are an end in themselves rather than a means to an end will be the fundamental ethos of engagement in Industry 4.0 organisations (Williams et al., 2014; Kuntonbutr et al., 2017; Parent & Lovelace, 2018; McNeil & Jeffery, 2020; Sony & Naik, 2020). This requires a positive environment giving the opportunity for dialogue, participation and enthusiasm where job demands and resources are in balance. *Creates an engagement culture* is therefore an important part of core management competence. At a strategic level being sensitised to the importance of culture—for example, in the newly merged Anheuser Busch-Inbev, resources were allocated to ensure this important part of the integration strategy (Steers et al., 2010). At operational level an engagement culture will be one in which encouragement is used regularly instead of criticism; in which trust is fundamental and individuals are respected as individuals. To this point, Charles Handy has written that trust is an integral part of keeping subsidiarity—through delegation and autonomy—intact. Amongst its characteristics are openness, community, collaboration and meaning. In today's context, applying social media platforms will have an impact on job satisfaction, with analytics from social media interactions used to indicate engagement levels and play an important role in engagement direction (Handy, 1996; Hlupic, 2014; Holland et al., 2016; Golestani et al., 2018; Parent & Lovelace, 2018). The model for engagement refers to the three elements covered earlier in this chapter. In the first place the psychology of work will be related to the manager's role in ensuring an individual's emotional presence. Secondly the sociology of work will rely on the manager recognising, articulating and enacting positive social relations and normative codes and diversity or inclusivity. Thirdly the organisation of work will be based on the organisation's vision, its structure, systems and processes, and its resource allocation (Mukherjee, 2020; Turner, 2020). The features of this competence are an understanding of employee engagement and its drivers, respect of diversity and equality of opportunity, empathy and communication skills.

- A contributory factor in the creation of an engagement culture is that of the ability of members of the workforce to develop and progress in their roles and future careers. Senge (1990) articulated the concept of learning organisations with the powerful statement that there are ways of working together that can be more satisfying and productive than traditional systems of management. The essence of the argument was that as the world becomes more interconnected and organisations become more complex and dynamic, then work must become more 'learningful' (Hecklau et al., 2016; Kirby, 2020). In the context of Industry 4.0 this assertion becomes even more powerful because of a world in a constant state of flux where skills quickly age. The new environment will demand a 'cognitive workforce', intelligent and analytical with verbal aptitude (vocabulary, spelling and reading), numerical aptitude (maths, arithmetic) and spatial aptitude (coordination, memory, decision-making, problem solving thinking, abstract reasoning, analytical thinking). In addition, members of the workforce will be digitally literate and digitally interactive. Nurturing these capabilities and the ability to adapt to change will be paramount objectives for all organisations. To facilitate this, an important aspect of core management competence will be *creates a learning culture* comprising of shared norms, values and assumptions about the benefits and opportunities of learning. Where a manager can empower people to learn and this becomes embedded into the organisational culture there are positive outcomes, including innovation, knowledge exploration and knowledge exploitation. It is also one of the factors behind the creation of 'good jobs' or the opportunity for people to create and develop their careers by gaining experience and building skills that give them options to progress over time (Schein, 1996; Hlupic, 2014; Gonzalez & de Melo, 2018; Naqshbandi & Tabche, 2018; Flores et al., 2020; Wilson, 2020; Williams, 2020). The manager has an instrumental role in all aspects of the learning culture. The articulation of the why of work and the translation of this into goals and objectives; and the creation of engagement and learning cultures provide a human resource infrastructure within which the potential for competitive advantage exists. However, other operational competences will be required concerned with the demographics of the workforce on the one hand and human resource practice on the other.

- The why of work, clarity of objectives and a culture that is inclined towards positivity and innovation by having an engaged, trained, workforce provide a solid basis on which to build. The context for these is set by the boundaries of the strategy of the organisation, the systems and processes to deliver the strategy, the underlying cultures that support the strategy and an environment in which people are able to relate their own roles to that of the organisation as a whole and enthuse about their contribution. The desired outcome is that they will apply their tacit and explicit knowledge to productivity, innovation, creativity and flexibility. The basis of this success is the right people in the right place at the right time with the right level of skills achieved through good human resource practice and alignment of people with the mindsets and skillsets to the values of the organisation (Jøranli, 2018; Latukha et al., 2018; Maisiri et al., 2019; Williams & Mihaylo, 2019). Hence a further aspect of management competence is *selects, recruits and retains the right people*. The selection will match individual skills and 'fit' with the organisation's strategic and operational needs. It will seek to ensure a balance in the skill mix which will include not only innovators or independent thinkers, but also action- or achievement-oriented individuals and traditional 'completer finishers' (Adler, 2007; Jøranli, 2018; Akuffo & Kivipõld, 2019; Saenz et al., 2019; Suzuki et al., 2019). The judgement of the manager will be the determining factor guided by organisational support such as traditional competence-based assessments and contemporaneously the use of social media-based recruitment or gamification ('to reach out to and engage with sought after talent'). Increasingly managers will have to take account of virtuality, contingent work arrangements, automation, transparency and globalisation in the selection process (Headworth, 2015; Moore, 2017; Eckardt et al., 2018; Kim & Ployhart, 2018; Ryan & Derous, 2019; Williams & Mihaylo, 2019). The competence will facilitate *a cultural, skills and aspirational fit that provides the basis for a sound psychological contract.* In return for this there will be an expectation that the employee will also feel an obligation to deliver work to their highest achievable level. A culture of engagement is an important step and efficient people management practices—such as selection and retention—will contribute to the creation of such a culture.

- Employee engagement is a multi-faceted construct. It is influenced by the organisation's strategy and stewardship on the one hand, and its rewards or benefits, training provision and well-being policies on the other. These might be regarded as the 'supply push' factors of engagement. In addition, 'demand pull' factors also have in important part to play. These will include such areas as overwork, not enough resources, inadequate work life balance or lack of understanding about the expectations of a particular job and the individual's role in delivering to those expectations. To do so means that the manager *provides role clarity.* This will stem from explicit knowledge about the work at hand, about organisational design or work-flow or facilitating the employee to craft the job—in which employees make self-initiated changes to the levels of their job demands and job resources to align them with their own capabilities and preferences. Where there is clarity, where there is empowerment, where there is the ability to craft the job, and the design of meaningful and motivating work, then there will be a positive impact on engagement (Hakanen et al., 2018; Milhem et al., 2019; Karkkola et al., 2020; Lesener et al., 2020; Turner, 2020). The manager's role is therefore to deal with cognitive expectations about the role (job design, work-flow, processural issues) as well as affective, emotional expectations that the employee might have about the role. Where these are addressed, they will enhance enthusiasm, motivation and absorption necessary for an engaged employee in an engaged team. Providing role clarity will impact on a number of criteria associated with employee engagement, including job satisfaction, being valued, the opportunity for involvement, communication and cooperation. The features of this competence are an understanding of organisational dynamics and the organisation of work, work-flows and job design and communication skills.

- The final area of knowledge and skills as part of this competence is *operates effectively in a multi-generational, multicultural environment.* The quality of the exchange between managers and members of the workforce—irrespective of generation or culture is one of the factors that can predict the quality of employee engagement and satisfaction. It is that managers actively engage with and have knowledge and skills in the dynamics of a multicultural environment. To do so effectively will require awareness, behavioural skills and continuous improvement based on learning and experience. These include empathy and a robust approach to fairness and equity (Chrobot-Mason, 2003; McGuire et al., 2007; Maddux et al., 2014; Huang, 2016; Prifti et al., 2017; Berisha, 2020). In all cases it means being able to engage with multiple generations and cultures to ensure that all points of view are recognised in an empathetic way. But this also has additional benefits since managing in a multicultural environment may also bring a 'critical contrast' (Maddux et al., 2014) to long-held beliefs, practices and assumptions in favour of innovation and new knowledge. The features of this competence are a recognition of the importance of culture, understanding different generational needs and a willingness and capability to accommodate both into a management outlook.

A desirable objective is an environment of transparency, trust and esteem, in which members of the workforce feel confidence with the result of motivated and integrated members of an organisation (Duden, 2011). The knowledge and skills outlined above represent steps towards these goals with strategic elements—the articulation of the why of work, a vision that will inform direction, the creation of a culture that fosters engagement and a positivity towards development in a learning organisation. In addition, more tactical or operational considerations are important—from the preparation of clear, implementable goals or objectives that provide the framework for the achievement of the vision and specific areas of competence in relation to people management practices with specific reference to attraction, recruitment and retention to acting as learning coach. Each of these contributors to the core management competence of engages and develops the workforce are aspects of managerial capability.

Attitudes and Behaviours for the Core Management Competence of 'Engages and Develops the Workforce'

An engaged employee is more likely to stay with and act as an advocate of the organisation in which they work. The knowledge and skills of the manager outlined above will go some way to creating such an environment. On the one hand they will do so by the application of 'hard' competences such as fairness and realism in objective setting and 'soft' competences such as communication, teamwork or cooperation and flexibility or adaptability (Flores et al., 2020). The knowledge and skills demonstrated in these areas will be complemented by important attitudes and behaviours:

- The organisational and managerial dynamics that create the foundation for employee engagement begin with articulating the why of work, a vision of where the organisation wants to be, a strategy for how it will get there and the allocation of sufficient resources to a workforce that has the right skills and is empowered to adapt and change as circumstances demand. The values to do so are 'the ways an organisation collectively thinks, acts, feels and expresses' itself in relation to its desired ends, which informs the first aspect of attitudes and behaviours and this is that the manager *is values driven*. Values are the deep enduring convictions about what is right or wrong, good or bad and acceptable or unacceptable aspects of management practice. They have the potential to shape behaviour and action by creating shared loyalties leading to cooperation (Chen et al., 2020). Motivation and engagement are positively associated with the use of a values-based system in which values are the sayings and doings, artefacts, symbols and rituals about what is normatively right or wrong. Where there is congruence between individual and organisational values there is a potential impact on job satisfaction, employee engagement, organisational commitment and employee turnover (Padaki, 2002; Gehman et al., 2013; Albu, 2018; Adla et al., 2020). Values will surface in organisational interactions that are implicit—specific choices or lines of action in accordance with a value—or explicit. Typically, amongst stated values will be accountability, fairness, honesty, integrity and transparency. They will contribute to winning hearts and minds, for inspiring others and for encouraging employees to be positive and enthusiastic through persuasion and through these the manager will make contact with what has been referred to as inner work lives—'perceptions, emotions, and motivations that they experienced as they made sense of their workday' (Stoner & Freeman, 1992; Hynes, 2012; Albu, 2018).

- Empathy, integrity, a positive mutual regard, and being able to work well with others are essential characteristics. These will determine how the manager is able to build and sustain personal relationships and the nature of personal interaction with members of the workforce. It is important therefore that the manager *demonstrates emotional intelligence*, which is a further aspect of attitudes and behaviour in relation to this competence. Goleman (2009) famously wrote that 'the daily challenge of dealing effectively with emotions is critical to the human condition because our brains are hard wired to give emotions the upper hand'. In this respect emotional intelligence is the ability to recognise and understand emotions in oneself and in others and the ability to use this awareness in behaviour and relationships. It is particularly relevant because 'the rules for work are changing. We're being judged by a new yardstick; not just how smart we are; or by our training and expertise, but also how well we handle ourselves and each other' (Goleman, 1998). For many, emotional intelligence has become the bedrock of good management. Those with high emotional intelligence are 'aware of their own emotions, tend to be more sensitive to the emotions and feelings of others, have higher ability to control their own emotions and would be able to direct their own emotions in positive directions'. And to demonstrate humility when it is necessary to do so (Liu & Cho, 2018; Yuan et al., 2018; Marr, 2019).

- Positive and open lines of communication between employees and managers are important for effective working relationships, can help to increase organisational identification and over time improve individual performance and productivity. Communication as a means of perceived organisational support has been shown to influence employee affective commitment and support employees through organisational change—where change communication informs, creates understanding, guides, calls for action and alters behaviour and reactions to change (Neves & Eisenberger, 2012; Shulga, 2020). Whilst these assumptions have held, contemporary environments add extra dimensions as the employment relationship, which is becoming increasingly personalised and adapted to individual needs. These considerations apply at two levels. In the first instance there is a positive relationship between communication of mission and performance and associated with this employee voice in the overall commitment to the organisation. The evidence also revealed the importance of the manager in this role. The second concerns the use of social media in the engagement 'equation'. Social media can play an effective role on the quality and impact of communication, which has been closely linked to affective commitment and job satisfaction. There is a significant positive relationship between social media use and employee voice. Employees who were engaged with social media at work reported positively about organisational commitment and reduced turnover intention. Furthermore, social media engagement with co-workers can positively affect intrinsic work motivation and proactive behaviour (Williams et al., 2014; Bizzi, 2020; Han & Xia, 2020). Dealing with these gives strong support therefore for an aspect of management competence which is *communicates effectively and encourages employee voice.* Communication will help to establish shared understanding and 'buy-in' from employees at all levels, which will lead to engagement and 'ultimately facilitate successful strategy implementation and thus organisational effectiveness'. The manager will be expected to continue with traditional methods of communication—physically present at team briefings or performance updates; as well as regular communication based on technology applications such as Zoom or Teams; and social media to strengthen network ties, shared vision and trust (Robertson & Kee, 2017; Tijunaitis et al., 2019; Nienaber & Martins, 2020). Communication from the manager can help to understand goals and strategies and to 'provide needed information on a timely basis that helps employees carry out their jobs'. This information includes 'positive job-related feedback, and conversations about support'. And for it to be effective, communication will be two way because upward communication allows employees to bring forward positive interventions—through tacit knowledge—as well as airing internal contradictions or problems. Increasingly social media as a 'user friendly and visible web-based communication arena inside an organisation in which coworkers and managers can communicate, interact, connect and make sense of their work and organisational life' can help to make communication visible with potentially positive organisational consequences (Neves & Eisenberger, 2012; Nienaber & Martins, 2020).

- The effective manager balances performance and objective achievement with the need to create an effective team and to build confidence and competence in each of the team's members. Key to this will be that the manager adopts person-focused behaviours and the ability to understand team needs and to apply corresponding management behaviour to address them. A convergence of several of the characteristics discussed above is important when considering a further aspect of the core competence of *builds high performance teams*. The challenge is extended as the definition of a team broadens to include virtual teams, network teams, parallel teams, project teams, work teams or action teams. In all contexts the team comprises of people with knowledge and skills directly related to achieving common goals and is characterised by direction, momentum and commitment—pulling together in the same direction to achieve something; a common approach and mutual accountability—where each team member is accountable for their actions—'aligned with and committed to a common purpose, who consistently show high levels of collaboration and innovation' (Cook, 2009; Moura et al., 2014; Hadjiev, 2018; Macpherson et al., 2019; Homan et al., 2020; Nienaber & Martins, 2020). The role of the manager in building these teams will be to engage team members in the why of work, vision and purpose; set specific goals; ensure clarity about the contribution of individuals and roles in the achievement of goals; consult and solicit options based on member knowledge (tacit and explicit); allocate resources in a way that is fair and efficient through rational decision making; communicating transparently and clearly the reasons for decisions and ultimately the outcomes of decisions; ensuring that there is diversity in the team and inclusivity in team dynamics and dealing with conflict or disagreement in an even handed way. The manager will use their emotional intelligence to nourish positivity to maximise the team's intelligence and the 'synergistic interaction of every person's best talents' (Goleman, 1998) whilst building a climate of trust and trustworthiness (Kim & Min-Hsun, 2015). A combination of factors will in turn contribute to the organisation's overall core competence and in turn that will impact on competitive advantage.

- Investment in learning, training and development satisfies a wide range of objectives—the strategic goals of the organisation by having a skilled and engaged workforce; the personal goals of individuals and the opportunity to develop into different roles in future and environment where 'employees can continuously develop to be their best'. In this culture the manager encourages learning for all and *acts as learning coach*, moving away from the 'leader-centric model' towards one of greater reciprocity. 'Past and more current research on management and leadership taxonomies has underscored the important roles or subsets of roles that managers and leaders play in providing support, training, coaching, mentoring, and promoting growth and employee development' (Ellinger, 2013; Kim and Min-Hsun 2015; Weinberg, 2016; CIPD, 2020b). The features of this competence are an understanding of the coaching process.
- When people are happy and well at work then organisations can benefit because there is a positive link between employee satisfaction, employee engagement and business performance. Workplace well-being has an important part to play in each of these areas, and so giving it attention will pay dividends. Positive workplace perceptions and feelings were associated with higher customer loyalty, higher profitability, higher productivity and lower rates of staff turnover. Well-being

creates a positive working environment leading to a positive impact on a range of organisational performance indicators. As well as reducing sickness, workplace well-being can improve operational performance, increase discretionary effort, trust and employee loyalty. So, 'although engaged employees invest a lot of their energy into their work, they are likely to gain even more in return', and thus they have surplus resources which contribute to their ongoing well-being and prevent them from burning out (Hakanen et al., 2018; Hesketh & Cooper, 2019). Effective well-being programmes can deliver benefits to people and businesses (as well as economies and wider society) and their importance was reinforced by the fast-changing world of work and the demands it places on employers and employees. The pandemic of 2020 has only accentuated these demands. But well-being goes beyond corporate programmes. Hence, a further aspect of management competence which is *cares for employee well-being* at two levels (Hynes, 2012; Simpkins & Lemyre, 2018). First in their individual attitudes and behaviours and second in developing 'underlying factors of the work environment' through contribution to stewardship—a meta-phenomenon that goes beyond interpersonal exchanges, being a more organisation-wide approach that 'emphasizes a sense of purpose toward the common good through the sharing of power, resources, and information across networks in working through complex issues'.

Employee engagement is positive proactive behaviour in the workplace and towards the organisation; motivated, emotionally attached employees who are able to bring their whole selves into the workplace; and integrated enlightened people management activities. Having engaged employees is highly valuable for organisations because those employees 'are most likely to be willing and capable of increasing their resources and also taking on new challenges in the future … engaged employees will behave more proactively in the future than satisfied employees by actively crafting their jobs (Hakanen et al., 2018). Its incidence will increase when there are managers in place who are empathetic towards the necessity of an engaged workforce and have the knowledge, skills, attitudes and behaviours to foster an environment for it to flourish. The core management competence—*engages and develops the workforce*—will require an awareness of the drivers of engagement and the levers of development. In the first place the business or service strategic drivers include creating a vision and making sure that this is fulfilled through shared purpose. It will require that the organisation is structured in a way to minimise intra department or team conflict and that the manager has a values-based approach to delivering objectives. Operational drivers of engagement include meaning, pride and a positive work environment. It means providing opportunities for job enrichment and role clarity and above all it means an understanding of the necessity of engagement and how to achieve it. Finally, the manager will be competent in the people management drivers of engagement, including the strength of team relationships, empowerment and the importance of employee voice (Turner, 2020). An engaged and fully developed workforce will deliver benefits to the organisation, to teams within the organisation and to individuals within those teams. The manager has a critical role to play in all three areas and their role is regarded as amongst the most important in any organisational dynamic. The features associated with this are enthusiasm, persistence, emotional intelligence and an understanding of individual behaviours, team dynamics and organisational dynamics.

References

Adla, L., Eyquem-Renault, M., & Gallego-Roquelaure, V. (2020). From the Leader's Values to Organizational Values: Toward a Dynamic and Experimental View on Value Work in SMEs. *M@n@gement, 23*(1), 81–101.

Adler, L. (2007). *Hire with Your Head.* John Wiley.

Akuffo, I. N., & Kivipõld, K. (2019). Influence of Leaders' Authentic Competences on Nepotism—Favouritism and Cronyism. *Management Research Review, 43*(4), 369–386.

Albu, O. B. (2018). Making a Difference: The Performative Role of Values in the Constitution of Organizations. *M@n@gement, 21*(2), 858–883.

Allahar, H. (2019). A Management Innovation Approach to Project Planning. *Technology Innovation Management Review, 9*(6), 4.

Al-Mannaee, N. S., & Ryan, J. C. (2018). Examining a Competency Model of Workplace Learning: An Assessment of Participants' Reactions. *International Journal of Work Organisation and Emotion, 9*(1), 107.

Bajorek, Z. (2020). *The Squeezed Middle.* IES.
Bakker, A. B. (2017). Strategic and Proactive Approaches to Work Engagement. *Special Issue: Employee Engagement, Organizational Dynamics, 46*(2), 67–75.
Bakker, A. B., & Demerouti, E. (2014). Jobs Demands Resources Theory. In P. Y. Chen & C. L. Cooper (Eds.), *Work and Wellbeing: A Complete Reference Guide, Volume III.* John Wiley & Sons, Ltd.
Barry, T., & Hunt Davis, B. (2020, July 8). *How to Reset the New Now.* Webinar.
Berisha, Besa Haxhiu. (2020). Managing across Generations: The Case of Bibita Group. *Dynamic Relationships Management Journal, 9*(1), 49–66.
Bizzi, L. (2020). Should HR Managers Allow Employees to Use Social Media at Work? Behavioral and Motivational Outcomes of Employee Blogging. *The International Journal of Human Resource Management, 31*(10), 1285–1312.
Black, C. (2008). *Working for a Healthier Tomorrow.* The Stationery Office.
Boyatzis, R. E. (1982). *The Competent Manager.* John Wiley and Sons.
Boyatzis, R. E. (2011). Managerial and Leadership Competencies: A Behavioural Approach to Emotional, Social and Cognitive Intelligence. *Vision (09722629), 15*(2), 91–100.
Bridger, E. (2014). *Employee Engagement.* CIPD.
Chen, C. X., Lill, J. B., & Vance, T. W. (2020). Management Control System Design and Employees' Autonomous Motivation. *Journal of Management Accounting Research, 32*(3), 71–91.
Chrobot-Mason, D. (2003). Developing Multicultural Competence for Managers: Same Old Leadership Skills or Something New? *The Psychologist-Manager Journal, 6*(2), 5–20.
Chrupała-Pniak, M., Grabowski, D., & Sulimowska-Formowicz, M. (2017). Trust in Effective International Business Cooperation: Mediating Effect of Work Engagement. *Entrepreneurial Business and Economics Review, 5*(2), 27–50.
Ciampa, D. (2017). What CEOs Get Wrong About Vision and How to Get It Right. *MIT Sloan Management Review, 59*(1), 86–88.
CIPD. (2016). *Preparing for the Future of Learning.* CIPD.
CIPD. (2019). *Employee Engagement and Motivation.* https://www.cipd.co.uk/knowledge/fundamentals/relations/engagement/factsheet#6227
CIPD. (2020a). *Coronavirus and the Workforce; Learning in a COVID World.* https://www.cipd.co.uk/news-views/changing-work-views/future-work/thought-pieces/coronavirus-workforce-learning
CIPD. (2020b). *Learning and Development Roles.* https://www.cipd.co.uk/careers/career-options/learning-development-roles

Cook, S. (2009). *The Effective Manager*. IT Governance Publishing.

Cunha, T. P., Méxas, M. P., da Silva, A. C., & Quelhas, O. L. G. (2020). Proposal Guidelines to Implement the Concepts of Industry 4.0 into Information Technology Companies. *The TQM Journal, 32*(4), 741–759.

Davies, A., Dodgson, M., Gann, D. M., & MacCaulay, S. C. (2017). Five Rules for Managing Large, Complex Projects. *MIT Sloan Management Review, 59*(1), 73–78.

Davies, G., Mete, M., & Whelan, S. (2018). When Employer Brand Image Aids Employee Satisfaction and Engagement. *Journal of Organizational Effectiveness: People and Performance, 5*(1), 64–80.

Duden, A. (2011). Trust and Leadership—Learning Culture in Organizations. *International Journal of Management Cases, 13*(4), 218–223.

Eckardt, R., Skaggs, B. C., & Lepak, D. P. (2018). An Examination of the Firm-level Performance Impact of Cluster Hiring in Knowledge-intensive Firms. *Academy of Management Journal, 61*(3), 919–944.

Ellinger, A. D. (2013). Supportive Supervisors and Managerial Coaching: Exploring Their Intersections. *Journal of Occupational and Organizational Psychology, 86*(3), 310–316.

Elliot, J. (2012). *Leading Apple with Steve Jobs*. Wiley.

Fareri, S., Fantoni, G., Chiarello, F., Coli, E., & Binda, A. (2020). Estimating Industry 4.0 Impact on Job Profiles and Skills Using Text Mining. *Computers in Industry, 118*, 103222.

Flores, E., & Xun Xu, & Yuqian Lu. (2020). Human Capital 4.0: A Workforce Competence Typology for Industry 4.0. *Journal of Manufacturing Technology Management, 31*(4), 687–703.

Garratt, R. (2000). *The Learning Organisation*. Harper Collins.

Gehman, J., Treviño, L. K., & Garud, R. (2013). Values Work: A Process Study of the Emergence and Performance of Organizational Values Practices. *Academy of Management Journal, 56*(1), 84–112.

Ghislieri, C., Molino, M., & Cortese, C. G. (2018). Work and Organizational Psychology Looks at the Fourth Industrial Revolution: How to Support Workers and Organizations? *Frontiers in Psychology, 9*, 2365. https://doi.org/10.3389/fpsyg.2018.02365

Goleman, D. (1998). *Working with Emotional Intelligence*. Bloomsbury.

Goleman, D. (2009). *Emotional Intelligence 2.0*. TalentSmart.

Golestani, A., Masli, M., Shami, N. S., Jones, J., Menon, A., & Mondal, J. (2018). *Real-Time Prediction of Employee Engagement Using Social Media and Text Mining*. 17th IEEE International Conference on Machine Learning and Applications (ICMLA).

Gonzalez, R. V. D., & de Melo, T. M. (2018). The Effects of Organization Context on Knowledge Exploration and Exploitation. *Journal of Business Research, 90*, 215–225.

Greenan, P., Turner, P. A., & Reynolds, M. (2017). Training Transfer: The Case for Implementation Intentions. *International Journal of HRD Practice, Policy and Research 2017, 2*(2), 49–56.

Ha, T. S. (Ed.). (2015). Learning Stories from IT Workers: Development of Professional Expertise. *Studies in Continuing Education, 37*(1), 79–98.

Hadjiev, K. (2018). Managing High Performance Virtual Teams. *VIII International Interdisciplinary Conference 'One World—Many Cultures.'* Kujawy and Pomorze University in Bydgoszcz, Poland.

Hakanen, J. J., Peeters, M. C. W., & Schaufeli, W. B. (2018). Different Types of Employee Well-Being across Time and Their Relationships with Job Crafting. *Journal of Occupational Health Psychology, 23*(2), 289–301.

Han, Q., & Xia, L. (2020). Social Media Use and Employee Innovative Behaviour: The Mediating Role of Employee Voice. *Social Behaviour and Personality: An International Journal, 48*(3), 1–7.

Handy, C. (1996). *Beyond Certainty*. Arrow Books.

Headworth, A. (2015). *Social Media Recruitment*. Kogan Page.

Hecklau, F., Galeitzke, M., Flachs, S., & Kohl, H. (2016). Holistic Approach for Human Resource Management in Industry 4.0. *Procedia CIRP, 54*, 1–6.

Hesketh, I., & Cooper, C. (2019). *Wellbeing at Work*. Kogan Page.

Hlupic, V. (2014). *The Management Shift*, Palgrave Macmillan, UK.

Holland, P., Cooper, B. K., & Hecker, R. (2016). Use of Social Media at Work: A New Form of Employee Voice? *The International Journal of Human Resource Management, 27*(21), 2621–2634.

Homan, A. C., Gündemir, S., Buengeler, C., & van Kleef, G. A. (2020). Leading Diversity: Towards a Theory of Functional Leadership in Diverse Teams. *Journal of Applied Psychology, 105*(10), 1101–1128.

Howlett, E. (2020). *A Learning and Development Revolution*. People Management, CIPD.

Huang, J. (2016). The Challenge of Multicultural Management in Global Projects. *Procedia—Social and Behavioural Sciences, 226*, 75–81.

Hynes, G. E. (2012). Improving Employees' Interpersonal Communication Competencies: A Qualitative Study. *Business Communication Quarterly, 75*(4), 466–475.

Jøranli, I. (2018). Managing Organisational Knowledge through Recruitment: Searching and Selecting Embodied Competencies. *Journal of Knowledge Management, 22*(1), 183–200.

Kahn, W. A. (1990). Psychological Conditions of Personal Engagement and Disengagement at Work. *Academy of Management Journal, 33*(4), 692–724.

Karkkola, P., Kuittinen, M., & Hintsa, T. (2020). Role Clarity, Role Conflict, and Vitality at Work: The Role of the Basic Needs. *Scandinavian Journal of Psychology, 60*(5), 456–463.

Khodakarami, N., & Dirani, K. (2020). Drivers of Employee Engagement: Differences by Work Area and Gender. *Industrial and Commercial Training, 52*(1), 81–91.

Kim, S., & Min-Hsun Kuo. (2015). Examining the Relationships among Coaching, Trustworthiness, and Role Behaviours: A Social Exchange Perspective. *Journal of Applied Behavioural Science, 51*(2), 152–176.

Kim, Y., & Ployhart, R. E. (2018). The Strategic Value of Selection Practices: Antecedents and Consequences of Firm-Level Selection Practice Usage. *Academy of Management Journal, 61*(1), 46–66.

Kirby, S. (2020). *5 Ways COVID-19 Has Changed Workforce Management,* World Economic Forum. https://www.weforum.org/agenda/2020/06/covid-home working-symptom-of-changing-face-of-workforce-management/

Kouzes, J. M., & Posner, B. Z. (2007). *The Leadership Challenge.* Jossey Bass.

Krishnaveni, R., & Monica, R. (2018). Factors Influencing Employee Performance: The Role of Human Resource Management Practices and Work Engagement. *International Journal of Business Performance Management, 4,* 450.

Kucharčíková, A., Mičiak, M., Bartošová, A., Budzeľová, M., Bugajová, S., Maslíková, A., & Pisoňová, S. (2021). *Human Capital Management and Industry 4.0.* EDP Sciences.

Kuntonbutr, C., Jaturat, N., Wilairatana, P., & Konosu, T. (2017). *The Management Vision for Innovation and Human Resource Development Affecting New Markets and New Products Development.* 6th IIAI International Congress on Advanced Applied Informatics (IIAI–AAI).

Kwon, K., & Kim, T. (2020). An Integrative Literature Review of Employee Engagement and Innovative Behavior: Revisiting the JD-R Model. *Human Resource Management Review, 30*(2), 100704.

Latukha, M., Golubkova, A., & Victoria, T. (2018). To be Involved or Not to be Involved? HRM Competences for Internationalization Process in Russian Companies. *Journal of East-West Business, 24*(4), 265–286.

Lesener, T., Gusy, B., Jochmann, A., & Wolter, C. (2020). The Drivers of Work Engagement: A Meta-analytic Review of Longitudinal Evidence. *Work & Stress, 34*(3), 259–278.

Liu, J., & Cho, S. (2018). Interaction Effect of Display Rules and Emotional Intelligence on Hotel Managers' and Non-Managers' Work Engagement. *International Journal of Contemporary Hospitality Management, 30*(3), 1903–1919.
Macpherson, A., Kiersch, C., & Antonacopoulou, E. (2019). Can Senior Management Sustain Engagement and Identification to Support Learning? Designing Communities and Defining Goals. *Journal of Strategy and Management, 13*(1). https://doi.org/10.1108/JSMA-07-2019-0136
Maddux, W. W., Bivolaru, E., Hafenbrack, A. C., Tadmor, C. T., & Galinsky, A. D. (2014). Expanding Opportunities by Opening Your Mind: Multicultural Engagement Predicts Job Market Success through Longitudinal Increases in Integrative Complexity. *Social Psychological and Personality Science, 5*(5). https://doi.org/10.1177/1948550613515005
Maisiri, W., Darwish, H., & van Dyk, L. (2019). An Investigation of Industry 4.0 Skills Requirements. *South African Journal of Industrial Engineering, 30*(3), 90–15.
Marr, B. (2019). The 10 Vital Skills You Will Need for the Future of Work. *Forbes.* https://www.forbes.com/sites/bernardmarr/2019/04/29/the-10-vital-skills-you-will-need-for-the-future-of-work/#52b6cb8e3f5b
McGuire, D., By, R. T., & Hutchings, K. (2007). Towards a Model of Human Resource Solutions for Achieving Intergenerational Interaction in Organisations. *Journal of European Industrial Training, 31*(8), 592–608.
McNeil, R., & Jeffery, R. (2020). We Can't Forget That People Are an End in Themselves Not a Means to an End. *Work*, CIPD, Summer 2020.
Meyer, J. P. (2017). Has Engagement Had Its Day: What's Next and Does It Matter? *Organizational Dynamics, 46*(2), 87–95.
Milhem, M., Muda, H., & Ahmed, K. (2019). The Effect of Perceived Transformational Leadership Style on Employee Engagement: The Mediating Effect of Leader's Emotional Intelligence. *Foundations of Management, 11*(1), 33–42.
Mintzberg, H. (2011). *Managing*. Prentice Hall.
Moica, S., Gherendi, A., Veres, C., & Moica, T. (2019). *The Integration of the Blended Learning Concept into Employee Training as a Factor in Shifting Mentalities towards the Industry 4.0 Approach*. 8th International Conference on Industrial Technology and Management (ICITM).
Molino, M., Cortese, C. G., & Ghislieri, C. (2020). The Promotion of Technology Acceptance and Work Engagement in Industry 4.0: From Personal Resources to Information and Training. *International Journal of*

Environmental Research and Public Health, 17(7), 2438. https://doi.org/10.3390/ijerph17072438

Moore, D. A. (2017). How to Improve the Accuracy and Reduce the Cost of Personnel Selection. *California Management Review, 60*(1), 8–17.

Moura, I. C., Dias, P. M., Dominguez, C. E., & Varajão, J. E. (2014). What Team Members Perceive as Important to Achieve High Performance: An Exploratory Case Study. *Procedia Technology, 16*, 1010–1016.

Mukherjee, A. S. (2020). 5 Musts for Next Gen Leaders. *MIT Sloan Management Review, 61*(4), 1–4.

Naqshbandi, M. M., & Tabche, I. (2018). The Interplay of Leadership, Absorptive Capacity, and Organizational Learning Culture in Open Innovation: Testing a Moderated Mediation Model. *Technological Forecasting and Social Change, 133*, 156–167.

Nawangsari, L. C., & Sutawidjaya, A. H. (2019). Talent Management in Mediating Competencies and Motivation to Improve Employee's Engagement. *International Journal of Economics and Business Administration (IJEBA), 1*, 140.

Neves, P., & Eisenberger, R. (2012). Management Communication and Employee Performance: The Contribution of Perceived Organizational Support. *Human Performance, 25*(5), 452–464.

Nienaber, H., & Martins, N. (2020). Exploratory Study: Determine which Dimensions Enhance the Levels of Employee Engagement to Improve Organisational Effectiveness. *The TQM Journal, 32*(3), 475–495.

Nonaka, I., & Hirotaka, H. (2008). *The Knowledge Creating Company*. Harvard Business Review Press.

Nonaka, I., Takeuchi, H., & Umemoto, K. (1996). A Theory of Organizational Knowledge Creation. *International Journal of Technology Management, 11*(7), 833–845.

Odhiambo, F. (2020). *The Awareness, Preparedness and Roles of the Workforce and Managers for the Fourth Industrial Revolution in Africa*. Consultancy Research Report.

Padaki, V. (2002). Making the Organisation Learn: Demystification and Management Action. *Development in Practice, 12*(3/4), 321.

Parent, J. D., & Lovelace, K. J. (2018). Employee Engagement, Positive Organizational Culture and Individual Adaptability. *On the Horizon, 26*(3), 206–214.

Park, Sunyoung, Shinhee Jeong, & Boreum Ju. (2018). Employee Learning and Development in Virtual HRD: Focusing on Moocs in the Workplace. *Industrial and Commercial Training, 50*(5), 261–271.

Popkova, E. G., & Zmiyak, K. V. (2019). Priorities of Training of Digital Personnel for Industry 4.0: Social Competencies vs Technical Competencies. *On the Horizon, 27*(3/4), 138–144.

Prifti, L., Knigge, M., Kiennegger, H., & Krcmar, H. (2017). *A Competency Model for 'Industrie 4.0' Employees.* 13th International Conference on Wirtschaftsinformatik, February 12–15, 2017, St. Gallen, Switzerland.

Qin Jun & Xiao Jing. (2017). *Innovation Research on the Emerging Engineering Talent Cultivation Mode in the Era of Industry 4.0.* International Conference on Industrial Informatics—Computing Technology, Intelligent Technology.

Ramirez, J. C. (2020). *Fourth Industrial Revolution Brings Challenge and Opportunity.* H.R. Executive. https://hrexecutive.com/fourth-industrial-revolution-brings-challenge-and-opportunity/

Rapaille, C. (2006). *The Culture Code.* Broadway Books.

Robertson, B. W., & Kee, K. F. (2017). Social Media at Work: The Roles of Job Satisfaction, Employment Status, and Facebook Use with Co-workers. *Computers in Human Behaviour, 70*, 191–196.

Romani, L., Barmeyer, C., Primecz, H., & Pilhofer, K. (2018). Cross-Cultural Management Studies: State of the Field in the Four Research Paradigms. *International Studies of Management & Organization, 48*(3), 247–263.

Ryan, A. M., & Derous, E. (2019). The Unrealized Potential of Technology in Selection Assessment. *Revista de Psicologia Del Trabajo y de Las Organizaciones, 35*(2), 85–92.

Saenz, M., Sarquis, A., & Albornoz, A. (2019). *Agility Competencies, a Vision from Digital Transformation.* 38th International Conference of the Chilean Computer Science Society (SCCC).

Saks, A. M. (2006). Antecedents and Consequences of Employee Engagement. *Journal of Managerial Psychology, 21*(7), 600–619. https://doi.org/10.1108/02683940610690169

Saks, A. M. (2017). Translating Employee Engagement Research into Practice. *Organizational Dynamics, 46*, 76–86.

Sandberg, S. (2013). *Lean In.* W.H. Allen.

Schaufeli, W. B., & Bakker, A. B. (2004). Job Demands, Job Resources, and Their Relationship with Burnout and Engagement: A Multi-sample Study. *Journal of Organizational Behavior, 25*, 293–315.

Schein, E. (1996). Culture: The Missing Concept in Organization Studies. *Administrative Science Quarterly, 41*(2), 229.

Schwarz, T. (2012). New Research: How Employee Engagement Hits the Bottom Line. *Harvard Business Review.* https://hbr.org/2012/11/creating-sustainable-employee.html

Senge, P. (1990). *The Fifth Discipline* (2006 edition). Random House Books.
Sharafizad, J., Redmond, J., & Morris, R. (2019). Leadership/Management Factors Impact on Employee Engagement and Discretionary Effort. *International Journal of Organization Theory & Behaviour, 23*(1), 43–64.
Shekar, L. S. S. C. (2015). Evaluation of Workplace Training: The Role of Emotional Intelligence, Self-Esteem, Motivation and Achievement. *International Journal of Business Excellence, 8*(6), 798.
Shulga, L. V. (2020). Change Management Communication: The Role of Meaningfulness, Leadership Brand Authenticity, and Gender. *Cornell Hospitality Quarterly, 61*(3). https://doi.org/10.1177/1938965520929022
Simpkins, L., & Lemyre, L. (2018). Organizational Stewardship: Examining a New Measure in the Stress and Well-being Framework. *Canadian Journal of Behavioural Science/Revue Canadienne Des Sciences Du Comportement, 50*(3), 144–155.
Slemp, G. R., Kern, M. L., Patrick, K. J., & Ryan, R. M. (2018). Leader Autonomy Support in the Workplace: A Meta-analytic Review. *Motivation and Emotion, 42*, 706–724.
Smith, A. (1776 [1986]). *The Wealth of Nations*. Penguin Books Edition.
Sofer, C. (1972). *Organisations in Theory and Practice*. Heinemann.
Sony, M., & Naik, S. (2020). Industry 4.0 Integration with Socio-technical Systems Theory: A Systematic Review and Proposed Theoretical Model. *Technology in Society, 61*(1), 101248.
Steers, R. M., Sanchez-Runde, C. J., & Nardon, L. (2010). *Management across Cultures*. Cambridge University Press.
Stepanenko, V., & Kashevnik, A. (2017). Competence Management Systems in Organisations: A Literature Review. *Proceedings of the XXth Conference of Open Innovations Association FRUCT, 776*(20), 427–433.
Stoner, J. A., & Freeman, R. E. (1992). *Management*. Prentice Hall.
Suzuki, M., Ando, N., & Nishikawa, H. (2019). Recruitment of Local Human Resources and Its Effect on Foreign Subsidiaries in Japan. *Management Research Review, 42*(8), 1014.
Takai, J., & Ota, H. (1993). Assessing Japanese Interpersonal Communication Competence. *The Japanese Journal of Experimental Social Psychology, 33*(3), 224–236.
Tijunaitis, K., Jeske, D., & Shultz, K. S. (2019). Virtuality at Work and Social Media Use among Dispersed Workers: Promoting Network Ties, Shared Vision and Trust. *Employee Relations: The International Journal, 3*, 358.

Toh, S.-Y., Cheok, J., & Mughal, S. A. (2019). *Reciprocal Fit Concept in Mission Statement Research*. 13th International Conference on Mathematics, Actuarial Science, Computer Science and Statistics (MACS).

Turner, P. A. (2018). *Talent Management in Healthcare*. Palgrave Macmillan.

Turner, P. A. (2020). *Employee Engagement*. Palgrave Macmillan.

U.S. Immigration Commission. (1910). *Report on Immigrants in Industries*. Government Printing Office.

Ulrich, D., & Ulrich, W. (2011). *The Why of Work*. McGraw Hill.

Vance, R. (2006). Employee Engagement and Commitment, *SHRM*. https://www.shrm.org/hr-today/trends-and-forecasting/special-reports-and-expert-views/Documents/Employee-Engagement-Commitment.pdf

Weinberg, A. (2016). The Preventative Impact of Management Coaching on Psychological Strain. *International Coaching Psychology Review, 11*(1), 93–105.

Williams, A. (2020). Betting Big on Employee Development. *MIT Sloan Management Review, 61*(3), 10.

Williams, R. I., Jr., Morrell, D. L., & Mullane, J. V. (2014). Reinvigorating the Mission Statement through Top Management Commitment. *Management Decision, 52*(3), 446–459.

Williams, J. C., & Mihaylo, S. (2019). How the Best Bosses Interrupt Bias on Their Teams: Strategies to Foster Equity and Inclusion. *Harvard Business Review, 97*(6), 151.

Wilson, H. (2020, July 27). Why Future Workers Will Crave L & D. *The Times*.

Yuan, L., Zhang, L., & Tu, Y. (2018). When a Leader Is Seen as Too Humble: A Curvilinear Mediation Model Linking Leader Humility to Employee Creative Process Engagement. *Leadership and Organization Development Journal, 39*(4), 468–481.

10

Management Competence for the Fourth Industrial Revolution: Integrates Multiple Systems and Processes and Seeks Continuous Improvement

Managers: A Community of Change Practitioners

The benefits of the complementarity of management decisions will only come about by effective integration of systems and processes.

Management is a 'constellation' of concepts and ideas, expanded in recent times by the demands of agile governance in organisations; the growth of workplace practices such as virtual working and the incidence of networks, matrices and 'swarms' as adhocratic structures replace bureaucratic ones. Organisational hierarchies, cascade communication and rigid long-term strategic plans now sit alongside more flexible approaches to business management. But it is the assimilation of new technologies that can present some of the most challenging scenarios for the management role—accentuated by forces for change emanating from Industry 4.0. Technology may be knowledge, but it is the community of practitioners that use it to elicit change. However, 'the great challenge of our time will be to absorb these changes in ways that do not overwhelm people or leave them behind. None of this will be easy' (Basalla, 1988; Friedman, 2006). Maintaining business continuity and achieving goals

P. Turner, *The Making of the Modern Manager*,
https://doi.org/10.1007/978-3-030-81062-7_10

and objectives, critical aspects of the managerial job, goes hand in hand with integration —which is the process of bringing together multiple systems or subsystems into a single whole and making sure that these subsystems function together in the wider business ecosystem. The objective is to incorporate a number of 'separate paradigms' into a network of interrelated domains that are mutually enriching, thereby creating a consistent entity to maximise the use of resources through an improved business model (Hlupic, 2014; Thomson et al., 2021). It recognises complementarity—the 'wholeness' of the business—as a key focus of management action, where complementary sets of business practices are able to yield superior outcomes than the sum of their component parts from synergies across the organisation. Its features are organisational constructs that are based on collaboration and are therefore multi-layered and multi-faceted. As Richard Rumelt (2011) has pointed out, building sustained competitive advantage requires constellations of activities that are 'chain linked'. Where each of these activities are maintained at a high level of quality (as exemplified by the excellence of IKEA's business processes), then the whole becomes resistant to imitation and can lead to a sustained period of success. Systems integration ensures the chain linking of business processes.

Both the benefits and challenges of integration have been recognised over time. The British factory owner Sir Richard Arkwright's letters to his colleague Samuel Oldknow during the First Industrial Revolution in the eighteenth century revealed the diversity of operations that needed to be brought together and the extent of his managerial interests and responsibilities. Subjects within the sphere of integration included not only the challenges of technology or maintaining a workforce but linking sales to credit management, stock control, supply chain management and cash flow—in the face of strong competitor activity—'the prospects look so dark for British manufacturers' (Arkwright-Oldknow Letters, 1783–1796). And all of this whilst trying to make the time to meet friends—*we can meet on Sunday morning by 9 or half past for breakfast. I will endeavour to be there.* In short, the day-to-day life of a manager repeated across time and geography. The 'tyranny of the production line,' such as that in the US automobile industry during the Second Industrial Revolution in the early twentieth century, didn't make the role any simpler or less demanding. Additional pressure resulted from the necessity to achieve targets but also to improve existing systems, adapt to new materials or methods, and integrate extensive administrative controls. The introduction of an assembly line in Henry Ford's factory was not an overnight process but one that 'unfolded' over many months, and the limitations of a single blueprint or bureaucratic system for compiling and assessing production knowledge meant that managers had to be agile and adept. Often inconclusive arguments about role clarity—who did what, when—reflected the challenges inherent during periods of integration (Wilson & Alan McKinlay, 2010). Managers in organisations during the Third Industrial Revolution, such as those at Toyota, had to balance integration to achieve long-term objectives against near-term goals of continuous improvement, and solving problems at their root cause (Liker, 2004). Systems integration required process engineering.

A feature of many of these technological developments was less about the heroic view of a single invention replacing all that had gone before—though there are examples of this—but more of an 'undivided continuum' in which each development complemented the other. Furthermore, the sheer complexity of systems required integration capability that went beyond installation and maintenance—Thomas Edison's new incandescent lamp during the 1880s required the integration of associated technical elements before it was fit for purpose, including generators and cables as well as intangible factors such as finance (Fox, 1996). The assertion of a sequence of challenge and response in technology development gains added weight if this assumption holds true and integration of technology becomes an essential practice in the achievement of a company's success. There are good reasons for the focus on this area because of the identified benefits which include flexibility, cost reduction, product speed to market improvement, success in projects or product design; and across the value chain from customer satisfaction to workforce engagement to reducing business uncertainty. Where managers are able to integrate new systems and then combine and recombine competences, there is the possibility of creating superior value for the organisation as a whole. This may often mean moving beyond the managerial frames—'the corporate equivalent of genetic coding'—that can so often inhibit integrative behaviour and fail to recognise the complementarity of managerial actions (Landes, 1972; Basalla, 1988; Hamel & Prahalad, 1994; Overmeer, 1997; Yasumoto, 2006; Keller & Marko, 2009; Kamogawa, 2010; Saxena & Jaiswal, 2013; Yee & Oh, 2013; Yang, 2015).

In the contemporary business context, integration has multiple meanings. First, it can be that of bringing in new technologies, systems, methods and processes in the most efficient and effective way. Second it can relate to continuous improvement to cement any advantages that have accrued. And third, it is not confined to technology but also has a human perspective—integrating the various needs and demands, points of view and control at the group and individual level, and recognition of the importance of the organisational environment which Mary Parker Follett (1930) described as 'where organism reacts to environment plus organism'. Undoubtedly, a core management competence for the Fourth Industrial Revolution is *integrates multiple systems and processes and seeks continuous improvement*. The definition of this competence is as follows:

> *[T]he ability to coordinate technology and human resource systems; integrate them into a coherent and meaningful whole; use them to create a competitive strategy and operations; whilst ensuring innovation and improvement in a continuous cycle.*

Managers with such competence are able to craft better interpretations of organisational complexity—valuable if in future, competitive advantage will be 'more of a system of highly advanced technologically and organisationally competitive advantages than a clearly identifiable, singular activity distinguishing a given company' (Orton, 1996; Adner & Helfat, 2003; Ogasawara, 2003; Bobrek & Sokovic, 2006; Karlsson et al., 2010; Yang, 2015; Watanabe, 2018; Adamik, 2019; Huy & Zott, 2019). Figure 10.1 shows where the competence of integration and improvement fits into the overall core management competence framework. Understanding the nature of this and the aspects of systems and processes to which improvement applies is important to identifying those facets which are most relevant to the modern manager. Three areas have been identified as being of importance. These are integration in systems to increase efficiency and effectiveness; secondly continuous improvement

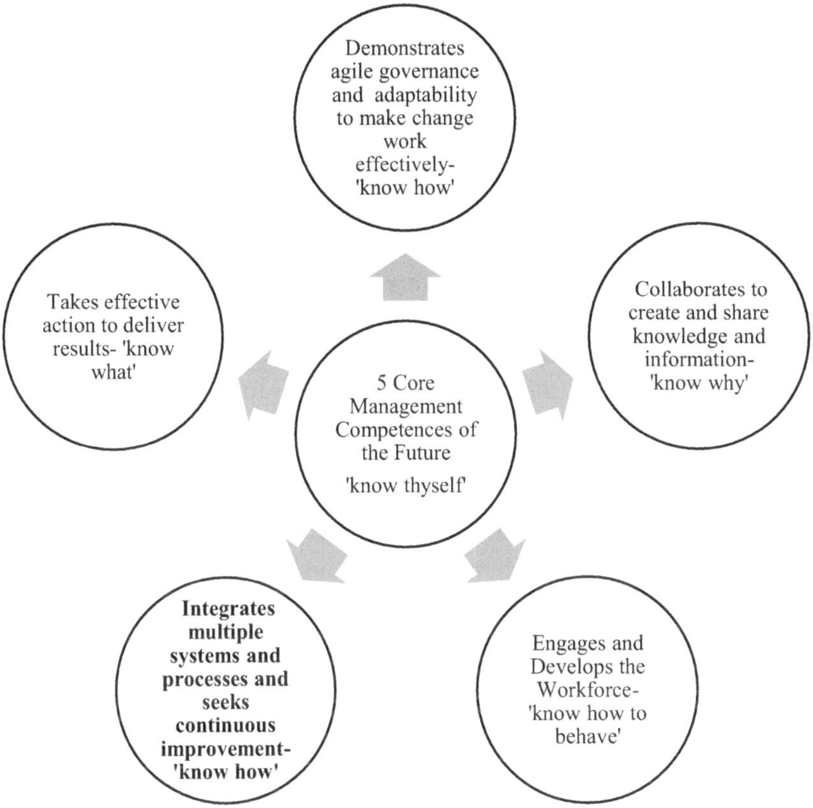

Fig. 10.1 Core management competences

and quality management; and thirdly the effective management of human resources during these events:

> *[C]apabilities with which managers build, integrate, and reconfigure organizational resources and competences.* (p. 1012)

> *Introduced the concept of dynamic managerial capabilities, defined as 'capabilities with which managers build, integrate, and reconfigure organizational resources and competences'.* (p. 1012)

Systems Integration: Character, Capacity and Technical Knowledge

The first of these—systems integration—refers to a level of technical understanding and has been a consideration for the attributes of business managers over the centuries as epitomised by John Gibbons' 1844 statement of competence as 'character, capacity and technical knowledge … are the three essentials, and I have placed them in the order of their importance. … character is the first requisite, cleverness and skill in his craft the second' (quoted in Pollard, 1965). These sentiments would have their adherents during the Second and Third Industrial Revolutions but more recently, a higher level of technology capability or awareness has become a condition for effective management as work has transitioned from labour centric to increasingly technology centric. The convergence of technologies anticipated by Industry 4.0 will accentuate this further placing a greater onus on the manager to understand how technologies and their applications will impact the working environment. Furthermore, whilst technological change was once largely associated with cost reduction through more efficient processes and could be implemented in a single instance or project, Industry 4.0 offers a different perspective. New systems and processes have a broader footprint and will demand multiple points of integration—often simultaneously in an ecosystem—the cyber–physical system—which 'unprecedentedly entangles the network and physical worlds'. Advances in machine learning, natural language coding, sensors, connectivity, cloud computing, nanotechnology, 3D printing and the Internet of Things will come together in a way that is transformative. In dramatic terms 'we have entered a nascent paradigm shift where science fictions have become science fact, and technology fusion is the main driver'. The implications of these forces are being felt across the commercial spectrum in industries as diverse as construction and footwear or services as diverse as health and finance, from technology start-ups or small- and medium-sized enterprises (SMEs), to established global corporations. They can apply in single organisations—such as BASF (with over 120,000 employees) with the concept of *verbund* or the optimum utilisation of resources, apply it as part of systematic strategy creation—or to whole industries. Explicitly, 'dynamic capabilities' include processes of reconfiguration and combination across multiple cells to form an integrated and profitable system. There is evidence that technology integration capability is important as a value-creation mechanism (Tanriverdi & Uysal, 2011; Nobre et al., 2014; Kudo, 2015; Morgan, 2019; You & Feng, 2020; Bongomin et al., 2020). The challenge for managers is to build such capability as part of their overall competence set because, whilst potential opportunities are exciting, 'making them happen is a demanding challenge' (Wheelwright & Clark, 1992). The challenge will be met by managerial competence.

Continuous Improvement: From Practice Observation to Scientific Analysis

Systems integration, if managed expertly, can provide the basis for new business models, products or services and better processes for delivering them. But, as demonstrated by those organisations in the Second and Third Industrial Revolutions who were not content to rest on their laurels, integration also provides the opportunity to cement any gains by continuously improving such processes. For most, this was experienced as performing operational activities as efficiently as possible, whilst simultaneously exploring, developing and improving on products, services and processes. The advent of Industry 4.0. reinforces this conclusion and 'hence, organisations need to be ambidextrous, i.e. being able to balance exploitation and exploration'. The second perspective—continuous improvement—is set within this context and once again will require managers who can demonstrate the necessary ambidexterity with the aim of making the organisation more effective, efficient and productive. Amongst the qualifications for so doing are understanding how workflows across a system, making improvements to this flow and resolving issues such as different priorities or interdepartmental tensions—making sure that there is continuous improvement without continuous conflict (van Aartsengel & Kurtoglu, 2013; Martin & Osterling, 2014; Fukuzawa, 2019; van Assen, 2020). When Henry Ford introduced the moving assembly line in 1913, for example, the company 'rejected the theoretical distillation of one best way in favour of continuous improvements resulting from practice'. From this point, continuous improvement became bywords in the new manufacturing processes that characterised the Second Industrial Revolution. The refinement of the concept into the production process gathered momentum and expertise and the Third Industrial Revolution from the 1960s saw its increasing sophistication through the quality management techniques and just in time systems that gained traction at first in Japan and then throughout the world (Hout & Michael, 2014; Link, 2018). The workplace-based management and fact-based reason that underpin its principles continue to resonate. In contemporary organisations continuous improvement is not regarded as an optional business strategy; 'it is the game today; a condition of survival.' There is support for the principle that 'truth exists in the *gemba* (the workplace or where the action is happening)' whereby continuous improvement arises from a combination of observation, measurement and analysis on the one hand and competent management on the other. It depends on the interactions and interdependencies within and across the organisation as a system. It is the ability to analyse these interconnections, identify systems improvements opportunities and convert these into reality through effective plans and actions—to ensure that the pace of improvement is aligned closely aligned to 'value stream improvement plans' (Ohno, 2013; Martin & Osterling, 2014; Kang et al., 2016). The success of emulating exemplars such as GE and Toyota, lies in 'the ability of the enterprise business to understand conditions' and adapt accordingly and to understand and measure where a change has led to improvement and to what extent (van Aartsengel & Kurtoglu, 2013; Graban, 2019). Continuous improvement has progressed from its origins as a practice-based observational process to one that increasingly involves more rigorous analysis and understanding. Its success depends on effective management of culture and values, performance, alignment and commitment and sustainability. Managers are urged to 'act as committed ambassadors'. The challenge is twofold. First to create an environment in which members of the workforce feel empowered to generate improvements from their tacit knowledge of the process (Tetik et al., 2019; van Assen, 2020). But then to convert that tacit knowledge to explicit knowledge available to everyone and readily processed. The manager's role will be to take continuous improvement from an art form to one based on art, science and common sense. And one that can be replicated and used across all systems and processes where relevant.

The Human Perspective: A Prerequisite for Technological Integration

In this respect there is support for the conclusion that business integration across systems and borders will depend to a great extent on human interaction (Hvolby & Trienekens, 2010; Kang & Moon, 2016)—inter alia, 'the methods, magnitude and frequency of communication and the nature of the information exchanged; co-ordination of the process of interactions and decision making between source and recipient; and the willingness of the partners to cooperate in the pursuit of mutually compatible interests instead of acting opportunistically' (Karlsson et al., 2010). During the period of the Third Industrial Revolution, production techniques associated with lean production, depended on members of the workforce being able to identify quality problems as they appeared; being able to solve the problems (either alone or in a problem-solving group), have a conceptual grasp of the production process and the skills to identify the root cause of problems. 'The attentiveness, analytical perspective, and creativity needed for incremental problem solving cannot be attained through close supervision or the elaborate control systems used to ensure compliance in a mass production system' (MacDuffie & Krafcik, 1992). The effectiveness of the new production systems relied upon the effectiveness of the people operating those systems. There are parallels with contemporary organisations and Taiichi Ohno's words continue to resonate. 'I don't think the *gemba* (workplace) changes easily' and it is essential to gain agreement of many people for change or integration to happen (Ohno, 2013). Even with the shift towards more cyber physical systems that are a feature of Industry 4.0. the increase in integration and strengthening of autonomous capabilities in industrial and commercial processes continue to have a human perspective at two levels. The first is the necessity of ensuring that individual members of the workforce have skills for the current environment and the opportunity to develop for future ones. These go back to the competence associated with creating an engagement and a learning culture. Hence understanding how employees 'can be better integrated to enable increased flexibility' in systems is a prerequisite to technological solutions to harness their full potential. The human interface will provide 'additional degrees of freedom to the systems' (Fantini et al., 2016). The second concerns the managerial competence to ensure that the 'human interface' has the right level of skill and motivation to deal with transformation that arises when integrating multiple systems or technologies. Competitive success depends on the ability to 'learn, innovate and change on an ongoing, sometimes radical basis' (Deiser, 2009). As noted in the previous chapter managerial skill and judgement towards the 'application of labour' will involve the interaction between people and technology in multiple ways. The assumption that 'people issues are business issues,' means not only providing a conducive work environment but ensuring that the skills required for integration and continuous improvement are in place to influence positively attitudes towards the organisation, relationships with colleagues and team members. The development of new technologies such as smart sensors, intelligent assistants, robots and automation will change the types of skills required in operational and development processes across the spectrum from lower to higher levels of skills, including both technical and soft skills (Bongomin et al., 2020).

Successful integration depends on core management competence beyond supporting and championing technology. Instead, managers are 'direct key actors,' which will require that they should understand the potential of the technology and combine this knowledge with their strategic understanding of the business. And having done so be aware that continuity of any business benefits depends on continuity of process improvement. The manager will foresee not only opportunities and needs, but also the practical implications of implementing new technologies (Devece, 2013), will access the right information and communicate that information effectively. They will have competence in planning and stakeholder management. And they will have competence in engaging a workforce to participate whole heartedly in the integration of new systems. This means that their focus should be on technology integration, continuous improvement *and* the human interface. Managerial knowledge, skills, attitudes and behaviours to fulfil this competence are therefore of paramount consideration.

Knowledge and Skills for the Core Management Competence of 'Integrates Multiple Systems and Processes and Seeks Continuous Improvement'

A manager's knowledge—the retention and utilisation of information, skills—the ability to demonstrate a sequence of behaviour towards a goal—attitudes and behaviours—the social manifestation of how a manager undertakes a role, will have a direct impact on the outcomes of the area for which the manager has responsibility. The specific aspect of competence dealt with by this chapter covers a range of technical competences as well as those relating to organisational dynamics, decision-making, adaptation and relational or motivation competences. These reflect both the complexity in business integration and continuous improvement, and the level of ambidexterity required to manage them successfully.

Competences will be based on both process-oriented and systems thinking as well as self-efficacy. The challenge of integration can take a variety of forms. For example, it could involve a process by which a new single source of technology is blended into existing systems or processes; or it could involve a new single source of technology replaces existing ones; or it could be based on two or more technologies or structures merging into a single entity. The complexities involved in each of these examples will be based on the nature of the extent of the integration—organisation wide, departmental, internal or external facing, and its processes—how new or different technologies are merged together (Peyrefitte et al., 2002; Houe et al., 2006; Ishiwatari et al., 2012). Recognising the implications of each of these examples will depend on relevant prior knowledge or the ability to access such knowledge.

Core management competence is causally related to performance and is enacted in a dynamic scenario determined by both the nature of the managerial job and the organisational environment in which that job takes place. Business integration spans technical competences, organisational competences, decisional competences, competences of interpretation and formalisation, adaptation competences and relational or motivation competences (Houe et al., 2006). It can be summarised as *integrates multiple systems and processes and seeks continuous improvement* and is shown as one of five core management competences included in Fig. 10.1. The knowledge and skills that feature in this area of 'know how' are discussed in more detail below:

- Awareness of new technologies, their applications and impact on the business model are important considerations. That the manager *understands technology applications,* the first aspect of core management competence is therefore a foundation on which other aspects of this competence can be built. Applications can cover a multitude of instances from innovative breakthrough to day-to-day and continuous improvement. For the practicing manager this means knowledge of technology applications as they affect operational goals and objectives but, because of the nature of Industry 4.0. from the position of the organisation as a whole. There is an association between managerial support for technology investment and application and value creation which is based on involvement, participation, attention and use. This is a 'sociocultural approach,' which integrates the individual and the collective (López-Muñoz & Escribá-Esteve, 2017; Deligianni et al., 2019; Lemmetty et al., 2020). It means being knowledgeable about technology not necessarily expert at technology. Most importantly it means an understanding of the unique context within which the technology is applied. Where that managerial support is based on an understanding of the technology involved and an awareness of its impact on the organisation or the area in which integration is taking place will improve the chances of success in the process.
- Converting the understanding of technology into sustainable applications will require that the manager *coordinates integration processes and actions,* including efficient planning methodologies to promote maxi-

mum benefit and efficient integrative processes to deliver it. It requires a focus on integration that is broad based-functional and technological, organisational and structural, socio-cultural and legal and financial. The input will be technology specification; efficiency, usability; the outputs will be increasing responsiveness, capacity and functionality (Koren, 2010; Morales et al., 2011; Schuh et al., 2013). Outputs will be based on 'generic' goals—higher-level strategic goals; related goals to specific areas such as production or operations and functions such as marketing, sales and procurement, but, as importantly, cross-functional goals and objectives to prevent a narrow or silo view of the process. Satisfying all of the requirements will be a combination of management competences from agility and adaptability to engagement and collaboration (Schmidt & Lyle, 2010; Schuh et al., 2013; Ma Shu-wen and Pan Wen an, 2013; Bannert & Tschirky, 2020). Social media has a part to play in coordination by encouraging employee participation in projects and idea sharing, strengthening ties with customers and improving communication with suppliers or business partners. Invaluable contributions which may lead to faster access to knowledge, a reduction in communication costs and a faster access to internal expertise (Chung et al., 2017).

- Since the quality of information that is available to those involved in integration will have an influence on the outcomes of that integration, it is important to ensure that organisational knowledge, embedded in routines, processes and systems, is garnered, organised and communicated. To do so will be enhanced by a manager who *seeks and disseminates information about integration.* Tacit knowledge from individuals and teams, relational knowledge from within or without the organisation (customers or other departments) and organisation-wide explicit knowledge will be accumulated through business processes, networks or communities of practice. This will inform implications of the proposed integration, its possible challenges and most importantly the available on which decisions will be made. It will be important for the manager to clarify where the information resides, who needs the information and how it should be communicated. In this respect 'useful knowledge' has been a concept that has stood firm over the generations as it provides the basis of practical applications on the one hand

and 'powerful forces for transformation' on the other. Knowledge relates to technology, processes and people and its exchange will enhance interoperability among devices and systems (Mokyr, 2009; Schneider, 2012; Cimini et al., 2020). The manager will be responsible for moving information beyond its traditional confines to ensure a holistic, organisation-wide perspective of what is available and what is required. This competence will be based on an interactive process, including communicating knowledge of the integration and its implications in a meaningful way to relevant audiences.

- The success of the 'take-up' will depend on how well the goals and objectives of integration match the wider goals and objectives of business areas. It is the role of the manager to see beyond the limited scope of single incidence integration (such as that relating to a specific unit) and where possible take an organisation-wide perspective. In this respect the managerial competence will include a*ligns integration to business outcomes* and is cognisant of an observation made some 30 years ago that 'intelligent reorganisation' requires the organisation to be regarded as a complete entity. Indeed the 'high-velocity organisation' has business outcomes as part and parcel of the role of every manager who will be always concerned with the way that the work of individuals, teams and technologies will contribute to not only the process of which they are a part but also the wider sphere—going beyond the limitations implied in the observation that 'what you see when you look at a corporation, heavily depends on where you sit' (Tomasko, 1993; Prencipe et al., 2005; Spear, 2009). Alignment will involve dialogue with and cooperation by multiple people across the organisation. Engaging multiple stakeholders is as much of a requirement of this competence as others. Internal stakeholders will be other managerial colleagues and employees, technology and functional specialists, and external stakeholders, including suppliers and customers. The Toyota Production System describes this process as *nemawashi*—literally translated as going around the roots—or laying the groundwork or foundation and building consensus towards business goals (Toyota, 2013). The manager's success will be very dependent on ensuring that stakeholders are persuaded by the necessity of the proposed changes, understand the implications for their part of the organisation and can see how change will be aligned to business outcomes.

- The purpose of the integration of new technologies, systems or processes or the commitment to continuous improvement is to enhance organisational outcomes such as financial returns or shareholder value, customer or employee satisfaction. Translating organisational objectives into meaningful ones for individual members of the workforce attracts the same consideration and is an important stage in the planning process undertaken by the manager who will have to reconcile two elements—day-to-day or business-as-usual objectives and integration objectives. Each of these will be set against the employee's personal values where 'values are stable dispositions that structure and guide specific beliefs, norms, and attitudes'. Hence the role of the manager goes beyond that traditionally covered by performance management processes and ensures that there is recognition of objectives from multiple sources, congruence between them and that these are set in the context of personal values since 'values can direct which goals are considered important' (Ungemach et al., 2018). This activity translates into an important aspect of the competence as *aligns departmental and personal objectives to integration.*
- The level of engagement on the part of individual members of the workforce will depend on the interaction between 'supply push' factors—such as worthwhile jobs, sustainable workload, proactive and positive line managers, culture and values alignment, terms and conditions of work, and 'demand pull' factors—such as overwork, lack of role clarity, lack of control, poor working environment, poor work-life balance, poor sense of culture, community or values (Turner, 2020). An important contributor to many of these factors is the level of resources that are allocated to the process. The balance between work demands and the resources necessary to fulfil those demands are explained by an important contributor to the subject of employee engagement the 'job demands resources model' which showed that 'work overload, emotional job demands, physical job demands, and work-home conflict are all risk factors for job burnout, but. … can be alleviated by job resources such as job autonomy, social support, qual-

ity of the relationship with the supervisor, and performance feedback' (Bakker & Demerouti, 2008, 2017). The model proposes a balance between expectations or demands of a job, or in this case, the process, and the resources applied to the completion of the job. And therefore, a key aspect of the process is that the manager *ensures sufficient resources for integration.* Of course, this aspect of competence applies to all situations and not just that relating to integration and improvement. But it is of particular interest here given the ambidexterity mentioned earlier which involves achieving existing goals whilst simultaneously attempting to incorporate new systems or processes. The process has key stages and levers that act as catalysts for change. These are grounded in both explicit knowledge and tacit knowledge in anticipating problems to work or jobs. This will be knowledge based on the one hand to identify a problem and a spirit of mutualism—supportive and collaborative environment—to fix it (Hlupic, 2014; Anand & Barsoux, 2017). Anticipating the impact and areas where there may be problems will help the manager to maintains course.

- Learning training and development represent a source of motivation for people in their existing roles but also a means to acquire new skills for future roles or responsibilities. It is towards the latter that effort on the part of the manager could be directed during periods of transition. In this respect an aspect of the competence of the manager will be *champions investment in new skill development.* This could relate to knowledge about the technologies used and how they are applied which would be an obvious area of attention during any integration, but it may also include knowledge of and the development of skills in organisational issues such as structure and how this works, product management, project management, or the nature of the supply chain or logistics. Successful engagement of members of the workforce will therefore be enhanced by the potential for development in new areas and the opportunity to expand knowledge accordingly (Blaga, 2020; Bongomin et al., 2020). The interconnectivity of organisational activity accentuates the need for knowledge in these facets of organisational life and the role of the manager as coach will be to ensure that the employee acquires knowledge and skills training to enable them to perform effectively.

- The pace of change in contemporary organisations means that integration is most likely to be the start of an ongoing process. And so, the emphasis given by managers to continuous improvement will be a critical factor to ensuring sustainable competitiveness—'the authority, technical support and resources needed to operate the necessary changes to improve quality' (Blaga, 2020). This will create a culture of seeking operational excellence and, what one commentator has called 'the relentless pursuit of doing things better' in which operating models are continuously reviewed to see if they can be improved, focuses on adding value and optimises the speed of output. It is the 'ability to relentlessly pursue improvements in performance and profitability' by focusing on value (Miller, 2014). The role of the manager is to use information—internal and external—about existing systems and processes and in the pursuit of adding value, an outlook which *seeks continuous improvement*. To do so requires a culture of openness, a *sunao* or open mind and the encouragement of innovative proposals and actions. The objective is an organisation that 'harnesses the best-known approaches currently available' but doesn't rest on that knowledge but actively seeks to improve them. It is 'a culture of discovery and discoverers' whereby the workplace not only creates products—physical or virtual—but keeps learning how to produce those products, such that learning and discovery become intrinsic to success (Spear, 2009). Continuous improvement relies on proactivity and the effective involvement of people in operational activity. It is the role of the manager to facilitate the environment within which this involvement can flourish.
- The human perspective of this core management competence provides the bedrock on which the success of the technology application and its planning rest. In so doing the engagement of the workforce is a critical factor and the role of the manager will be to navigate through any tensions between the organisation's objectives and the individuals' needs for 'recognition of their unique identities' (Vuori & Huy, 2016; Ramarajan & Reid, 2020). And so, *engages employees in the process of integration and change* and ensuring attention to the change is a critical factor. Employee Engagement has been articulated as a positive work-related state characterised by vigour, dedication and absorption; where

vigour concerns energy and resilience; *dedication* is about enthusiasm and being inspired, whilst a*bsorption* is the intense concentration in the work being undertaken; and the simultaneous employment and expression of a person's 'preferred self' in task behaviours that promote connections to work and to others, personal presence (physical, cognitive and emotional) and active, full role performance (Schaufeli & Bakker, 2004; Saks, 2006, 2017). Other interpretations include organisational engagement—the level of employee commitment to the organisation; work engagement; and job engagement. Engaging employees to the purpose and process and the need for continuous improvement will involve addressing three elements of the engagement construct. First, engagement as it relates to the psychology of work. This involves meaning at work—understanding and believing in the purpose of or need for the integration; emotional presence; the level of emotional or psychological resources to engage at that particular moment, that is, with its demands; and trust that the 'case' presented is real. The second element is the sociology of work. This means that work demands and resource supply are balanced and the employee has sufficient personal and material resources necessary to deal with the implications of integration; it means that expectations of employees are consistent with health and well-being; and it means that the physical and working environment is positive and sustainable. The third element is the organisation of work. This refers to the structure of the organisation, how it will change and how the allocation of resources or responsibilities will be impacted; the implications for ways of working and the competence of managers in making the integration work (Turner, 2020). In all respects the use of social media platforms can add value to the integration process through collaborative projects and the creation of content communities (Poba-Nzaou et al., 2016). Engaging members of the workforce is therefore as much of a priority for managers as the technical or process dynamics. Poor levels of employee engagement will thwart or slow down integration and improvement. High levels of engagement will have an impact on advocacy on the part of employees, efficiency in terms of processes and performance in terms of the organisation as a whole.

The role of the manager will be to apply elements of the knowledge and skills outlined above in the pursuit of maintaining the course of integration whilst allowing flexibility in the precise nature of the process through empowerment. To so will require the manager to be a master of ambidexterity. The level of competence will also be determined by their attitudes and behaviours as they execute the process of coordination and engagement necessary.

Attitudes and Behaviours for the Core Management Competence of 'Integrates Multiple Systems and Processes and Seeks Continuous Improvement'

The demonstration of knowledge and skills provide the manager with the conceptual basis of competence, but it will be the attitudes and behaviours that accompany these that will determine how well they are enacted—complementing the know-how with the 'know how to behave'. In this regard the management of integration goes hand in hand with the management of inclusion. This means inclusion of multiple areas of business on the one hand—to the goals and objectives of integration—and recognition of contributions of the workforce on the other. The context of integration, its purpose and potential benefits will be communicated throughout the organisation; and individual managers taking responsibility for delivering these outcomes in practice during the implementation of any process. The manager's capability in leading and inspiring will be an important factor in the link between operational activity and success. Where the manager is able to show 'agreeableness,' and openness to experience it will have a positive impact on both the ability to integrate new systems and processes, and, ultimately, organisational performance. But these attributes will also be complemented by empowerment, which is embodied in the psychological state of the employee brought about in part by the attitudes and behaviours of the manager (Morton et al., 2019; Shengli et al., 2019; Hayes et al., 2020):

- The first aspect is based on an assumption that access to information on the part of the workforce (from formal organisation-wide communication processes, from the manager as they seek and disseminate knowledge; from social media sources and some from colleagues), means that they are less of an audience in contemporary organisations and more of a community. Not only will they have tacit knowledge that will help in the integration process, but also ideas and opinions as to its improvement. So, with the practice of community comes the philosophy of openness—since communities need trust, information and understanding to be effective. For the manager, this means that an important aspect of attitudes and behaviour will be *maintains an open mind about ideas and suggestions for integration processes.* Perhaps a concept that epitomises this is that of *sunao* and having a *sunao mind*—a concept that views organisational life, in an open and constructive way. Attitudes and behaviours associated with this include seeing issues as they really are (and hence avoiding falling into the trap of making decisions based on their previous experiences, interests and any biases they may have). The view will facilitate an appropriate response to changing circumstances such as external market forces or internal restructures and will help managers to know when to introduce a new / different approach to a particular issue and when to leave things as they are (Turner & Kalman, 2014).
- Associated with the openness of *sunao,* and necessitated by the dynamic nature of integration, it is important that the manager *recognises opposing points of view* facilitated by collaboration and purpose (Hlupic, 2014). An environment of openness and trust and one in which the manager encourages employee participation and voice provide the basis for members of the workforce to contribute their own ideas. It is a form of praxis whereby opinions are formed and articulated. They are openly considered without prejudice and the manager will take the decision having evaluated several different points of view. As a result, conceptions will either be reinforced or revised depending on the outcome. There is no fear or blame attached to the rightness or the wrongness but there is an expectation that once a decision is taken then it will receive the support of all the members of the team. In such a boundaryless environment, the value of individual contribution is

encouraged, indeed, expected. Inevitably therefore there will be differing points of view about both the direction of a project and how to get there. It is recognition of opposing points of view and how these are dealt with that will form part of the managerial competence.

- A familiar trope associated with change is that it is 'the new normal'. And for many this new normal has opened the prospects of new ways of working and new roles or challenges as well as the potential for career development. The new normal, with greater transparency through widespread and more rapid dissemination of knowledge and information also means that, as signalled earlier, members of the workforce are no longer an 'audience' for change, watching from the sidelines until the change is complete and taking whatever is offered once outcomes have been decided. In fact, the 'new normal'—one in which the workforce is more of a community than audience with expectations of voice and participation, of contribution to integration or improvement and a willingness to be involved in their outcomes. It is therefore important that manager *builds a culture in which employees feel empowered.* Empowerment goes hand in hand with a sense of control and competence in one of two forms. First, structural empowerment refers to the organisational mechanisms which enable the delegation of responsibilities and decision-making powers from managers to employees. Second psychological empowerment is the increase in enhancement of feelings of self-efficacy by fulfilling the employee's ability in self-determination (Schein, 2017; Idris et al., 2018). Where the culture is aligned to the organisation's business objectives, strategy or value propositions, and where resources are allocated to the continued alignment employees will be encouraged to 'benchmark best practices, build networks, share learnings, and implement observed best practices' (Kelly, 2016). During integration and continuous improvement these sentiments will be important. The objective is to provide structure and a management ethos that reduces or eliminates barriers between the manager and members of the workforce, which will result in improved communication and knowledge sharing, thereby allowing employees greater participation in decision-making processes. Sense-making of organisational knowledge is a key management challenge (Deiser, 2009; Idris et al., 2018). Empowerment brings with it a sense of belonging, which in turn improves employee engagement, which in turn improves productivity and organisational outcomes. In order to achieve these desirable goals, the manager's role will be to encourage aspects of information sharing, and regard positively individual participation. Managers who empower stand a better chance of gaining cooperation.

- The challenge of alignment of organisational and individual objectives requires an ambidexterity on the part of the manager. However, even applying this skill to great effect may not always have outcomes that satisfy all stakeholders. Emotions can outrank rationality during change with a negative effect on outcomes. Emotions are feelings with or towards an identified cause, goal or target that emerge when we feel that we have a stake in the outcome of a particular event. At purely management level, the most senior managers could be wary of the impact of change on, for example, the views of shareholders, whilst others could be concerned with the reactions of internal groups—including peers. And where negative emotions are at play between groups of managers, this can hinder the process with a focus on only short-term goals rather than longer-term organisational objectives or position. Significantly, how a manager deals with emotions during periods of transition has organisation-wide implications. Emotions can be regulated before the emotion fully rises (by actively 'doing something to alter the relationship between person and environment'), or after they emerge (by 'blocking the emotion that they do not want to have or resolving problems that would exacerbate an undesired emotion'). The processes of integration, involving as they do a large number of simultaneous activities or projects that may or may not behave as expected are likely to introduce elements of tension for which emotions are inevitable (Vuori & Huy, 2016; Huy & Zott, 2019). This aspect of core management competence is that the manager effectively *deals with emotions arising from implications of integration*—through the process of emotional regulation, one that allows the manager to draw on their reserves of personal knowledge, skills and experience in dealing with any challenges through which strong emotions may emerge. The consciousness of the need to mobilise emotional regulation will have the psychological effect of helping the manager to cope, will have the sociological effect of providing support for employees in a rational way, and will have the organisational effect of helping managers to obtain discretionary support from other stakeholders, as well as eliciting their favourable legitimacy judgements (Haar et al., 2019; Huy & Zott, 2019) important for their continuing role.

- Regulating emotion and its impact on the rationality of decision-making will be important contributions to the ability of the manager to fulfil their objectives. An additional, associated factor is that of the nature of the relationship with stakeholders. If the manager is able to create an environment in which emotions are recognised and accommodated, then this will contribute positively to a further important aspect of competence which is *builds and sustains relationships to facilitate integration and improvement.* These relationships are based on trust and will depend on managerial capital that has been accrued through other aspects of competence whether this be knowledge of technology, knowing how the organisation works or rationality in decision-making. The characteristics are that people are confident in building informal networks, and in the organisation, there is a feeling of community where teamwork and collaboration are prominent—relationship building is a critical success factor (Hlupic, 2014). From an employee perspective, the theoretical underpinning of the concept stems from leader–member exchange to explain the quality of the social exchange relationship between the manager and the employee. Where this is constructive, their interactions will produce positive feelings, which will act as a reinforcement mechanism, encouraging manager and employee to maintain and strengthen the relationship. The benefits to the manager will be to facilitate a smooth process. To the employee a positive relationship will produce better and quality access in securing resource. And, associated with this is the impact on employee well-being since positive relationships at work 'shape greater meaningful work and this then influences happiness'. Supportive work relationships can improve the attachment of employees to the workplace and improve the quality of organisational life. They are the 'threads in the fabric of organisational life' and high-quality work relationships can be a powerful source of connection, engagement and vitality (Muldoon et al., 2018; Ehrhardt & Ragins, 2019; Haar et al., 2019). The manager will 'need to have the capacity to implement diverse courses of action simultaneously, including exploration and exploitation, incremental and radical, flexibility and control, and feed-forward and feedback learning'. But the impact of good interpersonal relationships is felt beyond the immediate manager-employee responsibility. Relationships with peers and managerial colleagues will smooth the process of integration. It will allow explicit knowledge to be shared between different units or teams. Relationships with and within teams will benefit from this aspect of managerial competence—a particularly important outcome because of the 'increasing reliance of organisations on teams to devise and implement organisational strategy' (Bucic et al., 2010). Building relationships is an aspect of managerial behaviour that goes hand in hand with dealing with emotions and having a *sunao mind* in day-to-day operational activity.

- It is important that the process of integration goes hand in hand with learning and this gives a further important element to management competence which is *coaches and trains for integration.* The complexity and the fluidity of the modern organisation will demand that tacit knowledge is converted into explicit knowledge easily and quickly. The incidence of integration will take place in a collaborative work environment which will combine the physical and virtual; the formal and informal. In the process they will bring together a dynamic configuration of people, processes, tools and applications. How the manager applies the competences outlined above will determine how well the integration is carried out. They will endeavour to enhance communication, cross-functional collaboration and rational, collaborative decision-making in their day-to-day activities (Mueller, 2010). A further aspect will be that of explicit knowledge transmission—having been made accessible to others across the organisation—and behavioural change coaching—allowing the manager to coach members of the team in the learning.

Amongst the many demands of Industry 4.0. on organisations and their managers are how to integrate multiple systems, continuously improve those systems once in place and ensure that the human resources who are responsible have today's and tomorrow's skills and are fully engaged with both the job in hand and the future direction. 'Principles' of execution' include prioritising, acting on the lead measures, keeping a compelling scorecard and create a cadence of accountability (McChesney et al., 2012) and *The Toyota Way* (Liker, 2004) offers a methodology. Where the manager is able to integrate information systems into business and human systems the potential for differentiation increases with the potential knock on effect on business performance. The organisational competence of integration is a source of competitive advantage (Mukai & Negoro, 2009). The above narrative is one in which the manager regards integration as a process, which includes multiple lines of enquiry and action, and requires tacit knowledge to become explicit through an environment of trust and openness. For it to be successful it will also require the manager to regard it as a cross organisational phenomenon especially because of the interconnectedness of modern organisations. It will require them to see integration in its totality. This core management competence will require managers to have both technical and people management knowledge and skills and to have attitudes and behaviours that are consistent with both. The excellence with which they deal with integration and continuous improvement will provide them with the basis for the next aspect of competence which is takes effective action to deliver results.

References

Adamik, A. (2019). Creating a Competitive Advantage in the Age of Industry 4.0. *Problemy Zarządzania: Organizational Management Issues in the Age of Industry 4.0, 17*(2 (82)), 13–31.

Adner, R., & Helfat, C. E. (2003). Corporate Effects and Dynamic Managerial Capabilities. *Strategic Management Journal, 24*(10), 1011–1025.

Anand, N., & Barsoux, J.-L. (2017). What Everyone Gets Wrong about Change Management: Poor Execution Is Only Part of the Problem. *Harvard Business Review, 95*(6), 78.

Arkwright-Oldknow Papers. (1783–1796). *Columbia Rare Book and Manuscript Library*. University in the City of New York.

Bakker, A. B., & Demerouti, E. (2008). Towards a Model of Work Engagement. *Career Development International, 13*, 209–223. https://doi.org/10.1108/13620430810870476
Bakker, A. B., & Demerouti, E. (2017). Job Demands–Resources Theory: Taking Stock and Looking Forward. *Journal of Occupational Health Psychology, 22*(3), 273–285.
Bannert, V., & Tschirky, H. (2020). Integration Planning for Technology Intensive Acquisitions. *R & D Management, 34*(5), 481–494.
Basalla, G. (1988). *The Evolution of Technology*. Cambridge University Press.
Blaga, P. (2020). The Importance of Human Resources in the Continuous Improvement of the Production Quality, *Procedia Manufacturing, 46*, 287–293.
Bobrek, M., & Sokovic, M. (2006). Integration Concept and Synergetic Effect in Modern Management. *Journal of Materials Processing Technology, 175*(1), 33–39.
Bongomin, O., Gilibrays Ocen, G., Oyondi Nganyi, E., Musinguzi, A., & Omara, T. (2020). Exponential Disruptive Technologies and the Required Skills of Industry 4.0. *Journal of Engineering* (2314–4912), 1.
Bucic, T., Robinson, L., & Ramburuth, P. (Eds.). (2010). Effects of Leadership Style on Team Learning. *Journal of Workplace Learning, 22*(4), 228–248.
Chung, A. Q. H., Andreev, P., Benyoucef, M., Duane, A., & O'Reilly, P. (2017). Managing an Organisation's Social Media Presence: An Empirical Stages of growth model. *International Journal of Information Management* 37(1, Part A), 1405–1417.
Cimini, C., Boffelli, A., Lagorio, A., Kalchschmidt, M., & Pinto, R. (2020). How Do Industry 4.0 Technologies Influence Organisational Change? An Empirical Analysis of Italian SMEs. *Journal of Manufacturing Technology Management, 3*.
Deiser, R. (2009). *Designing the Smart Organisation*. Jossey Bass.
Deligianni, I., Voudouris, I., Spanos, Y., & Lioukas, S. (2019). Non-linear Effects of Technological Competence on Product Innovation in New Technology-Based Firms: Resource Orchestration and the Role of the Entrepreneur's Political Competence and Prior Start-Up Experience. *Technovation*, 88. https://doi.org/10.1016/j.technovation.2019.05.002
Devece, C. (2013). The Value of Business Managers' 'Information Technology' Competence. *Service Industries Journal, 33*(7–8), 720–733.

Ehrhardt, K., & Ragins, B. R. (2019). Relational Attachment at Work: A Complementary Fit Perspective on the Role of Relationships in Organizational Life. *Academy of Management Journal, 62*(1), 248–282.

Fantini, P., Tavola, G., Taisch, M., Barbosa, J., Leitao, P., Liu, Y., Sayed, M. S., & Lohse, N. (2016). *Exploring the Integration of the Human as a Flexibility Factor in CPS Enabled Manufacturing Environments: Methodology and Results.* IECON 2016—42nd Annual Conference of the IEEE Industrial Electronics Society.

Follett, M. P. (1930). *Creative Experience.* Longmans, Green and Co.

Fox, R. (1996). *Technological Change.* Routledge.

Friedman, T. (2006). *The World is Flat.* Penguin Books.

Fukuzawa, M. (2019). Factory Strategy. *Annals of Business Administrative Science, 18*(5), 149–179.

Graban, M. (2019). *Measures of Success.* Constancy Inc.

Haar, J., Schmitz, A., Di Fabio, A., & Daellenbach, U. (2019). The Role of Relationships at Work and Happiness: A Moderated Mediation Study of New Zealand Managers. *Sustainability, 11*, 3443.

Hamel, G., & Prahalad, C. K. (1994). *Competing for the Future.* HBS Press.

Hayes, T. L., Oltman, K. A., Kaylor, L. E., & Belgudri, A. (2020). How Leaders Can Become More Committed to Diversity Management. *Consulting Psychology Journal: Practice and Research, 72*(4), 247–262.

Hlupic, V. (2014). *The Management Shift.* Palgrave Macmillan.

Houe, R., Grabot, B., & Geneste, L. (2006). Competence Management for Business Integration. *IFAC Proceedings, 39*(3), 217–222.

Hout, T., & Michael, D. (2014, September). A Chinese Approach to Management. *Harvard Business Review.*

Huy, Q., & Zott, C. (2019). Exploring the Affective Underpinnings of Dynamic Managerial Capabilities: How Managers' Emotion Regulation Behaviours Mobilize Resources for Their Firms. *Strategic Management Journal, 40*(1), 28–54.

Hvolby, H.-H., & Trienekens, J. H. (2010). Challenges in Business Systems Integration. *Computers in Industry, 61*(9), 808–812.

Idris, A., See, D., & Coughlan, P. (2018). Employee Empowerment and Job Satisfaction in Urban Malaysia: Connecting the Dots with Context and Organisational Change Management. *Journal of Organisational Change Management, 31*(3), 697–711.

Kamogawa, T. (2010). Structural Models that Manage IT Portfolio Affecting Business Value of Enterprise Architecture. *IEICE Transactions on Information and Systems, 93*(D9), 2566–2576.

Kang, S., & Moon, T. (2016). *Supply Chain Integration and Collaboration for Improving Supply Chain Performance: A Dynamic Capability Theory Perspective.* 49th Hawaii International Conference on System Sciences (HICSS).

Kang, N., Zhao, C., Li, J., & Horst, J. A. (2016). A Hierarchical Structure of Key Performance Indicators for Operation Management and Continuous Improvement in Production Systems. *International Journal of Production Research, 54*(21), 6333–6350.

Karlsson, C., Taylor, M., & Taylor, A. (2010). Integrating New Technology in Established Organizations: A Mapping of Integration Mechanisms. *International Journal of Operations & Production Management, 30*(7), 672–699.

Keller, T., & Marko, T. (2009). *Management Framework for Business Integration Projects.* IEEE Conference on Commerce and Enterprise Computing, 226–232.

Kelly, S. (2016). Creating a Culture of Continuous Improvement and Sustainable Management Systems at Abbott Diagnostics Longford. *Global Business and Organizational Excellence, 36*(1), 6.

Koren, Y. (2010). *The Global Manufacturing Revolution.* Wiley.

Kudo, S. (2015). Exploring Causal Relationship between IT Management Maturity and IT Effects—A Field Study in Akita Prefecture. *International Journal of Japan Association for Management Systems, 7*(1), 1–10.

Landes, D. (1972). *The Unbound Prometheus.* Cambridge University Press.

Lemmetty, S., Glăveanu, V. P., Collin, K., & Forsman, P. (2020). (Un)Sustainable Creativity? Different Manager-Employee Perspectives in the Finnish Technology Sector. *Sustainability, 12*(9), 3605.

Liker, J. K. (2004). *The Toyota Way.* McGraw Hill.

Link, S. (2018). The Charismatic Corporation: Finance, Administration, and Shop Floor Management under Henry Ford. *Business History Review, 92*(1), 85–115.

López-Muñoz, J. F., & Escribá-Esteve, A. (2017). An Upper Echelons Perspective on Information Technology Business Value. *European Research on Management and Business Economics, 23*(3), 173–181.

Ma Shu-wen & Pan Wen an. (2013). Impact of Relationship Strength and Integration Capability on the Efficiency of Knowledge Transfer among Technology Alliances in China. *Journal of Science and Technology Policy in China, 4*(2), 136–151.

MacDuffie, J. P., & Krafcik, J. F. (1992). Integrating Technology and Human Resources for High Performance. In T. A. Kochan & M. Useem (Eds.), *Transforming Organisations*. Oxford University Press.

Martin, K., & Osterling, M. (2014). *Value Stream Mapping*. McGraw Hill.

McChesney, C., Covey, S., & Huling, J. (2012). *The Four Disciplines of Execution*. Free Press.

Miller, A. (2014). *Redefining Operational Excellence*. Amacom.

Mokyr, J. (2009). *The Enlightened Economy*. Penguin Books.

Morales, E., Franch, X., Martinez, A., & Estrada, H. (2011). *Considering Technology Representation in Service-Oriented Business Models*. IEEE 35th Annual Computer Software and Applications Conference Workshops.

Morgan, J. (2019). Will We Work in Twenty-First Century Capitalism? A Critique of the Fourth Industrial Revolution Literature. *Economy and Society, 48*(3), 371–398.

Morton, S., Michaelides, R., Roca, T., & Wagner, H. (2019). Increasing Employee Engagement in Organizational Citizenship Behaviors within Continuous Improvement Programs in Manufacturing: The HR Link, *IEEE Transactions on Engineering Management. Engineering Management, 66*(4), 650–662.

Mueller, K. (2010). *The Role of Human Factors Integration and Change Management Coaching in Integrating Multidisciplinary Teams Working in Collaborative Work Environments*. SPE Intelligent Energy Conference and Exhibition.

Mukai, M., & Negoro, T. (2009). Contribution of Information Systems to Business Performance as an Embedded Factor of 'Differentiation Mechanism': A Case Study of Seven-Eleven Japan (Apcim2009 Best Papers). *Journal of Information and Management, 30*(3), 122–133.

Muldoon, J., Keough, S. M., & Lovett, S. (2018). The Mediating Role of Workplace Attitudes on the Leader–Member Exchange—Turnover Intention Relationship. *The Psychologist-Manager Journal, 21*(4), 229–248.

Nobre, F., Walker, D., & Brown, M. (2014). Ability Based View in Action; A Software Corporation Study. *Brazilian Administrative Review, 11*(2), 164–187.

Ogasawara, Y. (2003). *The Development of ICT and Business Model*. Abstracts of Annual Conference of Japan Society for Management Information. https://www.jstage.jst.go.jp/article/jasmin/2003s/0/2003s_0_31/_article/-char/en

Ohno, T. (2013). *Workplace Management*. McGraw Hill.

Orton, J. D. (1996). Reorganisational Learning. In B. Moingeon & A. Edmondson (Eds.), *Organisational Learning and Competitive Advantage*. Sage Publications.

Overmeer, W. (1997). Business Integration in a Learning Organization: The Role of Management Development. *Journal of Management Development, 16*(4), 245–261.

Peyrefitte, J., Golden, A., & Brice, J., Jr. (2002). Vertical Integration and Economic Performance: A Managerial Capability Framework. *Management Decision, 40*(3), 217–226.

Poba-Nzaou, P., Lemieux, N., Beaupré, D., & Uwizeyemungu, S. (2016). Critical Challenges Associated with the Adoption of Social Media: A Delphi of a Panel of Canadian Human Resources Managers. *Journal of Business Research, 69*(10), 4011–4019.

Pollard, S. (1965). *The Genesis of Modern Management*. Penguin Books.

Prencipe, A., Davies, A., & Hobday, M. (2005). *The Business of Systems Integration*. Oxford University Press.

Ramarajan, L., & Reid, E. (2020). Relational Reconciliation: Socializing Others across Demographic Differences. *Academy of Management Journal, 63*(2), 356.

Rumelt, R. (2011). *Good Strategy, Bad Strategy*. Profile Books.

Ishiwatari, Sae, Jing Tang, Loo geok Pee, & Junichi Iijima. (2012). Enhancing Business Process Understanding to Support Employee's Work, Abstracts of Annual Conference of Japan Society for Management Information, Session ID H1-7. https://doi.org/10.11497/jasmin.2012s.0.140.0; https://www.jstage.jst.go.jp/article/jasmin/2012s/0/2012s_140/_article/-char/en

Saks, A. M. (2006). Antecedents and Consequences of Employee Engagement. *Journal of Managerial Psychology, 21*(7), 600–619. https://doi.org/10.1108/02683940610690169

Saks, A. M. (2017). Translating Employee Engagement Research into Practice. *Organizational Dynamics, 46*, 76–86.

Saxena, A., & Jaiswal, M. P. (2013). Impact of Enterprise Systems on Firm Performance: A Business Integration Capabilities Perspective. *IUP Journal of Operations Management, 12*(3), 29–75.

Schaufeli, W. B., & Bakker, A. B. (2004). Job Demands, Job Resources, and Their Relationship with Burnout and Engagement: A Multi-Sample Study. *Journal of Organizational Behavior, 25*, 293–315.

Schein, E. (2017). *Organisational Culture and Leadership*. Wiley.

Schmidt, J. G., & Lyle, D. (2010). *Lean Integration; An Integration Factory Approach to Business Agility*. Pearson Education.

Schneider, M. (2012). Knowledge Integration. In N. M. Seel (Ed.), *Encyclopedia of the Sciences of Learning*. Springer.

Schuh, G., Bremer, D., Wellensiek, M., & Drescher, T. (2013). Method Towards a Scenario-Based Planning of Technology Exploitation. *Proceedings of PICMET'*13.

Shengli Dai, Yingchun Li, & Wei Zhang. (2019). Personality Traits of Entrepreneurial Top Management Team Members and New Venture Performance. *Social Behaviour and Personality: An International Journal, 47*(7), 1–15.

Spear, S. J. (2009). *The High Velocity Edge*. McGraw Hill.

Tanriverdi, H., & Uysal, V. B. (2011). Cross-Business Information Technology Integration and Acquirer Value Creation in Corporate Mergers and Acquisitions. *Information Systems Research, 22*(4), 703.

Tetik, M., Peltokorpi, A., Seppanen, O., & Holmstrom, J. (2019). Direct Digital Construction: Technology-Based Operations Management Practice for Continuous Improvement of Construction Industry Performance. *Automation in Construction, 107*, 102910.

Thomson, L., Kamalaldin, A., Sjödin, D., & Parida, V. (2021). A Maturity Framework for Autonomous Solutions in Manufacturing Firms: The Interplay of Technology, Ecosystem, and Business Model. *International Entrepreneurship and Management Journal*, 1. https://doi.org/10.1007/s11365-020-00717-3

Tomasko, R. M. (1993). Intelligent Resizing: View from the Top Down. *Management Review, 82*(5), 16.

Toyota. (2013). *Nemawashi-Toyota Production System Guide*. https://blog.toyota.co.uk/nemawashi-toyota-production-system

Turner, P. A. (2020). *Employee Engagement*. Palgrave Macmillan.

Turner, P. A., & Kalman, D. (2014). *Make Your People Before You Make Your Products*. Wiley.

Ungemach, C., Camilleri, A. R., Johnson, E. J., Larrick, R. P., & Weber, E. U. (2018). Translated Attributes as Choice Architecture: Aligning Objectives and Choices through Decision Signposts. *Management Science, 64*(5), 2445.

van Aartsengel, A., & Kurtoglu, S. (2013). *A Guide to Continuous Improvement Transformation*. Springer.

van Assen, M. F. (2020). Empowering Leadership and Contextual Ambidexterity—The Mediating Role of Committed Leadership for Continuous Improvement. *European Management Journal, 38*(3), 435–449.

Vuori, T. O., & Huy, Q. N. (2016). Distributed Attention and Shared Emotions in the Innovation Process. *Administrative Science Quarterly, 61*(1), 9–51.
Watanabe, Y. (2018). Design for Downstream to Integrate R&D and Downstream Opportunities. *The Annual Bulletin of Japan Academy of Business Administration*, 88.
Wheelwright, S. C., & Clark, K. B. (1992). *Revolutionising Product Development*. The Free Press.
Wilson, J. M., & Alan McKinlay, A. (2010). Rethinking the Assembly Line: Organisation, Performance and Productivity in Ford Motor Company, c. 1908–27. *Business History, 52*(5), 760–778.
Yang, C.-C. (2015). The Integrated Model of Core Competence and Core Capability. *Total Quality Management and Business Excellence, 26*(1/2), 173–189.
Yasumoto, M. (2006). Reconsidering Novel Technology Introduction Strategies. *Annals of Business Administrative Science, 5*, 67–98.
Yee, J. T., & Oh, S. C. (2013). *Technology Integration to Business*. Springer.
You, Z., & Feng, L. (2020). Integration of Industry 4.0 Related Technologies in Construction Industry: A Framework of Cyber-Physical System. *IEEE Access*.

11

Management Competence for the Fourth Industrial Revolution: Takes Effective Action to Deliver Results

Talent Is Not Recognised by Cause But by Effect

Managers know what counts and act accordingly.

Charles Clinton Spaulding, president of the North Carolina Mutual Insurance Company between 1923 and 1952, believed that 'in business, as in no other profession or occupation, the inevitable measurement of capability is results' (Prieto & Phipps, 2016). Warren Buffet, the 'Sage of Omaha', was very clear on the subject—'we want our managers to think about what counts', and what counted was the application of the manager's limitless potential to profitable achievements. There was an incentive to do so because Berkshire Hathaway managers generally had a stake in their company's success, 'we eat our own cooking' (Buffet, 2002). These philosophies mirror an aspect of the role of the manager that has changed little over 250 years, and Adam Smith's words in the *Wealth of Nations* (1776) continue to resonate—talent is recognised not by cause but by effect. Management action was the cause, delivering results the effect. For the eighteenth-century Scottish flax spinner William Brown, this meant 'produce good quality yarn, make a large quantity, keep costs

P. Turner, *The Making of the Modern Manager*,
https://doi.org/10.1007/978-3-030-81062-7_11

as low as possible, and keep the machinery in good working order' (Geraghty, 2003). To the owners and managers of the steam engine and boiler factory in Staffordshire in 1808, it meant 'executing well' to achieve quality at reasonable cost in their contract with Josiah Wedgewood; (Bateman and Sherratt, 1808) and during the Second Industrial Revolution, to the managers of the Baltimore and Ohio Railroad, it meant managers accounting for their actions at every level (Licht, 1995). As industrial and commercial society evolved, the scope of action was often determined by the organisation's structure and the associated policies and delegated decision-making authority, as in 1950s America, where 'the use of organisation charts to illustrate personal and departmental relationships and the flow of authority and responsibility in any structured situation' (Browne, 1950). In these examples, management action emanated from clarity about what was expected—centred on output, to the boundaries within which such actions can take place, increasingly determined by organisation structure and policy. Actions could be determined by managers influencing workforce behaviour 'through shaping their mindset in the hope that they will internalize the values and beliefs of the organisation and act in accordance with these', or by more technical forms—output-based criteria such as budgets or incentives (Gerdin, 2020).

In Japan's remarkable rise during the Third Industrial Revolution, Akio Morita, co-founder of Sony, for example, urged the company's managers to take action because 'a business that doesn't take advantage of its opportunities doesn't deserve to be called an enterprise' (Sony, 2020). Lee Iacocca asked his managers to 'keep acting like every decision, no matter how small, has a major impact on the vitality of the company' (Iacocca, 1994), and Indra Nooyi, Chair and CEO of PepsiCo, urged action after evaluating options by 'sweating the details' (Nooyi, 2014). The key words of *act, account, produce, quality, costs, impact, vitality* and *detail* have permeated managerial action consistently over time. In contemporary organisations this applies not only to functional or line management, but across the organisation as managers increasingly cooperate and collaborate outside of their immediate spheres of influence. The advent of Industry 4.0. accentuates the trend such that the lines of a line manager extend as much laterally as vertically. In this context, taking action to achieve results has qualities that would be recognised throughout time—understanding opportunity or priority, evaluating options, allocating resources appropriately, mobilising and motivating a workforce—but with the added dimensions of pace, space and scope. That is, the speed at which decisions need to be made, the broader horizon for the impact of decisions (organisation wide) and the wider frame of reference brought about by collaboration and cooperation. The implication of knowledge-intensive value creation processes means that the 'creation, organisation, mediation or practical use of knowledge outranges by far the disposal of physical assets' (Brödner, 2013). In Thomas Friedman's (2006) words: 'whatever can be done will be done. And much faster than you think. The only question is whether it will be done by you or to you.' The modern manager has additional, significant parameters in which to take action to deliver results. Whilst the end product of a scientific innovation might be a scientific paper, it is innovative technological activity that will create actual, made products. The President's Scientific Research Board conclusion in 1947 that strength lay in the practical application of scientific principles remains relevant today as the outputs of these scientific principles swamp society and industry in unprecedented volumes (Kirby et al., 1956; Basalla, 1988). Action on the part of organisations underlies this assumption and action on the part of managers brings it to life.

Amongst the innovations through which managers will have to craft their strategies, plans and actions are smart products, smart manufacturing processes, the 'Internet of Things', the availability of large amounts of process/product data for analysis, highly integrated enterprises (both horizontally and vertically) and the use of cyber–physical systems (Marion et al., 2020; Saxby et al., 2020). The panoply of responsibilities that are traditionally associated with the role of the manager, together with new technologies, the accentuation of the importance of collaboration, diversity and equality of opportunity, and the critical nature of the health and welfare of the workforce or environmentally friendly methods of production, adds extra dimensions to decision-making. For some this means acting in a traditional format through a well-structured hierarchy. For others it means acting as a fulcrum, positioned between external forces and internal business units. And for others still it means acting at the centre of a hub, coordinating multiple strands from multiple levels with managerial actions—rarely set in a static environment—moving, changing and flowing, because they are rooted in actual rather than conceptual situations. In all scenarios, sense-making will be a priority and gathering information, intelligence and insight to inform decisions will be the process (Deiser, 2009; Mintzberg, 2011; Rumelt, 2011; Teece, 2011; Teece, 2014; Derwik et al., 2016; Bag et al., 2021). All of these factors require the 'phronesis' of management—the practical wisdom of getting things done. There is some support therefore for Watson's (1994) observation: 'the essential rationale of the management of an organisation' is its long-term survival. If managers are there to achieve objectives by ensuring the efficient functioning of their business unit, *taking effective action to deliver results* becomes as much of a core management competence as adapting to change, collaborating, integrating new systems or engaging the workforce. The definition of this competence is as follows:

> *[T]he ability to achieve goals through action; the ability to take action through rational, inclusive decision-making; the ability to make rational decisions based on a combination of evidence, intuition and emotional intelligence.*

Actions may be taken through applying knowledge in a collaborative way; or being agile and adaptable in dynamic environments. Some managers will take action through workforce engagement; others by integrating new technologies, systems or processes into work-flow. All managers will seek to balance the achievement of strategic objectives with near-term ones. In Mitsui, whose business ranges from Iron and Steel to IT and Communications, the objectives are 'to improve business management expertise and to foster and deploy business management talent, while at the same time, prioritizing the allocation of management resources into businesses where profitability improvement can be realized' (Mitsui, 2020). The thesis of the *Making of the Modern Manager* is that each of the core management competences, or a combination of them, are important in the organisation's quest for competitive advantage. And as well as being a knowledge seeker and disseminator, systems integrator and talent facilitator, the manager will also be action oriented, a trouble shooter resolving issues such as resource allocation, differing points of view about ways and means, working within centralised or devolved decision-making, striking the balance between cost and capability (Armstrong, 2005; Brachos et al., 2005; Ballou et al., 2010; Gold, 2010; Shirahada, 2010; Palma & Pavez, 2017; Karltun et al., 2019; Shamim et al., 2019). At the same time, a new 'socio-technical configuration' means a move from a linear approach to decision-making and action to a more circular one taking account of *intelligence*—the identification of elements and pathways relevant to define future actions; *design*—the pathways to enact decisions in practical actions; *choice*—how to adapt decisions to the specific characteristics of context; and *review*—the evaluation and redefinition of decision processes (Del Giudice et al., 2016).

Management Action: Pace, Space and Scope

Frameworks of management competence have evolved from theories of management, and the praxis of management—how theory is enacted or realised—which in turn emerged as new ideas permeated the thinking of business owners, consultants and academics. Then came the practice of management—its repeated disciplines and activities. In the contemporary organisation management takes place on the intersection between these three where practitioners—'who shape the construction of practice'—use the growing body of knowledge and their practical wisdom, to bring management to life through action. The competences to be displayed will include such generic ones as business practice, technology proficiency and understanding as well as communication and engagement. A typology of competence might include 'competence-in-stock, competence-in-use, and competence-in-the-making' or within a typology that includes cognitive competence or work-related knowledge and the ability to apply it; functional competence the ability to perform work-based tasks; social competence or relational and communication skills; and meta-competence or personal and professional values. Of particular relevance to this section, is 'action style competence' which refers to the way in which goals are and how those goals are achieved. Charles Handy's seminal work on organisation listed the roles of the manager that encapsulate the action competence and included liaison, monitor, disseminator, disturbance handler, resource allocator and negotiator

(Bernstein, 1971; Handy, 1988; Lindgren et al., 2004; Kang et al., 2015; Iasbech & Lavarda, 2018; Igielski, 2020). The intersection of these various assumptions is presented through the core management competences as shown in Fig. 11.1. The fifth of these—takes effective action to deliver results—is the 'know what' and 'know how' of management; the 'actional competence' based on planning, crafting and visioning on the one hand, and mobilising resource on the other. It is a sharp focus on what counts

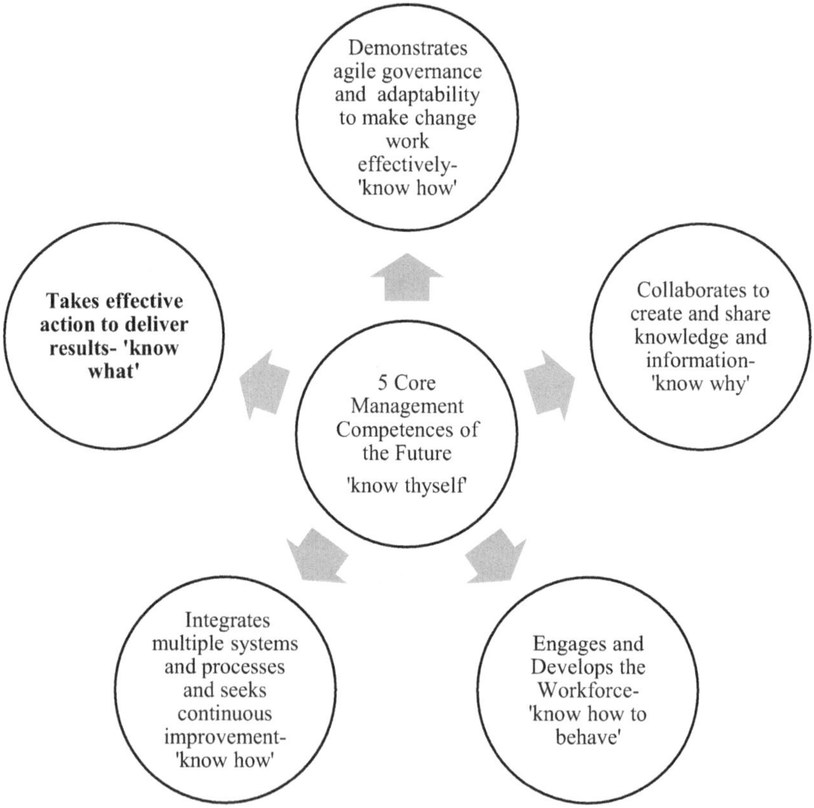

Fig. 11.1 Core management competences

and what must be done and depends on managers acting with purposeful, consistent, conscious and energetic behaviour which requires them to be determined, persistent and relentless; and to show a personal commitment towards a goal that cuts out distractions and overcomes difficulties (Eccles & Nohria, 1992; Bruch & Ghoshal, 2004; Mintzberg, 2011). Management is a bias for meaningful action towards a goal.

The practice of management and the application of core management competence take place in an organisational context, which today is full of competing demands and priorities in which the theoretical predictability of the hierarchy is increasingly replaced fluid organisational structures—an organisational environment which is more multidisciplinary, open, collaborative and multicultural (Cresnar & Nedelko, 2020; Dzwigol et al., 2020). The modern manager may have to operate in multiple structures as organisations become more 'strategically' agile and this will influence the competences required to do so. In addition, the manager will continue to act in search of goals simultaneously, these being 'Getting the organisation's work done', whilst ensuring that the psychological and social needs of the workforce are met where possible and then dealing with their own 'psychological and social needs'. Skills such as planning and goal setting and the organisation of activity are implemented by a dynamic capability 'to appropriate, adapt, integrate and reconfigure' for organisational effectiveness. The effect is that, in the first place, managers sometimes have to be logical and sequential in their actions—if this decision is taken then that will happen. But there are also circumstances where this is not possible—creating a paradox with which managers have to deal, and so in the second place—to 'maintain both distance and closeness, treat subordinates uniformly while allowing individualism, and ensure decision control while allowing autonomy'. The former will require a planned and systematic approach; the latter a 'paradox mindset' dealing with ambiguity by searching for solutions to problems, demonstrating cognitive complexity, being open to ambiguity and multiple experiences and treating competing demands as opportunities, they will 'confront conflict in a constructive manner to stimulate understandings' (Vaill, 1967; Sony & Naik, 2019; Waldman et al., 2019). It is part of the ambidexterity of the modern manager that they may build a sustainable model through continuity in some processes and change and transformation from innovation in others. Such a context raises three questions that are particularly important to the competence of takes effective action to deliver results; first, how does the manager determine what is important—what counts; second how does the manager mobilise resources to deliver against this once it has been articulated in terms of goals and objectives; and third how do they know when they have achieved them?

What Counts and What to Do About It

Managers are often faced with opaqueness, and complexity. A good understanding of what counts will help managers is essential in helping to navigate in the course of better decisions as they get to grips with large amounts of information (García-Sánchez and García-Meca 2020). These will be influenced by internal considerations such as organisation governance (strategy, stewardship and policy), innovation, operational excellence, the development of human capital, workforce health and well-being and diversity; to which the responses may be prioritising issues; resource allocation to 'hot button' issues or aligning the organisation's structure in a way that meets new challenges. External considerations about what counts may be inspired by shareholder value, competitor product development activity, increased competition, customer relationships or macro-economic change or opportunity or one of system shocks such as a pandemic; the response to which will include creating a greater emphasis on customer centric culture or increased support for innovation in processes, products or services in the quest for competitive advantage; or the health and safety of the workforce. Throughout all, the manager's competence—the 'interplay of knowledge, capacities and skills, motives and affective dispositions' (CMI, 2015; Škrinjarić & Domadenik, 2020) will be critical. More recently, what counts has been dealing with the human and business outcomes of COVID 19. Whether these remain high on corporate agendas will sit alongside either survival, as world economies struggle to cope with the output of the pandemic, or growth for those companies that maximised their competitive positions during it. From this exhaustive list, 'what counts' as a manager is essentially contextual. The answer will depend on the strategic priorities of the organisation—markets or customers, systems integration, innovation amongst others—and how these filter through directly to the area in which any particular manager has a remit and indirectly because that manager will most likely be in collaborative projects or programmes with others. The competence of the manager will be reflected in how, when and where they make decisions and what decisive action they take against the 'what counts' priorities of the organisation in which they work.

Goal Setting and Resource Allocation

The second area of importance concerns decision-making and actions to mobilise resources—an issue which has been heavily influenced by the theory and practice of goal setting, that is, the identification of a goal will bring with it the resource necessary for its achievement. In their influential work Locke and Latham (1990) articulated the importance of consciously set goals which resonated across participants, tasks, nationality, goal source, settings, experimental designs, outcome variables, levels of analysis (individual, group, division and organisational) and time spans. The work emphasised the importance of specific and attainable goals as a means of enhancing employee productivity, namely management by objectives—'people with specific, challenging goals reliably outperform those with do-your best goals because the latter type of goal is interpreted too subjectively' (Locke & Latham, 2019). The goals that managers can use to influence desired employee outcomes are performance goals— specific outcomes that employees agree to accomplish; learning goals—specific skills and knowledge areas that an employee agrees to master in order to pursue a specific performance goal successfully and behavioural goals; to define behaviours that a person needs consistent with the previous two. In addition, implementation intentions (as part of any learning activity) and their associated 'if/then' plans offer the chance to enhance goal achievement by giving situational cues in the workplace (Ford, 2017;

Greenan et al., 2017). A proposed framework to structure thinking in respect of this particular aspect of core competence and that was the use of 'SMART' in goal achievement. The concept, which became ubiquitous during the Third Industrial Revolution, is an acronym for Specific: target a specific area for improvement; Measurable: quantify, or at least suggest, an indicator of progress; Assignable: specify who will do it; Realistic: state what results can realistically be achieved given available resources; Time-related: specify when the result can be achieved (or variations such as *attainable, action oriented* or *achievable* for assignable; and *relevant* for realistic). SMART goals were a popular method of systematising performance management allowing managers to break down goals from the macro to the micro, assign them to individuals or teams and monitor key activities against them. The logicality and simplicity of this methodology explained its popularity since it was a methodology for clarity and action which when used effectively, brought order to an otherwise chaotic or random situation. More recently, and in response to the different pace, form, and organisational structures of Industry 4.0. with greater emphasis on multi-directional multi-stakeholder involvement in decisions, there are added foci on inclusivity in decision-making, ensuring that everyone is treated fairly, and an emphasis on relationships that nurture community and the integral common good—the components of which have been referred to as SMART 2.0 goals (Dyck, 2020). Hence the planned and systematic approach to decision-making against structured, well-thought-through goals has not been eliminated but encouraged to develop into one that is more inclusive and collaborative—two themes that feature in several of the competences associated with Industry 4.0. 'Strategies are not immaculately conceived in detached offices so much as learned through tangible experience' (Mintzberg, 2011). The use of social media offers additional choices about how to engage with diverse stakeholders by facilitating transparency and inclusivity in decision-making and action (Heavey et al., 2020). Part of this learned experience will come through collaboration with other managers or stakeholders in the organisation. In essence this means constant interaction between business functions such as design, marketing, engineering, purchasing and manufacturing.

Feedback: Measures and Achievements

The third area of importance concerns the systems and processes by which managers can obtain feedback about goal achievement, measures or resource utilisation and take decisions to sustain or modify their earlier actions. The options are broad and range from benchmarking, state-of-the-art or state-of-the-process type of measures through to more specific ones such as measures of customer satisfaction, zero defects or continuous improvement from a production quality perspective, employee engagement data from a workforce perspective. They can be objective measures involving the use of financial or accounting data, or subjective measures involving the perceptions of managers or members of the workforce in terms of how well their organisation is performing. All are likely to involve multiple levels of accountability (Arauz et al., 2009; Singh et al., 2016). Words like *practical* and *obtainable*, and compatibility with the organisation's overall goals (*alignment*) have resonated from the earliest days of management by objectives (see, e.g. McConkey, 1965) but continue to be relevant. Given the fast pace that is a feature of Industry 4.0 there is the added necessity of capturing the influence and significance of changes in the process. The rationale in this is that 'it is difficult for companies to make intelligent decisions unless management understands how the company and the industry are directing their changes'. Taking effective action to deliver results isn't a one off event and to attain first-rate performance, the modern manager will have the ability to adjust their plan of action based on external data such as changes in customer demand and competitor strategies; or internal such as process measurement or workforce data. These decisions will be based on sound tacit knowledge—a particular feature of management competence—but also contemporaneously 'machine learning can supply additional scrutiny and assessment outside the limitations of performance standards and predictors'. They will also have to seek and identify linkages between their decisions and those of the wider organisation paying attention to the social dimension of linkage—who is aware of and committed to the decision, and intellectual linkages—understanding of the impact of the decision on other areas, for example (Reich & Benbasat, 1996; Singh et al., 2016; Harrower, 2019).

In order to achieve its desired mission, vision or strategic position, the organisation will identify and where appropriate gain agreement from its stakeholders for a series of objectives against which its performance can be measured. From these will emanate multiple goals and multiple coalitions of constituents amongst whom are the organisation's managers to whom the task of operationalising strategic intent will fall (Locke and Latham 1990). These will determine that the manager's actions are not taken in a vacuum but as part of a virtuous cycle of challenge, response and adaptation. In Hamel and Prahalad's (1994) case study of Komatsu they drew attention to how the organisation achieved its Deming Prize-quality status in just three years by ensuring that the managers were clear about what counted when it came to the choice between quality and cost. Komatsu focussed on quality until it achieved world class standard. Having clear objectives, the managers were able to take actions not only for their own areas of responsibility but in the knowledge that the quest for quality was a company-wide initiative. Long-term corporate objectives were achieved by effective management action.

Goals will be established that will direct action and effort; and energise individuals or teams. The questions facing the contemporary manager relate to creating organisational structures, systems and cultures to deal with the new dynamics, opportunities and uncertainties; to creating 'robust designs' to deal with massive change (Deiser, 2009). And having answered these, what actions need to be taken to make them work effectively. The success of this process depends on the manager having knowledge and skills in how to go about taking effective action and deciding on which outcomes to focus; and attitudes and behaviours that ensure followership or collaboration in so doing.

Knowledge and Skills for the Core Management Competence of 'Takes Effective Action to Deliver Results'

The challenges of Industry 4.0. will require the manager to negotiate their way through a context of interoperability; dynamic capabilities; system partnering and knowledge partnering; decentralisation; real-time assessment of capabilities; network cooperation and the installation of smart networks, machines, processes, systems, products and supply chains. Amongst the competences required for such an environment are the ability to work in teams; the ability to seek and process information, the ability to organise the work of others through setting direction and the ability of the manager to organise their own work, set goals and create an action plan. But most of all in relation to Industry 4.0 it is the ability to function effectively in complex organisations (Igielski, 2020). It is incumbent on managers to recognise their own action styles, their strengths and limitations (know thyself) and how they impact on teams or business units and the organisation as a whole. The knowledge required will be related to the economic environment, business strategy, technology and organisational dynamics. Skills will be personal or social; some will pertain to communication or project management; some will be acquired through experience or practice; some will be based on intuition—always remembering the words of Chesley B. Sullenberger, in the context of his decision to land flight US Airways 1549 in the Hudson River off Manhattan in January 2009 after it was disabled by a collision with a flock of Canada geese—'not every situation can be foreseen or anticipated. There isn't a checklist for everything.' When must-do situations occur, managers will rise to the occasion (Schaffer & Stearn, 2015; Adamik, 2019; Marnewick & Marnewick, 2020). But what are the elements of knowledge and skill that make up the competence of effective decision-making and action?

- Making sense of the dynamics of the transformation that is taking place in the current business environment and how to respond, is an extremely demanding task for managers 'irrespective of size, role, and position in an existing ecosystem'. The basis of this sense making is the manager's cognitive foundation, which is 'a set of givens to any management decision—assumptions about the future, knowledge about alternatives and a view of the consequences of pursuing each alternative'. In the first place a 'management inclination'—knowledge and understanding of the implications of Industry 4.0. will provide a frame for decisions, focusing on particular issues and developing particular strategies, which will establish a context for everyone else working in the unit, in a way that is relevant and value adding. It will help to sense opportunities, develop and implement viable business models, build capability and craft strategic and operational responses in anticipation of the outcomes of the new environment or as they occur (Hertz, 1977; Allen, 2001; Mintzberg, 2011; Teece, 2016; Shamim et al., 2019; Belinski et al., 2020; Bettiol et al., 2020; Cunha et al., 2020; Penttilä et al., 2020). The inclination means competence will be acquired to master not only 'business as usual' but also complex situations—such as contradictory information, informal collaboration and abstract, dynamic and highly integrated processes (Škrinjarić & Domadenik, 2020). The knowledge that provides the foundation for this inclination will in turn inform the first aspect of core management competence—*understanding what counts* where the manager decides what they must do as opposed to what they might do. An observation made over 50 years ago still resonates—the underlying assumption is that a manager will manage more effectively the more thoroughly they understand 'the nature of the beast'. It concerns the manager's relationship to the system—what the manager knows, what the manager understands. In the first place, the manager will apply knowledge of the vision or mission of the organisation, its strategy and its key performance indicators—based on access to explicit knowledge through the organisation's public strategic intent; and tacit knowledge based on their own interpretation of the opportunities and challenges inherent in this—to determine priorities and areas of immediate versus longer-term action. To support this, modern managers have a wide range of knowledge sources, including systems for business or process control; integrated programming systems for production planning and control 'based on various linear, nonlinear, dynamic, integral models', project management models; workforce scheduling; investment and finance, including risk analysis. Secondly, they will ensure that their own and their teams' goals and objectives are aligned accordingly, and that there are plans to achieve them—identifying and prioritising what to do. The vision will give not only a sense of the future but also a sense of direction and a 'sense of discovery' (Vaill, 1967; Hamel & Prahalad, 1994; Oliveira et al., 2020). And all of these will take place with the inclination towards the opportunity and the things that must be done to take advantage of the opportunity.

- Industry 4.0 brings with it a new type of new organisational dynamic requiring 'systems thinking', that is, looking across the whole organisation to give a real understanding of the impact of change or transformation. Hence there is a strong emphasis on organisational skills in competence research which finds that in the contemporary organisation, with its complexities and dynamics it is important that the manager is able to take a holistic view of the influences on their decisions. And to go a stage further, with the advent social media and other new technologies, 'it is becoming more difficult to argue that one could not have known or at least have considered more alternatives, particularly negative unintended consequences that happen in addition to the intended positive ones' (Wilburn & Wilburn, 2016; Škrinjarić & Domadenik, 2020). More than ever, therefore, an important element of making effective decisions therefore is that of *demonstrates systems thinking*. In Senge's (1990) *Fifth Discipline* he was of the view that 'there are ways of working together that are vastly more satisfying and more productive than the prevailing system of management' and that systems thinking would accord better decision-making and ultimately better business results. 'You can only understand the system of a rainstorm by contemplating the whole, not any individual part of the pattern.' Here, a system is 'a complex social organization composed of people with distinct worldviews, conflicting interests and asymmetrical and unbalanced power of influence ... The system has subjective existence and is the product of individual perceptions.' The objective of systems thinking is to deal with complexity, by looking at the totality of the situation. A systems approach helps to overcome any barriers by providing multiple perspectives, in deciding and defining priorities—understanding what counts. It takes management beyond an emphasis on individuals alone to that of the social system of which they are a part. As organisations adapt to the new Industry 4.0 environment 'a reframing of prevailing sensemaking' (including in the application of social media to the business strategic level) goes beyond a simple process-solving approach, requiring instead, the manager to reflect on the wider implications of managerial decision-making (Ryden et al., 2015; Oliveira et al., 2020). Systems thinking requires the manager to take account of the totality of organisational systems.

- This aspect of competence will determine what the organisation needs to do to 'integrate, build and reconfigure' to address the changing environment. But the actions required are not automatic, 'they don't just happen … but rather result from value creation activities, including search, learning, R&D and managerially directed asset orchestration processes' (Bossidy & Charan, 2002; Teece, 2017). They will arise from a conscious decision to *build dynamic capabilities (*to deal with what counts) and is a further aspect of the core management competence. Some capabilities are about firms doing things right; but 'dynamic capabilities are about doing the right things, at approximately the right time, based on new product (and process) development, unique managerial orchestration processes, a change-oriented organisational culture and a prescient assessment of the business environment and technological opportunities'. They are patterns of collective activity through which organisations generate and modify their operational routines as they strive for improved effectiveness. The core capabilities of the organisation will include the competence, skill and knowledge of the workforce; technology systems that 'embed the knowledge resulting from the experience'; and most importantly that these are underpinned by supportive management systems, organisational structures and processes. Effective team working, as in other aspects of core management competence will be a key feature and in the contemporary organisation this can be enhanced by, inter alia, the effective use of social media to utilise each team member's expert knowledge to increase creative performance. The important functions of managers are to identify, assemble and orchestrate the organisation's assets (Teece, 2011, 2014, 2016, 2017; Ali et al., 2019; Garbellano & Da Veiga, 2019). Supportive management systems are engendered by managers who understand the importance of dynamic capabilities to success and have the knowledge to make them happen.
- Understanding what counts, systems thinking and building capabilities are based on what is actually happening in the organisation and what needs to happen. A key part of the role of the manager is to ensure that this reality is set in a context that members of the workforce can engage with and discuss specific things they have to do, and why. These assumptions form the basis of *takes meaningful action that*

genuinely matters. Such an aspect of competence will satisfy the requirement 'to sense and react to internal and external opportunities and threats, identify and evaluate current and potential competitors in the business environment very quickly. In fact, an organization's market agility heavily relies on its ability to access information and then act on it due to the information overload issues in the current big data era' (Li et al., 2021). This means meaningful action in relation to the manager's own objectives and responsibilities on the one hand, and meaningful action on the part of members of the workforce on the other. In respect of the latter, the onus is on the manager to relate the two ideals of meaningful action and meaningful work because 'broadly speaking, when something is meaningful, it helps to answer the question, "Why am I here?" It is the manifestation of 'the value of a work goal or purposes, judged to the individual's own ideals or standards.' For members of the workforce, meaningful work consists of four sources: 'developing and becoming self', 'unity with others', 'serving others' and 'expressing self'. Employees actively, and on an ongoing basis, evaluate the meaning of work. Individuals can experience inspiration towards an ideal, the desire to 'ever improve oneself and the conditions for others' through being able to discern and articulate the reality of their organisational context. The manager has a role to play in both of these desirable outcomes—identifying meaningful action—'watch any manager and one thing readily becomes apparent; the amount of time that is spent simply communicating—namely collecting and disseminating information for its own sake without necessarily processing it'—and then setting proximate goals, which are 'close enough to hand to be feasible. For the workforce, those who find meaning at work are more competent committed and contributing, which leads to increased customer commitment which in turn leads to better financial results. Where they are able to relate the meaning of their work to the meaning of the organisation then this will have positive outcomes (Bossidy & Charan, 2002; Lips-Wiersma & Morris, 2009; Ulrich & Ulrich, 2010; Mintzberg, 2011; Jurksiene & Pundziene, 2016; Adamik, 2019; Marnewick & Marnewick, 2020). The competence of the manager rests on them being able to convey meaning. That is meaning in relation to the organisation's purpose and goals, meaning in respect of the unit's contribution to those goals and meaning in respect of the individual in relation to both the organisation and the unit.

- Prioritising what counts, developing capabilities to deliver and taking meaningful action, provide essential building blocks for a further aspect of this competence which is *takes action in a coherent way.* The effectiveness of the organisational systems and processes will in turn depend on the competence of the manager in delivering coherent actions. The skill of the manager means joining up strands of activity whatever structure is in place and maintaining a narrative of continuity (Garratt, 2000; Rumelt, 2011; Adamik, 2019). And to do so in the face of the 'problematic preferences' or fluid participation that might occur ' depending on the amount of time and effort, participants devote to different domains. Achieving coherent actions against this backdrop means constantly adjusting, manoeuvring, and adapting (Cohen et al., 1972; Kindarto & Zhu, 2019). It involves steps that are coordinated with one another and work together in accomplishing the required outcome. It involves deploying resource, policies and manoeuvres that are consistent and coordinated.
- Interconnectedness and interoperability will enable different tasks to be carried out by 'different partners in separate geographic spaces, both intra and inter organisations' (Belinski et al., 2020). And so, taking coherent actions will necessitate that the manager *builds lateral relationships*—across, within and without the organisation—the greater the competence in collaboration and cooperation, the greater the ability to build relationships. To make progress against both will necessitate bringing together individuals (who may not be directly under the manager's control) to achieve wider organisational goals. Credibility in so doing will depend on competence in systems and processes, social and personal competences and the ability to work with and manage diverse teams and team members. Furthermore, the manager will spend not only on planning, decision-making and controlling, but also on networking and multi-layer communications in value loops as well as value chains (Derwik et al., 2016; Turner et al., 2016; Bugalska, 2019; Dyck, 2020; Marnewick & Marnewick, 2020). This aspect of competence is about making full use of the talents of members of the workforce within the direct remit of the manager, and of the talent

outside of this remit. The manager will seek to develop and maintain long-term relationships cross-functionally and inter-organisationally.
- The final area of knowledge and skill will be that the manager *pays attention to detail* (Turner et al., 2016; Yin et al., 2018). Since competent managers 'are able to use their knowledge of their organisational context and their colleagues/subordinates/seniors to influence those around them to adopt their point of view', it is important that the manager stays on top of both the environment in which the organisation, unit or team is operating and the performance against it—Aristotelian 'episteme' or insight. The knowledge gained will add to the ability of the manager to deliver results and its detail will support monitoring, control and optimisation across the whole of the production or service cycle (Rouleau & Balogun, 2011; Bredillet et al., 2015; Turner et al., 2016; Yin et al., 2018; Cunha et al., 2020). The manager will therefore need to have a grasp of detail of performance across their objectives on the one hand and against each element of the objective on the other—and will translate and adapt to specific situations and context.

Knowledge per se is not enough to deliver effective management practice; instead, it will require complementary attitudes and behaviours—a 'soft component' to match 'hard' technical or business process knowledge—including communication, courtesy, integrity, honesty, being nurturing or empathetic, self-control, reliability and a strong work ethic, together with willpower and energy (Robles, 2012; Fareri et al., 2020). Attitudes and behaviours are important because behavioural criteria can considerably add to the achievement of positive business or organisational outcomes.

Attitudes and Behaviours for the Core Management Competence of 'Takes Effective Action to Deliver Results'

The advent of Industry 4.0, demographic change and the unprecedented economic and social outcomes of COVID-19 have prompted the implementation of advanced technologies, new operating models, resilient strategies to minimise complexity and an emphasis on business continuity during times of transition (Verma & Gustafsson, 2020). The preceding narrative, proposed that successful management during such demanding times required proactivity using explicit and tacit knowledge—to understand how the change affects the strategy, services and products required to meet unprecedented or unexpected demands, and action to develop sustainable business practices. Each of these areas will be complemented by attitudes and behaviours that form a more holistic picture of the competence of effective actions to deliver results:

- In the first place, competence isn't just about having the ability to apply principles and techniques in practical situations it is also about having *the willpower to get things done* and executing this with disciplined action (Bruch & Ghoshal, 2004). This will be paramount as the manager becomes involved in conflict resolution, negotiating and expectation management, and problem awareness and solving. 'Being clear on the outcome you want' the inclination to getting things done, and strong directing and decision-making skills, spending time and being persistent. Implementation and implementation intentions as clear priorities will strengthen willpower (Peters, 1978; Miterev et al., 2016; Nijhuis et al., 2018; Tawse et al., 2019). Willpower means the willingness to meet new challenges as they arise and the willingness to overcome any obstacles that are encountered. Getting things done means collaboration, rational persuasion, consultation, inspirational appeals and the willingness to pursue the objectives of both exploitation and exploration simultaneously (Turner et al., 2016; Lam et al., 2017). The personal competence of 'managing self'—reflecting, time managing, dealing with stressful situations, prioritising and 'juggling' (Mintzberg, 2011) will each influence willpower.
- A factor in facilitating the achievement of organisational goals, the implementation of change or the delivery of transformation will be emotional commitment, resilience and versatility, strength of purpose in dealing with problems as they arise and a connection with team members. In this respect the manager will be consistent about articulating value, consistent in the way that they facilitate change and con-

sistent in the way they gain commitment or resolve issues. A combination of attributes will see behaviour in which the manager *acts with purposeful, consistent, conscious and energetic behaviour*, showing inner drive, taking pride in the job and striving for results (Huy, 2002; Bruch & Ghoshal, 2004; Kinley & Ben Hur, 2015; Derwik et al., 2016; Aušra & Birutė, 2019). This is the second aspect of attitudes and behaviours requiring deep personal involvement in the substance and detail of delivering business results.

- The purpose, energy and willpower behind managerial decision-making and action will inevitably be influenced by the manager's and the organisation's values and norms (Derwik et al., 2016; Lam et al., 2017; Garbellano & Da Veiga, 2019). Where the two are consistent with each other and where they also resonate with members of the workforce, the chances of success will increase. Hence an important part of competence is to *deliver value with values,* of which Indra Nooyi has said, 'you cannot deliver value unless you anchor the company's values. Values make an unsinkable ship.' Managers are role models. They need to show that they 'trust their subordinates, offer help and guidance, show appreciation to the subordinates, and solve problems adequately'. Their behaviours reflect their values, and they will try to elicit the same from their co-workers (Andersen, 2019; Backstrom, 2019). And so, demonstrating business acumen and an awareness of cost-benefit analyses will contribute to the delivery of shareholder value, but to optimise the effectiveness of action the intrinsic personal or social values and beliefs of the manager and members of the workforce are important—when an individual identifies strongly with the organisation it will influence behaviours that are more likely to result in task commitment. Managerial assumptions define values and in turn how they would perceive, think or feel. These values inform the 'ideas that managers draw on consciously in order to shape their actions', influence both the structure and the generation of ideas, and inform the areas to which managers directed their attention, determine the nature of the problem (or opportunity) and what are considered as reasonable or acceptable solutions. When behaviour and justifications or values are repeated successfully over time, both the organisation and the manager will retain them as reflexes or the 'right way to respond to a certain problem' (Schein, 2004). Wong & Kong, 2017; Chen et al., 2018). Organisational performance will be enhanced where hard data outcomes are combined with a supportive organisational culture which includes values and norms.

- Action means getting the job done. And the communication around the action should motivate and support people as they plan, solve problems or evaluate outcomes. In this respect sensemaking is accomplished through the ability of managers 'to craft and share a message. Building a shared vision, which are shared pictures of the future that will contribute to commitment rather than compliance' (Senge, 1990; Jameson, 2001). Hence for the participation of the workforce it is important that the manager *clearly communicates expectations.* Highlighting the end game, enhancing the probability of accomplishing a goal ('the extensive work needed to accomplish a challenging and meaningful task can provide feelings of deep satisfaction and psychological wellbeing') are both aspects of communication behaviour that the manager will employ (Rouleau & Balogun, 2011; Tortorella & Fettermann, 2018; Tawse et al., 2019). And having communicated expectations, achievement against those expectations at all levels—everyday progress. In the contemporary organisation, multi stakeholder management brings with it the need for effective communication both laterally and vertically; internally and externally—'communicating all round'. A working assumption behind this aspect of competence is that 'the whole is always more important than the parts' and the behaviour of the manager would be to ensure that everyone understands and is engaged with broader objectives as well as those at hand. The challenge is that of bringing both vision, values and strategy to life. Employee participation and collaboration between team members will help to generate a unified understanding of the team's goals (Wong & Kong, 2017; Belinski et al., 2020; Cunha et al., 2020; Dyck, 2020; Marnewick & Marnewick, 2020). Communicating expectations in the contemporary environment is all round, lateral and vertical.
- Managers will do all within their power to facilitate positive performance and act as a buffer for potential negative influences through problem resolution. Getting things done means enhancing individual/group efficacy and function; bettering firm efficacy and

performance; nurturing knowledge, skills and competences; and increasing people potential and growth. Management is a process which makes use of all available resources to achieve these four objectives and *enables performance driving activities* is therefore at the heart of this aspect of competence. In the first place it means ensuring that resources are balanced in a way that delivers continuity of production or service processes whilst at the same time maximising opportunity for innovation—providing for current and future value. It means supporting members of the workforce as they go about their roles and communicating, treating people with respect, encouraging other people's ideas and listening to ideas and suggestions in public fora are important facets of this. At the same time as acting as a motivator and facilitator the manager also takes on the mantle of barrier 'to prevent unwarranted distractions affecting the team performing the tasks' (Armstrong, 2005; Goldsmith, 2008; Deiser, 2009; Turner et al., 2016; Rana & Sharma, 2019). The competence will require an orientation to action and performance, utilisation of lateral relationships and most of all, because management is a constellation, 'controlling and doing and dealing and thinking and leading and deciding and more' (Mintzberg, 2011). Furthermore, as social media continue to define and shape 'the contours of the contemporary organisation' performance driving activities will include influence, analytics and insights, as well as the development of communities of interest or expertise in the creation of knowledge (McCosker, 2017). Enabling performance will come about by the manager's drive manifested by an action orientation, awareness of the impact of new media with which to engage and an inclusive approach to information acquisition for decision-making.

The creation of competitive advantage in an era of Industry 4.0 will be dependent on inter alia 'modern management methods; strategic analysis; active marketing; alliances and agreements; computerisation of management in the area of: brand, quality, logistics, knowledge; implementation of modern manufacturing technologies; development of unique product features; better fulfilment' (Adamik, 2019). Each of these requirements will in turn be dependent upon the manager taking effective actions to deliver results. Managers will make decisions based on their perceptions, knowledge and experience about their resources as they relate to their knowledge of the external environment. They will employ 'a bounded repertoire of implementation processes', amongst which are formal planning and control, participation in decision-making from key stakeholders and the definition of individuals' roles in the desired action. They will make decisions with a good understanding of their own action styles and the effect these will have on the workforce from whom they are both directly and indirectly responsible. Furthermore, these will not be isolated incidents; but linked by knowledge and understanding; cooperation and collaboration; communication and engagement (Partington, 2000; Enríquez-De-La-O, 2015). The competence of the manager in each of these areas will be a key source of competitive advantage.

References

Adamik, A. (2019). Creating a Competitive Advantage in the Age of Industry 4.0. *Problemy Zarządzania: Organizational Management Issues in the Age of Industry 4.0,* 2(82), 13–31.

Ali, A., Wang, H., & Khan, A. N. (2019). Mechanism to Enhance Team Creative Performance Through Social Media: A Transactive Memory System Approach. *Computers in Human Behaviour, 91*, 115–126.

Allen, D. (2001). *Getting Things Done*. Hatchette.

Andersen, J. A. (2019). Trust in Managers Revisited: Antecedents, Mediating Factors, and Consequences. *Dynamic Relationships Management Journal, 8*(2), 65–73.

Arauz, R., Matsuo, H., & Suzuki, H. (2009). Measuring Changes in Quality Management: An Empirical Analysis of Japanese Manufacturing Companies. *Total Quality Management & Business Excellence, 20*(12), 1337–1374.

Armstrong, M. (2005). *Armstrong's Handbook of Management and Leadership*. Kogan Page.

Aušra, G., Birutė, P., & Danguolė, S. (2019). Personal Qualities in the Context of Sales Manager Competence Development. *Economics and Culture, 16*(2), 46–57.

Bäckström, I. (1963 [2019]). Health-Related Quality Management Values: Comparing Manager and Co-worker Perceptions. *International Journal of Quality and Service Sciences, 11*(4), 588–603.

Bag, S., Gupta, S., & Kumar, S. (2021). Industry 4.0 Adoption and 10R Advance Manufacturing Capabilities for Sustainable Development. *International Journal of Production Economics, 231*, 107844. https://doi.org/10.1016/j.ijpe.2020.107844

Ballou, B., Heitger, D. L., & Schultz, T. D. (2010). The Actions-to-Value Framework: Linking Managerial Behaviour to Organizational Value. *Management Accounting Quarterly, 11*(4), 1–9.

Basalla, G. (1988). *The Evolution of Technology*. Cambridge University Press.

Bateman and Sherratt. (1808). *Steam Engine and Boiler Works, Letter Held in the Wedgewood Museum, Stoke on Trent*,

Belinski, R., Peixe, A. M. M., Frederico, G. F., & Garza-Reyes, J. A. (2020). Organizational Learning and Industry 4.0: Findings from a Systematic Literature Review and Research Agenda. *Benchmarking: An International Journal, 27*(8), 2435–2457.

Bernstein, R. J. (1971). *Praxis and Action*. University of Pennsylvania Press.

Bettiol, M., Capestro, M., Di Maria, E., & Micelli, S. (2020). At the Roots of the Fourth Industrial Revolution: How ICT Investments Affect Industry 4.0 Adoption, '*Marco Fanno*' Working Papers.

Bossidy, L., & Charan, R. (2002). *Execution; The Discipline of Getting Things Done*. Random House Business Books.

Brachos, D. A., Philippidou, S. S., & Soderquist, K. E. (2005). The Culture Model as a Mediation Framework between Managerial Cognitions and Actions: How Communities of Practice Can Drive Strategic Change. *International Journal of Information Technology and Management, 4*(3), 217–230.

Bredillet, C., Tywoniak, S., & Dwivedula, R. (2015). What Is a Good Project Manager? An Aristotelian Perspective. *International Journal of Project Management, 33*(2), 254–266.

Brödner, P. (2013). A Faustian Exchange: What Is to Be Human in the Era of Ubiquitous Technology? *Reflective Design of Technology for Human Needs.* 25th Anniversary Volume 28(1), 27–37

Browne, C. G. (1950). The Concentric Organization Chart. *Journal of Applied Psychology, 34*(6), 375–377.

Bruch, H., & Ghoshal, S. (2004). *A Bias for Action*. Harvard Business School Press.

Buffet, W. (2002). *The Essays of Warren Buffet*. Edited by L. A. Cunningham. Wiley.

Bugalska, A. (2019). Personality Predispositions and Competences. *International Journal of Contemporary Management, 18*(1), 7–36.

Chen, N., Chao, M., Xie, H., & Tjosvold, D. (2018). Transforming Cross-Cultural Conflict into Collaboration; The Integration of Western and Eastern Values. *Cross Cultural and Strategic Management, 25*(1), 70–95.

CMI. (2015). *The CEO Challenge.* Chartered Management Institute in Conjunction with the Conference Board, British Library Resources.

Cohen, M. D., March, J. G., & Olsen, J. P. (1972). A Garbage Can Model of Organizational Choice. *Administrative Science Quarterly, 17*(1), 1–25.

Cresnar, R., & Nedelko, Z. (2020). Understanding Future Leaders: How Are Personal Values of Generations Y and Z Tailored to Leadership in Industry 4.0? *Sustainability, 12*(11), 4417.

Cunha, T. P., Méxas, M. P., da Silva, A. C., & Quelhas, O. L. G. (2020). Proposal Guidelines to Implement the Concepts of Industry 4.0 into Information Technology Companies. *The TQM Journal, 32*(4), 741–759.

Del Giudice, M., Caputo, F., & Evangelista, F. (2016). How Are Decision Systems Changing? The Contribution of Social Media to the Management of Decisional Liquefaction. *Journal of Decision Systems, 25*(3), 214–226.

Derwik, P., Hellström, D., & Karlsson, S. (2016). Manager Competences in Logistics and Supply Chain Practice. *Journal of Business Research, 69*(11), 4820–4825.

Deiser, R. (2009). *Designing the Smart Organisation.* Jossey Bass.

Dzwigol, H., Dzwigol-Barosz, M., Miskiewicz, R., & Kwilinski, A. (2020). Manager Competency Assessment Model in the Conditions of Industry 4.0. *Entrepreneurship and Sustainability, 7*(4), 2630–2644.

Dyck, B. (2020). The Integral Common Good: Implications for Melé's Seven Key Practices of Humanistic Management. *Humanistic Management Journal, 5*(1), 7.

Eccles, R., & Nohria, N. (1992). *Beyond the Hype.* Harvard Business School, Press.

Enríquez-De-La-O, J. F. (2015). Resource-Based View and Dynamic Capabilities Resource-Based View and Dynamic Capabilities. *Vezetéstudomány/Budapest Management Review, 46*(11), 50–61.

Fareri, S., Fantoni, G., Chiarello, F., Coli, E., & Binda, A. (2020). Estimating Industry 4.0 Impact on Job Profiles and Skills Using Text Mining. *Computers in Industry, 118.* https://doi.org/10.1016/j.compind.2020.103222

Ford, R. C. (2017). Combining Performance, Learning, and Behavioural Goals to Match Job with Person: Three Steps to Enhance Employee Performance with Goal Setting. *Business Horizons, 60*(3), 345–352.

Friedman, T. (2006). *The World is Flat.* Penguin Books.

Garbellano, S., & Da Veiga, M. (2019). Dynamic Capabilities in Italian Leading SMEs Adopting Industry 4.0. *Measuring Business Excellence, 23*(4), 472–483.

García-Sánchez, I.-M., & García-Meca, E. (2020). Do Able Bank Managers Exhibit Specific Attributes? An Empirical Analysis of Their Investment Efficiency. *Administrative Sciences (2076–3387), 10*(3), 13–22.

Garratt, B. (2000). *The Learning Organisation*. Harper Collins.

Geraghty, T. M. (2003). Technology, Organization and Complementarity: The Factory System in the British Industrial Revolution. *The Journal of Economic History, 63*(2), 536.

Gerdin, J. (2020). Management Control as a System: Integrating and Extending Theorizing on MC Complementarity and Institutional Logics. *Management Accounting Research, 49*, 1–13.

Gold, J. (2010). *Problem-Based Leadership: Nurturing Managers during Turbulent Times*. Emerald.

Goldsmith, M. (2008). *What Got You Here Won't Get You There*. Profile Books.

Greenan, P., Reynolds, M., & Turner, P. (2017). Training Transfer: The Case for 'Implementation Intentions'. *International Journal of Human Resource Development, Practice, Policy and Research, 2*(2), 49–56.

Hamel, G., & Prahalad, C. K. (1994). *Competing for the Future*. HBS Press.

Handy, C. (1988). *Understanding Organisations*. Penguin Books.

Harrower, K. (2019). Algorithmic Decision-Making in Organizations: Network Data Mining, Measuring and Monitoring Work Performance, and Managerial Control. *Psychosociological Issues in Human Resource Management, 7*(2), 7.

Heavey, C., Simsek, Z., Kyprianou, C., & Risius, M. (2020). How Do Strategic Leaders Engage with Social Media? A Theoretical Framework for Research and Practice. *Strategic Management Journal, 41*(8), 1490–1527.

Hertz, D. B. (1977). Does Management Science Influence Management Action? *Columbia Journal of World Business, 12*(3), 105–112.

Huy, Q. N. (2002). Emotional Balancing of Organizational Continuity and Radical Change: The Contribution of Middle Managers. *Administrative Science Quarterly, 47*(1), 31–69.

Iacocca, L. (1994). *'I Gotta Tell You'; Speeches of Lee Iacocca*. Edited by M. W. Seeger. Wayne State University Press.

Iasbech, P. A. B., & Lavarda, R. A. B. (2018). Strategy as Practice and the Role of Middle Manager in Organizations: The Future of the Field. *Brazilian Journal of Management/Revista de Administração Da UFSM, 11*(4), 1125–1145.

Igielski, M. (2020). Manager's Competence Model in the Face of New Economic Challenges: Research Report. *Management (1429–9321), 24* (1), 114 2299-193X, 1429-9321. https://doi.org/10.2478/manment-2019-0038

Jameson, D. A. (2001). Narrative Discourse and Management Action. *Journal of Business Communication, 38*(4), 476–511.

Jurksiene, L., & Pundziene, A. (2016). The Relationship between Dynamic Capabilities and Firm Competitive Advantage: The Mediating Role of Organizational Ambidexterity. *European Business Review, 28*(4), 431–448.

Kang, Hyo-Jin, Kyung-won Chung, & Ki-Young Nam. (2015). A Competence Model for Design Managers: A Case Study of Middle Managers in Korea. *International Journal of Design, 9*(2), 109–127.

Karltun, J., Karltun, A., Havemose, K., & Kjellström, S. (2019, June 24–27). Positioning the Study of First Line Managers' Resilient Action Strategies. In *8th REA Symposium on Resilience Engineering: Scaling Up and Speeding Up*, Kalmar, Sweden.

Kindarto, A., & Zhu, Y. Q. (2019). The Future of Decision-Making Process in the Government's IT Project in Industry 4.0 Era, *5th International Conference on Science and Technology (ICST)* 1, 1–6.

Kinley, N., & Ben Hur, S. (2015). *Changing Employee Behaviour; A Practical Guide*. Palgrave Macmillan, UK.

Kirby, R. S., Withingto, S., Darling, A. B., & Kilgour, F. G. (1956 [1990]). *Engineering in History*. Dover Publications Edition.

Lam, M., Raja, M., Finstad-Milion, K., & Desilus, B. (2017). Getting Things Done: Proactive Influence Tactics in Mexico and the United States. *Global Journal of Management and Marketing, 1*(2), 46.

Li, H., Wu, Y., Cao, D., & Wang, Y. (2021). Organizational Mindfulness Towards Digital Transformation as a Prerequisite of Information Processing Capability to Achieve Market Agility. *Journal of Business Research, 122*, 700–712.

Licht, W. (1995). *Industrialising America*. Johns Hopkins University Press.

Lindgren, R., Henfridsson, O., & Schultze, U. (2004). Design Principles for Competence Management Systems: A Synthesis of an Action Research Study. *Management Information Systems Quarterly, 3*, 435.

Lips-Wiersma, M., & Morris, L. (2009). Discriminating Between 'Meaningful Work' and the 'Management of Meaning'. *Journal of Business Ethics, 88*, 491–511.

Locke, E. A., & Latham, G. P. (1990). *A Theory of Goal Setting and Task Performance*. Prentice Hall.

Locke, E. A., & Latham, G. P. (2019). The Development of Goal Setting Theory: A Half Century Retrospective. *Motivation Science, 5*(2), 93–105.

Marion, T. J., Fixson, S. K., & Brown, G. (2020). Four Skills Tomorrow's Innovation Workforce Will Need. *MIT Sloan Management Review, 61*(3), 8–13.

Marnewick, C., & Marnewick, A. L. (2020). The Demands of Industry 4.0 on Project Teams. *IEEE Transactions on Engineering Management, Engineering Management, IEEE Transactions on, IEEE Trans. Eng. Manage, 67*(3), 941–949.
McConkey, D. D. (1965). Management by Objectives: How to Measure Results. *Management Review, 54*(3), 60.
McCosker, A. (2017). Social Media Work: Reshaping Organisational Communications, Extracting Digital Value. *Media International Australia, Incorporating Culture and Policy, 163*, 122–136.
Mintzberg, H. (2011). *Managing*. FT Prentice Hall.
Miterev, M., Engwall, M., & Jerbrant, A. (2016). Exploring Program Management Competences for Various Program Types. *International Journal of Project Management, 34*(3), 545–557.
Mitsui. (2020). Company Profile. https://www.mitsui.com/jp/en/company/outline/profile/index.html
Nijhuis, S., Vrijhoef, R., & Kessels, J. (2018). Tackling Project Management Competence Research. https://doi.org/10.1177/8756972818770591
Nooyi, I. (2014). *Top 15 Quotes from PepsiCo CEO Indra Nooyi*. https://www.indiatvnews.com/business/india/top-15-quotes-from-pepsico-ceo-indra-nooyi-8157.html
Oliveira, B. G., Liboni, L. B., Cezarino, L. O., Stefanelli, N. O., & Miura, I. K. (2020). Industry 4.0 in Systems Thinking: From a Narrow to a Broad Spectrum. *Systems Research and Behavioural Science, 37*(4), 593–606.
Palma, J. F., & Pavez, H. R. (2017). Management, Innovation and Business Results under the Resources and Capabilities Theory. *RAN, 1*(3), 35–50.
Partington, D. (2000). Building Grounded Theories of Management Action. *British Journal of Management, 11*(2), 91–102.
Penttilä, K., Ravald, A., Dahl, J., & Björk, P. (2020). Managerial Sensemaking in a Transforming Business Ecosystem: Conditioning Forces, Moderating Frames, and Strategizing Options. *Industrial Marketing Management, 91*, 209–222.
Peters, T. J. (1978). Symbols, Patterns, and Settings: An Optimistic Case for Getting Things Done. *Organizational Dynamics, 7*(2), 3–23.
Prieto, L. C., & Phipps, S. T. A. (2016). Rediscovering Charles Clinton Spaulding's the Administration of Big Business. *Journal of Management History, 22*(1), 73–90.
Rana, G., & Sharma, R. (2019). Emerging Human Resource Management Practices in Industry 4.0. *Strategic HR Review, 18*(4), 176–181.

Reich, B. H., & Benbasat, I. (1996). Measuring the Linkage between Business and Information Technology Objectives. *MIS Quarterly, 20*(1), 55.
Robles, M. M. (2012). Executive Perceptions of the Top 10 Soft Skills Needed in Today's Workplace. *Business Communication Quarterly, 75*(4), 453–465.
Rouleau, L., & Balogun, J. (2011). Middle Managers, Strategic Sensemaking, and Discursive Competence. *Journal of Management Studies, 48*, 953.
Rumelt, R. (2011). *Good Strategy, Bad Strategy*. Profile Books.
Ryden, P., Ringberg, T., & Wilke, R. (2015). How Managers' Shared Mental Models of Business Customer Interactions Create Different Sensemaking of Social Media. *Journal of Interactive Marketing, 31*, 1–16.
Saxby, R., Cano-Kourouklis, M., & Viza, E. (2020). An Initial Assessment of Lean Management Methods for Industry 4.0. *The TQM Journal, 32*(4), 587–601.
Schaffer, R. H., & Stearn, J. M. (2015). The Rapid Results Package: Better Performance/Stronger Managers. *Business Horizons, 58*(6), 687–695.
Schein, E. H. (2004). *Organizational Culture and Leadership*. Jossey Bass.
Senge, P. (1990). *The Fifth Discipline*. Random House Business Books.
Shamim, S., Cang, S., Yu, H., Li, Y., Chen, L. Y., & Yao, X. (2019). *How Firms in Emerging Economies Can Learn Industry 4.0 By Extracting Knowledge from Their Foreign Partners? A Viewpoint from Strategic Management Perspective*. International Conference on Advanced Mechatronic Systems (ICAMechS).
Shirahada, K. (2010). Improving Automobile Technical Personnel's Goal Commitment: Investigation of Managerial Actions Based On Individual Potentials. *International Journal of Automotive Technology and Management, 10*(4), 345–360.
Singh, S., Darwish, T. K., & PotoAnik, K. (2016). Measuring Organizational Performance: A Case for Subjective Measures. *British Journal of Management, 27*(1), 214.
Škrinjarić, B., & Domadenik, P. (2020). Examining the Role of Key Competences in Firm Performance. *International Journal of Manpower, 41*(4), 391.
Smith, A. (1776 [1986]). *The Wealth of Nations*. Penguin Books Edition.
Sony. (2020). *Sony Corporation of America*. https://www.sony.net/SonyInfo/CorporateInfo/History/SonyHistory/1-10.html
Sony, M., & Naik, S. S. (2019). Ten Lessons for Managers While Implementing Industry 4.0. *IEEE Engineering Management Review, 2*, 45.
Tawse, A., Patrick, V. M., & Vera, D. (2019). Crossing the Chasm: Leadership Nudges to Help Transition from Strategy Formulation to Strategy Implementation. *Business Horizons, 62*(2), 249–257.

Teece, D. J. (2011). *Dynamic Capabilities and Strategic Management*. Oxford University Press.

Teece, D. J. (2014). A Dynamic Capabilities-Based Entrepreneurial Theory of the Multinational Enterprise. *Journal of International Business Studies, 45*, 1.

Teece, D. J. (2016). *Dynamic Capabilities and Entrepreneurial Management in Large Organizations: Toward a Theory of the (Entrepreneurial) Firm*. EBSCOhost.

Teece, D. J. (2017). Towards a Capability Theory of (Innovating) Firms: Implications for Management and Policy. *Cambridge Journal of Economics, 41*(3), 693–720.

Tortorella, G. L., & Fettermann, D. (2018). Implementation of Industry 4.0 and Lean Production in Brazilian Manufacturing Companies. *International Journal of Production Research, 56*(8), 2975–2987.

Turner, N., Swart, J., Maylor, H., & Antonacopoulou, E. (2016). Making It Happen: How Managerial Actions Enable Project-Based Ambidexterity. *Management Learning, 47*(2), 199–222.

Ulrich, D., & Ulrich, W. (2010). *Meaning at Work*. McGraw Hill.

Vaill, P. B. (1967). Management Language and Management Action. *California Management Review, 10*(1), 51–58.

Verma, S., & Gustafsson, A. (2020). Investigating the Emerging COVID-19 Research Trends in the Field of Business and Management: A Bibliometric Analysis Approach. *Journal of Business Research, 118*, 253–261.

Waldman, D. A., Putnam, L. L., Miron-Spektor, E., & Siegel, D. (2019). The Role of Paradox Theory in Decision Making and Management Research. *Organizational Behaviour and Human Decision Processes, 155*, 1–6.

Watson, T. J. (1994). *In Search of Management*. Thomson Business Press.

Wilburn, K. M., & Wilburn, H. R. (2016). Asking 'What Else?' To Identify Unintended Negative Consequences. *Business Horizons, 59*(2), 213–221.

Wong, J. W.-C., & Kong, S.-H. (2017). What Does the 'Inner World' of Chinese Managers Tell Us About Their Management Values, Thoughts and Practices? An Ethnographic Study. *Asia Pacific Business Review, 23*(5), 625–640.

Yin, Y., Stecke, K. E., & Li, D. (2018). The Evolution of Production Systems from Industry 2.0 through Industry 4.0. *International Journal of Production Research, 56*(1/2), 848–861.

12

The Making of the Modern Manager: Core Management Competences and Their Attributes

Management: A Palimpsest of Overlapping Activities

There are few concepts in the field of business or commerce that have such a broad reach as that of management.

On the one hand, management is clearly defined as planning, organising, integrating and coordinating. On the other, it is a palimpsest of overlapping responsibilities, responsive and fluid. For some it is intertwined with leadership, inspiring people to achieve goals or objectives—with significant influence functions (strategy, stewardship, policy). For others it is concerned with business administration—making sure that processes and people are in place, that budgets are agreed and met, that operational plans are well ordered—covering the day-to-day delivery of departmental goals. It can take place in Weberian hierarchical structures, or, in the contemporary digitally mediated world, in networks or 'swarms'. It can be viewed at the very top of the organisation as governance or strategy, at its middle as operations or tactics, or at its centre as hub coordination. Management covers the abstract—such as culture change, and the physical—such as making a production line flow smoothly. And through all of these functions, management is required for both transformation

P. Turner, *The Making of the Modern Manager*,
https://doi.org/10.1007/978-3-030-81062-7_12

and continuity. In each of the Four Industrial Revolutions that have swept the world from the middle of the eighteenth century, 'philosophers and speculators' have reflected on the impact of transformation on the nature of work, the workforce to deliver it and the skills of the people required to plan and organise its production; the latter being known variously as executives, directors, managing partners, agents, foremen, underagents, overmen, corporals, supervisors or stewards, but collectively as managers. Nils Bohr wrote in 1929 that 'as our knowledge becomes wider, we must always be prepared therefore to expect alterations in the points of view best suited for the ordering of our experience' (Bohr, 1929). The rich experience of managers over the past two centuries provides evidence from which to formulate such a point of view.

During the First Industrial Revolution, Charles Babbage (1832) summarised its impact—'the vast extent and perfection to which we have carried the contrivance of tools and machines'. At this time the antecedents of modern management were present in the new mills and factories that sprang up around small towns in England during the eighteenth century—informed by the division of labour as articulated in Adam Smith's seminal work of classical economy, *The Wealth of Nations*, in 1776—then extended by such as the *meisters* in the Krupp Factories in Germany—who arranged 'all things at the shop-floor and also had much influence on the workers' labour conditions' (Tanaka, 1992). During the Second Industrial Revolution in the early part of the twentieth century, centred mainly on the United States, Geddes (1915) forecast that the world would witness a 'new economic order' in which 'palaeotechnic' economics would be replaced with 'neotechnic' economics, 'bringing the potentialities of wealth and leisure beyond past utopian dreams'. Large manufacturing complexes came to dominate American towns and cities, and production lines, most notably at Ford, provided the narrative for an American system of manufacturing, once again requiring managers to adapt to long production runs and a working environment that was radically different to that which had gone before. Over the past 60 years, during the course of the Third Industrial Revolution, managers have been involved in incorporating innovative ideas and practices first in Japanese organisations as they took advantage of global economic opportunity and achieved significant market share in targeted key sectors; followed by those in Asian Tiger and Asian Dragon countries, and subsequently in China and India as they became leading world economies into the twenty-first century. Key to this was the transformational potential of new technologies and automation; a point reinforced by evidence from the many corporate members of the Japanese Industrial Robot Association—in 1977 more than 100 Japanese companies were producing robots (Drucker, 1954; Hasegawa, 1979; Seeck & Kuokkanen, 2010). Throughout these revolutions, the most 'significant management and organisation paradigms' were built around scientific methods or a human relations school, based on structural analysis, organisational culture and responsibilities relating to innovation, transformation and change. Commentaries were largely positive exhortations to embrace the new ages and the driving force of technology. 'Whenever civilisation has gone through a major technological revolution, the world has changed in profound and unsettling ways. But there is something about the flattening of the world that is going to be qualitatively different from the great changes of previous eras; the speed and breadth with which it is taking hold' (Friedman, 2006). And so to the present day, where far-reaching change, a Fourth Industrial Revolution, is permeating all aspects of commerce—known as Industry 4.0. In its scale, scope and complexity, it is 'unlike anything humankind has experienced before' (Schwab, 2016). A feature of each of these transitions, transformations or upheavals, which have included not only technological change but the effects of global pandemics amongst their ranks (inter alia 1918, 1957, 1968, SARS and MERS, and in 2020, COVID-19), is that organisations have had to react to survive and pro-act to flourish.

Throughout, managers were responsible for ensuring that the right strategy was underpinned by the right technology, and that the right people in the right place at the right time, with the right skills, had the resources and an environment in which innovation, adaption and action could take place. The role of the manager in Industry 4.0, like many of their historical counterparts, is to ensure that their organisations respond to the rapidity of transformation, initiating and adopting approaches to integrate new technologies, establishing new forms of organisation and meeting new sets of expectations from stakeholders whether they be shareholders or members of the workforce. Advances in both process and product technology provide the theoretical basis for the competitiveness of organisations but it is the competence of managers that will convert this into reality. In contemporary organisations the forces for change include the urgency to ensure diversity in race and gender to allow those with talent to 'defy the challenges, acquire the necessary competences and shatter the glass ceilings'. Increasing gender and racial diversity in management and leadership will result in positive outcomes across organisations (Abernathy & Corcoran, 1983; Tanaka, 1992; Idris et al., 2012; Pozzi, 2014; Albino & Wisdom, 2020; Odhiambo, 2020). The making of the modern manager—a long and illustrious process—continues. And so, over time, managers have had to respond to the political, economic, social, technological or environmental challenges that were taking place in whatever commercial environment their organisations operated. Understanding the nature of these challenges is important in understanding the competences required to deal with them.

Four Industrial Revolutions and Management Challenges

The First Industrial Revolution from the mid-eighteenth to the mid-nineteenth century reflected many of the early management challenges as organisations integrated new technologies and ideas into their processes. During this time, a series of inventions, a surge in innovation and a commitment to improvement in key industries, backed by favourable institutions, transformed the British economy. Its characteristics were mechanisation, standardisation of systems and processes and mutually reinforcing dynamics across industrial, commercial and infrastructure sectors. Subsequently the economies of France, Germany and others in Europe grew in response to endogenous pressures towards change; and as a reaction to new methods which were being developed in Britain. Europe became the epicentre for technological and processural transformation. The production logic of the type of factory organisation that emerged at this time was irrefutable, but questions remained about how to convert the logic into practice and achieve productivity gains. Challenges were those of significant growth; of making the most of advanced industrial technologies and of putting in place new systems and processes—whilst dealing with a complex mix of demographic and social influences. Technological adaptation created the need for more capital to fund new machinery, which in turn led to the need for better production planning, which in turn led to challenges related to the cultural shift to large manufacturing operations. In parallel, an unprecedented level of workforce planning came about in response to challenges in recruitment and retention, in motivation and direction and in performance management—implementing hard and fast rules of performance, timekeeping and behaviour. At the same time, there were the problems caused by the frequent pandemics as urbanisation brought poor living conditions. The role of the manager emerged from these forces in a sequence of challenge and response. On the one hand, there was the necessity to acquire knowledge about new technology; on the other, the necessity to apply that knowledge to new systems and processes; to attract, select and recruit a workforce; the need to maintain a fluid approach to adapting to change; and finally, to be innovative in exploiting land and capital. Each of these factors contributed to the development of the concept of management in its 'modern' incarnation. Hence, it was not only technological innovation but the challenge of incorporating such innovation into day-to-day production or service systems and processes that created a successful management outcome.

During the nineteenth century through the first half of the twentieth a Second Industrial Revolution, once again powered by technology developments, saw the rise of the United States as the dominant world economic power. In 1876 Bell invented the telephone; Edison and Swan perfected the design of the light bulb in 1879; then came automatic signals on railways, new processes in steel mills; the elevator and structural steel improvements which enabled the development of the first skyscrapers—the Chrysler Building was erected in 1930, the Empire State Building in 1931. Furthermore, it was the age of motion pictures, the electric generator; the internal combustion engine and the first airplane flight. The jet engine, the electron microscope, frozen foods and instant coffee, all came out of this period. It was the age of mass production as large industrial developments replaced smaller workshops or craft operations. The use of pure science by engineers in industries from bridge building to shipbuilding; applied science in business methods such as accounting and management and an increase in competition with more companies in 'ever widening markets' came together to bring about a reshaping of the world economic order. The management challenges once again centred on the impact of technology as electricity replaced steam to power factories and new inventions demanded new techniques of production—which in turn created the need to integrate new technology, plan new systems and processes, develop new organisational forms and recruit, train and retain a workforce. The pressure was on to keep expensive manufacturing installations running at capacity whilst coordinating the procurement of raw materials and distribution of finished goods; and ensuring that there was a sufficient supply of skilled and willing labour. Managers had to maximise opportunity from technology by integrating inventions, delivering the benefits of innovation and ensuring continuous improvement once the new technologies had been installed. They did this with few precedents and no play book, balancing the objective of short-term profit for the owners and shareholders of the companies in which they worked, whilst at the same time ensuring their own performance and long-term stability. These process challenges were compounded by the human challenges of mass production and mechanisation. The restructuring of factories involved the transformation of the flow of work on the shop floor as well as social reorganisation, different work arrangements and new patterns of specialisation on the part of both workers and management, which took significant experimentation and learning. Mass production technologies and forms of business organisation gave rise to new social organisations of work and a radically changed world of jobs and occupations. Managers also faced significant losses in their human resources caused by pandemic, in the early twentieth century. The management challenges facing those working in companies in the United States during the Second Industrial Revolution covered the whole gamut of technological innovation and human resource management practice. As a result, management became more structured, more systematic, more scientific and more professional. By 1920, 65 American Business Schools awarded over 1500 business degrees annually; by 1950 over 600 American higher education institutions offered courses which were attended by over 370,000 students. The Second Industrial Revolution saw the rise of American Corporations and their business methods, and the ascendancy of American management thought.

As the US economy developed in the post war period, new corporations of unprecedented size, complexity, breadth and international scope began to emerge. From the 1950s a Third Industrial Revolution began, defined by scale and geography; but also by technology—the miniaturisation of electronics and the integration of telecommunications and computing; microchips, computer-aided design and computer-aided manufacturing (CAD/CAM), fibre optics, lasers, holography, biogenetics, word processors, robotics and engineered materials—notwithstanding space exploration and its technological spin offs. The Third Industrial Revolution became increasingly known as the *information revolution* or the *digital revolution*. But it was also the harbinger of economic change and globalisation which created opportunity in the fortunes of Asian economies, the companies of which achieved prominence in a multiplicity of industries and sectors with notable economic performance from Japan, the rapid and significant economic growth in the economies of Singapore, Hong Kong, South Korea and Taiwan, Indonesia, Malaysia and Thailand, and the incredible growth of the Chinese and Indian economies. From the 1960s, organisations faced some testing questions: what long-term vision to pursue, what objectives to set to achieve the vision, what practical knowledge and skills were required to achieve both, how to achieve competitive advantage, and in which markets? Management challenges at this time can therefore be seen at three levels. The first was on the scale of change. The challenge facing Asian organisations during this period was how to gain a foothold and then an advantage against well-established competitors in burgeoning growth markets. The second challenge was that of the pace of change—the impact of technology was rapid and overwhelming. The third challenge was adaptability to change. An additional consideration is one that was episodic throughout the first Three Industrial Revolutions and that was the nature of short and immediate shocks that impacted on society and the commercial organisations within them—war, economic recession—or the incidence of epidemic or pandemic illnesses that struck indiscriminately.

And so, to the management challenges of the Fourth Industrial Revolution which will see momentous technological advances merge the physical, digital and biological worlds. Socio-cultural change—Society 4.0—will occur through the application of digital applications across many aspects of life and community, accentuated by a compelling emphasis on equality and diversity in race and gender; and the impact on life and work of COVID-19. In parallel, industrial and commercial developments—Industry 4.0—will transform industrial systems and processes by incorporating innovative technologies. Physical assets will be integrated into digital processes in smart factories or connected offices or workspaces. Its features will be *digital energy* using digital technologies to efficiently manage the generation and distribution of energy from traditional as well as renewable resources; *digital health*—digitisation will have a significant role in improving healthcare by comprehensive monitoring of health status, better preventive care, more accurate diagnosis and efficient delivery of treatment; *digital transportation* and autonomous vehicles; *digital communication*—using sophisticated wirelessly connected smartphones; e-commerce web services and image and voice recognition and chatbots; and *digital production*. The impact on work and the organisation of work will be significant. To thrive in this new complex environment, it is argued that managers will need to collect and disseminate vast amounts of information; adapt new technologies so that the best possible technical solution is applied; be agile and adapt to a shifting organisational structure and be able to deal with constant change, uncertainty and disruption (Marnewick & Marnewick, 2020). These unprecedented social dynamics will require human ingenuity of the highest order because the management challenges will span technology and human resources through the union of physical systems with virtual systems in a business environment which has unprecedented pace and continuity of change. Interoperability, virtualisation, decentralisation, real-time capability, service orientation and modularity will be the fundamentals, how to achieve flexibility and responsiveness in response to this and how to manage a newly skilled, re-skilled or upskilled, diverse and technologically competent workforce will be key challenges. But it will not be enough to deal with change as a singular event, instead, the 'inchoate' nature of the transformation means that the process by which the Fourth Industrial

Revolution will occur is in a continuous sequence that is likely to last for years or even decades. The differentiator of the Fourth Industrial Revolution is its scale and scope—massive and global—the pace and continuity of change—dynamic and real time and the sheer ubiquity of its many strands of change—vertical and horizontal applications.

There were some consistent way points in management challenges over the Four Industrial Revolutions. The first was the impact of technology and how to integrate new developments into an organisation's systems and processes; the second was that of continuous improvement in order that any advantage could be maintained; the third was to ensure that organisational design, structure, policy and process were appropriate for the environment in which any organisation operated; and the fourth was the human resource challenge of the right people, in the right place, at the right time, with the right level of skills, and the right attitudes and behaviours to deliver organisational objectives.

Four Industrial Revolutions and Management Responses—Theory and Practice

The conclusion is that management is a rich and diverse field of study, with a confluence of factors influencing its development. In the First Industrial Revolution, for example, managers gained their skills on the job, had little in the form of training and learned from the sequence of challenge and response as new technologies or methods were introduced. The demands of the Second Industrial Revolution meant that there was an awareness that more was needed other than the rule of thumb and so evolved the origins of *scientific management* mainly in the United States. Scientific management consisted of standardisation, systematic work study and high levels of productivity. First tried in the Detroit factories of Henry Ford, its popularity in the early years of the twentieth century rested upon impressive increases of workplace productivity. Mass production led to economies of scale and scope, lower unit costs and higher levels of quality and such methods gained credence throughout the industrialised world from the early years of the twentieth century. At this time there was a hunger for knowledge about management principles and processes. For example, the Rowntree management conferences during the 1920s, which encapsulated a strand in management thinking that was 'liberal, human-centred and forward-looking'. The conferences were the brainchild of Benjamin Seebohm Rowntree, who had visited Boston just after World War I to meet some of the more progressive thinkers in American management, such as Henry Dennison and Edward and Lincoln Filene, 'who were actively encouraging their fellow business leaders to come together and share knowledge'. After 1921, the conferences centred on Balliol College, Oxford, with subjects such as 'scientific salesmanship as a factor in regularising the demand for goods; need movement study dehumanise industry; Industry as a service and controlling production within the factory (Witzel et al., 2018). An increase in understanding of the dynamics of more complex organisations and from both research and practice, social factors were seen as critical to effective performance which led to the emergence of *behavioural management* theories. These recognised that social factors (human interaction) in cooperative systems were features of the contemporary business environment and that people and their interactions were as important as systems and processes inspired by technology efficiency. The role of human dynamics in organisations was recognised and the role of the executive or manager as a part of this dynamic was articulated creating a significant contribution to behavioural or humanistic perspectives of management theory. The third aspect of the development of management theory concerned *management science*, which emerged at the peak of the humanistic or behavioural era of management theory during the 1950s. It was based on understanding that the operating environment, the operating technologies in that environment and the scale and scope of the organisation in that environment would be influential in both the structure of an organisation and the demands of its stakeholders. In management science 'professional managers were assigned responsibility for planning, setting goals defining problems and making decisions. The methodological cornerstone was a contingency approach with unobtrusive control devices such as job specification, internal career ladders and operating routines monitoring performance.' The structured, planned or systematic approaches to management sometimes didn't take into account the unpredictability or 'messiness' of the working environment a factor in

Mintzberg's iconoclastic approach based on the reality of management action; 'how do we make sense of the vast array of activities that constitute managing?' From this emerged *management as practice*, where management was not uniquely a science nor uniquely a profession, instead, it was a practice that could be learned through experience and context—'a good deal of craft, with the right touch of art alongside some use of science'. The role of the manager was one of action, of perpetual awareness of the environment, of constant needs to adapt and respond. A further aspect of management as practice emerged during the Third Industrial Revolution as Japanese corporations introduced a whole new set of processes and additions to the language of management which included total quality management, continuous improvement, decision-making by consensus, identifying problems at the root cause and dealing with them accordingly, just-in-time systems; *jidoka*, or 'automation with a human touch'; *kanban*, a production tool helping just-in-time production; and *poka yoke* or mistake proofing. There was an emphasis on responsiveness, improvisation, flexibility and speed and the idea of adaptive translation were features of the approach to management in Asian companies that were as important to their success as Taylor's *scientific management* to that of US companies in earlier periods. And more recently the Internet has reframed roles in the lives of individuals and in the workplace. Social media platforms, originally introduced to facilitate the communication of personal and professional interests have become 'expansive, dynamic and enable the sharing of several types of content' (Ruparel et al., 2020). The impact of social media on organisations and the management of those organisations stretched from communication during change through to the creation and dissemination of knowledge; through to creating a learning culture. Its full effects are being realised at an exponentially increasing rate.

It's possible to conclude that management is a distinct and identifiable organisational function. It can be manifested in human form—amongst those appointed to the task during the First Industrial Revolution were managing partners, agents, foremen, under-agents, overmen, corporals, supervisors and stewards—each of whom had managerial responsibilities, extended in subsequent revolutions to include line manager, supervisor, principal, controller, comptroller, administrator, overseer or officer during the Second as the function took shape.

And during the Third, Executive or Director titles in some organisations were synonymous with the manager title in others. Management is also a set of activities that come together to achieve a goal, and these can include inter alia, planning, organising, allocating resources, monitoring and motivating the workforce. In all cases, the definition of management and what a manager actually does, how they think and behave are articulated in the form of management competences and the related attributes to these competences.

The conventional narrative of the history of modern management begins with Adam Smith, progresses through F.W. Taylor, through human relations and behavioural theories through practice, to the current concept of management based on agility, speed of response, accessing and applying knowledge and the ability to integrate new technologies into process and structure. Additional inputs to the development of the concept have focussed on philosophical and ethical foundations, conservation, sustainability and cultural specificity in organisational forms (Cummings et al., 2017; Lord & Pierides, 2019). Each of the revolutions brought developments in the theory and praxis of management through different shades of ownership and control—from 'Personal', in the early stages of industrialisation, through 'Personal-Proprietal' through a 'Managerial' phase from the 1940s to the 1970s to a 'Managerial-Financial' phase since the 1980s (Wilson & Thomson, 2009). And each of the revolutions brought with it questions about the nature of management and the competences required to fulfil a management role. From Richard Arkwright to Taiichi Ono, management and those who fill the roles have evolved and adapted to meet the challenges of the dynamics of businesses throughout the world.

Four Industrial Revolutions—Management Competences

There is evidence that over the Four Industrial Revolutions management can be situated in its organisational, geographic or temporal context and no domain of management can be independent of the organisation in which that activity takes place. This gives a narrative to the idea of *contextual competences* or a combination of knowledge, skills, attitudes and behaviours that are relevant to a point in time that were necessary to do the managerial job successfully and efficiently at that time. Amongst these were knowledge and skills in setting up a factory based on water-power from fast-flowing rivers, establishing long-run production lines, and recruiting and retraining workers from other industries to run them. Or attitudes and behaviours in which individualism was subsumed into a greater whole, instilling the culture of quality circles, in which the organisation resembled an organism with information going from the head to the hands and feet and back. More recently technical knowledge and skills in adapting social media to employee engagement is a contextual competence of Industry 4.0. Contextual competences provide the individual with an indication or map of the behaviours and actions that were valuable in delivering organisational objectives at a point in time. They formed the language of performance management in an organisation.

But there are limitations to this context only view of management. Knowledge and skills about how to adapt to change and how to collaborate with others, and attitudes and behaviours about acquiring and disseminating information or taking action to deliver results have traversed time and can be identified in any of the periods under consideration. Though the methods may have changed, the necessity has not. Hence the thesis that there are *core competences* to which managers can look as they navigate or craft their ways through the complexities of revolution. Core Management competence is a combination of knowledge, skills, attitudes and behaviours that are consistent over time, produce an ability to do the managerial job successfully and efficiently, contribute to effective performance and ultimately organisational success. The core competence of the individual can therefore be defined as a 'specific, identifiable, definable and measurable knowledge, skill, ability and/or other deployment related characteristic (e.g. attitude, behaviour, physical ability), which a human resource may possess and which is necessary for, or material to, the performance of an activity within a specific business context. These may include generic skills such as Complex Problem Solving, Critical Thinking, Creativity, People Management, Coordinating with Others, Emotional Intelligence, Judgement and Decision-Making, Service Orientation, Negotiation and Cognitive Flexibility. At management level, to thrive and prosper, to create abundance in their organisations, managers will require core competences, that is, those things that are causally related to effective performance, consisting of *knowledge*—the retention and utilisation of information, *skills*—the ability to demonstrate a sequence of behaviour towards a goal, and *attitudes* and *behaviour*—how the social manifestation of how a manager undertakes a role. They are the *know-how, know why, know what* and *know how to behave* of management and are part of a three-way interaction with the nature of the job and the organisational context. Over the course of the industrial revolutions, five 'core competences' were identified. These, and their constituent parts, are shown in Fig. 12.1. and are proposed as a model that may be relevant as the Fourth Industrial Revolution gathers momentum.

The first of the core management competences, 'demonstrates agile governance and adaptability to make change work effectively—'know thyself', is borne out of the fact that industrial revolutions were rarely single-issue affairs. Whilst the inventions of scientists or risk taking by entrepreneurs are the events that are remembered it was the operationalisation of inventions or process improvements that gave form and function. Managers realised ideas and put them to work often through a sequence of challenge and response, adapting the approach or design as learning of its operation accumulated.

This competence has stood the test of time and applies as much today as in previous eras because Industry 4.0 will require more agile procedures and processes, in extremely complex, dynamic environments. Organisational systems will need to be efficient, flexible and able to find the right management and control principles. Hence this competence is part of the know-how of management and may be defined as 'the ability to respond to change in a dynamic and flexible way; aligning change methodologies to the needs of the unit; whilst identifying the ramifications of change for areas outside of the unit and influencing or shaping the organisation and its processes accordingly'. *Change objectives are the drivers; agile governance is the enabler, change processes are the tools.*

The second of the core management competences—*collaborates to create and share knowledge and information*—is the 'know why' of management. This may be defined as 'the ability to disseminate knowledge by connecting individuals and teams and inspire them to collaborate in

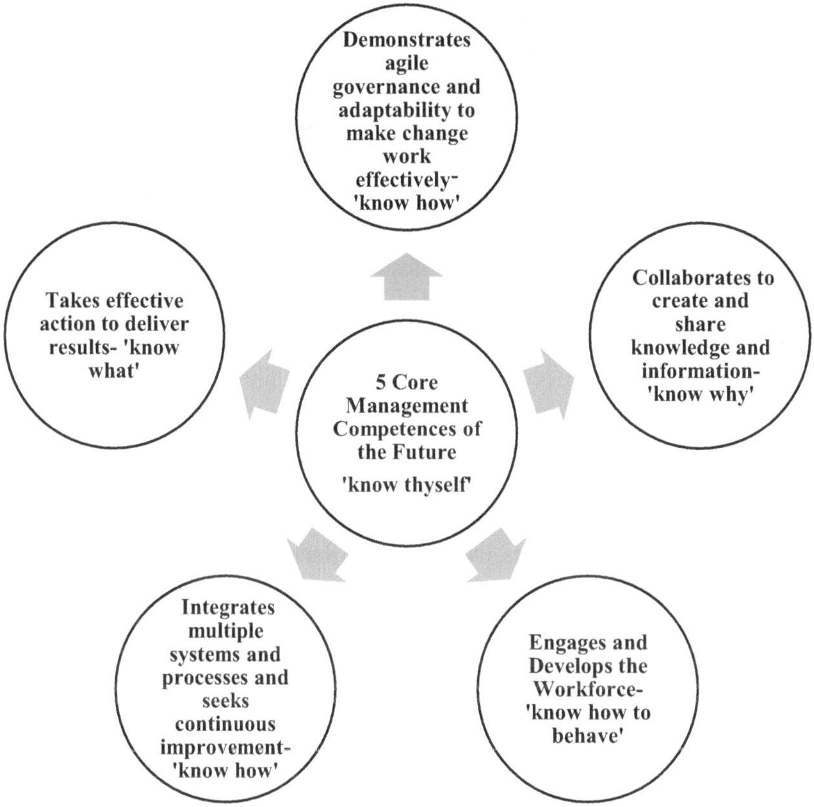

Fig. 12.1 Five core management competences

working towards common goals'. During each of the revolutions the acquisition and dissemination of knowledge have been priorities not only to scientists and technologists but to managers, whose use of both explicit and tacit knowledge was fundamental to the success of transformation and change. Increasingly, as the Fourth Industrial Revolution gathers momentum, collaboration and cooperation both within and without organisations will become more important. In this respect collaboration also relates to the capacity to engage people who aren't in the manager's immediate sphere of influence and inspire or persuade them to common goals—a requirement in network or project-based objectives. Knowledge is an incredibly valuable asset; collaboration is the key to maximising its use. It is on these assumptions that the second core management competence is based and informs the 'know why' of management. The role of the manager will be to engage members of the workforce in the importance of collaboration, ensure that there is a culture of collaboration, a process to maximise collaboration, systems for capturing knowledge as a result and a workforce where employees have the relevant information and insight to make well-informed decisions. The manager will have an understanding of the technology and be able to identify where it can be applied. It will be the remit of managers to ensure that these work to maximum effect. The core management competence on how to apply this principle will enhance not only internal operational performance but also strategic advantage.

Managers have to deliver results. It is their main function. To do so they have to ensure that the workforce under their area of responsibility also delivers the requirements of the business units in which they work. Over time as people management knowledge increased, how managers dealt with human resources moved from ordering, hectoring, cajoling to controlling and directing, through to coaching and engaging—yet always with the same desired output. The core management competence of 'engages and develops the workforce' represents the know how to behave. This may be defined as 'the ability to create a positive working environment and inspire individuals to apply themselves with intelligence, energy, resilience, enthusiasm and concentration; whilst providing the means for their personal and professional development'. The facets of this competence include clarity of purpose and contribution through to performance management and workforce development. The modern manager will apply this competence to motivation, goal achievement and high performance on the one hand and diversity of opportunity, security of the workplace, and good health and well-being on the other because employee productivity is not purely due to technology or the environment, but to the positivity in the employee experience. For an organisation to gain and keep competitive advantage, 'it is essential that human capital investment be made along with technology investment, so it is possible to increase productivity and competence'.

Many aspects of the technological or organisational change emanating from Revolution were complex and multi-faceted and as such required significant management nous to ensure that they were dealt with efficiently. This represents the 'know how' of management and is 'total innovation management'—the management of a value network that integrates strategy, technology, structure, process, culture and people at all levels of organisation. In this context integration depends on the manager's competence at collaboration, at engagement and agility the quality of which will go in some way to determining the achievement of a common purpose, through unity of effort. To deal with these dynamics, a management competence for the Fourth Industrial Revolution is *integrates multiple systems and processes and seeks continuous improvement*. This may be defined as 'the ability to coordinate technology and human resource systems; integrate them into a coherent and meaningful whole; use them to create a competitive strategy and operations; whilst ensuring innovation and improvement in a continuous cycle'. In future, competitive advantage (4.0) will come about by the integration of multiple systems which create 'competitive advantages' rather than a clearly identifiable, singular activity. Understanding the nature of this integration and the aspects of systems and processes to which improvement applies is important to identifying those facets of competence which are most relevant to the modern manager. The important elements for consideration are systems integration, continuous improvement and the effective management of human resources during these events. This competence will require *character, capacity* and *technical knowledge*.

If managers are there to achieve objectives by ensuring the efficient functioning of their business unit, *taking effective action to deliver results* becomes as much of a core management competence as adapting to change, integrating new systems or engaging the workforce. This may be defined as 'the ability to achieve goals through action; the ability to take action through rational, inclusive decision-making; the ability to make rational decisions based on a combination of evidence, intuition and emotional intelligence'. Managers are accountable for achieving goals; managerial decisions will determine how the organisation 'creates, shapes and deploys' its capabilities; and these managerial decisions will be influenced by the level of core management competence. For some managers this means applying knowledge in a collaborative way; for others it means agility or adaptability to changing environments. Some managers will be outstanding at workforce engagement; others at integrating new technologies, systems or processes into work-flow. Each of these core management competences, or a combination of them, is important in the organisation's quest for competitive advantage. And as well as being a knowledge seeker and disseminator, systems integrator and talent facilitator, the manager will also be a trouble shooter resolving issues such as resource allocation, differing points of view about ways and means, working within centralised or devolved decision-making, striking the balance between cost and capability, and meeting short-term operational deliverables whilst enabling longer-term development activities. This final core management competence concerns not input to the role of the manager but output from it and has been fundamental in which ever historical period they operated—the ability to convert strategy into actionable plans and outcomes. This is the 'know what' of management establishing priorities, delivering objectives in a targeted way (arising from years of performance management) managing time and overcoming obstacles.

Four Industrial Revolutions—Competence Attributes and Requirements

The questions facing those involved in the subject of management are how to bring competence or capability to life; how can the theoretical construct of competence be articulated through meaningful behaviours that managers demonstrate; how can the potential of competence be realised through applying knowledge; how can competence be demonstrated through action. Particularly, how can the learning from the management experiences of previous times be articulated as competence attributes and requirements as managers face up to the challenges of the Fourth Industrial Revolution—these are the detail of the specifics of knowledge and skill or of attitudes and behaviour that the manager would need or need to display in order to fulfil the competence identified. The argument put forward in this book is that core management competences result from a combination of cognition, intuition and emotional intelligence; from explicit and tacit knowledge; from the know how to behave as well as the know what and know how; 'a subtle blend of interpersonal skills and personal credibility', an understanding of the political dynamics of formal and informal networks and an understanding of both context and strategy. This means that the core competences of the manager can be captured in part, by objective lists of activities but it is also constituted by the 'subjective meaning' through lived experience (Sparrow, 2000; Partington et al., 2005). And so a further aspect of the analysis was to categorise each of the competences into know how, know why, know what and know how to behave and identify what attributes or requirements were relevant to each. Table 12.1 is a matrix that combines both competence and knowledge and brings together the specifics within each of the intersections. It reflects a combination of theoretical and the 'lived experiences' of managers as they have navigated their way through the transformation and change that accompanied each of the industrial revolutions to date. From this matrix, it is possible to see the growing importance of people management, reflected in 'know how to behave'. Whereas once, a workforce would be managed by command and control methods, today's manager must combine emotional intelligence, understanding human dynamics, understanding organisational dynamics and collaboration to get things done. Demographic change and its impact on culture and attitude mean that more refined and subtle methods of leading a workforce are required based on engagement and persuasion—especially in areas of scarcity such as in managing and retaining digital talent or the ability to maximise the resource in a multi-cultural, multi-generational environment. In an age of diversity and employee voice knowing how to behave is an imperative. There is an equally strong indication in respect of an understanding of technology applications. Knowing what to do is one part of competence but knowing how to do it is of equal importance and this is where a significant change has taken place. It will no longer be enough for the manager to wait upon the delivery of a new technology system after its completion by technology specialists. Instead the manager will have enough knowledge of the technology to be able to influence its development and will be expected to do so. The manager will not be an expert technologist but will have knowledge of technology applications. The third stand-out is a greater expectation of knowing why

Table 12.1 Core management competences—attributes and requirements

	Demonstrates agile governance and adaptability to make change work effectively	Collaborates to create and share knowledge and information	Engages and develops the workforce—know how to behave	Integrates multiple systems and seeks continuous improvement—know how	Takes effective action to deliver results—know what
Knows what to do	– Defines and prioritises what is crucial – Understands technology applications – Influences change across the whole system – Anticipates systems behaviour – Transfers knowledge	– Facilitates a knowledge management orientation – Acts as knowledge disseminator – Acts as knowledge seeker – Implements collaborative processes – Engages stakeholders in knowledge creation	– Articulates the why of work – Translates the vision into short-term actionable plans – Selects, recruits and retains the right people	– Aligns integration to business outcomes – Seeks and disseminates information about integration – Aligns departmental and personal objectives – Builds and sustains relationships	– Understands what counts – Builds dynamic capabilities – Demonstrates systems thinking – Clearly communicates expectations
Knows when to do it	– Maintains course and manoeuvrability – Has a sense and respond mindset – Optimises resource deployment	– Keeps teams from being mired in debate	– Focuses on output as well as input	– Coordinates integration processes and actions – Seeks continuous improvement – Ensures sufficient resources for integration	– Pays attention to detail

Knows why it is being done	– Focuses on outcomes	– Integrates diverse bodies of knowledge into a coherent whole – Uses knowledge to create value for stakeholders – Communicates the value of knowledge effectively	– Articulates the why of work – Provides role clarity – Communicates effectively and encourages employee voice	– Recognises opposing points of view – Maintains an open mind about ideas and suggestions for integration processes	– Takes meaningful action that genuinely matters – Delivers value with values
Knows how	– Aligns the technological domain with the organisation's objectives – Implements n-step process change – Coaches for change – Recognises the importance of teamwork	– Understands organisational dynamics – Uses political skills to secure commitment to collaboration – Uses judgement in connecting sources of knowledge	– Builds high performance teams – Acts a learning coach	– Understands technology applications – Anticipates problems to work or jobs – Coaches and trains for integration – Deals with emotions arising from integration	– Takes action in a coherent way – Has the willpower to get things done

(*continued*)

Table 12.1 (continued)

	Demonstrates agile governance and adaptability to make change work effectively	Collaborates to create and share knowledge and information	Engages and develops the workforce—know how to behave	Integrates multiple systems and seeks continuous improvement—know how	Takes effective action to deliver results—know what
Knows how to behave	– Handles situations and problems – Demonstrates self-awareness – Adopts a positive attitude – Works effectively in multi-cultural environments – Develops effective relationships – Adjusts social behaviour	– Makes rational decisions – Acts as a role model for collaboration – Promotes a collaborative environment – Helps others to learn	– Creates an engagement and learning culture – Combines professional and management credibility – Is values driven – Cares for employee well-being – Effective in a multi-cultural environment – Demonstrates emotional intelligence	– Engages employees in the process of integration and change – Builds a culture in which employees feel empowered – Champions investment in new skills development	– Builds lateral relationships – Acts with purposeful, consistent, conscious and energetic behaviour

something is being done. Whereas once the manager may have been part of an audience watching the strategy of their organisation emerge through strategy specialists, confidential reports and closed-door board discussions, they will in future want to be involved in the setting of that strategy and will expect to be included. The pace of change, the nature of opportunity and the short time from strategy to delivery that are features of the contemporary organisation means that the separation that used to exist between leading and managing or strategy and implementation is now less pronounced. And finally, the manager's competence in knowing what to do, what to prioritise and what is needed across the system to achieve goals are as important as any aspect of competence.

Conclusion—The Making of the Modern Manager

Technological transformation has been the underlying feature of each of the Four Industrial Revolutions to date, prompting revolution in organisation which in turn has prompted revolution in the way work is undertaken which in turn has prompted social change impacting on the demographics of the workforce on the one hand and expectations, attitudes and behaviour on the other. Against this powerful convergence of forces, the role of the manager has been transformed from the command and control methods of earliest forms of factory production to the application of science to management methods to greater recognition of the human factor and behavioural methods to the present day, calling for agile governance, collaboration and emotional intelligence. The theory, praxis and practice of management have evolved through countless interactions. Adam Smith, Frederick Taylor, Henri Fayol, Mary Parker Follett and Chester Barnard were pioneers of the field; Peter Drucker and Henry Mintzberg often cited for their influence. But the canon of management has not always been confined to narrow boundaries. In this respect, the influence ofTaiichi Ohno or Zhang Ruimin, Hou Weigui, or Lu Guanqiu must surely be considered in the evolution of the subject. And greater acknowledgement must also be given to the points of view of successful managers such as Charles Clinton Spaulding who, writing in 1927, saw cooperation and teamwork and management accountability as 'necessities' for the conduct of a successful business operation (Prieto & Phipps, 2016). Management as practice became management as science then became management as profession then management as practice. The competences required were contextual, their relevance ebbing and flowing with the prevailing economic or technological winds. Effective managers adapt to and are comfortable with change. But effective managers also understand that there are core competences on which they will need to draw whether these are capability in knowledge or people management, or agility or collaboration or the ability to integrate multiple processes. The making of the modern manager is undoubtedly a story influenced by a rich and diverse confluence of forces and the evolution of the competences required to do the job bear the hallmarks of significant theoretical development and significant practice experience.

When Samuel Smiles published his *Self Help* guide he extolled the virtues of *patient labour and application* and the acquisition of knowledge, urging his readers to practice *wisely and diligently*. If this path was followed it would bring out a person's individual character and stimulate the action of others. Attention, application, accuracy, method and *despatch* (purpose, speed and efficiency) would, if implemented effectively, produce desired business outcomes (Smiles, 1859). About 150 years later, some of these sentiments would perhaps not be lost on Henry Mintzberg (2011), whose description of the competences of managing included leading individuals, prioritising, administering, scheduling, timing, seeing and sensing. The experiences over the past 250 years has shown that management competence can't be regarded solely in the abstract. Nor is it a checklist of attributes against which managers or potential managers can be assessed and ultimately judged. Separating the theoretical from the practical gives an unclear picture and there is support for Tony Watson's assertion that 'it is a foolish and dangerous error to maintain barriers between thinkers and doers in any kind of human activity' (Watson, 1994). Instead, management competence is derived from the multi-faceted role of the managers operating in complex environments. It is concerned with knowledge and action often simultaneously. It is concerned with planning and forecasting and problem solving. It is concerned with strategic workforce management and emotional intelligence.

Management competence is not just the know what or the know why; it is the know-how and the know how to behave.

Some of the core competences of managers have stood the test of time, though their methods have changed drastically. It is argued in this book that agility, collaboration, workforce management, integration and action will continue to be relevant as the Fourth Industrial Revolution accelerates past the systems and processes that have gone before.

References

Abernathy, W. J., & Corcoran, J. E. (1983). Relearning from the Old Masters: Lessons of the American System of Manufacturing. *Journal of Operations Management, 3*(4), 155–167.

Albino, J., & Wisdom, J. P. (2020). Introduction to the Psychologist-Manager Journal Special Issue on Women Psychologists in Management and Leadership. *The Psychologist-Manager Journal, 23*(3–4), 135–138.

Babbage, C. (1832). *On the Economy of Machinery and Manufacture.* John Murray.

Bohr, N. (1929). *Atomic Theory and the Description of Nature.* Published by Cambridge University Press, 1961.

Cummings, C., Bridgman, T., Hassard, J., & Rowlinson, M. (2017). *A New History of Management.* Cambridge University Press.

Drucker, P. (1954). *The Practice of Management.* Butterworth-Heinemann Edition (2007).

Friedman, T. (2006). *The World is Flat.* Penguin Books.

Geddes, P. (1915). *Cities in Evolution.* Williams and Norgate.

Hasegawa, Y. (1979). New Developments in the Field of Industrial Robots. *International Journal of Production Research, 17*(5), 447.

Idris, N., Hong, T. S., & Mansor, N. N. A. (2012). A Qualitative Inquiry of Women Managers' Competence Acquisition. *Procedia—Social and Behavioural Sciences, 40*, 395–403.

Lord, G., & Pierides, D. (2019). Review: A New History of Management. *Academy of Management Learning and Education, 18*(3), 521–525.

Marnewick, C., & Marnewick, A. L. (2020). The Demands of Industry 4.0 on Project Teams. *IEEE Transactions on Engineering Management, 67*(3), 941–949.

Mintzberg, H. (2011). *Managing.* Prentice Hall.

Odhiambo, F. (2020). *The Awareness, Preparedness and Roles of the Workforce and Managers for the Fourth Industrial Revolution in Africa.* Consultancy Research Report.

Partington, D., Pellegrinelli, S., & Young, M. (2005). Attributes and Levels of Programme Management Competence: An Interpretive Study. *International Journal of Project Management, 23*(2), 87–95.

Pozzi, D. (2014). An Elastic Managerial Revolution: Family, Managers and Multidivisional Organisation at Pirelli (1943–56). *Business History, 56*(5), 765–788.

Prieto, L. C., & Phipps, S. T. A. (2016). Rediscovering Charles Clinton Spaulding's "The Administration of Big Business". *Journal of Management History, 22*(1), 73–90.

Ruparel, N., Dhir, A., Tandon, A., Kaur, P., & Islam, J. U. (2020). The Influence of Online Professional Social Media in Human Resource Management: A Systematic Literature Review. *Technology in Society, 63*, 101335.

Schwab, K. (2016). *The Fourth Industrial Revolution: What it Means, How to Respond.* World Economic Forum. https://www.weforum.org/agenda/2016/01/the-fourth-industrial-revolution-what-it-means-and-how-to-respond/

Seeck, H., & Kuokkanen, A. (2010). Management Paradigms in Finnish Journals and Literature between 1921 and 2006. *Business History, 52*(2), 306–336.

Smiles, S. (1859). *Self Help.* Penguin Books Edition, 1986.

Sparrow, P. R. (2000). Strategic Management in a World Turned Upside Down: The Role of Cognition, Intuition and Emotional Intelligence. In P. C. Flood, T. Dromgoole, S. J. Carroll, & L. Gorman (Eds.), *Managing Strategy Implementation.* Blackwell.

Tanaka, Y. (1992). Changing Roles of the Factory-Meister in the Fried. Krupp Co. 1850–1870. *Socio Economic History, 58*(3), 339.

Watson, T. J. (1994). *In Search of Management.* Thomson Business Press.

Wilson, J. F., & Thomson, A. (2009). *The Making of Modern Management.* Oxford University Press.

Witzel, M., Booth, A., & Pistol, R. (2018). *Rowntree and the Search for a British Approach to Management.* https://blogs.lse.ac.uk/businessreview/2018/06/14/rowntree-and-the-search-for-a-british-approach-to-management/

Index

P. Turner, *The Making of the Modern Manager*,
https://doi.org/10.1007/978-3-030-81062-7

The manufacturer's authorised representative in the EU is Springer Nature Customer Service Centre GmbH, Europaplatz 3, 69115 Heidelberg, Germany. If you have any concerns regarding our products, please contact ProductSafety@springernature.com

Printed and bound by CPI Group (UK) Ltd, Croydon, CR0 4YY
30/09/2026
02225701-0017